# Third Cinema, World Cinema and Marxism

# Third Cinema, World Cinema and Marxism

*Edited by Ewa Mazierska
and Lars Kristensen*

BLOOMSBURY ACADEMIC
NEW YORK · LONDON · OXFORD · NEW DELHI · SYDNEY

BLOOMSBURY ACADEMIC
Bloomsbury Publishing Inc
1385 Broadway, New York, NY 10018, USA
29 Earlsfort Terrace, Dublin 2, Ireland

BLOOMSBURY, BLOOMSBURY ACADEMIC and the Diana logo
are trademarks of Bloomsbury Publishing Plc

First published in the United States of America 2020
This paperback edition published 2022

Volume Editor's Part of the Work © Ewa Mazierska and Lars Kristensen
Each chapter © of Contributors

Cover design by Eleanor Rose | Cover image: Still from Soy Cuba
(I Am Cuba, 1964), dir. Mikhail Kalatozov © ArenaPAL

All rights reserved. No part of this publication may be reproduced or transmitted in
any form or by any means, electronic or mechanical, including photocopying,
recording, or any information storage or retrieval system, without prior
permission in writing from the publishers.

Bloomsbury Publishing Inc does not have any control over, or responsibility for,
any third-party websites referred to or in this book. All internet addresses given in
this book were correct at the time of going to press. The author and publisher
regret any inconvenience caused if addresses have changed or sites have
ceased to exist, but can accept no responsibility for any such changes.

Library of Congress Cataloging-in-Publication Data
Names: Mazierska, Ewa, editor, author. | Kristensen, Lars Lyngsgaard Fjord,
editor, writer of introduction.
Title: Third cinema, world cinema and Marxism / Ewa Mazierska, Lars Kristensen.
Description: New York ; London : Bloomsbury Academic, 2020. |
Includes bibliographical references and index.
Identifiers: LCCN 2020009513 | ISBN 9781501348273 (hardback) | ISBN 9781501348297
(pdf) | ISBN 9781501348280 (ebook)
Subjects: LCSH: Motion pictures–Political aspects. | Motion pictures–Social
aspects. | Motion pictures–Political aspects–Developing countries. | Motion
pictures–Developing countries. | Communism and motion pictures. | Postcolonialism
in motion pictures.
Classification: LCC PN1995.9.P6 T485 2020 | DDC 791.4309172/4–dc23
LC record available at https://lccn.loc.gov/2020009513

| ISBN: | HB: | 978-1-5013-4827-3 |
| | PB: | 978-1-5013-7384-8 |
| | ePDF: | 978-1-5013-4829-7 |
| | eBook: | 978-1-5013-4828-0 |

Typeset by Integra Software Services Pvt. Ltd.

To find out more about our authors and books visit www.bloomsbury.com
and sign up for our newsletters.

# CONTENTS

List of Figures   vii

Defining Third Cinema and World Cinema   1

## PART 1  Revisiting films

1  Exporting cinemarxism in the 1960s: The case of *Soy Cuba*  *Andrei Rogatchevski*   25

2  Brazil's open cities: Mimicry, sexuality and class dynamics in the urban landscape of 1960s cinema  *Bruce Williams*   63

3  'Unreal city': The aesthetics of commitment in *Pratidwandi* and *Interview*  *Koel Banerjee*   83

4  The Peruvian Kuntur group: A Marxist-Indigenist filmmaking practice  *Isabel Seguí*   99

## PART 2  Comparative readings

5  The legacy of the furnaces: The twenty-first century documentaries of Fernando Solanas  *Mariano Paz*   121

6  Third Cinema after the turn of the millennium: Reification of the sign and the possibility of transformation  *Paulina Aroch Fugellie and André Dorcé*   141

7  We have never been transnational: The female condition in socialist realism, postsocialism and Third Cinema  *Lucian Tion*   163

## PART 3 Third Cinema versus World Cinema

8 Dialogical encounters on the cinema of revolution: *Save the Children Fund Film* and *Metalepsis in Black* David Archibald and Finn Daniels-Yeomans 189

9 Newsreel Front: A revived vision of Third Cinema in Slovenia Andrej Šprah 213

10 Listening to the future: The film-philosophy of Abderrahmane Sissako William Brown 235

11 Class, gender and ethnicity in Alfonso Cuarón's *Roma* Ewa Mazierska 255

12 'After' or back to Third Cinema? Plebeian film, the national popular, fingernails and the resilient behemoth Enrique Uribe-Jongbloed and Toby Miller 273

*Index* 290

# LIST OF FIGURES

1.1 Mourning the dove  36

1.2 Demo a la Rodchenko  46

1.3 American sailors chasing a Cuban woman  48

2.1 Norma Bengell and Gabriele Tinti in *Night Games*  73

2.2 Urban São Paulo following an evening of fun and games  73

2.3 Oduvaldo Vianna Filho and Isabella in *The Dare*  76

2.4 Ada's visit to the factory in *The Dare*  78

4.1 Meeting at the headquarters of the Tupac Amaru Revolutionary Agrarian Federation of Cusco (FARTAC). On the wall, portraits of Lenin and José Carlos Mariátegui, an influential Peruvian Marxist public intellectual  108

4.2 Newspaper publicity 'Laulico Wanted Dead or Alive'  110

4.3 In the banner, the three basic Inca moral principles, *Ama Llulla, Ama Quella, Ama Sua* (do not be a liar, do not be idle, do not be a thief)  112

6.1 Cameraman Leonardo Henricksen is shot by the military as he recorded the failed coup on Allende  151

6.2 Salvador Allende's broken glasses  154

6.3 Floating wagoner  156

7.1 Tian Hua in her first role as the white haired girl  169

7.2 Raquel Revuelta playing the first of the three Lucias  172

7.3 The brooding universe of socialist oppression  176

8.1 Jaramogi Oginga Odinga in *Save the Children Fund Film*  196

8.2 Ngũgĩ wa Thiong'o in *Save the Children Fund Film*  197

8.3 **Ben Kantai** in Save the Children Fund Film  198

8.4 Graffiti on unspecified university campus in South Africa. Screen grab from *Metalepsis in Black*  204

8.5 **Extreme close-up on conference delegates in** *Metalepsis in Black*. **Screen grab from** *Metalepsis in Black*  209

9.1 *Karl Marx Among Us*, 2013, black & white, sound, videostill. Copyright: Jurij Meden & Newsreel Front  217

9.2 *1717 Km of Summer*, 2009, black & white and colour, sound, videostill. Copyright: Jurij Meden & Newsreel Front  219

9.3 *Karl Marx Among Us* (To be or not to be), 2013, black & white, sound, videostill. Copyright: Jurij Meden & Newsreel Front  222

9.4 *Newsreel 55*, 2013, black & white and colour, sound, videostill. Copyright: Nika Autor & Newsreel Front  225

9.5 *Newsreel 62*, 2015, black & white and colour, sound, videostill. Copyright: Nika Autor & Newsreel Front  227

9.6 *Newsreel 62*, 2015, black & white and colour, sound, videostill. Copyright: Nika Autor & Newsreel Front  228

11.1 Cleo and Pepe. Screen grab from *Roma* (dir. Alfonso Cuarón, 2018)  260

11.2 Granny and Cleo being upheld. Screen grab from *Roma* (dir. Alfonso Cuarón, 2018)  261

11.3 Defence against the revolution. Screen grab from *Roma* (dir. Alfonso Cuarón, 2018)  261

# Defining Third Cinema and World Cinema

This collection offers a re-examination of the theories and practices of Third Cinema. There are two principal reasons why we decided to look at Third Cinema about a half a century after this concept was first coined. One of them is a wish to fill a gap in research by presenting facets of Third Cinema which were previously neglected or underplayed, such as its manifestations in the Second World and the relationship between Third and other types of cinema, such as queer cinema and Fourth Cinema. The second reason is political – demonstrating the relevance of this concept to describe political struggles which take place in contemporary cinema and the world at large. This happens with an awareness that 'Third Cinema' is not a term with which the general public or even current students of film studies are familiar. In popular consciousness, 'Third Cinema' has been replaced by 'World Cinema': both terms referring primarily to films produced outside of Hollywood and Europe, yet carrying different connotations, with Third Cinema being addressed to the disadvantaged people and focused on liberating them from economic oppression, and World Cinema addressing a 'global consumer' and eschewing any unifying narrative or political cause. As a starting point, let's briefly reconstruct the main ideas behind the concept of Third Cinema and the reasons why they fell out of fashion.

## Third Cinema and Marxism: Points of contact

From several manifestoes which laid the foundations of Third Cinema, the most important is one written by Fernando Solanas and Octavio Getino,

'Towards Third Cinema', originally published in 1969 in the Cuban-based magazine *Tricontinental* (Solanas and Getino 2000). In it, the authors provide the by-now well-known taxonomy of cinema, dividing it into First, Second and Third Cinema, with the First being the cinema of spectacle, produced chiefly in Hollywood, and the Second being auteurist cinema. Third Cinema differs from them on several accounts. One of them concerns geography: Third Cinema is mainly produced in the Third World, in 'developing countries', arising from colonial oppression. Another characteristic of Third Cinema is its active character: its goal is encouraging and assisting people in their political struggles, as opposed to merely representing the world or creating enticing spectacles. Hence, Third Cinema cannot be reduced to a collection of 'Third Cinema Films'; it has to involve its viewers. As Solanas put it at a round-table discussion in 1978:

> We realized that the most important thing was not the film and the information in it so much as the way this information was debated. One of the aims of such films is to provide the occasion for people to find themselves and speak about their own problems. The projection becomes a place where people talk and develop their awareness. We learnt the importance of this space: cinema here becomes humanly useful. (quoted in Chanan 1997: 373)

Third Cinema is associated with projections in public spaces or it is assumed that thanks to such projections private spaces become spaces of political discussion and action. For this reason, the wholeness of films is of a relatively little importance for their creators. They do not mind if the projections of their films are stopped, to allow for discussion; on the contrary, they welcome it. This also means that Third Cinema's theory co-exists with practice and they feed each other. It is not an accident that it is the practice of making and distribution of *La Hora de los hornos* (*The Hour of the Furnaces*, 1968) that motivated its authors into writing their manifesto. Here one can see a parallel between Solanas and Getino's position and Marx's 11th 'Thesis on Feuerbach': 'Philosophers have hitherto only interpreted the world in various ways; the point is to change it' (Marx and Engels 1947: 199). To paraphrase Marx, Solanas and Getino could say, 'Filmmakers have hitherto only represented the world; the point is to change it' and, of course, they cannot change it by themselves; they have to involve the viewers. The change is meant to consist of liberation, primarily from inequalities resulting from capital accumulation, of which colonialism is the most extreme manifestation.

Another characteristic of Third Cinema is its local character and rejection of universalism. Films belonging to this category and theories pertaining to them do not address the 'human subject' and 'human condition' as such, but a man or a woman entangled in specific historical circumstances and affected by many factors, of which class is the most important. This means, as Getino asserted in his later article, that Third Cinema is aligned with 'national culture' understood as 'the ensemble of the popular classes' (quoted in Chanan 1997: 378). This point is very important in contemporary times when nationalism or even suggesting that a 'national dimension' should be taken into account when assessing political positions and the decision of citizens is regarded as a sign of backwardness and the scourge of contemporary leftism: populism. Again, we can see a parallel between the concept of Third Cinema and one of Marx's 'Theses of Feuerbach', namely the 8th Thesis: 'All social life is essentially practical. All mysteries which lead theory to mysticism find their rational solution in human practice and in the comprehension of this practice.'

Finally, an important feature of Third Cinema is its formal characteristics: imperfection and openness. Perfection was rejected on practical and essential grounds. Militant filmmakers simply did not have the financial and technical means to compete with eye-catching spectacles from Hollywood or even auteurist films produced in France or Argentina. Moreover, the beautifully controlled surface of commercial cinema was seen by them as a way of lulling the audience into passive consumption, which was antithetic to the political goals of revolutionary filmmakers. As Julio García Espinosa stated in his manifesto, 'For an imperfect cinema': 'nowadays, perfect cinema – technically and artistically masterful – is almost always reactionary cinema' (Espinosa 2000: 286). This also meant rejecting the socialist realism of Soviet cinema, which lacked revolutionary qualities on the basis of being 'closed' films.

Openness, as Robert Stam observes in relation to *The Hour of the Furnaces*, lies first of all in its process of production.

> *The Hour of the Furnaces* is open... in its very structure as a text, operating by what might be called tendentiously aleatory procedures. At key points, the film raises questions – 'Why did Peron fall without struggle? Should he have armed the people?'– and proposes that the audience debate them, interrupting the projection to allow for discussion. Elsewhere, the authors appeal for supplementary material on the theme of violence and liberation, soliciting collaboration in the film's writing. The 'end' of the film refuses closure by inviting the audience to prolong the text: 'Now it is up to you to draw conclusions to continue the film. You have the floor.' (Stam 1998: 256)

Openness, however, as Stam observes, does not mean ideological hesitation or the authorization of a plurality of equally legitimate reading. 'Its messages are stridently unequivocal; its ambiguities, such as they are, derive more from the vicissitudes of history than from the intentions of its authors' (Stam 1998: 256).

Again, one can see here a similarity between the form of Third Cinema films and the work of Marx. The majority of Marx's works come across as sketchy and unfinished, leading to thousands of volumes (including this one), trying to complete his theories and move them forward, adjusting to new historical circumstances. They are also stylistically heterogeneous, on occasion being scientifically dry, elsewhere using propagandist language or sounding like poetry. However, despite their openness and heterogeneity, practically nobody (and this includes both advocates and critics of Marxism) accuses its author of sending its readers mixed political messages.

## The world politics after Third Cinema's inception

From the perspective of politics, the time when Third Cinema was born was special. As Stam puts it, 'the late 1960s were, virtually everywhere, the hour of the furnaces and *The Hour of the Furnaces*, quintessential product of the period, forged the incandescent expression of their glow. Tricontinental revolution, under the symbolic aegis of Frantz Fanon, Ché Guevara, and Ho Chi Minh, was deemed imminent, waiting to surprise us around the next bend of the dialectic' (Stam 1998: 255).

Revolutions of different colours were also taking place in Europe, in cities such as Paris, Prague and Warsaw, whose inhabitants demanded more political freedom, in the workplace, in public places and on the streets. The 1970s was still a period of political upheaval, yet its character was different. Rather than the rise of uprisings, the decade saw a rise in terrorist activities, civil wars and the imposition of what Stam describes as 'subfascist regimes'. A decade later, a new world order was born: that of neoliberalism, whose first manifestations were the victories of Margaret Thatcher in the United Kingdom and Ronald Reagan in the United States. David Harvey, its leading analyst and critic, defines neoliberalism as a version of capitalism, in which accumulation of capital is achieved by ruthless dispossession consisting of (1) privatization and the commodification of public assets; (2) financialization, so that any commodity can become an instrument of economic speculation; (3) management and manipulation of crises; and (4) state redistribution, by which wealth and income is distributed upwards, from lower to upper classes and from poorer to wealthier countries and regions (Harvey 2005: 160–2). These characteristics were antithetical to the programmes of the revolutions of the 1960s, as well as to the principles on which the politics and economy of the Second World was based.

At the end of the 1980s the West, which adopted neoliberalism, was enlarged by countries which previously constituted the Eastern Bloc, such as Poland, Hungary and Bulgaria, giving the impression that communism was a failed project and there was no alternative to national and global development through capitalist accumulation. This mindset is well captured by the words of Ella Shohat:

> The period of so-called 'Third World euphoria' – a brief moment in which it seemed that First World leftists and Third World guerrillas would walk arm in arm towards a global revolution – has given way to the collapse of the Soviet communist model, the crisis of existing socialisms, the frustration of the hope-for tricontinental revolution (with Ho Chi Minh, Frantz Fanon, and Che Guevara as talismanic figures), the realization that the wretched of the earth are not unanimously revolutionary (nor necessarily allies to one another), and the recognition that international geo-politics and the global economic system have obliged even socialist regimes to make some kind of peace with transnational capitalism. (Shohat 1992: 100)

The march of neoliberal capitalism was abetted by an alliance between neoliberalists (described also as globalists) and a large section of the political forces, which identified itself as left, for example the Labour Party under Tony Blair and Gordon Brown and the SPD in Germany under Gerhardt Schröder and his successors. Rather than fighting the capitalist enemy, such politicians, who typically described themselves as 'centre-left', embraced it with a greater zeal than their conservative predecessors. They pronounced that there is no viable alternative to neoliberal model and there should be no discussion about economic inequality, because what really matters is the growth of the economy, which benefits the entire society. They also declared that the adversarial model of politics became obsolete – so categories of right and left were no longer needed. Such a way of conducting politics, in which the bulk of citizens are de facto deprived of political choice, Chantal Mouffe aptly describes as 'post-politics', to underscore its democratic deficit (Mouffe 2018, 2019).

The same scenario was also played in many countries outside Europe, which embarked on a programme of deregulation of industry and privatization of state assets, often in exchange for receiving a loan from the World Bank or the International Monetary Fund. Such decisions, as in Europe, were rationalized by the claim that there was no viable alternative. Mexico is a case in point. As Harvey notes, in 1984 the World Bank granted a loan to this country in exchange for structural neoliberal reforms, which resulted in falling income per capita at the rate of 5 per cent per year and the value of workers' real wages between 40 and 50 per cent, as well as a decline of state expenditure on public goods (Harvey 2005: 100).

In other countries of the 'Global South', where the left managed to cling to power, it was significantly weakened by corruption, high levels of crime and economic ineptitude, in part reflecting the difficulty of pursing socialist policies while surrounded by countries where capitalism rules and whose governments are bent on destroying socialism inside and outside its borders. The histories of countries such as Venezuela and Brazil in the last two decades well illustrate this trend. Another interesting trend is South Africa, discussed in this book by David Archibald and Finn Daniels-Yeomans, where the end of apartheid and colonial rule, marked by the universal elections in 1994, did not result in the universal improvement of the position of the majority of black citizens, only a small proportion of them. On the contrary, the overall standard of living, life expectancy and unemployment rate of the black majority worsened under the rule of the 'black' government, leading to, among other things, conflicts with migrants coming from other African countries. This situation does not suggest that colonialism is acceptable when it serves the economic interests of the colonized, but it points to the fact that colonial struggle does not bring liberation if it is not accompanied by class struggle.

The global victory of neoliberalism, as Marx predicted in *The Communist Manifesto*, brought with it the weakening, if not erasure, of many negative traits of the previous systems, such as patriarchy, racism and religious bigotry. This did not result from neoliberalism being 'progressive per se' but from the fact that any factors which weaken free trade, such as strong borders between countries with their control of the flow of workers, are opposite to the goals of capitalism, which is an unlimited accumulation of surplus value. This achievement of neoliberalism had several far-reaching consequences. One of them was a widespread perception that the victory of neoliberalism equals entering a 'post-ideological age', in which clinging to the previously dominant ideas such as nationalism or even locking the market into a nation-state is a sign of backwardness. Such a view was most conspicuously espoused in the works of Francis Fukuyama with his thesis of the end of history (Fukuyama 1992). The result is a marginalization of the concept of class in historical and political studies and even political discourse after the 1970s (Meiksins Wood 1986; Rowbotham and Beynon 2001; Mazierska 2015: 9–45) and especially from the 1990s onwards. Another consequence is an alliance of neoliberalism and those political forces whose ostensible goal is liberation of oppressed minorities, such as LGBT people, ethnic minorities, (illegal) migrants and women and even people concerned with climate change (Eistenstein 2005; Fraser 2009). As David Harvey observes, 'the modern embrace of multiculturalism and women's rights within the corporate world, particularly in the United States, provides some evidence of capitalism's accommodation of these dimensions of social change, even as it re-emphasises the salience of class divisions as the principle dimension for political action' (Harvey 2010: 258). This accommodation even affected the semantics of contemporary Western political discourse. 'Leftism' and 'progressivism' are no longer associated with socialism but with cultural diversity and defence of minority rights within a neoliberal framework or even it is argued that these political ideals can be defended only within neoliberal framework, given that they are supposedly under threat from 'neofascists' (Streeck 2017: 11). Equally, standing up for socialism and arguing that it is easier to defend it within one country than globally is associated with such movements as far-rightism or at best populism (Streeck 2017, 2019).

Such 'neoliberal leftism', grafted onto identity politics, not only shows little sympathy to the workers in the First World but sees them as the remnants of the old system and an obstacle to the introduction of the utopia of 'cultural diversity' and 'fair competition'. In relation to that, Wolfgang Streeck wrote sarcastically in the context of recent elections, particularly in Europe: 'There were plenty of voters who simply did not understand that international solidarity among workers in the twenty-first century meant that it was their duty to open up their own job to unrestrained global competition' (Streeck 2017: 14) – a comment which can be also applied to South African workers, protesting against an influx of migrants from other African countries.

However, as Streeck observes, the proletarians fought back by punishing the 'neoliberal left' in elections in Europe and globally, choosing political forces which promise them at least some measure of protection against neoliberal globalization, such as tighter borders, so that they do not need to compete with migrants and tariffs, which results in domestic production being more profitable. Such a programme is currently realized by the government of Donald Trump, and, meaningfully, he is attacked from the left more for 'demonizing migrants' and 'starting a trade war with China', which negatively affects the stock market and introduces some friction into an otherwise frictionless global capitalism, than for his disdain for socialist values. The victory of Brexit was largely a victory for those trying to disentangle Britain from the European Union, an organization which perfectly fits Marx and Engels' description of the super-state as a modern state, whose executive is merely a 'committee for managing the common affairs of the whole bourgeoisie' (Marx and Engels 2008: 36), a description which Streeck develops in his writings.

Identity politics and multiculturalism are also an important aspect of World Cinema. To this concept and its difference from Third Cinema, we will now turn.

# Third and World Cinemas in a new world order

Cinema, being part of superstructure (to use Marxist vocabulary), reflects its base. This can be seen in the trajectory of Third Cinema, understood both as a concept and as a practice. In the 1960s and the early 1970s those who practiced it had a sense of being at the forefront of global cinema and politics, offering models of cinematic engagement which could be applied locally and which eventually would change film production and reception across the world and assist political struggles of the victims of political and economic oppression. In the subsequent decade or so, this programme was realized in specific countries, paying great attention to the national specificity and emphasizing that the 'natural' habitat of Third Cinema is the Third World. This opinion was conveyed by publishing an influential book by Teshome Gabriel, *Third Cinema in Third World: The Aesthetics of Liberation*, in 1982. Such confinement of Third Cinema to the Third World rendered it more focused, yet also more parochial, suggesting that Third Cinema is of little interest to those living in the First and Second Worlds.

It can be added that the idea of 'Third World' is closely connected to the concept of 'developing countries'. It includes 'lagging behind' and a need to 'catch up' with the 'developed countries', some of which were the old colonies and address the legacy of colonialism and the consequences of postcolonialism. From this perspective Third Cinema is never solely a matter of and for the Third World; it always, explicitly or implicitly, concerns the rest of the world.

In 1996, the filmmaker John Akomfrah declared at a conference for African cinema that Third Cinema is dead, and apparently this declaration was accepted by the audience without objections (Wayne 2001: 2; Ekotte and Koh 2009: 2). Even if Akomfrah's statement was exaggerated, we have to agree that by the end of the last century, Third Cinema lost much of its novelty, power and confidence. This is reflected in the Third Cinema films of the later period (the 1990s and later) frequently focusing on the past, taking issue with historical struggles, rather than those taking place 'here and now'. In recent years we also find attacks on Third Cinema for its supposedly totalitarian character, namely usurping the place of the only spokesperson for the cinemas produced in the Third World and the identities of its creators. A symptomatic, from this perspective, is a recent article by Ivo Ritzer, who claims:

> Third Cinema claimed to represent the oppressed masses, but in fact, it remained throughout in the hands of an educated elite, ironically almost always trained in Europe. Its aesthetics of didacticism and pretension have come under attack and appeared less and less appealing to a new generation of African filmmakers.
>
> Since the model of Third Cinema has led to an ideological one-way street, as well as to an aesthetic exhaustion, the multiplicity of new forms of cinematographic practices diversified what might be regarded as African cinema today. For sure, African cinema can no longer be understood as Third Cinema. While the so-called Africanness of African cinema in the age of Third Cinema was defined by its very Third Worldism (and hence

by the anticolonial struggle), today the question of Africanness in African cinema is probably more complex than ever before. (Ritzer 2018: 22–3)

Such accusations, in our opinion, are unjust, given that the authors of Third Cinema manifestoes never claimed to represent the whole or even the majority of film production in the Third World. On the contrary, they saw their films as a minority with a specific film production (South American, African, Argentinian) or even a project – something which was meant to happen. However, it is true that the attention of critics directed to this phenomenon gave an impression that Third Cinema dominates in countries such as Argentina and Senegal. For example, in the anthology *Film and Theory* (Stam and Miller 2000), the majority of contributions about cinema from Third World Countries concerns Third Cinema.

At the same time as Third Cinema, rightly or (more often) wrongly came under attack, new terms and concepts entered into circulation in film studies, such as transnational cinema and even more so world cinema, on occasion written in capital letters, to underscore its distinctiveness. Over the last decade, such concepts have overshadowed Third Cinema. Their dominant status is reflected in the large number of volumes with 'world' or 'transnational' cinema in their titles, such as *Remapping World Cinema* (Dennison and Lim 2006), *Transnational Cinema: The Film Reader* (Ezra and Rowden 2006), *World Cinemas, Transnational Perspectives* (Ďurovičová and Newman 2010) and the Routledge journal *Transnational Cinema* (2010–2018, now *Transnational Screens*).

We can list two (perhaps only seemingly) contrasting approaches to World Cinema. One, which derives from the idea of World Literature, as described by Goethe and Marx, emphasizes the fact that World Cinema is about film production from the periphery as seen by Western eyes and largely for their benefit. Stephanie Dennison and Song Hwee Lim write:

> World cinema is analogous to 'world music' and 'world literature' in that they are categories created in the Western world to refer to cultural products and practices that are mainly non-Western. While the historical trajectories of their origins and developments may not have been totally identical, their relationship to non-Western cultural products and practices in terms of consumption and reception of the latter in the Western world bear striking similarities that lend themselves to a comparative study. (Dennison and Lim 2006: 1–2)

Dennison and Hwee Lim thus recognize the fact that cinema is not democratic and the best the researcher can do is to bring films from the periphery to the attention of the international audience. At the same time, Song Hwee Lim in his subsequent article has acknowledged that the periphery and the centre might change places, as illustrated by a growing power of China and

Chinese cinema in relation to the United States and American cinema (Lim 2019: 2–4).

The second approach is espoused by Lucia Nagib, who proposes a different definition of World Cinema on the grounds that the previous concepts perpetuate Western hegemony and are negative. She states:

> World cinema is simply the cinema of the world. It has no centre. It is not the other, but it is us. It has no beginning and no end, but is a global process. World cinema, as the world itself, is circulation.
>
> - World cinema is not a discipline, but a method, a way of cutting across film history according to waves of relevant films and movements, thus creating flexible geographies.
> - As a positive, inclusive, democratic concept, world cinema allows all sorts of theoretical approaches, provided they are not based on the binary perspective. (Nagib 2006: 31)

Although we salute Nagib for her boldness in writing a scholarly manifesto and her desire to democratize film studies, we doubt her programme is realistic and from a Marxist perspective, which we espouse, desirable. To begin with, claiming that 'world cinema is simply the cinema of the world' does not solve the issue of hierarchies within global film production and discourses tackling them, most importantly 'Hollywood versus the rest', as well as within peripheral cinema itself. To change these hierarchies, one needs much more than the will of film scholars; it requires significant transformation in what, in Marxist discourse, is described as 'the base', namely the property relations, the technical division of labour and so on, both within the economies of film production and consumption as well as in the wider world. As long as capitalism remains the hegemonic system within the global economy, the type of cinema represented by Hollywood (spectacular, presenting the adventures of an individual hero) will dominate global film production and consumption. Moreover, the fact that World Cinema, as world economy, is a circulation, which might affect the hierarchies between, for example, national and global cinemas as well as individual films, does not change the fact that the system is hierarchical and that the units comprising it compete for a better position in relation to the centre. Second, saying that World Cinema is a method does not preclude it being a discipline, as methods often delineate disciplines. For example, fun studies or production studies, which constitute subfields of film studies, are defined by their methods rather than by geographical regions. Moreover, focusing on 'relevant films and movements' brings a distinct risk of choosing those films and movements which are relevant for 'central' (Western) scholars, because those of them who do not speak the language in which a given peripheral film was made will have to settle for films which are 'translated' through being subtitled and widely available, being shown in cinemas, sold on DVD or on internet platforms, as noted by Kwame Anthony Appiah in his seminal essay 'Is the Post-in Postmodernism the Post-in the Postcolonial' (1991) in relation to art. By the same token, 'relevant films and movements' are inevitably those which constitute a canon or are on the way to receiving canonical status. This brings us to Nagib's third point – 'World Cinema' conceived this way is not democratic, because it reflects on and adds to the hierarchies existing in film studies, which largely mirror those existing in the global economy and politics. In summary, we believe that Nagib's programme does little to change the existing 'pecking order' in cinema and film studies, largely because it is impossible to engage in any discipline (especially in humanities) without using a specific map.

What is important, from our perspective, in the debates on World Cinema are the changing parameters of discussions in comparison with those on Third Cinema. Authors engaging with the concept of World Cinema are mainly concerned with the hierarchies within cinema and cinema studies, even if, like Nagib, they purport to reject these hierarchies; the way reality is depicted in films is of lesser importance for them. Opting for World Cinema is also about rejecting a binary perspective and instead embracing diversity and plurality, which presumably also includes ideological diversity and political plurality, not unlike in post-political model espoused by Tony Blair, as previously mentioned. In research on World Cinema, transnationalism, rather than nationalism, is foregrounded, with issues such as multilingualism, international coproduction, exhibition at film festivals receiving much attention. Furthermore, the bulk of authors engaging in studies of transnational cinema reject nationalism, linking it to populism, racism, bigotry and simply immorality. Hence, Lim, in the previously quoted article, writes that insistence of the transnational (which he equates with rejecting nationalism) 'becomes a political position' (Lim 2019: 8). For sure, it is a political position, but it cannot be equated with socialism. As we have already argued, trans-and pan-nationalism is often used as a cover to introduce neoliberal order, not least because pan-national institutions are less susceptible to democratic scrutiny than national ones. This fact is recognized by some film authors covered in this book, such as Fernando Solanas (see Marano Paz's chapter in this collection), who in his recent films adopts an openly nationalist position, in part out of solidarity with the fellow Argentinians and in part out of awareness that supporting any form of transnationalism on the capitalist terms (and these are the only terms currently on offer) equals transferring more power from the ordinary people to capitalist institutions, such as multinational corporations.

The main question perplexing researchers of World Cinema is how to change the dynamics between the centre and the periphery, Hollywood and the rest of cinema. One answer is to add value to World Cinema by acknowledging its contribution to global film production by appreciating local stylistic innovations and new characters. Another answer is to deconstruct the centre, by seeing it as polycentric and reflecting the influences from the periphery (Iordanova, Martin-Jones and Vidal 2010). Generally, the big question for World Cinema scholars is how to render global cinema more democratic.

Rejecting binarism can be seen as a noble moral stance, pointing to the scholars' respect for different cultures and styles of filmmaking. However, embracing plurality and inclusiveness does little to help the masses excluded from participation in politics and culture due to their poverty or colonial legacy. Instead, what might help them is an analysis of their condition, which leads to identifying the enemies and the means to fight them, as suggested in the Getino and Solanas' manifesto. In other words, winning political battles is about dividing the world into allies and foes, hence embracing a binary perspective, dreaded by the advocates of World Cinema. These foes are mentioned in some of the chapters. They include multinational companies, which exert immense power over national governments and show no loyalty towards local workers, supranational organizations such as the IMF, which force the governments to introduce economic reforms impoverishing local populations, the banking system, local elites which prioritize foreign interests over the national ones and corrupt politicians.

The difference in approach affects other disparities between Third and World Cinema. Third Cinema is primarily addressed to the people whom it represents: the oppressed suffering from income inequalities and colonialism. Its ultimate purpose is a call for action, in the conviction that if the oppressed do not take their affairs in their own hands, nobody will do it for them. Third Cinema thus typically advocates revolution. By contrast, the privileged topic of World Cinema, due to being addressed largely to First World audiences, is migration (both illegal and legal) from peripheral countries to the developed countries of the First World. By the same token, the consumption of World Cinema in the West suggests gazing at the 'wretched' and underscoring the role of Westerners in helping them by, for example, facilitating their transfer from Africa to Europe, as opposed to pointing to the agency of the inhabitants of Africa or Asia in transforming their circumstances. Although presented as 'progressive cinema', World Cinema films are often made from a colonial perspective and normalize the status quo, in which the Third World remains forever a recipient of First World's assistance.

Through its very interest in the (old) Third World and a sympathetic attitude to its inhabitants, World Cinema competes with Third Cinema. This raises a question in relation to how Third Cinema makers should react to prevent being obliterated by World Cinema. One strategy is suggested by Teshome Gabriel in his article aptly titled 'Third Cinema Updated: Exploration of Nomadic Aesthetics & Narrative Communities'. In this article Gabriel recognizes the need for Third Cinema to adapt, because the world has changed, with the Second World no longer existing.

The tactics of Third Cinema have changed, becoming based less on oppositional strategies than on more complex, more mixed, more ironic, forms of resistance. Similarly, the communities that are constituted around Third Cinema have also become less fixed, more heterogeneous, as different cultural forms and memories have come to be juxtaposed and combined. In a sense, Third Cinema has become an increasingly *creolized* form, in much the same way that peoples from various parts of the Third World have found themselves intermingling in the metropolitan centers of 'developed' countries. Indeed, the myths and stories from these different cultures have not only been combined with one another, but with aspects of Hollywood and European cultures as well. These narrative communities are dynamic and changing, open to diverse cultural influences. They are complexly multicultural and, for the most part, non-exclusionary. Unlike Hollywood, they do not rely on the figure of the Other to define themselves. (Gabriel undated)

In the same article Gabriel advocates a Third Cinema which is multiple – Third Cinemas rather than Third Cinema – and uses a plethora of screen media, as opposed to only (celluloid) film (Gabriel undated).

Gabriel's programme for an invigorated Third Cinema seems to be similar to the programmes of World Cinema and postmodern art, with its emphasis on championing multiculturalism and identity politics at the expense of class politics. It even reveals an uncanny resemblance to that offered by neoliberal apologists, such as Fukuyama, who picture the world in its allegedly post-ideological state, when liberal democracy has won over other political positions and worldviews, previous contradictions are overcome, there is no conflict, only plurality of perspectives (Fukuyama 1992). As we mentioned earlier, citing Streeck, such a programme is rejected by a large proportion of the working class, seeing it as antithetical to their class interests.

We thus doubt that such a deflated Third Cinema would be able to capture the imaginations of the disadvantaged populations living in the First and Third World and stand up to the powerful neoliberal enemy. Instead, we propose that, in order to survive and flourish, Third Cinema has to be more rather than less confrontational, namely identify the communities which it purports to represent, especially in the Third World, and its enemies; explain the damage they inflict on them in terms of standard of living, political sovereignty, culture and natural environment; and seek solutions. Such cinema does not need to be simplistic or focus on only one form of oppression. On the contrary, it should elucidate how different forms of oppression intermingle, magnify or cancel each other. However, it needs to acknowledge the existence of inequalities and a need to oppose them.

Such cinema can look back, towards battles which the disadvantaged won and lost, but should not limit itself to indulging in history and memory but only use them to offer lessons for the future. Similarly, as much as possible, it should search for new forms of expression, but not merely for the sake of aesthetic experimentation but to reflect on and forge new ways of resistance to capitalist domination. It should be made with an awareness of its overlap but also of its difference from World Cinema.

## Structure and chapter description

This book has two principal goals. One is to revisit what can be described as the original or historical Third Cinema, drawing attention to its aspects which were omitted by previous scholarship. The second goal is to look at newer examples of films and cinematic phenomena which lend themselves to what we describe as a 'Third Cinema' approach. These are not necessarily Third Cinema productions proper (if such films can at all be made nowadays) but films which encourage questions about the distribution of political power in the Third World and between First and Third Worlds, decolonialization and neocolonialism, both in material reality and in cinema, and the difference between Third and World Cinemas. This approach affected the structure of this collection, which is divided into four parts.

In the first part we focus on films which were previously omitted from discussions about Third Cinema or are tackled here from perspectives which were previously marginalized. They include relations between Third Cinema, Second Cinema and cinema produced in the socialist world, the connection between class emancipation and liberation from oppression related to gender and sexual orientation, as well as the critical discourse around Third Cinema. Implicitly or openly, this part poses the question of the canon of Third Cinema, arguing for extending it, both for the sake of what can be described as 'cinematic justice', namely acknowledging the place of certain previously critically neglected films in the struggle for class liberation, as well as, for pragmatic reasons, namely breathing new life into a discussion about Third Cinema, which, as we mentioned earlier, is seen as moribund.

This part begins with Andrei Rogatchevski's consideration of *Soy Cuba* (1964) by Mikhail Kalatozov – a USSR-Cuban co-production on the subject of the Cuban revolution, a widely recognized masterpiece, yet initially treated with relatively little sympathy in the country which was its subject, namely Cuba. In his analysis of this film, which can be described as proto-Third Cinema, Rogatchevski accounts for the reasons of this disappointment, presenting in detail the production context of Kalatozov's film and the similarities and differences between Third Cinema and cinema produced in the Soviet Union and the socialist part of Europe. As his theoretical framework, he uses the theory of accelerated cultural development by Georgi Gachev, according to which the development of a nation (country) is conditioned by neighbouring nations or countries, which have already gone a long way in accumulating substantial experience of social and cultural development, arguing that Cuba's development was conditioned on that of the Soviet Union and *Soy Cuba* testifies to this. The originality of this chapter thus lies in drawing attention to the specificity of Soviet colonialism in relation to the developing world and its manifestations in cultural production.

Chapters 2 and 3 deal with representation of the interface between class identity and other markers of human identity and simultaneously explore the relationship between Third and Second Cinemas. First Bruce Williams discusses two films, belonging to Brazilian *Cinema Novo* – Walter Hugo Khouri's *Night Games* (1964) and Paulo César Saraceni's *The Dare* (1965) – using the concept of mimicry, as developed by Homi Bhabha. *Night Games* relates the adventures of two men of different social classes who explore the night life of São Paulo's gritty centre, in search of socialites and prostitutes. *The Dare* focuses on a love affair between the wife of a factory owner and a young, left-wing journalist. Williams argues that these films give an insight into the reality of class and sexuality immediately prior to the military coup in 1964, which initiated some twenty-one years of dictatorship and, at the same time, draw on European modernist cinema of Michelangelo Antonioni, as a way to depict the minds of the characters and acknowledge these authors' debt towards European cinema and culture.

Koel Banerjee examines the first films from the respective Calcutta Trilogies of Satyajit Ray and Mrinal Sen, *The Adversary* (1970) and *Interview* (1970), as a reworking of Third Cinema by two leading Indian cinematic auteurs, using Adorno's concept of committed art. Like Williams, Banerjee locates these films in a specific political context, when the Indian left witnessed a moment of crisis in 1969, when, under the leadership of Charu Majumder, a radical faction split from the Communist Party of India to form the Communist Party of India-Marxist-Leninist (hereafter, CPI-ML). Supported by young university students of West Bengal, the CPI-ML, popularly known as the Naxalites, mobilized landless peasants into armed conflict with landlords, moneylenders and government officials and the government retaliated with brute force, perpetrating civil and human rights violations, including detention without counsel, torture and staged shootouts. However, the author argues that these films, and Ray's production especially, shy away from overt political cinema by focusing on the plight of individual, on occasion politically hesitant, characters.

The first part closes with Isabel Seguí's consideration of the Kuntur group, consisting of director Federico García and producer Pilar Roca, who have been active in the production of films in Peru since the 1970s. Although their work was imbued by the Marxist-Indigenist ideology of the time, it is overlooked in the process of creating Third Cinema's canon. Seguí looks at possible reasons for this exclusion, pointing to a Westernised type of film criticism that has been pervasive in Peru, especially 'cahierist' critics publishing in the influential journal *Hablemos de cine*. At the same time she argues for their canonization by examining their first three films: *Where the Condors Are Born* (1977), *Laulico* (1980) and *The Huayanay Case: Part Testimony* (1981), which were the cinematic embodiment of the collaboration between leftist urban intellectuals and Peruvian indigenous peasant communities and grassroots leaders.

The next part of the collection consists of two chapters which compare the early and late work of directors whose names are at the centre of the first wave of Third Cinema. First Mariano Paz examines the twenty-first-century documentaries of Fernando Solanas as the legacy of his seminal work, *The Hour of the Furnaces* (co-directed with Octavio Getino), looking at their production context, reception and their textual characteristics. Paz draws attention to the large body of work produced by Solanas in this period, amounting to a total running time of 942 minutes, making this a significant film corpus, exceeding a duration of *The Hour of the Furnaces*. The author observes that in terms of their form, the new Solanas's films are more conventional, but they are animated by the same spirit as *The Hour of the Furnaces*, namely recognition of the injustice inflicted on the majority of Argentinian people by such forces as multinational corporations and the inept, corrupt or pro-capitalist governments. Paz also notes new motives in these films, such as the destruction of the natural environment and transport infrastructure, as well as nationalism, which can be regarded as a testimony to Solanas's attachment to Peronism and a recognition that if socialism is to win anywhere, it needs first to be local, before it can move globally.

Paulina Aroch Fugellie and André Dorcé compare two films made by Chilean director Patricio Guzmán: *La insurrección de la burguesía* (the first part of the trilogy *La batalla de Chile*) (1975) and *Salvador Allende* (2004). The authors investigate to what degree the critical potential of the 1960s and 1970s persists today and in what ways it has been depoliticized, its critical edge converted into reified signs of emancipation. They do so, drawing on the concept of melodrama as both transformative and conservative form. They argue that the first film under consideration employs melodrama as a transformative tool, presenting and heightening the drama of class struggle, in which filmmakers not only recorded political conflicts but became its actors and victims. The second film, on the other hand, uses it in a conservative way, looking at the past conflicts from a safe distance. By the same token, Aroch Fugellie's and Dorcé's take on Third Cinema today is more pessimistic than Paz's, as they recognize, if not the impossibility, then at least great difficulty of producing political cinema under neoliberalism.

In common with Rogatchevski, Lucian Tion argues in favour of exploring connections between Third Cinema and films produced in the socialist world, because exchanges between postcolonial and socialist cultures led to aesthetic borrowings that deeply impacted the themes and look of the cinemas of Asia, Latin America and Eastern Europe. Hence, Third

Cinema should theoretically be connected with socialist realism. Moreover, this hybrid continuum of anti-imperialist filmmaking, in turn, influenced postsocialist cinema. To make this point, in his chapter he looks at three films: Humberto Solas's *Lucia* (1968), which is a Cuban film; concurrent with the Third Cinema, Wang Bin's *The White Haired Girl* (1950), which is a staple of Chinese socialist realism; and *4 Months, 3 Weeks and 2 Days* (2007), Cristian Mungiu's postsocialist film from Romania. Tion compares these three films from the perspective of representing women's emancipation (or the lack thereof), seen by him as a litmus test of progressiveness of cinematic movements.

The third part of the collection is devoted to contemporary Third Cinema films. It begins with David Archibald and Finn Daniel-Yeomans entering a dialogue about two films: *Save the Children Fund Film* (1971), directed by Ken Loach, and *Metalepsis in Black* (2016), by Aryan Kaganof. *Save the Children Fund Film* is not a contemporary film, given that it was produced in 1971, but it is a new film in the sense of being available to the audience only from 2011; before that date, it was consigned to the British Film Institute's archive. Commissioned in 1969 by Save the Children charity from Ken Loach, nowadays regarded as the ultimate British socialist filmmaker and one of the most transnational, the film failed the expectations of its sponsors by presenting charitable giving as a form of imperial control. Released nearly half a century later, *Metalepsis in Black* chronicles an academic conference that took place in South Africa in 2016. Focusing on the *#RhodesMustFall* and *#FeesMustFall* protests, two student-led movements that emerged in 2015 united by a demand to decolonize South Africa's higher education system, Archibald and Daniel-Yeomans argue that the two films are connected by taking issue with the question of class, race, colonialism and decolonization. Their chapter is also a form of transporting the ideas of Third Cinema into academic writing through eschewing the traditional form of an academic essay and instead offering a dialogue between two scholars which is meant to provoke rather than offer a definite political and aesthetic position.

A dialogue between Archibald and Daniel-Yeomans is followed by a chapter authored by Andrej Šprah, who examines a number of Slovenian newsreels under the banner Newsreel Front, produced around 2010 as a way to respond to the economic crisis and to revive Third Cinema in this country. An additional impulse for this endeavour was the publication of a 2009 translation into Slovenian of Solanas and Getino's 'Towards a Third Cinema'. Šprah argues that these politically committed films strive to operate in accordance with some of the fundamental principles of Third Cinema, such as creating work that the system cannot assimilate and the necessity of a committed film reception that considers the viewer as an active co-participant in the film act. They also draw on specific Yugoslav experience, most importantly the heritage of political cinema of former Yugoslavia, such as Black Wave, 'black documentary' of the Belgrade school and alternative film of the 1970s.

The next chapter, written by William Brown, examines the work of Abderrahmane Sissako, who, from the late 1990s, has been among the most prominent contemporary African filmmakers, particularly celebrated in the West. Brown argues that Sissako's cinema well illustrates imbalances of power between the global South, particularly northwest Africa and the global North resulting from economic difference. He also considers Sissako's films, especially his more recent productions, such as the Oscar-nominated *Timbuktu* (2014), which is a co-production between France and Mauritania, as an example of World Cinema, created for Western viewers, enjoying peripheral films in the festival circuit. By the same token, he poses a question whether Sissako's films and arthouse cinema more generally can be truly political.

The last part of the book considers films and cinematic practices which do not really belong to Third Cinema but lend themselves to what can be described as 'Third Cinema critique', on the account that they either involve flagrant exploitation of labour of people from Third World or represent such work. First Ewa Mazierska discusses *Roma* (2018), an Oscar-winning film, directed by Mexican director Alfonso Cuarón. *Roma* is set in Mexico in the early 1970s and focuses on the struggles of a disadvantaged worker during a period of political upheaval in Mexico. Mazierska suggests that dealing with such topic could be a great opportunity to revive Third Cinema and bring its ideals to a wider audience. However, in important ways *Roma* is antithetical to Third Cinema, because it promotes preservation of the status quo, by focusing on the supposed solidarity of people from the Third World across any class or ethnic divide and the positive role played by the wealthy in the lives of the poor, who can be easily misguided and manipulated. By the same token the author regards Cuarón's film as an epitome of a conservative World Cinema.

The final chapter in this part and the entire collection is written by Enrique Uribe-Jongbloed and Toby Miller. Drawing on political economy and ethnography, they examine the specificity of labour relations pertaining to films produced in the Global South, most importantly 'plebeian films' and 'runaway productions'. Their argument is twofold. On the one hand, they argue that the concept of 'plebeian films' returns the attention to modes of production, textual features and audience interests, which were key features of Third Cinema but, on the other hand, that this concept is corrupted by Hollywood's New International Division of Cultural Labour (NICL), which co-opts national and regional cinema industries by exploiting their labour markets. There are two predominate ways in which this neo-colonial exploitation happens: (1) by degrading, or ignoring, home-brew film production as not cinema, which means that it does not count in the statistics or distribution chains as a 'real' cinema, and (2) by staging 'runaway production' of First Cinema that undercuts national or regional labour markets. They argue that 'runaway productions' are based on precarious and exploitative labour, which ensures the conditions offered by this region are attractive to both Hollywood and local filmmakers. However, as film workers state in the interviews conducted by Uribe and Miller, clear hierarchical divisions are created where local production is taking second priority. Uribe-Jongbloed and Miller's chapter thus encourages us to look back at Third Cinema by researching its industrial aspects – a challenge which was met by Andrei Rogatchevski in his examination of *Soy Cuba*.

Together, the authors of this collection point to similarities and connections between Third Cinema films produced on different continents and in different countries, as well as between Third Cinema and other movements, such as socialist realism, oppositional cinema in Eastern Europe and Fourth Cinema. At the same time, however, they emphasize the importance of a national and local context for the production and reception of films. This reflects the recognition that if there is to come any significant political change whose goal is to reduce economic and social inequalities, it will have to be national first before it has a chance to become transnational, because globalization has been hijacked by neoliberal forces, which perfidiously implement a 'race to the bottom' and abolish workers' protection in the name of rationality, progress and even global justice.

# Bibliography

Appiah, Kwame Anthony (1991), 'Is the Post-in Postmodernism the Post-in Postcolonial?', *Critical Inquiry*, 2: 336–57.
Chanan, Michael (1997), 'Special Report: The changing geography of Third Cinema', *Screen*, 4: 372–88.
Dennison, Stephanie and Song Hwee Lim, eds (2006), *Remapping World Cinema Identity, Culture, and Politics in Film*, London: Wallflower Press.
Eisenstein, Hester (2005), 'Dangerous Liaison? Feminism and Corporate Globalization', *Science & Society*, 3: 487–518.
Ekotte, Frieda and Adeline Koh, eds (2009), *Rethinking Third Cinema: The Role of Anti-colonial Media and Aesthetics in Postmodernity*, Münster: Lit Verlag.
Ezra, Elizabeth and Terry Rowden (2006), *Transnational Cinema: The Film Reader*, London and New York: Routledge.
Fraser, Nancy (2009), 'Feminism, Capitalism and the Cunning of History', *New Left Review*, 56: 97–117.
Fukuyama, Francis (1992), *The End of History and the Last Man*, London: Penguin.
Gabriel, Teshome H. (1982), *Third Cinema in Third World: The Aesthetics of Liberation*, Ann Arbor, Michigan.
Gabriel, Teshome H. (undated), 'Third Cinema Updated: Exploration of NomadicAesthetics & Narrative Communities', http://teshomegabriel.net/third-cinema-updated (accessed 15 July 2019).

Garcia Espinoza, Julio (2000) [1979], 'For an Imperfect Cinema', in Robert Stam and Toby Miller (eds), *Film and Theory: An Anthology*, 286–97, Malden and Oxford: Blackwell.

Harvey, David (2005), *A Brief History of Neoliberalism*, Oxford: Oxford University Press.

Harvey, David (2010), *The Enigma of Capital and the Crises of Capitalism*, London: Profile Books.

Iordanova, Dina, David Martin-Jones, and Belén Vidal, eds (2010), *Cinema at the Periphery*, Detroit: Wayne State University Press.

Lim, Song Hwee (2019), 'Concepts of transnational cinema revisited', *Transnational Screens*, 1: 1–12.

Marx, Karl and Friedrich Engels (1947), *The German Ideology: Parts I and III*, New York: International Publishers.

Marx, Karl and Friedrich Engels (2008) [1848], *The Communist Manifesto*, London: Pluto Press.

Mazierska, Ewa (2015), *From Self-fulfilment to Survival of the Fittest*, Oxford: Berghahn.

Meiksins Wood, Ellen (1986), *The Retreat from Class: A New 'True' Socialism*, London: Verso.

Mouffe, Chantal (2018), 'Populists Are on the Rise but This Can Be a Moment for Progressives Too', *The Guardian*, 10 September, https://www.theguardian.com/commentisfree/2018/sep/10/populists-rise-progressives-radical-right (accessed 1 November 2019).

Mouffe, Chantal (2019), 'Centrist Politics Will Not Defeat Boris Johnson's Rightwing Populism', *The Guardian*, 1 October, https://www.theguardian.com/commentisfree/2019/oct/01/centrist-politics-boris-johnson-rightwing-populism (accessed 1 November 2019).

Nagib, Lucia. (2006), 'Towards a positive definition of World Cinema', in Stephanie Dennison, Song Hwee Lim (eds), *Remapping World Cinema: Identity, Culture and Politics in Film*, 26–33, London: Wallflower Press.

Ritzer, Ivo (2018), 'The Relational Politics of Media Culture in the Age of Post-Third Cinema', *Africa Today*, 1: 22–41.

Rowbottom, Sheila and Benyon Huw (2001), 'Handing on Histories', in Sheila Rowbottom and Huw Benyon (eds), *Looking at Class: Film Television and the Working Class in Britain*, 2–24, London: Rivers Oram Press.

Shohat, Ella (1992), 'Notes on the "Post-Colonial"', *Social Text*, No. 31/32: 99–113.

Solanas, Fernando and Octavio Getino (2000) [1969], 'Towards a Third Cinema', in Robert Stam and Toby Miller (eds), *Film and Theory: An Anthology*, 265–86, Malden and Oxford: Blackwell.

Stam, Robert (1998), 'The Two Avant-gardes: The Hour of the Furnaces', in Barry Keith Grant and Jeannette Sloniowski (eds), *Documenting the Documentary*, 254–68, Detroit: Wayne State University Press.

Stam, Robert and Toby Miller, eds (2000), *Film and Theory: An Anthology*, Malden and Oxford: Blackwell Publishers.

Streeck, Wolfgang (2017), 'The Return of the Repressed', *New Left Review*, 104, https://newleftreview.org/issues/II71/articles/wolfgang-streeck-the-crises-of-democratic-capitalism (accessed 17 August 2019).

Streeck, Wolfgang (2019), 'The European Union Is a Liberal Empire, and It Is about to Fall', *Brave New Europe*, 6 March, https://braveneweurope.com/wolfgang-streeck-the-european-union-is-a-liberal-empire-and-it-is-about-to-fall (accessed 17 August 2019).

Wayne, Mike (2001), *Political Film: The Dialectics of Third Cinema*, London: Pluto Press.

*World Cinemas, Transnational Perspectives*. Ed. by Nataša Durovicová, Kathleen E. Newman, London: Routledge, 2010.

# PART ONE

# Revisiting films

# 1

# Exporting cinemarxism in the 1960s: The case of *Soy Cuba*

## Andrei Rogatchevski
## (UiT The Arctic University of Norway)

Mikhail Kalatozov's *Soy Cuba* (I Am Cuba 1964), a Soviet-Cuban cinematic rendition of several human interest stories, put together to explain why the 1959 Cuban revolution had to happen, is largely recognized today as 'one of the masterpieces of world cinema' (Gott 2005). Co-scripted by Enrique Pineda Barnet and Evgeny Evtushenko, it consists of four novellas, linked by partially overlapping characters, a female voiceover and a build-up of protest emotions, resulting in a triumphant procession of rebellious masses to the tune of the Cuban national anthem. The first two stories – those of the Havana dweller Maria/Betty, prostituting herself to rich foreigners, and the tenant farmer Pedro, deprived of his livelihood by his landowner – can be called the novellas of abuse, while the last two – those of the freedom fighters Enrique (a student) and Mariano (a peasant) – the novellas of countering the abuse.[1]

Complete with the scenes featuring abject poverty, exuberant luxury, heroic deeds and tragic deaths, *Soy Cuba*'s fragmentary mini-plots feel

---

[1] In his interview to the Soviet press, Pineda Barnet claimed that the four stories represented four different stages of the Cuban revolution, and semi-jokingly labelled them 'Cuba that they wanted to buy', 'Cuba that they wanted to bleed dry', 'Cuba, whose mutinous spirit they wanted to kill' and 'Cuba that took up arms to liberate itself' ('Ia – Kuba' 1964a: 1). All translations are mine, unless indicated otherwise.

rather clichéd in both their melodramatic form and their propagandistic content.² As one Western critic put it, 'the police are shown to be book-burners and killers. The common man is always decent, and students are on the side of the angels' (Nangle 2001: 28). A Soviet critic's opinion was not much different: 'Take, for example, the film's first novella. This is a banal... story, often told in diverse films and novels, about a nice virtuous woman, who is in love with a nice virtuous man but has to turn to prostitution – and what a drama ensues! Evtushenko has not added anything new to this set of literary circumstances' (the film critic Georgy Kapralov in 'Ia – Kuba' 1965: 30).

It was mainly owing to Kalatozov and the extraordinary vision of his cameraman Sergei Urusevsky that *Soy Cuba* became 'an epic and poetic account that transcends its subject matter' (Gott 2005) and possibly 'one of the top three best-photographed films ever made' (Hudson 2006: 28).³ According to Alexander Calzatti, Urusevsky's chief camera operator on *Soy Cuba*, 'it was really a cameraman's film because everything was orchestrated for the camera' (Turner 1995). As Sergio Corrieri, a *Soy Cuba* actor, put it, 'light was the main protagonist in this film' (*Soy Cuba, o Mamute siberiano* 2005: 00:48:19–00:48:22). *Soy Cuba* was mostly shot with a handheld Éclaire CM3 Camiflex, often passed on from one assistant to another to ensure the fluidity and continuity of movement, as well as constant changes of the points of view (together representing an omnipresent and protean *perpetuum mobile*).⁴ Urusevsky's much preferred 9.8mm lens 'afforded him enormous opportunities, such as enhanced sharpness and easy transition from closeups to general view' (the cameraman Nikolai

---

²The full version of the script, published in the Moscow magazine *Znamia*, is even more overblown, practically in every respect. The scenes that mercifully did not make it to the film include a striptease; a visit of three American tourist couples to a casino and a dog-racing track; a mass brawl between American sailors, on the one hand, and Enrique and Cuban women and stevedores, on the other (see FIGURE 1.3); a multiple bus crash in protest against expensive public transport fares; an arrest and murder at a sugar mill; an episode in which a peasant woman lends her child to a female partisan messenger to make the messenger look innocuous and thus ensure her safe passage to Fidel Castro through the territory frequented by government patrols; a group of *guerrilleros* risking their lives to feed children some oranges; and a blind old man shooting at Batista's soldiers (Evtushenko 1963: 4, 6–8, 27, 37–38, 69–70, 83–8).
³Here's how Pineda Barnet described the manner in which the script had been developed: Kalatozov, Urusevsky, Evtushenko 'and I would gather at a round table and a general conversation would begin. Kalatozov, for instance, would ask what Cuban peasants were like. I would start explaining... Then Evtushenko and I would go to different rooms and work at our desks. Two drastically different versions of the script would often emerge. At this point Kalatozov and Urusevsky would intervene. They'd select what they were content with from both versions. We'd shout ourselves hoarse, naturally. Kalatozov acted as an arbiter' ('Ia – Kuba' 1964a: 1).
⁴Cf.: 'Urusevsky is a virtuoso of the kinetic camera – he dances with it, wanders about space with it, even goes underwater with it' (Iordanova 1997: 125).

Prozorovsky in 'Ia – Kuba' 1965: 28). The infrared stock, used in several sequences, occasionally inverted the black-and-white colour scheme (ideal for portraying both the struggle between good and evil[5] and the racial harmony on the island), so that 'beauty and foreboding [were] conveyed in about equal measure' (Turner 1995). In Calzatti's opinion, Cuba has never looked so spectacular on the screen (Turner 1995).

It is therefore all the more surprising that, despite the initial big interest and warm welcome at the opening nights in Santiago de Cuba and Havana on 24, 26 and 30 July 1964 (to coincide with the eleventh anniversary of Castro's attack on the Moncada Barracks),[6] the film gained only a week-long distribution in Cuba and a rather mixed response from the Cuban critics. While Teresa Ruiz in the newspaper *Revolucion* claimed that 'the film has much of Urusevsky and Kalatozov but little of Cuba' (quoted in Espinosa Domínguez 2012: 111), Josefina Ruiz in the magazine *Verde Olivo* insisted that 'for the first time we have seen a real Cuban cinema that has paradoxically been produced by foreigners' (quoted in Galt 2011: 216–17).[7] The reception in the USSR, where the film was premiered simultaneously, was not altogether dissimilar. During the discussion of *Soy Cuba* by Soviet industry professionals, the cameraman Sergei Poluianov succinctly expressed a widely held opinion: 'I am thinking of how this was filmed.... [Yet] I have not learned anything about the people of Cuba. When a house is burning [in the novella about Pedro], I am interested in the aesthetic effect of the flames but am not touched by the plight of the person who is forced to set his house on fire' ('Ia – Kuba' 1965: 27).[8] By contrast, the journalist Aleksandr Isbakh's impressions after a Moscow screening were perhaps closer to what Kalatozov and Urusevsky had aspired to achieve: 'A history of the Cuban people's struggle for life, happiness and freedom has passed before us on the screen... The film has touched me' (Isbakh 1964: 9). Still, in Soviet Russia, *Soy Cuba* did not stay in circulation for too long either and more or less disappeared off the radar until its surprise re-emergence at the Telluride and San Francisco film festivals almost thirty years later. Subsequently released on video and DVD under the auspices of Francis Ford Coppola and Martin Scorsese, it is now admired even by many of those who disagree with its

---

[5]Cf. 'the absolute good is represented by the anti-government elements, while absolute evil is clearly the government, its defenders and the socio-economic system that gives it life' (Garcia Osuna 2003: 170–1).

[6]A. V. Barinov, a deputy head at Goskino, recalled: Santiago de Cuba's 'biggest cinema, seating approximately 1,500, could not fit in all those who wanted to attend the first screening. People were standing in the doorways, aisles and along the walls. Many scenes were accompanied by enthusiastic applause' ('Ia – Kuba' 1964b: 4).

[7]For a representative range of the Cuban reviews of the film, see Garcia Borrero 2001: 327–8.

[8]For Soviet articles about *Soy Cuba*, see Antropov and Barykin 1979: 155–6.

political message, and features regularly in the academic discourse and on the film school curriculum.

Why was *Soy Cuba* deemed contentious enough by the Cuban and Soviet authorities to consign it to oblivion (if not for an outright ban)? And, being a major co-production with a well-established partner at an early stage in the development of post-1959 Cuban film industry, which role, if any, did it play in the formation of the so-called 'imperfect cinema' (the Cuban variety of Third Cinema, see Chanan 2005: 245) as a concept and a practice? There appears to be a number of possible answers to both questions. I will group such answers, some of which have already been suggested before, under five categories (the financial, the aesthetic, the ideological, the postcolonial and the co-productional) in order to undertake a critical appraisal of all the principal explanations that I am aware of and to identify the most convincing ones, while at the same time trying to separate *Soy Cuba*'s intentions and accomplishments from the way these intentions and accomplishments were perceived.

For my main theoretical framework, I have chosen the theory of accelerated cultural development by Georgi Gachev, a Soviet philosopher of Bulgarian origin. According to him, an accelerated 'development of a nation (country) is conditioned by a neighbouring nation or nations, which have already gone a long way in accumulating a substantial experience of social and cultural development' (Gachev 1989: 15). The word 'neighbouring' should not of course be understood strictly in the sense of one nation or country sharing a territory or a border with another. A colonial rule, no matter how far the distance is from a colony to a metropole, can arguably serve, up to a point, as an example of a condition for acceleration. So can a nation or country that has become a world leader in a particular aspect of a widely and obviously useful social and cultural know-how, and therefore a natural model to follow by other nations or countries. Accelerated development can simultaneously involve many sides of life in the affected country or nation but can also be, at least initially, confined to just one feature.

Gachev's book is not at all about Cuba, but its early version was written in the late 1950s and early 1960s, when Cuba was often front-page news and Castro's coming under the Soviet patronage (partly to ensure the implementation and lasting effect of his rapid socio-economic reforms) was seen by many as beneficial.[9] Besides, Cuba had already been through phases of accelerated development in the past, which has been testified to by

---

[9]Needless to say, not only the USSR but other countries of the Eastern bloc also acted as Cuba's patrons, quite a few of them being more economically and technologically advanced than Cuba.

the Cuban anthropologist Fernando Ortiz.[10] This makes the application of Gachev's theory to the situation in the 1960s' Cuba fully legitimate, especially as far as the post-1959 Cuban film industry is concerned. Filmmaking under Castro began from a fairly low starting point only to become, a few years later, 'one of the strongest... in Latin America, thanks to... the great help from socialist countries' (Julio Garcia Espinosa in Kozin 1964: 19). Co-productions were used as an instrument of accelerated development. In addition to *Soy Cuba*, a 1963 Czechoslovak-Cuban (*For Whom Havana Dances*) and a 1964 GDR-Cuban (*Preludio 11*) feature films should be singled out. These and other relevant examples – including several Cuban films of the period and Third Cinema-related theoretical publications by Cuban directors – will be referred to throughout the chapter, as and when appropriate.

## *Soy Cuba*'s excessive production costs

Instituto Cubano del Arte e Industria Cinematograficos, or ICAIC, founded in March 1959, comprised 'everything, from film studios and cinemas to domestic and international distribution' (Kozin 1964: 19), as well as 'a state committee for filmmaking, a filmmakers union and an educational establishment' ('17 dnei na Kube' 1964: 3). Meant to monopolize under the state ownership whatever was related to cinema production and consumption, it also received annual state funding to the tune of 7 million US dollars, which included salaries for *c.* 1,000 employees and production costs for *c.* forty documentaries, five to ten animated cartoons, four to six feature films and fifty-two weekly newsreels (see Burton 1997: 134). For 1964 – the year of *Soy Cuba*'s release – eight feature films, sixty documentaries and twelve animations were planned, and in the five years since the revolution, a total of eighteen features were made (see Kozin 1964: 19).

These figures look reasonably impressive, given that most if not all of the film industry professionals plying their trade in Cuba before 1959[11] left the country fairly soon after the revolution and had to be replaced with a

---

[10]Cf.: 'The whole gamut of culture run by Europe in a span of more than four millenniums took place in Cuba in less than four centuries. In Europe the change was step by step; here it was by leaps and bounds... At one bound the bridge between the drowsing stone ages and the wide-awake Renaissance was spanned. In a single day various of the intervening ages were crossed in Cuba; one might say thousands of "culture-years", if such measurement were admissible in the chronology of peoples' (Ortiz 1947: 97–8).

[11]Said to be in the region of 30–35, see Kozin 1964: 19. Burton (1997: 125), however, mentions 8,000.

largely inexperienced staff who subsequently learnt their métier on the job.[12] However, to put the statistics into perspective, the biggest Latin American film industry (Mexican) produced 'about seventy [feature] films a year' at the time (Brook 1961: 78), while ICAIC's entire annual budget amounted to 'less than the cost of a single big-budget movie in Hollywood' (Chanan 2004: 89).

It was in this atmosphere of financial frugality[13] and comparative amateurishness that the highly qualified Soviet members of the *Soy Cuba* crew[14] arrived on the island to make the film, commanding seemingly unlimited resources.[15] The Soviets stayed for a total of twenty months,[16] if one includes the fact-finding period, when many audio interviews with Cubans (and Fidel Castro himself) were recorded (see 'Ia – Kuba' 1964a: 1; and Iordanova 1997: 125). In the opinion of Raul Garcia (*Soy Cuba*'s sound assistant, who was also cast as Enrique), 'it was the longest shooting for a feature film in Cuba' (*Soy Cuba, o Mamute siberiano* 2005: 00:31:41–00:31:46), where the average filming period in those days lasted from eight to twelve weeks. Kalatozov laid the blame for shooting delays on Hurricane Flora (see 'Ia – Kuba' 1964b: 4), which ravaged Cuba's western provinces in October 1963.[17] Yet it is undeniable that in their pursuit of perfection as they understood it, the *Soy Cuba* crew – consisting of sixteen Russians and, by different accounts, fifty to seventy Cubans, all working hard, for up to sixteen hours a day and seven days a week (see 'Ia – Kuba' 1964a: 1; Turner 1995; and Iordanova 1997: 125) – did take their time on the sets, which, to make matters even worse, were occasionally inundated with a high number of additional participants. Thus, one famous 'nearly three-minute complex

---

[12]According to Matuskova (2017: 183), ICAIC's 'improvisation and the overall lack of organization mirrored the government's way of managing Cuba in those early years'.

[13]It was apparently from the French New Wave that Cuban and other Latin American directors learnt 'how to produce a film with limited resources' (Schroeder 2002: 2). There were exceptions, however. The phantasmagorical farce *El otro Cristobal* (1963), made in Cuba by the Frenchman Armand Gatti and submitted as Cuba's entry at Cannes, reportedly left the ICAIC's production department without a single nail (see Matuskova 2017: 184). It is these circumstances that Tomas Gutierrez Alea is probably hinting at when he jokes in Gatti's presence during the 1962 debate on modernity in art, arranged by the *Cine cubano* journal: Gatti 'talks about the material problems of the cinema, that is to say, the problems that he faces in the capitalist countries with producers, and how these can be overcome more easily in socialist countries, although I do not think that all of them have been completely overcome' ('Que es lo moderno en el arte?' 1963: 47; translation by Kirsty Jane Falconer).

[14]In 1958, Kalatozov was awarded a Palme d'Or at Cannes for his previous film, *The Cranes Are Flying*.

[15]Turner 1995 estimates the *Soy Cuba* budget to be 600,000 US dollars but this is probably on the low side.

[16]Some information about their sojourn can be found, for example, in Urusevsky's postcards from 1961 to 1962 to his wife Bella Fridman, who was also part of the *Soy Cuba* team (see 'Cartas desde Cuba (1961–1962)' 1983).

[17]For the footage of devastation and the Castro brothers helping personally to sort out the flood's aftermath, see Santiago Alvarez's 1963 documentary *Ciclon*.

opening shot on the hotel roof required seventeen takes and involved around one hundred extras' (Iordanova 1997: 126). For the closing scene, 5,000 Cuban army soldiers had to be moved from the Oriente province to Havana on the orders of Raul Castro (Espinosa Dominguez 2012: 114), which left the province unprotected. The infrared film stock (then manufactured solely for the use of the Soviet Army) did not make things go any faster. Calzatti recalls: 'We had no infrared meter, and no infrared marks on the lens, so many times the results were unpredictable... What you see in the film is okay, but we shot much footage to select from. Each scene was done 15 or 20 times, so it never was filmed spontaneously' (Turner 1995). Urusevsky's peculiar aesthetic preferences did not speed the shooting process up either. Once he stopped filming 'for almost three days waiting for clouds to show up' because he thought that 'a sky without clouds [was] uninteresting' (*Soy Cuba*'s construction chief Juan Varona in *Soy Cuba, o Mamute siberiano* 2005: 00:49:31–00:49:36, 00:49:53–00:49:54).

Even though 'the Cubans considered it a matter of honour to help the picture' (Kalatozov in 'Ia – Kuba' 1964a: 1), many of them must have thought that *Soy Cuba* was an unaffordable luxury.[18] The ICAIC founder and first president Alfredo Guevara diplomatically called the length of *Soy Cuba*'s production period 'extravagant' (*Soy Cuba, o Mamute siberiano* 2005: 00:58:50). In Matuskova's analysis (2017: 67), for the cash-strapped Cuban film industry, *Soy Cuba* served as a glaring example of practices to avoid. When reading the essay 'For an Imperfect Cinema' by Julio Garcia Espinosa,[19] a Third Cinema manifesto published in 1969 to say that 'imperfect cinema is no longer interested in quality or technique' (Garcia Espinosa 2014: 229), it is hard to ignore the feeling that *Soy Cuba* had something to do with it.[20] As John Mraz (2002) put it, 'the material conditions of film production in Cuba were no doubt... important to the type of cinema that evolved there... The fact that Cuban cineastes were making films in an underdeveloped country with little prior experience was crucial in their commitment to an "imperfect cinema", which might be summarized as cheap, portable, rough and dedicated to transforming reality.'[21]

---

[18]Paid for by the Soviet state, of course – which brought to Cuba its 'own transport and equipment, so as not to tie up ICAIC's limited facilities and halt its other productions; by informal arrangement, the equipment was then left behind in Cuba when they finished' (Chanan 2004:166), to be re-used by the island's film industry.
[19]He was then not only a Cuban film director of note but also Alfredo Guevara's deputy at ICAIC, i.e. an official who oversaw parts of the ICAIC budget.
[20]For his part, at the 1962 *Cine cubano* debate about modernity in art, in the presence of Garcia Espinosa and other reputable Cuban and foreign filmmakers, Kalatozov professed: 'My personal point of view is that a modern filmmaker should fully master the art of form' ('Que es lo moderno en el arte?' 1963: 37; translation by Kirsty Jane Falconer).
[21]Cf. also: 'Cuban filmmakers were making the films that it was possible for them to make, and... their experimental "philosophical" approach was a direct result of a dire lack of funding' (Smith Mesa 2011: 88).

Although such words as 'cheap', 'portable' and 'rough' are obviously inapplicable to *Soy Cuba*, it may well be the case that Kalatozov and Urusevsky were not averse to the idea of transforming reality by cinematic means, with their restless camera clearly not only urging the viewer to identify with the (Cuban) revolutionary cause but also attempting to spur him or her into revolutionary action.[22] This is not far off from what the Cuban filmmaker and theoretician Tomas Gutierrez Alea says in his 'Viewer's Dialectic' (1982), which Smith Mesa (2011: 90) calls 'an extension' of Garcia Espinosa's 'For an Imperfect Cinema': Cuban film 'should contribute in the most effective way possible to elevating viewers' revolutionary consciousness and to arming them for the ideological struggle which they have to wage against all kinds of reactionary tendencies' (Gutierrez Alea 1997: 110). Yet the *Soy Cuba* production mode was not something that Cuban filmmakers could ever adopt – and that made Kalatozov and Urusevsky vulnerable to accusations of elitism (not bourgeois but socialist elitism, yet elitism nonetheless), on the grounds of both their exuberant visual style (that could be easily deemed expensive and pretentious) and the limitations that this style necessarily imposed on their potential audiences. And for proto-Third Cinema proponents, elitism in any shape or form was an anathema. Garcia Espinosa (2014: 223, 229) declared:

> There can be no new and genuinely qualitative jump in art, unless the concept and the reality of the 'elite' is done away with once and for all... The only thing [the imperfect cinema] is interested in is how an artist responds to the following question: What are you doing in order to overcome the barrier of the 'cultured' elite audience which up to now has conditioned the form of your work?.[23]

## *Soy Cuba*'s controversial aesthetics

Judging by the available evidence from film reviews, public debates and reminiscences, the fact that *Soy Cuba*'s camera 'repeatedly challenges danger, convention and even the laws of gravity' (Turner 1995), and thus

---

[22]Cf.: 'In several sequences, the camera shows the masses "from [the] inside", where the spectator looking at the screen feels that that [s/he is] becoming a member of those Cuban masses; the spectator is marching with them, participating in what is going on [on] the screen. The camera persuades the spectator to join the Cuban revolutionary masses, to get involved, and to take an active position by the side of the Revolution' (Smith Mesa 2011: 138).

[23]Cf. also: Jean-Luc Godard 'managed to make anti-bourgeois cinema but he couldn't make people's cinema' (Gutierrez Alea 1997: 114). Perhaps this could also be read as a jibe against Gatti's *Cristobal*, which was very anti-bourgeois but unlikely to score high with the wider public.

attracts the attention to Kalatozov and Urusevsky's skills as auteurs at the expense of revolutionary Cuba, tended to irritate, rather than excite, many contemporary viewers in Cuba and the USSR.[24] Writing in the journal *Bohemia* in August 1964, the critic Luis M. Lopez noted 'the superficiality in [Kalatozov and Urusevsky's] approach to the reality we know so well, overwritten by their distorted portrayal' (quoted in Espinosa Dominguez 2012: 111). *Soy Cuba*'s production secretary Yolanda Benett echoed this sentiment four decades later: 'I had the feeling [Kalatozov and Urusevsky] wanted to show a reality that didn't actually exist' (*Soy Cuba, o Mamute siberiano* 2005: 01:02:52–01:02:55). Sergio Corrieri asserted that Cubans could not recognize themselves in *Soy Cuba* because the film presented the country and its people 'through a Slavic prism' (*Soy Cuba, o Mamute siberiano* 2005: 01:05:49–01:05:59). Yet in Soviet Russia, too, critical voices repeatedly stated that the image of the Cuban revolution 'drowns in the abundance of visual effects' (Bleiman 1965: 3) and that viewers 'are not allowed to forget about [Urusevsky's] craftsmanship even when [in the last novella] a child dies in a bomb explosion. We are invited to admire how brilliantly the scene has been shot. And this, I beg your pardon, is insulting. A child's death, a broken love, a poor man's grief, a desperate nation's wrath can't be a reason for narcissism' (the film director Grigory Chukhrai in 'Ia – Kuba' 1965: 36).[25]

It is evident that many ordinary Cubans 'understood the film at that sensitive and euphoric time as diminishing the historical importance of the Revolution... because it had placed too much weight on the aesthetic aspects instead of the agents of change' (Matuskova 2017: 115). As for Cuban filmmakers *per se*, likewise, their reaction to *Soy Cuba* was obviously influenced to a substantial degree by their belief that 'being a director with a distinct voice was less important than the sense of belonging to a collective emancipatory project with national and continental dimensions' (Schroeder 2002: 2).

However, it is also apparent that *Soy Cuba* was modelled on Sergei Eisenstein's unfinished film *Que viva Mexico*, which also had a multipart structure encompassing some of Mexico's dramatic historical and revolutionary time periods (see, for instance, Smith Mesa 2011: 124; and

---

[24]What appears to be overlooked at the time of the film's release is that 'the fluid, floating movement of the camera... emphasizes the theme of connectedness – the rootedness of Cuba's people in its land – and thus usefully introduces the rural backdrop of the final story, which points to the joining of the urban and rural arms of the revolutionary movement' (Thakkar 2014: 96).

[25]A quarter century later, another fault was found with *Soy Cuba*: it 'clearly aestheticises poverty. The peasant farms of the second and fourth episodes are gardens of Eden, the sugar cane (shot from below...) a great shining forest stalked by giant peasants' (Paul Julian Smith 1999: 45).

Harte 2013: 8). During their work on the script of *Soy Cuba*, Kalatozov reportedly made Pineda Barnet watch *Que viva Mexico* again and again (see Matuskova 2017: 101). Cinematographic parallels can be drawn between the two films revealing 'the interplay of shadow and light, the indolent and enchanting spirit of the South' (Iordanova 1997: 125). It is also worthy of note that *Soy Cuba* consciously imitates the aesthetics of Eisensteinian silent cinema in keeping dialogue to a minimum[26] and using the *typage* principle when casting actors, many of them non-professionals,[27] sometimes in key roles (such as Luz Maria Collazo playing Maria/Betty), so that 'characters borrowed from real life turn into allegorical images' (Bleiman 1965: 3), for example Maria/Betty personifying mistreated Cuba. So why could not Cuban filmmakers, many of whom held Eisenstein in high esteem,[28] see the connection between *Soy Cuba* and Eisenstein's legacy and show a more nuanced appreciation of Kalatozov's film?

One explanation may be that 'where Eisensteinian form is often... understood primarily in terms of montage, *Soy Cuba* proposes the fluidity of the long take' (Galt 2011: 226). Another explanation

---

[26]Cf.: 'various characters... remain practically mute, uttering words only sparingly and in a way that seems more akin to emphatic silent intertitles than live dialogue' (Harte 2013: 6). This notwithstanding, at least one Soviet critic opined that the film 'could be more... laconic' (Isbakh 1964: 9).

[27]Cf.: 'students played student parts, peasants played peasant parts and so on' (Kalatozov in 'Ia – Kuba' 1964a: 1)

[28]Cf.: 'Filmmakers such as Eisenstein... achieved the status of classics and were the first and most important point of reference for the younger generation of filmmakers in Cuba who were interested in promoting the social mission of the moving image' (Smith Mesa 2011: 98). For one, Gutierrez Alea first read Eisenstein in the late 1940s and this became a 'key moment in [his] development as a filmmaker' (Smith Mesa 2011: 166). Together with Alfredo Guevara, Santiago Alvarez and Julio Garcia Espinosa, Gutierrez Alea was a student of Jose Manuel Valdes Rodriguez (1896–1971), the founder of the first film course at the University of Havana in 1939. Valdes Rodriguez met Eisenstein in Moscow in 1934, wrote about him and purchased copies of his films. The awareness of early Soviet cinema in pre-Castro Cuba was also disseminated through *Cuba y la URSS* (1945–52), the journal of the Instituto de Intercambio Cultural Cubano Sovietico, of which Valdes Rodriguez was a member; and by the Communist film critic and author Mirta Aguirre (1912–80) and the film section of the Nuestro Tiempo cultural society, founded in 1950, to which Alfredo Guevara, Gutierrez Alea and Garcia Espinosa belonged (see Smith Mesa 2011: 62–6, 74). In his 'Viewer's Dialectics', Gutierrez Alea wrote (1997: 113): 'Soviet cinema attained a real closeness to the movement of radical social transformation which was taking place... It was destined for the masses, and popular, because it expressed the interests, aspirations and values of broad sectors of the population which at the time were carrying history onward. That first moment of Soviet cinema left a deep imprint on all filmmaking that was to follow and, today, the most modern filmmaking continues to drink from its fountains and nourish itself from that cinema's explorations, experiments and theoretical achievements that still have not been completely tapped'. It has to be noted, however, that Eisenstein's influence on Cuban filmmakers was 'less technical than ideological... The stylistic resemblances between... Soviet expressive realism and Cuban cinema in the 1960s... are slight' (Schroeder 2002: 14).

(a complementary one) is that, no matter how hard *Soy Cuba* tried to follow in Eisenstein's footsteps in 'the hope that Soviet cinema [would] once again be what it [had been] thirty years ago' (Cabrera Infante 1991: 323), in Cuba, Kalatozov's film was primarily associated with Socialist Realism,[29] which revolutionary Cuban filmmakers disliked for its excessive prescriptiveness and didacticism[30] and tended to juxtapose to what they praised as the 'cinema of October' – that is, early Eisenstein and Pudovkin (see Mraz 2002) – oblivious to the fact that Eisenstein and Pudovkin were not altogether alien to Socialist Realism either.

According to Chanan (2005: 244), for Cuba of the 1960s, Socialist Realism in cinema was a bit 'like a mirror image of Hollywood: stereotyped characters, formulaic plots with happy endings, naturalistic photography and continuity editing, avoidance of controversial subject matter, a Victorian code of sexual morals, in short, a mass-culture product addressed to the lowest common denominator of popular taste'. With the exception of Urusevsky's camerawork (qualifying *Soy Cuba* as 'elitist') and the unhappy endings in three out of four novellas in the film (making the happy ending of the fourth novella, i.e. the revolution's success, even happier), many of *Soy Cuba*'s features answer Chanan's description. Let me adduce only one example. In the third novella, the police have to fire eight gunshots at Enrique to make him collapse. The film critic Luiz M. Lopez takes issue with this scene, which he judges to be unrealistic and derived from the Soviet cinema tradition, when a single shot is often enough to kill a baddie,[31] while many close-range shots, even by a firing squad, cannot always seem to get a Bolshevik,[32] 'sustained, despite the bullets, by the force of [his] ideas' (Lopez 1964: 25).

---

[29] Cf., for example: in *Soy Cuba*, 'the saga of the Cuban revolution was... recreated in the purest style of socialist realism' (the narrator's voiceover in *Soy Cuba, o Mamute siberiano* 2005: 00:59:32–00:59:36).

[30] Thus, Ambrosio Fornet (2007), a Cuban film critic and scriptwriter, defined Socialist Realism as 'pedagogy and hagiography, methodologically oriented toward creating "positive heroes" and the strategic absence of antagonistic conflicts in "among the people"'. Garcia Espinosa's manifesto 'For an Imperfect Cinema' has been seen as 'a negation of Socialist Realism' (Smith Mesa 2011: 165). Neither Gutierrez Alea was a fan of Socialist Realism. In his contribution to the 1962 *Cine cubano* debate about modernity in art, he made a point (in Kalatozov's presence) that for a long time Soviet art had been coming out of the 'norms that tried clearly to establish what socialist art ought to be, and in many cases – it is very clear to everyone – ended up in what I would call socialist idealism, as opposed to what many believed was socialist realism' ('Que es lo moderno en el arte?' 1963: 47; translation by Kirsty Jane Falconer).

[31] E.g. at the end of Grigory Chukhrai's 1956 film *The Forty-First*, also photographed by Urusevsky.

[32] Like in Aleksandr Alov and Vladimir Naumov's 1958 film *Wind*, designed by *Soy Cuba*'s production designer Evgeny Svidetelev.

Lopez finds such a 'schematism detestable' (Lopez 1964), quite in line with the Cuban filmmakers' 'dominant wish' at the time, that is, 'non-conformity: to keep their cinema free, free from left wing clichés and conventions as much as from those on the right' (Brook 1961: 79). As far as left-wing clichés are concerned, Gutierrez Alea felt confident enough to challenge some of them in his film version of *Twelve Chairs*, a 1928 Soviet satirical novel by Il'ia Il'f and Evgeny Petrov, which the director successfully adapted to post-revolutionary Cuba as *Las doce sillas* (1962). In one film scene, an artist proposes to paint politically themed murals in a rail workers' club, which include an eagle symbolizing imperialism, wounded by an archer representing Cuba. Schroeder (2002: 16) appropriately calls this 'a parody of socialist realism, an inside joke'. It may even be a dig specifically at *Soy Cuba*, whose fondness for using humans and animals as emblematic images sometimes borders on the ridiculous. For instance, *Soy Cuba* depicts a mass demonstration at the University of Havana, triggered by a chance killing, by the police, of a snow-white dove (serving here as a symbol of innocence brought to death by injustice). The dead dove is carried in front of the indignant crowd who are singing the Cuban national anthem as a form of protest (see Figure 1.1). As Lopez noted ironically in connection with this scene, it was not a dove that mobilized protest actions in Batista's Cuba but people's hatred of tyranny (see Lopez 1964: 25). Even though *Las*

FIGURE 1.1 *Mourning the dove*

*doce sillas* was released a year and a half ahead of *Soy Cuba*, it may well be that Gutierrez Alea as an ICAIC insider knew enough about Kalatozov and Urusevsky's film (in preparation since 1961), to poke fun at its somewhat kitschy style long before it hit the screens.

As Matuskova (2017: 124) put it, the Cuban filmmakers at the time looked for a screen 'language that was more literal, more materialistic as well as realistic, and... symbolic, poetic renditions seemed foreign, exaggerated, fabricated, and even inappropriate to them'.[33] Such aesthetic preferences were closer to Italian neorealism than to Socialist Realism[34] (although, of course, these two traditions are not mutually exclusive[35]). Some Cuban filmmakers, such as Alfredo Guevara, Garcia Espinosa and Gutierrez Alea, even studied at the Centro Sperimentale di Cinematografia in Rome (the latter two subsequently co-directed Cuba's first neorealist film, a short called *El Megano*, 1954 – co-written by Guevara). Gutierrez Alea's first full-length independently directed feature, *Historias de la revolucion* (1960), also consisting of several (three) novellas about the 1959 Cuban revolution, is modelled after Roberto Rossellini's *Paisan* (1946), a six-part neorealist war drama about the liberation of Italy by the Allies and partisans in 1943–45. *Historias* were even photographed by *Paisan*'s cameraman Otello Martelli. According to Schroeder (2002: 13), *Paisan* served as an inspiration for *Historias* because it provided a safer 'bitty' option for an inexperienced cast and crew and an opportunity to deal with different aspects/phases/localities of the revolution. It is conceivable that Kalatozov watched *Historias* (it was screened in the USSR), which may have influenced *Soy Cuba* in some way.[36] After all, *Historias* display three principal features of the revolutionary struggle on Cuba, namely, 'city, country and their coming together' (Schroeder 2002: 13) – and this is exactly what *Soy Cuba* does.[37] Furthermore, the traits

---

[33]Pineda Barnet admitted that *Soy Cuba*'s 'melodramatic, exaggerated structure... made me feel responsible and guilty' after the film's release (*Soy Cuba, o Mamute siberiano* 2005. 01:02:19–01:02:32).

[34]Cf.: a 'neo-realist approach is the thing that suits [Cuban film art] at the moment' (Brook 1961: 79).

[35]Cf.: 'the strand of film and critical theory that led from the Soviet Union of the 1920s to Italy in the 1930s was taken up in Cuban cinematic discourse of the 1960s and '70s' (Salazkina 2012: 113).

[36]Upon their release in Cuba, *Historias* were watched by one million viewers, which was quite a success for the then Cuban population of just over seven million.

[37]In Evtushenko's published script (1963: 68), the mention of wounded people on stretchers en route to Sierra Maestra is reminiscent of the second novella in *Historias*. *Soy Cuba* was definitely influenced by yet another Cuban portmanteau film, *Cuba '58* (1962), also about the run-up to the 1959 revolution. The film was co-directed by Jorge Fraga and Jose Miguel Garcia Ascot. In 'Que es lo moderno en el arte?' 1963: 37, Kalatozov compliments Fraga's segment 'Ano nuevo', which proves that he knew the film. What is actually reflected in *Soy Cuba*, however (see its third novella), is the fat repulsive policeman and the dispersal of student demonstrations by water cannons from Garcia Ascot's segment 'Un dia de trabajo'.

that Schroeder (2002: 14) lists as typical of neorealism – the use of non-professional actors, shooting on location, 'the episodic form and the dignity and sacredness of everyday life' – are characteristic of *Soy Cuba*, too. In other words, despite an observable lack of congruence between them, *Soy Cuba* and Cuban cinema of the 1960s actually had a great deal in common.

There is one more important feature that *Soy Cuba* and Cuban cinema of the 1960s share, namely 'an irrepressible frenzy of filmic bricolage licensed by that supreme act of bricolage, the Cuban revolution' (Chanan 2005: 236–7). This bricolage has found expression, for example, in hybrid genres, such as documentary features – through 'adding documentary footage to the fictional narrative' (Smith Mesa 2011: 182), like in *Historias de la revolucion* – and, in the case of *Las doce sillas*, an eclectic mix of visual styles, 'stretching to animated vignettes and silent-film pastiche' (Brooke 2008: 93). Similarly, in *Soy Cuba*, there can be found elements of thriller (especially in the third novella, about Enrique's assassination attempt on a police chief), melodrama (throughout), epos (thanks to the fragmentary nature of the grand-scale narrative about heroic deeds) and myth (about the creation of a new world from pieces of an old one), as well as – like in the scene when Enrique in slow motion is throwing a stone at the police – some 'operatic timing... [that] prompted some of [the film's] Cuban collaborators to reject it as contrary to Cuba's real-life tempo' (Nagib 2007: 86). At variance with what these collaborators were saying, it is in fact possible to claim that 'Kalatozov's film... is "all mixed as one" (*todo mezclado*), like the ICAIC film productions, or like Cuban identity itself' (Smith Mesa 2011: 142). This is entirely in keeping with Gachev's theory (1989: 29), which posits that accelerated cultural development 'rarely gives us final, fully matured and developed types and forms. Instead, it is replete with transitional phenomena, in which one form already grows into another before reaching maturity. Everything here is boiling, wandering and slipping away from customary categories'. As *Soy Cuba* is a collaborative product of its time, no wonder that it is to all intents and purposes a miscellany.[38]

Yet there is at least one fundamental quality that sets *Soy Cuba* apart from the Cuban milieu that co-spawned it. According to Alfredo Guevara, the Cuban filmmakers' primary task after the revolution was 'to demystify cinema for the entire population;... to reveal all the tricks, all the recourses of the language; to dismantle all the mechanisms of cinematic hypnosis' (quoted in Burton 1997: 128–9). According to Burton, this was necessitated by 'the conviction that all forms of artistic expression carry an ideological dimension. If this ideological bias is veiled in the vast majority of art works

---

[38]The Cuban-Czechoslovak co-production *For Whom Havana Dances* (1963) also 'tried to combine too many genres. [Its director Vladimir Cech] wanted the film to be fictional but also documentary, melodramatic but political. He wanted to create a fictional film, yet the extent of [his] carnival sequences is excessive' for a feature (Matuskova 2017: 194).

produced in capitalist societies,... it should be made explicit in the artistic production of a revolutionary socialist regime [such as Cuban]' (Burton 1997: 129). Alas, such a mission would have been impossible to carry out with regard to *Soy Cuba*, of which even the highly experienced film director Martin Scorsese said (to Calzatti) 'that he didn't want to go to his grave without knowing how it had been done' (Espinosa Domíngues 2012: 114).

## *Soy Cuba*'s dogmatic ideology

Let me now examine the ideological roots of *Soy Cuba*'s rejection by the Cubans (as well as the Soviets). At first glance, the Soviet and the Cuban views on the role of cinema in post-revolutionary society were quite similar and should not have led towards any major disagreement. Lenin's adage 'of all the arts, cinema is the most important for us [Bolsheviks]' (Boltianskii 1925: 19) is often quoted and widely known. According to Chanan (2005: 235), Lenin's point of view was prompted by cinema's 'ability to reach a widespread and largely illiterate population [in Russia] with a vivid portrayal of great propaganda value' by virtue of being 'a terrific instrument for the enormous job of educating [the masses] in the basic tenets of the communist state'.

Equally, the law on the formation of ICAIC, published in *Gaceta oficial de la Republica de Cuba* on 24 March 1959, read:

> Cinema constitutes, by merit of its characteristics, an instrument of opinion and formation of individual and collective conscience and it can contribute to making the revolutionary spirit more profound and limpid, and to sustain its creator encouragement... Cinema is the most powerful and suggestive means of divulgation and artistic expression, and the most extended vehicle of education and popularization of ideas.[39]

The speed at which ICAIC was founded, merely three months after the revolution, points at the priority that Castro's government attached to the matter.[40] This is hardly surprising, given that in 1960, approximately 120 million cinema admissions were registered in Cuba, averaging at seventeen visits per person per year (Chanan 2004: 18). It would have been inconceivable not to utilize such a popular medium without delay.[41]

---

[39] The translator is unknown. The translation is slightly amended.
[40] Cf.: 'The ICAIC [has] always [been] the filmic voice of the Revolution and the cinematic front of the socio-political project of the Cuban Communist Party under the formula: the Cuban Revolution = ICAIC = Cuban cinema' (Smith Mesa 2011: 26).
[41] Another reason for such a prompt launch of ICAIC was perhaps Alfredo Guevara's personal friendship with Fidel Castro.

The issue of illiterate population (roughly estimated at about a quarter of the total but in the countryside reaching up to 43 per cent) also loomed large, especially in remote rural areas.

Contributing to the elimination of illiteracy in Cuba were the so-called *cines moviles*, or mobile cinemas, that screened films primarily to those in geographical isolation who rarely if ever watched movies before. This was arranged partly to homogenize, mobilize and modernize Cuban society by recourse to advanced technology, and partly 'to help educate "the masses" in understanding Marxist aesthetics and ideology' (Falicov 2010: 106) – not unlike what Soviet agit-prop trains did in the 1910s to the 1930s. The launch of mobile cinemas in 1961 roughly coincided with the announcement that Cuba was to become a socialist country, so it is not entirely surprising that many mobile cinemas were in due course mounted on the Soviet army trucks.[42]

The USSR assisted Cuba not only in distributing the films that had already been made. It also offered Cubans help in making new films, through training Cuban cadres in Moscow and Leningrad (see '17 dnei na Kube' 1964: 3) and shooting motion pictures in and about Cuba, for example Roman Karmen and Vasily Kiselev's eight documentaries of 1960–63 (the 1961 *Blazing Island* perhaps being the best known), as well as *Soy Cuba* itself. Smith Mesa (2011: 31) explains:

> As part of the Soviet cultural offensive on the world, cinema played a leading role, and politics would be placed at the centre of cinematic discourse. In the struggle for cultural supremacy during the Cold War, the USSR and the Eastern Bloc countries understandably supported the cinematic independence movements within the colonized 'Third World' nations because this undermined the power of the enemy: the West.

This of course was also true of the nations that had recently liberated themselves from (semi-) colonialism. Films by post-revolutionary Cuba and the Eastern bloc were meant to replace the commercial Hollywood and Latin American productions at Cuban cinemas as soon as practicable. 'From the very beginning the communists understood films to be the main weapons of Soviet ideological dissemination in Cuban intellectual life' (Smith Mesa 2011: 53–4).[43]

---

[42]In the first year of their operation, mobile cinemas organized over 4,500 screenings for a total of 1 to 2 million viewers (see Falicov 2010: 106). Mobile cinemas had outlived their purpose only by the 1980s.

[43]However, Soviet and East European films, as a rule, did not do well at Cuban cinemas, so their screenings had to be televised instead (see Smith Mesa 2011: 150, 289). As for the domestic fare, 'of the 130–140 feature films annually premiered in Cuba to supply the 510 theatres on the island, only about 3 percent are national products' (Burton 1997: 137).

The initiative with regard to filming *Soy Cuba* came from the Soviets and was gratefully accepted by ICAIC. In the words of Alfredo Guevara, 'that was the birth of our new cinema, the days of its founding... We needed help. We looked for it everywhere. Let everyone come! Let them all be different and no one should put a label on us' (*Soy Cuba, o Mamute siberiano* 2005: 00:11:53–00:12:48).[44] Still, it looked as if fellow Marxists[45] were particularly welcome,[46] at least initially. Soon it transpired, however, that the Cubans and the Soviets were preaching and practicing 'different Marxisms' (Chanan 2005: 233). As the prominent Marxist Cuban philosopher Fernando Martinez Heredia recalled (2001: 375), 'along with Soviet oil and weapons we received the products and influence of the Soviet theorized ideology known as Marxism-Leninism... Soviet... communist texts were widely read; they contained a rigidly dogmatic theory at the service of an ideology of legitimation and obedience'. For their part, Cuban Marxist intellectuals very much preferred questioning the Marxist doctrine and developing it creatively, rather than taking it as gospel.[47]

Garcia Espinosa's and Gutierrez Alea's contributions to the 1962 *Cine cubano* debate about modernity in art are symptomatic in this respect. In the presence of his fellow film directors from Czechoslovakia (Vladimir Cech), the GDR (Kurt Maetzig) and the USSR (Kalatozov) – all engaged in making co-productions with Cuba – Garcia Espinosa said:

If the Marxists take Marxism... as the highest expression of thought, we could say, and I think that in some way we have lapsed into this, that the artists who adopt this philosophy, or who live in a country the system of which corresponds to this philosophy, are supposed to be the more forward-thinking artists and therefore the artists who make more modern art. However, it is evident that it is not like that. It is certain that

---

[44] According to Garcia Espinosa in Kozin (1964: 19), 'since the revolution, there have been 18 feature films made [by ICAIC] (including co-productions)' with different countries. It is not certain if the Uruguayan Ugo Ulive's *Cronica Cubana*, released in Cuba in the summer of 1964, is included in this number, but if it is, the co-productions in this period amount to five and make up over a quarter of the total. For a brief introductory list of these co-productions, arranged chronologically, see Cumana (undated: 2–4).
[45] It was from Alfredo Guevara that Fidel Castro learnt about Marxism.
[46] They did not necessarily have to come from the Warsaw Pact countries. Marxists from the capitalist West were also invited. Thus, at the 1962 *Cine cubano* debate about modernity in art, the French film director Armand Gatti characterized himself as 'a Marxist [residing] in Paris, [which] is not the same as in Prague, Warsaw, Berlin or Moscow... Personally, I am still in the combat phase, you [the socialist countries' dwellers] are already in the construction phase' ('Que es lo moderno en el arte?' (1963): 40; translation by Kirsty Jane Falconer).
[47] With regard to filmmaking in post-revolutionary Cuba, it has been articulated thus: 'Cuban cinema [is] a product of Marxism-Leninism and the fact of living in a world in transformation. Surrounded by dramatic changes, Cubans believe in the possibility of generating real alternatives, and they demonstrate that belief in their films' (Mraz 2002).

there can be an artist who considers this philosophical attitude his own, who lives in a socialist country, and yet who is less modern than an artist from a capitalist country. ('Que es lo moderno en el arte?' 1963: 40; translation by Kirsty Jane Falconer)

What was this statement about if not doubting the validity of Marxism as a universally applicable know-how that supposedly guaranteed its adherent keeping up with (or even getting ahead of) the world's progress?

Taking his turn to speak, Gutierrez Alea warned the gathering about 'the risk of theorising too much, of trying to find a clear answer, free of contradictions: that is to say, an answer in which all the contradictions have been thoroughly elucidated using the master key of Marxism' and thereby 'fixing a priori standards for what should be done in the camp of socialist art' ('Que es lo moderno en el arte?' 1963: 47; translation by Kirsty Jane Falconer). At that particular point in time, people like Garcia Espinosa and Gutierrez Alea clearly must have felt that they should not sacrifice their artistic vision for a Marxist principle – but should instead modify this principle to suit their artistic vision.

It has to be pointed out that Garcia Espinosa's and Gutierrez Alea's statements were made during the Cuban Missile Crisis, which left many Cubans with a sense of betrayal after Khrushchev had made a deal with President Kennedy bypassing the Cuban leadership. Castro himself reportedly said shortly afterwards: 'So we fought for freedom – and what have we got? We used to take orders from the Americans, and now we are taking orders from the Soviets' (Evtushenko in Volkov 2018: 262). The crisis created quite a rift between the Cubans and the Soviets, affecting the Cuban attitude towards the official Soviet variety of Marxism. Mindful of the fact that Marx taught 'not to go from one form of domination to another but to end all forms of domination' (Martinez Heredia 2001: 381), Cubans did not part with Marxism altogether but embraced one of its alternative forms, namely the writings of the Italian Communist Antonio Gramsci, who was translated into Spanish and taught widely across the country between the mid-1960s and the early 1970s.[48] According to Martinez Heredia (2001: 377–8), in the absence of the domestic tradition of Marxist thought, Gramsci suited Cubans precisely because he was 'a critic of the Soviet version of Marxism,... offered the possibility of a creative Marxist philosophy' and appealed, among others, to those who, 'though searching for aesthetic Marxist fundamentals consistent with the country's cultural needs and problems, were at odds with "socialist realism", the texts on "Marxist-Leninist aesthetics" and the concrete manifestations of dogmatism'.

---

[48]Cf.: 'Cuban Marxism [...] has been generally closer to Gramsci' (Chanan 2005: 238).

Although Gramsci took hold in Cuban higher education only after *Soy Cuba*'s release, it did not mean that the film's underlying Marxist matrix (advocating 'the inevitability of the revolution', Bleiman 1965: 3) could not be challenged in Cuba from a Marxist standpoint. Thus, in his review, Lopez (1964: 24) stressed that the Marxist stance assumed by *Soy Cuba* was weakened by the film's insistence that the *Granma*'s landing (i.e. the revolution) had to happen because the farmer Pedro lost his mind and Maria/Betty could not marry her beloved, once he found out that she was a prostitute. In other words, *Soy Cuba* was accused of oversimplifying issues, and its melodramatic approach to Cuban history, of being superficial and patronizing.[49]

It also has to be remembered that 'Cuban Revolutionary leaders introduced Marxism-Leninism into the Cuban Revolutionary message by grafting it onto the images, symbols, values and concepts of Cuban nationalism' (Medin 1990: 530). However, in the third novella in *Soy Cuba*, in the scene of a police search at a student flat, it is Lenin's 1917 book *The State and Revolution* that dominates the screen, and not the mini bust of Jose Marti, which is also present. The segment afforded to the book is at least ten times longer that the one focusing on the bust, and the book is repeatedly photographed as part of a continuous moving close-up shot, while the bust can only be seen in the background and is easy to miss. As Hosek notes, the fact that 'the Soviet production depicted Lenin rather than Marti as germinal for the Cuban nationalist movement of the 1950s,… undoubtedly influenced [Cuban] assessments of [its] aesthetic quality as well' (Hosek 2012: 75).

On the Soviet side, ideological recriminations emerged mostly because 'Kalatozov's propaganda… [was] undercut by the uncontrollable aesthetic delight of his visual style' (Smith 1999: 46). The film director Chukhrai, for example, resented the fact that,

> while telling us about the exploiters of the Cuban people, *Soy Cuba*'s authors are carried away by the comfort and splendour of Havana hotels, and suggest that we too should admire the holidaying Yankees. And not only to admire them but to take a swim in a luxurious pool together with a charming female stranger. And not only to swim with her but also to take a dive in order to see what she looks like under water and how beautifully her legs work. ('Ia – Kuba' 1965: 35)

---

[49]Cf. a much later British review that makes a partly similar point: 'the exotic paradise of Cuba gets to play Virgin Nature to the Marxism that promises industrialisation among its other benefits' (Smith 1999: 45).

While aiming to portray the rich Americans' pastime on Cuba as repulsive, *Soy Cuba* in fact presented it as seductive. In Paul Julian Smith's estimation (1999: 45), 'the camera is clearly consumed by the urban decadence it so stylishly documents... The impossibly glamorous prostitutes, wasp-waisted and beehived, embody a Caribbean cool the revolutionaries, however romantically unkempt, can hardly rival'. *Soy Cuba* dutifully showed Havana slums, too, but it was its impression of Havana as an epitome of hip modernity that tended to stick with the viewing public. And this created yet another ideological problem for *Soy Cuba*: 'in the first and third story Havana appeared more modern than Moscow, and its images hardly justified all the material aid that was pouring to Cuba from the Soviet Union' (Matuskova 2017: 86).

The fact that *Soy Cuba* apparently did not feature at the international festival circuit and did not get much of a distribution outside Cuba and the USSR is also attributed to ideological grounds: the picture's militant tone (evident especially in the last novella), its 'invitation to take [up] arms... might have been one of the issues the Soviet state encountered with the film and could have been behind its ejection from international film festivals. It is unlikely that the Soviet leadership would agree to spread a message that contradicted the image of the world peace keeper they were building for themselves' (Matuskova 2017: 122–3).

## *Soy Cuba*'s ambivalent (anti-)colonialism

As far as Third Cinemas are concerned, it often so happens that 'the question of aesthetic labour is posed within the matrix of issues specific to the postcolonial experience' (Salazkina 2012: 115). It makes perfect sense to examine *Soy Cuba*'s imagery and reception from this point of view,[50] especially given that the Soviet Union tended to (re-)colonize the countries that were drawn into its geopolitical orbit. (Re-)colonization took cultural forms, too, sometimes much to the chagrin of those at the receiving end of the process. Thus, the USSR's pursuit of film co-productions with the Eastern Bloc in the 1950s,

> internationalizing the 1930s Soviet cultural formula – "national in form, socialist in content" –... was not well received by Bloc members,

---

[50]I am using the definition of colonialism by the Estonian art historian Jaak Kangilaski, as cited in Mazierska, Kristensen and Näripea (2014: 3): 'the most important characteristic of colonialism is the fact that the coloniser and the colonised come from different cultural and ethnic backgrounds, and that the colonisers have regarded their language and culture as higher than those of the colonised, and have seen their dissemination as progressive'

many of whom had already excelled in national cultural industries and had well-developed national styles… [Still,] within the Bloc, historical memory and boots on the ground gave the Soviet presence a political and economic asymmetry that conditioned both the manner of the overtures of cooperation and their reception. (Siefert 2016: 163)

On the strength of the evidence presented in and around *Soy Cuba*, was the Soviet Union trying to achieve something similar in the early 1960s in the Caribbean?

The film's title already raises suspicion of an appropriation attempt, colonial style. If one considers the Russian version of the title, *Ia – Kuba* (I Am Cuba), it is possible to translate it back into Spanish as 'Yo (I) – Cuba, a position taken by the Soviet filmmaker in relation to the "new" meaning of Cuba, which is essentially a form of political definition' (Smith Mesa 2011: 137). In other words, the film's title could be perceived as a kind of identification of the author (Kalatozov) with his subject, in the spirit of Gustave Flaubert's 'Emma, c'est moi' – performed not so much individually but on behalf of the Soviet Union staking a claim on Cuba, as it were.

The fact that it is meant to be Cuba itself that speaks in the film, ostensibly on its own behalf, with a female voice, did precious little to alter the above-named perception: 'Even though the voice belonged to Cuba's very own [actress] Raquel Revuelta and words to the Cuban poet Pineda Barnet, the combination of the film's title and melodramatic recitation of a reiterative and very didactic text gave the impression that who spoke in the film was the Soviet filmmaker, not the Cubans' (Matuskova 2017: 96). The film's multilingual nature seems to strengthen the argument in favour of cine-colonisation in progress: 'The unseen narrator speaks in Spanish and Russian, whereas the subtitles are in English… The trilingual approach epitomizes Spanish, American and Russian efforts to control Cuba… All of the credits appear in Russian – which foretells the imposition of Soviet influence as the new master who has replaced the United States' (Deaver 2008: 84–5). Furthermore, *Soy Cuba*'s opening aerial shot, taken from 'the perspective of outside in' (Matuskova 2017: 97), seems to suggest[51] 'the Soviet arrival to a new land, an aestheticising of Soviet foreign politics, a cinematic integration of Cuba within the so-called "socialist camp", the Soviet realm. Kalatozov's film may be seen as the Soviet cinematic conquest of Cuban reality' (Smith Mesa 2011: 128).

Other *Soy Cuba* shots have also come under scrutiny for a more or less hidden colonial (and simultaneously male chauvinist) agenda. According to Nagib (2011: 143–4),

---

[51] In agreement with Emma Widdis's point (2003: 122) that 'the aerial shot expresses control over the landscape, rendering it tame'.

In *I Am Cuba* colonial domination is presented from the outset as the invasion of a virgin land... The camera seems to be constantly diving into and penetrating this woman-country from above or outside, and investigating its interior with a foreign, admiring gaze, as seen... [in] the opening sequence, in which a small canoe standing for a degraded present-day version of Columbus's ship, penetrates the flooded slums.

From Rosalind Galt's (2011: 226–7) comparison of an angled downward shot (in the third novella) – a bird's eye view of Enrique's funeral procession (see Figure 1.2) – to Rodchenko's 1928 photograph 'Assembling for a Demonstration', it is possible to infer a symbolic visual expression of Soviet superiority (exemplified by Rodchenko as a chosen pattern to follow) over the Cuban nation, since the procession down below carries a Cuban national flag.

Even the infrared sequences upon closer examination reveal little else but the 'Russian snow over Cuba, that is, the view of a tropical country through foreign, northern eyes' (Nagib 2011: 148). To sum up, it does look as if in *Soy Cuba* 'the "new" Soviet Union... attempted to frame the "new" Cuba in the context of its own policy of internationalism, which implied dependency, paternalism and some unavoidable exoticism' (Matuskova 2017: 127).

Yet when one examines the testimonies of the Cuban members of the *Soy Cuba* cast and crew about their time on the project, there does not seem

FIGURE 1.2 *Demo a la Rodchenko*

to be any confirmation of colonial-style inequality within the team, even though the Russians occupied most of the top positions. Miguel Mendoza, the film's production manager, recalled: 'we formed such a monolith collective, an outsider would have struggled to distinguish a Cuban from a Russian' ('Ia – Kuba' 1964a: 15). Raquel Revuelta, in whose voice Cuba speaks to the film's audience, did not mention anything about her script monologues that could be interpreted as exploitative in the colonial sense: 'Evtushenko and Pineda Barnet wrote a wonderful text; when I read it, I feel emotional' ('Ia – Kuba' 1964a).

Cuban voiceovers had been implanted in foreigners' films about Cuba before, to lend them an extra authentic feel. For instance, Joris Ivens's *Cuba, pueblo en armas* (1961) – a short documentary with re-enactment scenes, about the People's Militia's fighting counterrevolutionaries in the Escambray Mountains – is ostensibly narrated by a Cuban militia member. At least in *Soy Cuba* the Cuban roles were played by the Cubans, which was not always the case with another contemporary co-production (with the GDR), *Preludio 11* (1964), directed by Kurt Maetzig. In this feature, inspired by the Bay of Pigs incident, about a botched attempt by US-sponsored Cuban émigrés to infiltrate Cuban territory to wage an anti-Castro insurrection, German actors were engaged in the majority of leading Cuban parts. Even though this casting decision was purely practical[52] and not intended as a surreptitious exercise in cultural colonialist takeover,[53] it did look on screen as if 'supremacist attitudes inflected [political] solidarity' quite a bit (Hosek 2012: 72). The rank-and-file soldiers, played by the Cubans, were subordinate to an officer, played by a German, which could leave an impression that 'Northern politics and whiteness lead and Southern people of colour follow' (Hosek 2012: 73). Moreover, the fact that *Preludio*'s female lead (Cuba's Aurora Depestre) in the event became an 'object of German desire,'[54].. resonates with colonialist narratives in which the relationship between North and South is articulated as the relationship between a benevolent masculine colonizer and a feminine colonized' (Hosek 2012: 73).

---

[52] The East German film studios 'DEFA hoped that familiar stars would draw GDR audiences... Maetzig believed that it would be easier to work with Germans' (Hosek 2012: 72).

[53] Being a mere satellite of the USSR, East Germany could not have possibly harboured colonialist plans of its own. Its interest in Cuba was primarily generated by the empathy with the country's bold anti-capitalist stance, as well as the shared issues of political and economic refugees and a fear of military invasion. Having said that, it also has to be admitted that for *Preludio 11* 'the GDR supplied the funds, materials, and most of the personnel and, by both German and Cuban accounts, dominated its production', treating Cubans 'more as apprentices than co-workers' (Hosek 2012: 68).

[54] One of her love interests, a Cuban character called Quintana, is played by the GDR's Armin Mueller-Stahl Figure 1.3 visualises colonizers.

And what about *Soy Cuba*? An authoritative opinion posits that Kalatozov, far from acting as a colonizer, wilfully submitted to the primacy of things Cuban. To prove the point, the opening credits sequence is invoked once again:

> In the Cuban version of the film, the first visual image of *Soy Cuba* is the words 'Instituto Cubano del Arte y Industria Cinematograficos presenta'. These words themselves constitute a cinematic message. Kalatozov recognised his film first and foremost as a creation of the nascent Cuban film industry, as part of a cinematic discourse from the New Cinema World: the *Third Cinema*. This is accompanied by the sound effect of the Cuban bongos, whereby Kalatozov made the drums speak, introducing the Afro element of Cuba and Carlos Farinas's prelude. (Smith Mesa 2011: 126)[55]

Another opinion utilizing the same sequence defends Urusevsky's much maligned camerawork by claiming that, for example, its 'low angles... are suggestive of the land's POV. The people in the film, seen from below, can be read as manifestations of that land, as if they have grown directly from it... The overwhelming impression of the opening sequence is what Scorsese has said about it: "The main character is the country, the land, the soil"' (Thakkar 2014: 90–1). For the cited scholar, Urusevsky's 'camera represents

FIGURE 1.3 *American sailors chasing a Cuban woman*

---

[55]Prior to his work on *Soy Cuba*, Farinas had studied at the Moscow Conservatoire (in 1961–63), and composed music for the first novella in *Historias de la revolucion*.

the very land of Cuba itself' (Thakkar 2014: 92), not a penetration of the land by a foreign intruder.

And *Soy Cuba*'s genuine and considerable effort expended in order to relate to Cuba's inhabitants seemed to have resonated at least with some viewers on the island. Mr Barinov, a deputy head of Goskino, thus spoke of the applause he witnessed at the film's premiere in Cuba:

> This applause pleased us [the Soviets in attendance] not only as a manifestation of the high appreciation of the work of Soviet and Cuban filmmakers, but also as a confirmation of the authenticity and reliability of the events displayed on the screen. After all, our spectators – the participants in the storming of the Moncada Barracks, the bearded revolutionaries who courageously fought in the Sierra Maestra mountains, peasants, students – are themselves characters in this film. ('Ia – Kuba' 1964b: 4)

It is not therefore altogether surprising that *Soy Cuba* sometimes can actually serve as an illustration of 'how important the audiovisual culture of the Soviet bloc was in [the] process of [Cuba's] decolonisation' (Smith Mesa 2011: 19).

To try and discern, to what extent *Soy Cuba* denoted decolonization and/or colonization, it makes sense to look briefly at the Soviet Union's track record in assisting the underdeveloped territories within and beyond its own to build up their film industries. It is probably true that the USSR's role in developing national cinemas in its Central Asian republics in the 1920s to 1940s, when filmmakers' routines of technological and ideological knowledge transfer were established, could be referred to as a form of 'cultural imperialism' (Mowell 2014: 72), even though the enforcers of this transfer 'started off by denouncing imperial colonial practices and "the profit-oriented perpetuation of exoticized and eroticized oriental imagery"' (Sarkisova 2017: 37). Beginning from the mid-1920s (and in some places, such as Kirghizia, from the late 1930s), for over a decade ethnic Russian, Ukrainian, Belarusian and Jewish film professionals, often visiting from Moscow and Leningrad, acted as tutors to previously non-existent Central Asian film practitioners, while establishing film studios, cinema networks (including bringing films to rural areas and nomads, not unlike mobile cinemas in Cuba) and training courses for the locals in all aspects of filmmaking, and shooting documentaries and features for them and with them, until they became able to do so themselves (for details, see Abul-Kasymova et al (1969–75)). The chief aim was, by cinematic means, 'to spread Soviet propaganda among the "Oriental population", and to introduce them and their way of life to the rest of the Soviet Union' (Chomentowski 2013: 33).

As a result, especially at an early stage in this '"enlightening" mission, [which] rested on a presumed teleological development "from backwardness towards civilization", where modernity, knowledge and progress arrived from the centre' (Sarkisova 2017: 38), the Central Asian films were often scripted, directed and even acted in by the people who did not know enough about local history, customs and everyday life. At a later stage, this asymmetrical collaboration (especially fruitful in 1941–44, when Mosfilm and Lenfilm were evacuated to Kazakhstan and the Central United Film Studios, or TsOKS, were formed there in the wake of their temporary merger on the basis of the Almaty studios[56]), brought about some generally acknowledged successes, for example, two films by Dziga Vertov (*Kazakhstan to the Front*, 1942; and *In the Alatau Mountains*, 1944). However, the growing numbers and proficiency of the local filmmaking cadres were accompanied by the 'cultivation of a national Soviet identity in film, [which] entailed not just the exaltation of Marxist-Leninist ideals but also the promotion of Russian and Slavic ways of life, and to a degree the dismissal and denigration of Eastern, non-European cultures including those of Central Asia' (Mowell 2014: 72).

After the Second World War, Soviet Russia also lent a helping hand to the fledgling film industries of Albania and North Korea, co-producing two features, *The Great Albanian Warrior Skanderbeg* (1953, directed by Sergei Iutkevich) and *Brothers* (1957, co-directed by Ivan Lukinsky and Cheon Sang-in).[57] How relevant for Cuba was this well-established pattern of Soviet behaviour towards the developing countries (or parts thereof)? To begin with, Cuba in the 1960s, while a developing country, was not quite in the same league as Albania and North Korea in the 1950s (not to speak of Central Asia in the 1920s to 1940s) but a reasonably 'highly developed island, rich in material comforts and populated by a cosmopolitan and naturally cultivated people who have always lived surrounded by foreigners, whose intellectuals travelled much' (Brook 1961: 78). The Cuban film industry, while comparatively small, still managed to produce about '150 features in its six decades of pre-revolutionary history' (Burton 1997: 126),[58] or two and a half films annually (in Central Asia, such an industry had to be built from scratch). Under Castro, 'from 1961 to 1967, the ICAIC produced 35 feature films; between 1968 and 1985 it produced 73 feature films; and during the period 1986–1991 it produced 52 feature films' (Smith Mesa 2011: 37), that is, five features annually, on average, over thirty years – a double increase on the pre-revolutionary period, but nevertheless relatively modest overall.

---

[56]In the Second World War years, 80 per cent of Soviet feature films were made there.
[57]On them, see Rogatchevski (2016) and Gabroussenko (2019) respectively.
[58]For a full list of films of all genres made in Cuba in 1897–1960, see Douglas 2008.

Size is not everything, however. Even though late Soviet film industry released 120–150 feature films per year, in an imaginary competition between Cuba's David and the USSR's Goliath, Cubans could still hold their own, sometimes beating the Soviets on their home turf. The already mentioned *Las doce sillas*, Gutierrez Alea's 1962 adaptation of a cult Soviet book, is vastly superior to any of its three Soviet film and TV screen versions attempted in the 1960s and 1970s. His magic touch has Cubanized the Soviet satire of the late 1920s by turning it into 'a light version of *choteo*, Cuba's national brand of corrosive humour' (Schroeder 2002: 16). A total of 1.7 million viewers, that is, a quarter of the entire population, turned up at the Cuban cinemas to watch two loveable rogues (a master, disenfranchised by the revolution, and his ex-servant) hunting for a treasure concealed somewhere in a twelve-chair dining-room set. While in the Soviet original the master kills his partner in crime in order to avoid treasure sharing, in the Cuban version both stay alive: 'as a representative of the working class, the servant's death... makes no sense for the Cubans' (Smith Mesa 2011: 172). In the final scene, the former servant joins a game of baseball played by strangers, while his ex-master simply runs away. 'The message is clear: Those who stay in Cuba must join the game of the Revolution, or else leave the island' (Schroeder 2002: 12). Such significant departures from the venerable literary prototype demonstrate how independent, not subservient, some Cuban filmmakers could be when dealing with some of the most compelling and highly revered specimens of Soviet culture, so soon after becoming acquainted with this culture in the first place.[59]

Such an unconstrained attitude by a recipient culture towards a donor culture (the latter on this occasion learns more about itself from the way it has been modified by the former) is fully commensurate with Gachev's theory of accelerated development, according to which not only the developing nations 'enrich themselves by accepting the modern forms of industrial production, spiritual culture and everyday life. The most advanced countries of the modern world discover something valuable in the contact with the so-called "backward" peoples, too... Accelerated development is mutually beneficial' (Gachev 1989: 6–7). Either because of Cuba's natural cultural resilience vis-à-vis the USSR[60] or because of its geographical distance from

---

[59]Curiously, a worthy attempt to adapt *Twelve Chairs* the novel to another cultural setting, this time the American, was undertaken by the film director Mel Brooks in 1970. Brooks set out to show that 'the desire to accumulate wealth and its destructive consequences, as depicted by Il'f and Petrov, are universal' (Mulcahy 2016: 192). Brooks's Americanization of *The Twelve Chairs* was not complete, though, as the action still took place in the USSR in the late 1920s.
[60]Gutierrez Alea's Cubanization of *Twelve Chairs* succeeds where Kalatozov's imitation of Cubanness in *Soy Cuba* ultimately fails (cf.: 'For me, the Cuban people are absent from the film. Its action can be just as well transferred to another country' (Kapralov in 'Ia – Kuba' 1965: 30)).

the USSR, or because for most of the 1960s the USSR tried to be a little more diplomatic about forcing its viewpoint on its socialist allies anyway,[61] 'the Soviet influence over Cuba was by no means of a coercive or assertive type as in Eastern Europe' in the 1940s and 1950s (Smith Mesa 2011: 12) and the Soviet-Cuban relations were not so much of a one-way traffic but more of 'a system of give and take' (Smith Mesa 2011: 14). This is probably a reason why *Soy Cuba* reveals an ambivalent tension of both colonizing and decolonizing tendencies. Not too keen on replacing their semi-colonial dependence on the United States with the Soviet one, in their assessment of *Soy Cuba* the Cubans were perhaps more likely to exaggerate what seemed to be in the film a manifestation of the propensity to colonize and to downplay the indications of the opposite trend.

## *Soy Cuba* as a heterotopian co-production

*Soy Cuba* is therefore a repository of self-contradictory components, which could partly be attributed to its belonging to a socialist mode of film co-production (in itself a subset of transnational cinema) that strives to empower a young(ish) or re-born film industry, on the one hand, and to promote socialism, on the other.[62] Both objectives may well get in the way of an anti-(neo)colonial nationalist sentiment by posing a threat of Soviet domination (see Matuskova 2017: 8–9).[63]

Socialist co-productions with the USSR as a partner were a means of 'Bloc-building through blockbusters… The imperative of realizing co-productions may have bred internationalist compromises but was part of the overall goal of achieving a Soviet ideological film art' (Siefert 2016: 178, 180). This was acutely felt in the East European subdivision of Second Cinema, which displayed a notable 'hostility towards "transnationalism,"… inevitably associated with the enforced internationalism imposed by the Soviet Union on its satellite countries during the Communist regimen' (Mazierska 2012: 483).

It has to be noted that such a reaction is not only dictated by and limited to the realities of the socialist world during the Cold War but is

---

[61]Cf.: 'Stalin's successors… did not simply warm up the old model of spreading world revolution and Soviet communism. The Soviet Union after 1953 combined ideas of socialist internationalism of the 1920s with the "cultural internationalism" of the 1950s. The new Soviet leadership opened the country to the world in order to spread, if much more cautiously than the early Bolsheviks, their model of society across the globe' (Rupprecht 2015: 9–10).
[62]In 1966–70, 24 films of various genres were co-produced in the USSR with socialist countries, 3 with developing countries and only 8 with capitalist countries (see Siefert 2016: 177).
[63]The term 'nationalism' as I use it here is free of negative connotations. Cubans 'are nationalistic without being jingoistic' (Brook 1961: 79).

part of a larger picture of internal incongruities of transnational cinema and international co-productions as a whole. Transnational cinema tends to be viewed as something 'above and beyond lobbying for an indigenous cinema' (Romanelli 2016: 27), and international co-productions more often than not emerge as hybrids that in general are not easily 'understood by national audiences' (Romanelli 2016: 42). As has been remarked by Mazierska, Kristensen and Näripea (2014: 28), 'international co-productions, typically between neighbours represented on-screen,[64]... often have a transnational life, being shown at international festivals and often gaining more recognition beyond their "natural borders"... However, the opposite phenomenon can be [also] observed: films about us and our neighbours hang in a transnational no man's land, being neglected by both sets of its potential viewer'.

One of the reasons for such a fall between two stools, as it were, is that owing to their hybrid nature co-productions are predisposed to manufacturing the so-called heterotopias, that is, places that are 'created out of real but incompatible spaces and existing outside the normal political, cultural, or even physical order. Such a result can be partially explained by the difficulties of shooting the films far from home' (Mazierska 2012: 501). In that sense, *Soy Cuba* is a typical heterotopia, recognized as such (without using the actual term) immediately upon its release by both Cuban and Soviet filmgoers. It is not coincidental that Luis M. Lopez's review of the film was titled 'No Soy Cuba' ('I Am Not Cuba'), while Teresa Ruiz called *Soy Cuba* 'paradoxically anti-local (it reflects what is Cuban via a foreign mentality) and anti-cosmopolitan (it does not reflect what is universal in humanity via the specifics of Cuba)' (quoted in Espinosa Dominguez 2012: 111). On the Soviet side, Grigory Chukhrai summed it up when he said: 'despite all the incomparable qualities of *Soy Cuba*, one main thing is missing from it, namely revolutionary Cuba' ('Ia-Kuba' 1965: 37). Of much later and therefore more balanced appreciations of *Soy Cuba* pointing at its heterotopianism, it is worth quoting Galt (2011: 213) (*Soy Cuba* is a 'conflict of Latin American and European models of cinematic Marxism') and Matuskova (2017: 131) (Kalatozov and Urusevsky 'did not impose their European vision or blindly transfer Soviet cultural symbols to their film. They found a way to consolidate both the Cuban national gaze and the vision connected with Soviet internationalism').

Heterotopian features can also be spotted in other Cuban co-productions of the period. Thus, Hosek (2012: 74–5) reports on *Preludio 11*'s reception in the GDR and Cuba, clearly conditioned by heterotopianism: the film was

> unpopular in the GDR and attendance fell quickly... The disjunction between the putative and de facto verisimilitude of this true-to-life, larger-

---

[64]Or perhaps by faraway political allies, as in the case of Cuba and the Soviet Union.

than-life, solidarity, adventure film may have left audiences dissatisfied...
In Cuba, *Preludio 11* was not well received despite Spanish dubbing.
The film was criticized for those characteristics meant to appeal to GDR
audiences: tropical exotic, revolutionary romantic, and focus on the
mercenaries.[65]... Audiences found their situation inaccurately represented,
and the European actors left them alienated.[66]

Cumana (undated: 3) quotes from a review of *Preludio 11* in the Cuban
newspaper *Hoy* of 6 February 1964: 'Maetzig does not know the Cuban
countryside or the Revolution (except in theory). Therefore, if we strike out
the word "revolution" and eliminate the name of "Cuba", the film would
be (and actually is) a story of adventures in the Philippines, Nicaragua or
Madagascar seen by a person from the Moon.'

Another example is a Cuban-Czechoslovak co-production *For Whom
Havana Dances* (1963), directed by Vladimir Cech. It centres on the plot
to stage an explosion on board a ship in Havana's harbour, timed for the
Havana carnival, so that the plotters can escape by boat to Miami unnoticed,
while people are distracted by the carnival and the explosion's aftermath.[67]
On the issue of heterotopia, it has been observed that Havana in this film
looks a little too American:

> The Czech filmmaker was, perhaps, overly impressed by the American
> style of life of Havana... The film, for example, has some overlong
> sequences depicting a tour of Havana by car, most of them in the modern
> area of Vedado, providing a wide range of information about the US
> material culture of the houses and modern urban areas of the city in the
> early 1960s. (Smith Mesa 2011: 112)

In addition, a contemporary review (by Luis M. Lopez, writing in *Bohemia*)
registered 'dollops of touristy dazzle from carnival parade' (quoted in
Espinosa Dominguez 2012: 110). All things considered, 'Cubans did not

---

[65]Cf.: 'instead of focusing on praising the travails of the victors as Cuban films did, [Maetzig] decided to "dissect" and discredit the enemy. He analyzed the triumph of the Revolution through their eyes rather than the victors, which had not been done in Cuban cinema before' (Matuskova 2017: 260).

[66]Cf.: In *Preludio 11*, a Cuban dubbing 'for a German actor who has his own particular gestures, gave the effect of something false and imposed' (Smith Mesa 2011: 115).

[67]This story bears a vague similarity to parts of the fifth novella ('Carnival') in Evtushenko's script (1963: 45–67) of *Soy Cuba*, about a group of rebels – a florist, a boxer, a joiner and an astronomer – attacking a prison where arrested revolutionaries are kept, during the Havana carnival (the arrested are freed but their liberators die in the process). Most of this novella has been dropped from the final version of *Soy Cuba*, possibly because of the parallel with *For Whom Havana Dances* – but also perhaps because it would have made Kalatozov's film too long overall.

recognize themselves in the characters and found the film inauthentic. This aspect did not remain hidden to the Czechoslovaks either' (Matuskova 2017: 189), when the film was shown there.

*El otro Cristobal* (1963) by the Frenchman Armand Gatti is as heterotopian as they come.[68] According to one reviewer, it looks like a 'Brazilian Cinema Novo film made in Bollywood' (Uzal 2019). The film's madcap action takes place simultaneously in heaven and in an imaginary Latin American country, which has as much or little of Cuba as, say, of Panama in it. *Cristobal* also mentions non-existent Latin American countries, such as El Sombrero and Nicoviento, and renames the USA 'Norte'. In Matuskova's interpretation (2017: 191), 'Gatti in *El otro Cristobal* did not even pretend to assimilate his representation to the reality. His film was an allegory and was about the entire Latin America'. A proper Latin American co-production, *Cronica Cubana* (1963) by the Uruguayan Ugo Ulive (a fictionalized account of Cuban revolutionary history from Castro's takeover of Havana on 1 January 1959 up until his victory at the Bay of Pigs), could have been expected to be more authentic. Yet in the opinion of Jose de la Colina, writing for *Revolucion* on 20 July 1964, in the film 'no one, or almost no one, seems to be Cuban. The actors move slowly, with great composure; there are long periods of silence and intense looks, in the best tradition of the Argentine or Mexican melodrama' (quoted in Cumana (undated): 3; one of Ulive's co-scriptwriters, Osvaldo Dragun, was Argentinian).

# Conclusions

Of the factors that have been advanced as affecting the creation and appreciation of *Soy Cuba* (the financial, the aesthetic, the ideological, the postcolonial and the co-productional), all five appear convincing enough, especially when taken as a group. Judging by the rich and varied context I have analysed (the contemporary co-productions with Cuba by other countries, some of Cuba's and the USSR's own films of the period, as well as Soviet co-productions with other socialist and developing countries, or parts of such countries), it does not seem possible to attach any particular significance to one specific factor. The five factors' role in the matter has transpired to be demonstrably combined. One can subdivide these factors into constants and variables, though.

It looks as if in the bigger scheme of things, neither financial, nor aesthetic, nor ideological, nor postcolonial factors could be decisive in and of themselves. Let me briefly examine the financial factor first. Although not

---

[68]Incidentally, Kalatozov knew this film and was influenced by it. For more detail, see Velitchko and Rogatchevski 2020.

in the same order of magnitude as *Soy Cuba*, *El otro Cristobal*'s production costs were admittedly still quite substantial (Gatti blamed the 1962 naval blockade of Cuba by the United States for the difficulties in supplying his crew with the materials needed to film the project) and Czechoslovakia 'ended up paying much more for the production [of *For Whom Havana Dances*] than intended to' (Matuskova 2017: 183). Yet, as a rule, the costs of other co-produced Cuban films under consideration in this chapter, to the best of my knowledge, were comparatively modest and kept more or less within budget. This did not, however, preclude such films from being treated as insufficiently Cuban.

The same applies to the aesthetic factor. All other co-produced films I have looked at in addition to *Soy Cuba*, with the exception of the ambitious and experimental *Cristobal*, appear rather ordinary and pedestrian by comparison with Kalatozov's 'tropical delirium' (Hoberman 1995: 57). Yet, by and large, this did not make their acceptance by Cuban viewers any easier. The ideological factor also was not uniform for all the films in question: if the Soviet, East German and Czechoslovak co-productions could be safely assumed to be based on, and propagating, the foundations of the Soviet variety of Marxism, the same could not be said of *Cristobal* and *Cronica Cubana* – but all these films were received unfavourably regardless. The colonial factor can only be categorized as a variable, too. In Cuba, the hypothetical colonial dependence on Latin American countries or France did not seem to be any more of an issue than such a dependence on the GDR or Czechoslovakia.[69] Still, the non-Soviet co-productions were largely judged to be just as inauthentic as *Soy Cuba*. It appears that only the co-productional factor with the concomitant heterotopianism was shared by all of the five films probed here, however cursorily, and this factor was powerful enough to cause on its own these films' overwhelming public rejection.[70]

Why was the number of Cuban co-productions in the first half of the 1960s so high, why did it promptly go down shortly afterwards and did co-production as a film form correlate in any way with the Third Cinema as it was proclaimed in Cuba? The evolution of Cuban cinema in the 1960s has been described as 'the broad and initially uncritical assimilation of foreign models, the virtually unlimited hospitality to visiting artists and intellectuals,

---

[69]Cf., for example: 'Cuba had much more in common with Czechoslovakia than the USSR. Czechoslovakia was a small country with limited resources like Cuba. It shared with Cuba a similar history of fight for preserving national identity and resistance against a hegemonic power because it had a long history of being under an imperial rule. The Soviet Union was the last of the many "conquerors" of the Bohemian lands... Czechoslovak assistance was more "palatable" for the Cubans and less threatening... Overall, the Czechoslovak State Film was instrumental in building the technical base for the Cuban film industry' (Matuskova 2017: 134, 141).
[70]Cf.: These films were 'schematic at best, with a penchant for the exotic that reveals the foreign point of view behind the cameras' (Garcia Osuna 2003: 42).

and the attentive quest for their approval', which, as the decade was drawing to a close, 'gave way to a more critical stance and to the growing influence of artistic inspiration from national sources and other Third World countries... in preference to the developed sector' (Burton 1997: 132). In the atmosphere of the first half of the 1960s, when learning fast from any available foreign film experts (as long as they held left-wing views) was one of the industry's chief priorities, co-productions naturally played a seminal role as a kind of laboratory experiment where a more or less negative result could still count as something useful.[71] However, as the second half of the 1960s became 'marked by the nation's attempt to develop autonomously through an accelerated economic project' (Martinez Heredia 2001: 382), a clearer vision of a national model for cinema has been formed – defined as 'imperfect cinema' – and co-productions, although they did not stop altogether, got reduced to more customary levels.[72]

The 1960s co-productions peter out in line with Gachev's observation that accelerated development first occurs an

> outbreak, an impetus – and the speed is at its maximum precisely at the initial moment when a contact and interaction with a more developed culture takes place, so that the first years are booming; but then the momentum slows down, and the peoples affected, becoming more closely linked to the modern level of civilization, develop more evenly and almost at the same pace as the surrounding lands, although waves from the first impulse continue to roll and influence the current state of affairs at any given moment. (Gachev 1989: 425–6)

Significantly, it is not only the pace that the developing country often adopts from its chief influencer but also the general direction of change. Unsurprisingly, therefore, in the late 1960s to the 1980s, as the Cuban revolution embarks on a process of institutionalization, Cuban cinema gradually turns away from experimentation and focuses more on the 'communication of ideological messages dictated by political goals, which is generally seen as a defining feature of Soviet cinematic discourse' (Smith Mesa 2011: 284).

Co-productions return to Cuba in astonishing numbers in the 1990s, comprising over 75 per cent of the ICAIC budget (see Getino 2007: 190), when the Soviet Union falls apart and reneges on its financial sponsorship

---

[71]Cf. Garcia Espinosa's assessment in Kozin (1964: 19): the collaboration over *Soy Cuba* was 'very useful for the Cuban national film industry'; and Juan Varona's acknowledgement: 'The experience gained in working on a foreign coproduction is never lost' (*Soy Cuba, o Mamute siberiano* 2005: 01:17:34–01:17:42).

[72]On the 1969 Cuban-Japanese feature *Kyuba no koibito*, directed by Kazuo Kuroki, see Cumana (untitled): 6.

obligations to Cuban economy. At this point in time, co-productions become the principal way of ensuring that filmmaking continues to happen[73] – not unlike in pre-Castro Cuba, when co-productions with Mexico functioned as a catalyst (if not a life-support machine) for the domestic film industry. The Third Cinema sentiments have retained their relevance for the post-1990s period, too, the 'imperfect cinema' being reformulated in 2004 by the renowned Cuban film director Humberto Solas as 'cinema for the poor'. This time around, however, Third Cinema, Cuban style, establishes itself not in opposition to the relatively rich and developed countries of the capitalist West and the socialist East but in solidarity with the like-minded filmmakers operating on a shoe-string wherever they are.[74] But that is another story.

## Acknowledgement

I would like to express my profound gratitude to Kirsty Jane Falconer, Jean-Jacques Hocquard, Sergey Lavrentiev, Ekaterina Rogatchevskaia, Pavel Straka, Anatole Velitchko and Elise Øksendal for their invaluable help with my work on this chapter.

## Bibliography

'17 dnei na Kube' (1964), *Sovetskii ekran* 9: 3.
Abul-Kasymova, Kh. et al., eds (1969–75), *Istoriia sovetskogo kino 1917–1967*, vol. 1, 1917–1931: 698–720; vol. 2, 1931–1941: 453–90; vol. 3, 1941–1952: 226–32, 247–9. Moscow: Iskusstvo.
Antropov, V. N. and E. M. Barykin, eds (1979), *Sovetskie khudozhestvennye fil'my: Annotirovannyi katalog*, vol. 5 (1964–1965), Moscow: Iskusstvo.
Bleiman, M. (1965), 'Povod dlia ser'eznykh razdumii', *Sovetskaia kul'tura*, 29 April: 3.
Boltianskii, Grigorii (1925), *Lenin i kino*, Moscow-Leningrad: Gosudarstvennoe izdatel'stvo.
Brook, Peter (1961), 'The Cuban Enterprise', *Sight and Sound*, 30 (2): 78–9.
Brooke, Michael (2008), 'Cuban Cinema Collection', *Sight and Sound*, 18 (3): 93.
Burton, Julianne (1997), 'Film and Revolution in Cuba: The First Twenty-Five Years', in Michael T. Martin (ed.), *New Latin American Cinema*, vol. 2, 123–42, Detroit: Wayne University Press.

---

[73]On some of these co-productions, see Cumana (undated: 7–8).
[74]Cf.: '"cinema of the poor" does not mean cinema which lacks ideas or artistic quality, it means a cinema with a tight budget which is produced in outsider or less developed countries as well as in the bosom of the culturally and economically guiding societies' (Humberto Solas in Scott MacKenzie 2014: 319).

Cabrera Infante, Guillermo (1991), *A Twentieth Century Job*, trans. Kenneth Hall and the author, London: Faber.
'Cartas desde Cuba (1961–1962)' (1983), *Cine cubano* 104: 71–87.
Chanan, Michael (2004), *Cuban Cinema*, Minneapolis and London: The University of Minnesota Press.
Chanan, Michael (2005), 'Cinemas in Revolution: 1920s Russia, 1960s Cuba', in Mike Wayne (ed.), *Understanding Film: Marxist Perspectives*, 232–46, London: Pluto Press.
Chomentowski, Gabrielle (2013), 'Vostokkino and the Foundation of Central Asian Cinema', in Michael Rouland, Gulnara Abikeyeva and Birgit Beumers (eds), *Cinema in Central Asia: Rewriting Cultural Histories*, 33–44, London and New York: I.B. Tauris.
*Cronica cubana* (1964), [Film] Dir. Ugo Ulive. Cuba: ICAIC.
Cumana, Maria Caridad (undated), 'Contradictions and Paradigms of Cuban Cinema after the Revolution in the Eyes of Foreign Filmmakers', *Academia.edu*, https://www.academia.edu/4543041/Paradigmas_de_la_mirada_de_cineastas_extranjeros_en_el_cine_cubano_despues_del_triunfo_de_la_Revolucion_eng (accessed 8 September 2019).
Deaver Jr., William O. (2008), '*I Am Cuba*: The Quest for Self-determination and Identity', *Journal of Commonwealth and Postcolonial Studies*, 15 (2): 84–92.
Douglas, Maria Eulalia (ed.) (2008), *Catalogo del cine cubano 1897–1960*, Havana: Ediciones ICAIC.
*El otro Cristobal* (1963), [Film] Dir. Armand Gatti. Cuba/France: ICAIC and Test Film.
Espinosa Dominguez, Carlos (2012), 'The Mammoth That Wouldn't Die', in Jacqueline Loss and Jose Manuel Prieto (eds), *Caviar with Rum: Cuba-USSR and the Post-Soviet Experience*, 109–17, New York: Palgrave Macmillan.
Evtushenko, Evgeny (1963), 'Ia – Kuba: Poema v proze', *Znamia*, 3: 3–89.
Falicov, Tamara (2010), 'Mobile Cinemas in Cuba: The Form and Ideology of Traveling Exhibitions', *Public: Art, Culture, Ideas*, 40: 104–08.
Fornet, Ambrosio (2007), 'The Five Grey Years: Revisiting the Term', trans. Alicia Barraqué Ellison, in *POLEMICA: The 2007 Intellectual Debate*, https://translatingcuba.com/the-five-grey-years-revisiting-the-term-ambrosio-fornet/ (accessed 4 September 2019).
Gabroussenko, Tatiana (2019), '"Brothers": The Banned North Korean-Soviet Film Ruined by Juche Politics', *NKnews.org*, 13 August, https://www.nknews.org/2019/08/brothers-the-banned-north-korean-soviet-film-ruined-by-juche-politics/ (accessed 7 September 2019).
Gachev, G. (1989), *Neminuemoe: Uskorennoe razvitie literatury*, Moscow: Khudozhestvennaia literatura.
Galt, Rosalind (2011), *Pretty: Film and the Decorative Image*, New York: Columbia University Press.
Garcia Borrero, Juan Antonio (2001), *Guia critica del cine cubano de ficcion*, Ciudad de La Habana, Cuba: Editorial Arte y Literature.
Garcia Espinosa, Julio (2014), 'For an Imperfect Cinema (Cuba, 1969)', trans. Julianne Burton-Carvajal, in Scott MacKenzie (ed.), *Film Manifestos and Global Cinema Cultures: A Critical Anthology*, 220–30, Berkeley-Los Angeles-London: University of California Press.

Garcia Osuna, Alfonso J. (2003), *The Cuban Filmography, 1897 through 2001*, Jefferson, NC: McFarland.
Getino, Octavio (2007), *Cine iberoamericano: Los desafios del nuevo siglo*, Buenos Aires: Ediciones CICCUS.
Gott, Richard (2005), 'From Russia with Love', *The Guardian*, 12 November, https://www.theguardian.com/film/2005/nov/12/cuba (accessed 28 August 2019).
Gutierrez Alea, Tomas (1997), 'The Viewer's Dialectic', trans. Julia Lesage, in Michael T. Martin (ed.), *New Latin American Cinema*, vol. 1, 108–31, Detroit: Wayne State University Press.
Harte, Tim (2013), 'Monumental Melodrama: Mikhail Kalatozov's Retrospective Return to 1920s' Agitprop Cinema in *I Am Cuba*', *Anuari de filologia: Llengues i literatures modernes* 3: 1–12.
Hoberman, J. (1995), 'Cuban Curios', *Premiere* 8 (8) (April): 57, 59.
Hosek, Jennifer Ruth (2012), *Sun, Sex and Socialism: Cuba in the German Imaginary*, Toronto: University of Toronto Press.
Hudson, Simon (2006), 'Cuba's Potemkin', *Film Ireland*, 109 (March/April): 28–9.
'Ia – Kuba' (1964a), *Sovetskii ekran* 15: 1, 15.
'Ia – Kuba' (1964b), *Sovetskaia kul'tura*, 8 August: 4.
'Ia – Kuba' (1965), *Iskusstvo kino* 3: 24–37.
Iordanova, Dina (1997), '*I Am Cuba* by Y. Yevtushenko, E. Pineda Barnet, M. Kalatozov and S. Urusevsky', *Russian Review*, 56 (1): 125–6.
Isbakh, Aleksandr (1964), 'Govorit Kuba: Zametki pisatelia', *Sovetskii ekran* 19: 8–9.
Kozin, V. (1964), 'Kuba, ekzotika i fil'my', *Sovetskii ekran* 21: 18–19.
*Las doce sillas* (1962), [Film] Dir. Tomas Gutierrez Alea. Cuba: ICAIC.
López, Luis M. (1964), 'No *Soy Cuba*', *Bohemia*, 21 August: 24–5.
Martinez Heredia, Fernando (2001), 'Gramsci in 1960s Cuba', trans. Alex Martin. *Nepantla: Views from South*, 2 (2): 373–85.
Matuskova, Magdalena (2017), 'Cuban Cinema in a Global Context: The Impact of Eastern European Cinema on the Cuban Film Industry in the 1960s', PhD diss., University of California, Los Angeles.
Mazierska, Ewa (2012), 'International Co-productions as Productions of Heterotopias', in Aniko Imre (ed.), *A Companion to East European Cinemas*, 483–503, Chichester/Malden, MA: Wiley-Blackwell.
Mazierska, Ewa, Lars Kristensen and Eva Näripea (2014), 'Postcolonial Theory and the Postcommunist World', in Ewa Mazierska, Lars Kristensen and Eva Näripea (eds), *Postcolonial Approaches to Eastern European Cinema: Portraying Neighbours On-Screen*, 1–39, London: I.B. Tauris.
Medin, Tzvi (1990), *Cuba: The Shaping of Revolutionary* Consciousness, Boulder, CL: Rienner.
Mowell, Barry (2014), 'Political, Economic and Historical Foundations of Central Asian Cinema', in Sevket Akyildiz and Richard Carlson (eds), *Social and Cultural Change in Central Asia: The Soviet Legacy*, 72–86, London and New York: Routledge.
Mraz, John (2002), 'October's Offspring: Soviet Cinema and the Cuban Film Institute', *Film Historia Online*, XII (3), http://www.publicacions.ub.edu/

bibliotecaDigital/cinema/filmhistoria/2002/october.htm (accessed 31 August 2019).

Mulcahy, Robert (2016), 'Chasing the Wealth: The Americanization of Il'f and Petrov's *The Twelve Chairs*', in Alexander Burry and Frederick H. White (eds), *Border Crossing: Russian Literature into Film*, 188–201, Edinburgh: Edinburgh University Press.

Nagib, Lucia (2007), 'Panamericas Utopicas: Entranced and Transient Nations in *I Am Cuba* (1964) and *Land in Trance* (1967)', *Hispanic Research Journal*, 8 (1): 79–90.

Nagib, Lucia (2011), *World Cinema and the Ethics of Realism*, New York: Continuum.

Nangle, John (2001), 'Video Views', *Classic Images*, 310 (April): 27–8.

Ortiz, Fernando (1947), *Cuban Counterpoint: Tobacco and Sugar*, trans. Harriet de Onis, New York: Alfred A. Knopf.

*Preludio 11* (1964), [Film] Dir. Kurt Maetzig. East Germany/Cuba: DEFA and ICAIC.

'Que es lo moderno en el arte? Referencia el cine' (1963), *Cine cubano*, 3 (9) (January): 31–49.

Rogatchevski, Andrei (2016), 'Sergei Iutkevich: The Great Albanian Warrior Skanderbeg (Velikii voin Albanii Skanderbeg, 1953)', *KinoKultura*, Special Issue 16, http://www.kinokultura.com/specials/16/R_skanderbeg.shtml (accessed 7 September 2019).

Romanelli, Claudia (2016), 'French and Italian Co-productions and the Limits of Transnational Cinema', *Journal of Italian Cinema and Media Studies*, 4 (1): 25–50.

Rupprecht, Tobias (2015), *Socialist Internationalism after Stalin*, Cambridge: Cambridge University Press.

Salazkina, Masha (2012), 'Moscow-Rome-Havana: A Film-Theory Road Map', *October*, 139: 97–116.

Sarkisova, Oksana (2017), *Screening Soviet Nationalities: Kulturfilms from the Far North to Central Asia*, London: I.B. Tauris.

Schroeder, Paul A. (2002), *Tomas Gutierrez Alea: The Dialectics of a Filmmaker*, New York and London: Routledge.

Siefert, Marsha (2016), 'Second World Cinema: Soviet Film Outreach from 1955–1972', in Babiracki, Patryk, and Austin Jersild (eds), *Socialist Internationalism in the Cold War: Exploring the Second World*, 161–93, London: Palgrave Macmillan.

Smith, Paul Julian (1999), 'Reviews', *Sight and Sound*, 9 (8): 45–6.

Smith Mesa, Vladimir Alexander (2011), 'Kinocuban: The Significance of Soviet and East European Cinemas for the Cuban Moving Image', PhD diss., University College London.

*Soy Cuba* (1964), [Film] Dir. Mikhail Kalatozov. USSR/Cuba: Mosfilm and ICAIC.

*Soy Cuba, o Mamute siberiano* (2005), [Film] Dir. Vicente Ferraz, Brazil: Tres Mundos Producoes.

Thakkar, Amir (2014), 'Who Is Cuba?: Dispersed Protagonism and Heteroglossia in *Soy Cuba/I Am Cuba*', *Framework: The Journal of Cinema and Media*, 55 (1): 83–101.

Turner, George E. (1995), 'The Astonishing Images of *I Am Cuba*', *American Cinematographer*, 76 (7): 77–82, https://ascmag.com/articles/flashback-soy-cuba (accessed 29 August 2019).

Uzal, Marcos (2019), '*El otro Cristóbal* sort enfin des limbes', *Libération*, 17 September.

Velitchko, Anatole, and Andrei Rogatchevski (2020), 'Sud'ba dvukh kinomamontov: *Ia – Kuba* i *Novyi Kolumb*'. In press.

Volkov, Solomon (2018), *Dialogi s Evgeniem Evtushenko*, Moscow: AST.

Widdis, Emma (2003), *Visions of a New Land: Soviet Film from the Revolution to the Second World War*, New Haven and London: Yale University Press.

# 2

# Brazil's open cities: Mimicry, sexuality and class dynamics in the urban landscape of 1960s cinema

*Bruce Williams*
*(William Paterson University of New Jersey)*

Brazil of the 1960s was a country divided and plagued by national angst; a privileged elite feared a popularist uprising inspired by international communism. This crisis of the ruling class was exacerbated by pressure from the United States; both the Kennedy and Johnson administrations chided President João Goulart's failure to support the US isolation from Havana. As a tragic consequence, the Brazilian upper crust, whose own interests were closely tied to the State, supported a military coup in 1964, which initiated some twenty-one years of dictatorship. The coup notwithstanding, 1964 and 1965 were particularly significant for Brazilian cinema; two films of this short period, unlike so many products of Brazilian *Cinema Novo*, foregrounded issues of social class in an *urban* setting. Walter Hugo Khouri's

*Noite vazia* (Night Games 1964)[1] and Paulo César Saraceni's *O desafio* (The Dare 1965) investigate this struggle in a discourse highly reminiscent of European new wave canon, particularly the films of Antonioni. While Khouri's film is more akin to the studio system, Saraceni's is decidedly aligned with the tenets of *Cinema Novo*. When read through the lens of Homi Bhabha's notion of mimicry and, perhaps more importantly, the Brazilian concept of Anthropophagy, the importance of these films becomes evident. Indeed, Khouri and Saraceni attest to the subversive potential of works that give back to the dominant discourse something similar, 'but just a little different'.

## Not just an imitation: Mimicry and anthropophagy

Drawing upon Bhabha's theories of the phenomenon, mimicry as a discursive practice implies at once resemblance and menace. Hamid Naficy discusses the use by minorities of

> certain defensive, resistive, and pleasurable performance strategies as creative means of fashioning new and empowered identities that counter their sociopolitical subalternity and cultural marginalization. Of these, mimicry, passing, posing, camp, drag, sly civility, doubling, and masquerade depend on the existence of an original something that is turned into something else, a copy of the original. Put another way, they depend on repeating an original as the same with a difference – a difference that often implies criticism of that which is being imitated. (Naficy 2001: 269–71)

Nonetheless, in the postcolonial context, the mere notion of imitation is problematized, and herein lies the subversive power of mimicry. Naficy makes a clear separation between the two concepts. He argues:

> imitation involves identification with the other to the point of producing whole, identical subjects, where the original and the copy match... Mimicry, on the other hand, involves the kind of overimitation or underimitation of the other that, in its surplus or deficit and in its

---

[1]*Night Games*, it is important to note, has been known under numerous titles, which include both *Eros* and *Eros, the Bizarre* in the United States and *Men and Women* in the United Kingdom. Its French title, *Les Célibataires*, although at first appearing misleading in light of the marital status of the male protagonists, serves to underscore the dynamics of the bachelor pad in which the film takes place.

irony, produces partiality of identity, where there is a slippage between the original and its copy. It is in this slipzone of unfitting that the critical tensions of exilic mimicry and irony can be deciphered. (Naficy 2001: 285)

Bhabha, further, explores such strategies as essential to the mimetic process in that 'the discourse of mimicry is centered around an ambivalence... Mimicry is thus the sign of a double articulation, a complex strategy of reform, regulations and discipline, which "appropriates" the Other as it visualizes power' (Bhabha 1994: 123–4).

While Bhabha speaks of mimicry primarily in the postcolonialist framework of British imperialism, both Bhabha and Naficy discuss the notion in *multi-racial* contexts. Bhabha argues that even when individuals have the overall appearance of white, there may well be a feature that betrays them and denies them access to privilege (Bhabha 1994: 123–5). Khouri and Saraceni play with this deceptive whiteness, both with regard to the physical attributes of their protagonists and the European visual processes they choose to employ. Rare as the mimetic subversion of *Night Games* and *The Dare* may be, however, it is not a *completely* isolated occurrence in Latin American cinema.

A case in point is María Luisa Bemberg's *Miss Mary* (1986), whose protagonist is a sexually repressed British governess hired to educate the children of a very wealthy Argentine family. In this film, the culturally colonialized Argentines imitate the cultural colonialists, the Brits, and this process reveals the full scope and complexity of mimeses when considerable likenesses are at play. (One must recall, moreover, that the film was released only four years after the Falkland Islands conflict, and the British issue was still very raw among many Argentines.) What is especially significant (and compelling!) in the case of *Miss Mary* is the physical resemblance between the Argentine family and the British protagonist, for this similarity becomes the driving force of the film's dramatic development.[2] It is the cultural colonializer, the British governess, who is subservient to the Argentine upper crust. Albeit imitating her language and education, the elite, nonetheless, ostracize her. In this respect, *Miss Mary* is a paradoxical work in which the colonializer finds herself subservient to those who mimic her. The Brit may be of the very ethnic and cultural background that the family emulates, but she is merely a governess.

---

[2] For a lengthy discussion of such processes of similarity and difference, see Bruce Williams (2003), 'Julie Christie Down Argentine Way: Reading Repression Cross-Nationally in Bemberg's *Miss Mary*'.

Issues of social class trump, in this case, those of cultural colonialism. The film reverses the commonly held assumptions of social class and power relations in the neo-colonial context. In the case of *Night Games* and *The Dare*, such processes can be extended from diegetic characters to the overall aesthetic and thematic underpinnings of the films.

From a Brazilian theoretical framework, mimicry recalls theories put forth in 1928 by Brazilian poet and playwright Oswald de Andrade, who described the dynamics of cultural colonialism in 'O manifesto antropófago'/'The Cannibal Manifesto'. The Manifesto represented one of the most radical forms of Brazilian Modernism inasmuch as its author draws upon anthropophagical practices of the Tupinambá Amerindians to iconoclastically evaluate the anti-colonialist stance of 1920s Brazilian literature. The Tupinambá, who ingested their enemies in order to assume their strength, serve for Andrade as a model whereby Brazilian artists and writers could consume European culture, digest it and engender a uniquely Brazilian product. Yet, despite its radicalism, the ensuing cultural movement, known as Anthropophagy, does not imply isolationism and actually envisions a continued dialogue between Brazil and the First World (Williams 1999: 202). To this effect, Erdmute Wenzel White has stressed Anthropophagy's indebtedness to, for instance, Dada and Surrealism, which she argues provided Oswald de Andrade and others with creative processes capable of producing the emancipation of art. Ella Shohat and Robert Stam (1994) echo a similar stance:

> By appropriating an existing discourse for its own ends, anthropophagy *assumes* the force of the dominant only to deploy that force, through a kind of artistic jujitsu, *against* domination. Such an 'expropriation' steals elements of the dominant culture and redeploys them in the interests of oppositional praxis... many alternative esthetics have in common the twin anthropophagical notions of revalorizing what has been seen as negative and of turning strategic weakness into strategic strength. (Shohat and Stam 1994: 328)

Although a number of Brazilian films, such as Joaquim Pedro de Andrade's *Macunaima* (1969), Nelson Pereira dos Santos's *Como era gostoso o meu francês* (My Tasty Little Frenchman, 1971) and Jorge Bodansky's and Orlando Senna's *Iracema: uma transa-amazônica* (Iracema 1974) overtly recur to cannibalist or, at least, indigenous motifs, Anthropophagy can serve as a model for the most urban of films. Stam (1989) separates Anthropophagy from its indigenous context and views it as another name for Kristeva's 'intertextuality' or Bakhtin's 'dialogism' and 'carnivalization', but this time in the context of neocolonial domination (Stam 1989: 125). In the specific case of twentieth-century Brazil, the neo-colonialist dynamics bear upon Europe and the United States and play out in both the cultural and the economic spheres.

## Tropicalism and urban spaces

Shohat and Stam draw a parallel between Anthropophagy and the Tropicalist movement of the late 1960s, to which both *Night Games* and *The Dare* are clear predecessors. They argue that the favoured technique of Tropicalism 'was an aggressive collage of discourses, an anthropophagic devouring of varied cultural stimuli in all their heterogeneity' (Shohat and Stam 1994: 310). A fusion of *aesthetic* internationalism and *political* nationalism, Tropicalism was characterized by an 'aesthetic of garbage', which implied

> an aggressive sense of marginality, of surviving within scarcity, of being condemned to recycle the materials of dominant culture. A garbage style was seen as appropriate to a Third World country picking through the leavings of an international system dominated by First World capitalism. (Shohat and Stam 1994: 310)

A 2016 retrospective of the works of Brazilian artist Hélio Oiticica held at the Carnegie Museum of Art in Pittsburgh looked back fifty years to the birth of Brazilian Tropicalism. The exposition recreated an Oiticica installation titled 'Tropicália', which was displayed in Rio de Janeiro in 1967, and which arguably marked the birth of the tropicalist movement. The installation consisted of an island constructed from sand and pebbles on which were found two-caged Amazonian parrots and two box-like structures. The latter structures were made from cloth, burlap and wood and were designed to recall the makeshift favelas overlooking Rio de Janeiro. Visitors to the installation could walk through the structures. At the Carnegie, Caetano Veloso's song, also titled 'Tropicalia', played in the background. The song speaks of the contrast between Brazil's newly founded modern capital, Brasília, and a child begging in the street. Assessing the Carnegie installation, Elisa Wouk Almino emphasizes, 'The Tropicália aesthetic – bright, lively, impassioned – was shaded with dark undertones, partially masked for censorship reasons. But artists were also optimistic – ready, as Oiticica put it, to "plunge into the shit", dissecting the guts of this diarrhea [Brazil]' (Almino 2016).

'Tropicalia' appeared in London at the Tate Museum in November 2017. There, it was accompanied by a screening of tropicalism films, including Glauber Rocha's *Terra em transe* (Land in Anguish 1967), which has been deemed one of the seminal works of the movement, and Rogério Sganzerla's

*O bandido da luz vermelha* (The Red Light Bandit 1968), known for its garbage aesthetics.[3] The website for the Tate exposition asserts that even though 'Tropicália' suffered censorship from the military government, it was revolutionary in nature and influenced the cinema of the following decades. The site describes Tropicalism:

> Works associated with the movement indulged in pastiche, parody and a reflexive style of filmmaking that flirted with the kitsch products of Hollywood in a knowing way, offering a subtle critique of political and cultural dominance in its different forms. Today, a new generation of young filmmakers looks back on Brazil's national cinema, while at the same time creating work that responds to the various crises facing the country today: historical amnesia, drastic social inequality and ecological catastrophe. (Tate Museum 2017)

Although stemming from a few years prior to Tropicalism and lacking the pastiche and kitsch of the movement, *Night Games* and *The Dare* anticipated a good deal of the thematic concerns that would soon characterize the urban spaces of Brazilian cinema. The aesthetics of the films, however, are considerably distinct from those of Brazilian films of just a few years later and evoke Italian cinema of the early 1960s. They send back to Europe, just a little bit of itself, yet all the while infused with astute study of issues of social class in Brazil.

## Smiles of a São Paulo night

*Night Games*, although produced by a small company, Kamera Filmes, was, nonetheless, distributed by Vera Cruz, Brazil's foremost studio. The intentional framing of visuals coupled with the film's overall high-quality production values constitute two of the Vera Cruz hallmarks it displays (Rolim and Leite Trindade 2016). A film of remarkable visual dynamics, it was chosen as Brazil's official entry to the Cannes festival in 1965, where it initially tied with Richard Lester's *The Knack... and How to Get It* for the Palme d'Or.

---

[3]Rogério Sganzerla's *The Red Light Bandit* is a seminal work of an avant-garde cinema often deemed outside of or running parallel to *Cinema Novo*. The experimental discourse of the film drew the attention of Brazil's concrete poets, given its complex interweaving of divergent cinematic codes (Haroldo de Campos, personal contact, 1978). Another highly experimental director of this period was Júlio Bressane, whose *Matou a família e foi ao cinema* (Killed His Family and Went to the Movies 1969) was also a key example of 'garbage aesthetics'. These two films shared some of the thematics of *Night Games* in that they reflected the sordid side of Brazil's urban centres.

The mere fact that it ranked so high indicates the impressive level of support it garnered from the jury.[4] It lost due to a tie-breaking vote by the jury's president, Olivia de Haviland. Another member of the jury, *nouveau romancier* Alain Robbe-Grillet lauded the film and actually cited its opening sequences in his *L'Éden et après* (Eden and After 1970) and, to a lesser extent, in *'N' a pris les dés* ('N' Took the Dice 1971).[5] The French filmmaker was inspired by the abstract elements of *Night Games*, and a comparison between *Eden and After* and *Night Games* underscores the extent to which Khouri's work, like Robbe-Grillet's, is an undisputable example of *auteur* cinema.

In Brazil, *Empty Night* met with scathing comments by Glauber Rocha, who attacked the film's escapism, moral ambiguity and deliberate obscurity. Rocha states: 'If Khouri insists on remaining in the dangerous position of the "alienated conscious of his alienation", he will be converting himself into an intellectual servile to any state based on lie and injustice' (Rocha [1963] 2003: 120). Joanna Malecka situates Rocha's comments within the overly restrictive and ideologically informed programme of early *Cinema Novo*, of which Rocha became one of the major figures and propagandists (Malecka 2012: 61). Indeed, Khouri's intense psychological, personal and academic style is more akin to *second cinema*, as defined by Fernando Solanas and Octavio Getino in their groundbreaking essay 'Toward a Third Cinema', than to the radical discourse of guerrilla cinema. Solanas and Getino assert that such film directions as 'the so-called "author's cinema", "expression cinema", *nouvelle vague*, and *cinema novo*, or conventionally the second cinema [constituted, in any case] a significant step forward inasmuch as it demanded that the film-mater be free to express himself in non-standard language, and inasmuch as it was an attempt at cultural decolonization' (Solanas and Getino 1969: 120).[6] For Solanas and Getino, despite the strides

---

[4]English-language publicity for the film's screening at Cannes used the British title, *Men and Women*.
[5]Robbe-Grillet's *Eden and After*, albeit having somewhat of a story line, was based on the theories of twelve-tone music. It is structured around a number of themes that repeat throughout the film, although these are not always easily recognizable. In a 1977 discussion of *Eden and After* following a screening of the film at the University of Pennsylvania, the director confessed that he himself could no longer remember just what the themes were. Nonetheless, the twelve-tone structure serves as the film's structuring device, and this formal mechanism trumps any notion of cause and effect. *'N' Took the Dice* was made from outtakes of the earlier film and abandons the twelve-tone process, reconstructing the rudimentary story of *Eden and After* in a considerably more linear fashion. Similarities between *Night Games* and *Eden and After* are notably more evident. The irony is that, despite having influenced the more abstract elements in *Eden and After*, *Night Games* is by far the most linear of the three works. Its story line is more clearly developed than that of *'N' Took the Dice'*.
[6]It is significant to note that Solanas and Getino deem *Cinema Novo* an example of second, or *auteur* cinema.

made by the second cinema, it is still trapped within the conventional system of capitalism. Nonetheless, although akin to European *auteur* films, *Empty Night* is strongly rooted in the socio-political context of Brazil at the time of the military coup.

Rocha's indictment of Khouri is obviously tied to the similarity of *Night Games* to the work of Antonioni and other European directors. Advocating for a radical break with the shallow Brazilian films of the 1950s, Rocha disdained as well *auteur* cinema. (Mimicry as a critical lens would only become a theoretical concept some thirty years later, and hence, in his naïveté, Rocha delegated his compatriot to the realm of unadulterated imitation.) His misguided suppositions can be rectified by reading *Night Games* within the historical context of Brazil's economic boom of the 1950s, which Malecka employs to frame her study of *Night Games*. She stresses that even the 1954 suicide of President Getúlio Vargas did not damper Brazil's faith in the future or its healthy economy. Brazil, moreover, thrived under the administration of Vargas's successor, Juscelino Kubitschek, whose predominantly economy-driven ideology of social progress encouraged in Brazil dreams of a just and more egalitarian state. Yet much of this dream was a glitz and glitter illusion (Malecka 2012: 62). Particular characteristic of this 'Brazilian dream', as Jaison Castro Silva notes, was that it was articulated in a specifically architectural language (Castro Silva 2009). Kubitschek's opening of the futuristic capital city, Brasília, served as a symbol of his bold promises of 'fifty years progress in five' (Denison and Shaw 2004: 81) and was greeted with general confidence (Malecka 2012: 62).

Malecka further examines the agenda of the Instituto Superior de Estudos Brasileiros (the Higher Institute of Brazilian Studies, which was created by Kubitschek in 1955) and had a strong influence on the early development of *Cinema Novo*. The propaganda of the institute supported Kubitschek's capitalist agenda. Describing the role of the enlightened and economically privileged bourgeoisie in this plan, Malecka affirms:

> Their role was to spread the new-ideology among the lower classes chiefly through the medium of the cinema. The task for the new national cinema was to oppose the foreign influenced *chanchadas* and spread the message of the developmentalism to the rural areas. The depictions of rural underdevelopment in early *Cinema Novo* stem from this agenda. (Malecka 2012: 62)

Malecka underscores the proximity of the release of *Night Games* to the military coup and to the squelching of freedom of speech and human rights that accompanied it. She views it as a 'transition point between the two periods, and as a preamble to a significantly more pessimistic phase within Brazilian cinema' (Malecka 2012: 62). Its liminal position notwithstanding, the film's critique of the bourgeoisie is far subtler than that of Saraceni's

*The Dare*. As Randal Johnson has asserted, not a single film of the period from 1960 to 1964 critically examined the 'supposedly progressive sector that was to lead the country along the road to development' (Johnson 1984: 100). He looks ahead one year to *The Dare* as one of the first films that did.

*Night Games* relates the adventures of two men of different social classes who once a week fuck their way through São Paulo's gritty centre in empty meetings with prostitutes or adventurous socialites. On the event in question, they bring two hookers to their inner-city *garçonière* for an evening of blue movies and even bluer fun. The film's heightened eroticism caused critics to deem it a soft-core imitation of Antonioni's trilogy. Yet this assumption, as was Rocha's condemnation of Khouri, was a blatant oversimplification. The interpersonal dynamics of the two male protagonists reflect the power plays of contemporaneous Brazilian society, particularly inasmuch as it is Luis (Mário Benvenutti), the older man – also of a higher socio-economic standing – who calls the proverbial shots and manipulates his handsome younger companion (Gabriele Tinti) in a way not unlike his treatment of the prostitutes (Norma Bengall and Odete Lara). The dialogue and physical dynamics of the two men in essence invite a queer reading – and this is noted by Malecka – in which stunning young Tinti plays boytoy to his older companion as the two switch female partners over the course of the evening.

The erotic intent of *Night Games* is anticipated by its title sequence, which is comprised of images from the *Kama-Sutra*. Such a visual choice affords the viewer a clear picture of just what the 'night games' will entail. If one translates the Portuguese title literally, we are also privy to the sexual nature of the 'empty night'. The images appear decayed and crumbling, and this mirrors the void into which the protagonists will ultimately fall. In the *Kama-Sutra*, moreover, sexual depictions are anonymous; there is no mention of who the participants are. Hence, the facelessness of the diegetic encounters is underscored. According to Rolim and Leite Trindade, Walter Khouri's stated goal was to make a film about São Paulo which explores sexual impulse and its effects on human behaviour (Rolim and Leite Trindade 2016).

Following the opening credits, there is a montage of urban images of twilight and nocturnal São Paulo. The shots of traffic, street lights, vestibules and abstracted high-rises are devoid of people, yet show locations to which the narrative will soon travel. And this montage is accompanied by sparse, dissonant music by Rogério Duprat.[7] Rolim and Leite Trindade argue that, in the outdoor sequences, the greyish colours of the São Paulo images imbue the city with an 'otherness', as if it were in a land far away from

---

[7] It is this abstract and almost cubistic opening montage that so strongly influenced Robbe-Grillet. This is particularly evident in the opening sequences of *Eden and After*. The primary distinction is that, the initial images notwithstanding, *Night Games* develops in a far more linear fashion.

the military coup. For Rolim and Leite Trindade, the modern buildings of the city function as if they were the film's protagonists (Rolim and Leite Trindade 2016). The film's celebration of modern architecture underscores the construction dynamics of the Kubitschek era.[8]

Of all of Antonioni's films, it is *L'Eclisse* that is most closely evoked by *Night Games*. Saraceni's opening montage is, in a number of ways, a flip-flop of the final montage of the earlier film, once Monica Vitti has been erased from the narrative. *L'Eclisse* ends without principal characters, dialogue or narrative, yet presents places which the protagonists have visited. As Brunette argues, what we see is the 'remainder or inherent excess of the previously coded narrative' (Brunette 1998: 87). *Night Games* conversely begins with such excess, and its haunting opening attests to the emptiness of the night we will soon follow once we meet the predators.

Following the opening montage, we are introduced to Luis's home in an affluent neighbourhood of São Paulo. As he prepares for his ritual romp through the bars and night clubs of the city, his son plays with the horn of his luxury automobile. Several key pieces of information are revealed here. The viewer becomes aware not only of the man's social status but also of the fact that he is married with a family. The young boy's tooting the horn suggests that he too will someday follow in his father's footsteps; machismo will not skip a generation! The car, moreover, is a special toy through which its owner shows mastery over the events that will soon transpire.

Luis subsequently drives to a high-rise apartment complex, which appears like one of the anonymous edifices of the opening montage. In a window, we see Nelson standing with a woman, probably his wife, although this is never made clear. Nelson's residence suggests a certain level of success, but far from that of his companion. The two set forth on their evening exploits.

In the microcosm of the *garçonière*, the socio-economic dynamics of mid-1960s Brazil are played out. Evident are the dynamics of class and gender that paved the way for the coup and subsequently held the regime in place. Through the fissures of the narrative, a homoeroticism emerges which anticipates Brazilian films of the 1980s and deconstructs the *machismo* implicit in the empty encounters. The hookers, who are merely numbers to be chalked up on Luis's tally of anonymous exploits, question whether he is even interested in them. Nelson is decidedly another story. After all, he

---

[8]Here, once again, we find a parallel with *Eden and After*. In the Bratislava sequences of the film, the director does now choose the picturesque city centre. Rather, he opts for images of a factory and modern buildings. The interior shots evoke Mondrian, and render Café Eden, where the protagonists engage in drug usage and sado-masochistic rituals, an undefinable space and could be in virtually any urban centre. In his 1977 talk at the University of Pennsylvania, Robbe-Grillet stressed that the Bratislava locations were designed to evoke a Paris, but an unrecognizable one. The same is true of the São Paulo of *Night Games*. As Rolim and Leite Trindade assert, the level of abstraction appears as though they were images of another world.

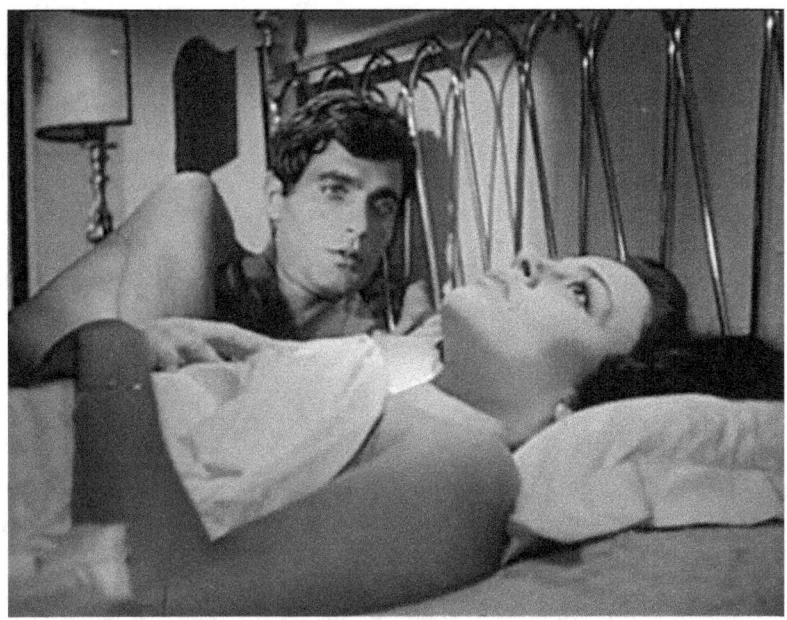

FIGURE 2.1 *Norma Bengell and Gabriele Tinti in* Night Games.

FIGURE 2.2 *Urban São Paulo following an evening of fun and games.*

is Luis's regular comrade in arms in the weekly adventures. His job is to fuck on demand, and it is Luis who pulls the strings. In Brazil of the 1960s, homosexuality was clearly a less-spoken concept than it would become a little over a decade later (Figure 2.1 and 2.2).

What initially may appear to be ersatz Antonioni is, in all actuality, a scathing depiction of the urban underbelly of Brazil. São Paulo's underbelly and a bold interrogation of Brazilian masculinity. Nonetheless, Khouri's mimicry is considerably more implicit than that of Saraceni, and this may well explain the different levels of acclaim, or lack thereof, that the two films met with in Europe.[9]

## Rio de Janeiro in a time without sun

A more radicalized mimicry of European cinema is found in *The Dare*. Made in a record fourteen days following the coup, the film was held up by Brazilian censors for five months prior to its screening out of competition at Cannes. Generating strongly mixed opinions upon its initial screening, *The Dare* attempts to reveal, through its male protagonist, a leftist writer, the plight of intellectuals caught up in the political transformation following the coup. It is in the political message that the film's greatest distinction from *Night Games* is to be found. Khouri's film explores the social dynamics and human toll of Brazil's economic miracle. Nonetheless, there is no direct discussion of political issues, and it is only through such indicators as urban architecture and clothing that the viewer ascertains the film's diegetic time. In contrast, *The Dare* overtly textualizes its immediate context. Constant references are made to the military coup, and the freshness thereof is most obvious. Unlike the São Paulo of *Night Games*, which could easily be a stand-in for any urban metropolis, and which slowly, but surely, invites the spectator to discover the Brazilianness of the setting, the Rio de Janeiro cityscape of *The Dare* is immediately evident. The latter film's inscription of social class is not only shown through images but, of equal importance, class issues are openly discussed between the film's protagonists, and such issues ultimately destroy the love affair between the young writer and the wife of an industrialist.

Of Italian heritage, Saraceni was trained in Rome, and during the course of his formative years, he became personally acquainted with Italian directors, among these Antonioni, whose influence on his cinematographic style is unmistakable. *The Dare* evokes European cinema in its preference

---

[9] In an exploration of Khouri's background, Malecka explains that the director was influenced by the *Nouvelle Vague*, Italian directors *and* existentialism. Most other sources tend to ignore the influence of Italian cinema on Khouri, merely alluding to his Lebanese and Italian background.

for longshots and methodical blocking, which foreground the socio-economic context of the locations depicted. The extended dialogues between its protagonists, moreover, are especially akin to the *cinéma d'auteur*. The lovers, Ada (Isabella) and Marcelo (Oduvaldo Vianna Filh), often appear in longshots, separated by a small line of negative space, foregrounding their alienation one from the other. When alone, Ada is frequently depicted, standing near the centre of the frame, against the background of the sparse interior of the apartment where the couple meet in the film. Saraceni further pays homage to Neo-Realism, this evidenced by handheld shots, location filming and use of non-actors, particularly in a factory sequence. Lacking the studio lustre of *Night Games*, the film's dialogue is periodically overridden by ambient sound, and a Brechtian separation is attained between the film and its spectators.

Nonetheless, to conflate *The Dare* with European cinema would be to miss its mimetic process altogether. The film, which boldly textualizes the crisis of the left following the military coup, is a decidedly historicized and contextualized work. More than any other Brazilian film of the 1960s, it documents the onslaught of the military government from the point of view of the urban intelligentsia. Its time specificity is most evidenced by the youthful passion of the protagonists as they confront, albeit in different ways, a defining moment in Brazilian history. *The Dare*, moreover, weaves an intricate tapestry of divergent Brazilian cultural references, and these stem primarily from the strong literary and intellectual leanings of Marcelo. We hear the *Bachianas brasileiras* of Villa Lobos, which provide a Brazilian response to baroque music; the politically charged songs of Maria Bethânia[10] and Zé Keti, which anticipate the tropicalist tendencies of a few short years later; and, the poetry of Jorge de Lima, a key figure of Brazilian Modernism.[11]

Although it is never made clear whether the lovers' meeting place is neutral turf or Marcelo's own apartment, the young writer clearly has had a hand in its décor. In contrast to the elegant and *intentional* design of the furnishings of the home that Ada shares with her husband, the apartment's space is sparsely furnished, and in the bedroom, several posters are precariously nailed to the wall. These evoke leftist tendencies, both Brazilian and international. Above the bed is a poster of Picasso's *Guerica*, and on

---

[10]It is essential to note that Bethânia is the sister of Caetano Veloso, a leader of the tropicalist movement.
[11]Brazilian Modernism must not be conflated with the Modernism of Spanish America. Ushered in 1922 by an exhibition of the paintings of Anita Malfatti held at São Paulo's municipal theatre, it sought to re-inscribe the European avant-garde into an authentically Brazilian discourse. Aside from Jorge de Lima, other poets associated with the movement include Mário de Andrade, Manuel Bandeira and Murilo Mendes. Oswald de Andrade's 'Cannibal Manifesto' represents Modernism in its most radical manifestation.

another wall, there hangs a film poster of Glauber Rocha's *Deus e o diabo na terra do sol* (Black God, White Devil 1964), which, released only a few short months prior to *The Dare*, has been deemed a seminal work of the rural tendency of *Cinema Novo*.

Rocha's film explores power structures in Brazil's impoverished Northeast, and such dynamics are not unlike those at play in the urban spaces of *The Dare*. In bed, the lovers listen to Villa Lobos's *Bachiana brasileira* #5.[12] Such a musical choice recalls the complex mélange of highbrow and popularist discourses of Rocha's film (Figure 2.3).

In a *cinema vérité* sequence, protagonist Marcelo attends a performance of *Opinião*, a show starring Maria Bethânia, which represented a transformation in Brazilian popular music from the romantic vision of early 'bossa nova' to a more politicized and radical expression, particularly strong

**FIGURE 2.3** *Oduvaldo Vianna Filho and Isabella in* The Dare.

---

[12]Although only the piece is credited only by name, it is most likely the 1958 recording conducted by the composer featuring the Orchestre National de la Radiodiffusion Française and Catalonian soprano Victoria de Los Angeles. Like the artwork on the wall of the apartment, the recording is a synthesis of Brazilian and European discourses. It is possible that no complete credit for the music was given due to the low-budget, guerrilla-film conditions under which *The Dare* was made. In a like manner, no credit is provided either for the Mozart music the lovers listen to, and which continues extra-diegetically as Ada returns home.

in the wake of March 1964.¹³ The show, photographed from the perspective of what appears to be a diegetic spectator, combines the discourses of Brazil's impoverished Northeast with those of the *favelas*, from which the samba itself had sprung. The songs are revolutionary and boldly allude to recent events; its title, *Opinião*, is in and of itself politicized. Two numbers from the show are actually performed in part in the sequence; these include Zé Keti's 'Notícias do jornal' and Maria Bethânia's 'Carcará'. The selection of the two performers is not random; Bethânia represents the Northeast, while Keti is a native of Rio de Janeiro. During the performance, there are several cuts to the diegetic audience and specifically to close-ups of Marcelo's face, which reveals profound emotion and the solidarity the protagonist obviously feels with the performers and their radical statement. Despite the politicized nature of the two songs heard in part, the title song of the show becomes an unspoken statement. Although not performed in *The Dare*, the lyrics of 'Opinião' as sung by Zé Keti speak to the climate of the film. 'You can arrest me/You can beat me/You can leave me without food/I won't change my opinion/I won't come down from the *morro*' (my translation).

The dichotomy leftist/bourgeoise that characterizes the love relationship is, nonetheless, not entirely simple. Although the film opens with Ada driving Marcelo to the love nest – like Luis in *Night Games*, the richer character is in the driver's seat – she is not necessarily in control of the relationship. Through Marcelo, Ada has come to doubt her husband's capitalist agenda, and by extension, that of Brazil at large. Her questioning remains, nonetheless, on a rather rudimentary level. She is limited by her own lack of cultural exposure, a fact underscored by her failure to recognize the poetry of Jorge de Lima or, more likely, not even to know who the poet was! Following her break with Marcelo, Ada visits her husband's factory and contemplates the workers as they clock out and leave the premises. She appears mystified by this daily ritual, yet her stance, which alternates between facing the workers and facing with them, may well indicate an attempt at solidarity. In the film's final sequence, Marcelo recalls her image. Yet the Ada of his thoughts does not reciprocate his gaze. Rather, she looks in the same direction as he does, as if trying to see the world from his perspective (Figure 2.4).

The initial months of the life of *The Dare* were indeed turbulent. The censors made minor cuts in dialogue which did not affect the film's integrity, yet this process held up the release. When initially screened in Rio de Janeiro on 17 May 1966, it met with mixed reactions. Expecting strong support from the left and anger from the mainstream, Saraceni organized a debate at the Clubinho dos Artistas, which was attended by such noted Brazilian cultural figures as poet Décio Pignatari, film critics Jean-Claude Bernadet and Paulo

---

¹³*Opinião*, which remained on stage in Rio de Janeiro from December 1964 through August 1965, would continue on to São Paulo, where a theatre would be named after it.

FIGURE 2.4 *Ada's visit to the factory in* The Dare.

Emílio Salles Gomes, writer Lygia Fagundes Telles and underground filmmaker Rogério Sganzerla. For the artistic community, *The Dare* was recognized as another important film by the young and aspiring director. In Rio, the film was awarded a prize by the World Historian's organization; in Brasília, it met with fifteen minutes of applause during the Week of Brazilian Cinema. Rejected as the official Brazilian entry to Cannes, the film was saved by French critics, who demanded that it be screened 'out of competition'. Unable to attend the festival himself, Saraceni sent his wife, the film's star, Isabella, to appear and speak on his behalf. Having been barred from a screening of *Modesty Blaise* because of her less-than-modest attire, Isabella had engendered a degree of notoriety which would actually serve to predispose audiences favourably to the film and its cause.[14] When *The Dare* met with several minutes of standing ovation, the actress burst into tears as she related the rapidity with which the film was made.[15] Given the scathing critiques of *Night Games* the previous year, the immediately warm and favourable reaction to *The Dare* attests to a genuine attempt on the part of international audiences to understand the complex situation of the Brazilian left. Such favourable reception is most impressive given that Saraceni's film is one of extensive dialogue, replete with Brazilian cultural and literary references.

---

[14]Isabella was the stage name of Isabella Cerqueira Campos (1938–2011). In Saraceni's 1993 memoir, her name is spelled in its Portuguese form, 'Isabela'.
[15]For more details on *The Dare* in Europe, see Saraceni 1993, 183–218.

## Concluding remarks

*Night Games*, through the mimicry of European cinematic codes, unravels the class and sexual dynamics of Brazil's urban underbelly. The very name *Boca do Lixo*, or 'Garbage Mouth', which denotes the seediest section of the centre of São Paulo, underscores the deprecating way in which more respectable members of society view the realm of marginality that the film's prostitutes call home. In a like manner, upper-class playboy, Luis, not only degrades the women he encounters but, moreover, renders his male companion (of a noticeably more modest class) a mere sex toy. Perhaps Khouri's mimicry was too subtle for international audiences in 1964; the film, although the subject of recent academic analyses, initially met with mixed reviews outside of Brazil. The relative success of *The Dare* in Europe vis-à-vis *Night Games* may well be explained by the increased familiarity Europeans were starting to have in the mid-1960s with Brazilian culture through popular music, *Cinema Novo*, and the like. Continental audiences were now finding inroads into the political reality of Brazil. More militant than its predecessor, *The Dare* drew upon European discourses to hurl back at the Continent a taste of Brazil's cultural and political reality. Urban São Paulo and Rio de Janeiro, class dynamics and power structures, the homoerotic underpinnings of Brazilian hyper-masculinity are the Brazilian realities which are returned to Europe in anthropophagical mimicry. Khouri, whose film discourse attests to a thorough familiarity with Antonioni and other European directors, and Saraceni, who overtly lays bare his Italian film training, both cite and rework their masters. They give back to Europe, and elsewhere, for that matter, an uncompromising vision of urban Brazil in all its complexities and contradictions – Antonioni, perhaps, but radically different.

## Acknowledgement

This chapter is dedicated to the memory of Claude L. Hulet, 1920–1917, an internationally recognized scholar of Brazilian literature and a corresponding member of the Brazilian Academy of Letters. Claude was my doctoral mentor and urged me to find academic autonomy.

## Bibliography

Almino, Elisa Wouk (2016), 'Tripping through Hélio Oiticica's Mythical World,' *Hyperallergic* (28 December), https://hyperallergic.com/345190/tripping-through-helio-oiticicas-mythical-world/ (accessed 31 March 2019).

Andrade, Oswald de (1928), 'Manifesto antropófago', *Revista de Antropofagia*, 1 May: 3, 7.
*Bachiana braasileira #5* (1958), [phonograph record] Heitor Villa-Lobos, Orchestre Nsational de la Radiodiffusion Française, New York City: Angel Records.
Bhabha, Homi (1994), *The Location of Culture*, New York: Routledge.
Brunette, Peter (1998), *The Films of Michelangelo Antonioni*, Cambridge: Cambridge University Press.
Castro Silva, Jaison (2009), 'Metrópole e melancholia: A ansiedade pela captação da realidade urbana no cinema brasileiro dos anos 1960', *ANPUH – XXV Simpósio nacional de história – Fortaleza, 2009*, https://anpuh.org.br/uploads/anais-simposios/pdf/2019-01/1548772192_15180292116840cac3ac698f6393f94c.pdf (accessed 19 March 2019).
*Como era gostoso o meu francês/My Tasty Little Frenchman* (1971), [Film] Dir. Nelson Pereira dos Santos, Brazil, Rio de Janeiro: Luiz Carlos Barreto, K.M. Eckstein, Nelson Pereira dos Santos, César Thedizo.
Dennison, Stephanie and Lisa Shaw (2004), *Popular Cinema in Brazil*, Manchester: Manchester University Press.
*Deus e o diabo na terra do sol/Black God, White Devil* (1964), [Film] Dir. Rocha Glauber, Brazil, Rio de Janeiro: Copacabana Films.
*Iracema: uma transa-amazônica* (1974), [Film] Dir. Jorge Bodansky and Orlando Senna, Brazil, Rio de Janeiro, Slop Films and Zweites Deutsches Fernsehen.
Johnson, Randal (1984), 'Brazilian Cinema Novo', *Bulletin of Latin American Research*, 3 (2): 95–106.
*The Knack...and How to Get It* (1965), [Film] Dir. Richard Lester, London: Woodfall Film.
*Macunaíma* (1969), [Film] Dir. Joaquim Pedro de Andrade, Brazil, Rio de Janeiro: Difilm, Filmes do Sêrro, Grupo Filmes, Condor Filmes.
Malecka, Joanna (2012), 'Walter Hugo Khouri's Voyeuristic Games with His Audience in *Noite vazia*', *Studia Humanistyczne AGH*, 11 (1): 61–8.
*Matou a família e foi ao cinema/Killed His Family and Went to the Movies* (1969), [Film] Dir. Júlio Bressane, Brazil, Rio de Janeiro: Júlio Bressane Produções Cinematográficas.
*Miss Mary* (1986), [Film]. Dir. María Luisa Bemberg, Argentina, Buenos Aires: GEA Cinematográfica.
*Modesty Blaise* (1966), [Film] Dir. Joseph Losey, UK, London: Modesty Blaise, Ltd.
Naficy, Hamid (2001), *An Accented Cinema: Exile and Difference in Filmmaking*, Princeton: Princeton University Press.
*'N' a pris les dés/'N' Took the Dice* (1971), [Film] Dir. Alain Robbe-Grillet, France, Paris, Bratislava: Como Films and Hranych Filmov.
*O bandido da luz vermelha/The Red Light Bandit* (1968), [Film] Dir. Rogério Sganzerla, Brazil, São Paulo: Filmes Urânio.
*O desafio/The Dare* (1965), [Film] Dir. Paulo César Saraceni, Brazil Rio de Janeiro: Mapa Filmes, Produções Cinematográficas Imago.
*Porto das Caixas* (1962), [Film] Dir. Paulo César Saraceni. Brazil, Rio de Janeiro, Produções Cinematográficas Imago.
Rocha, Glauber ([1963] 2003), *Revisão crítica do cinema brasileiro*, São Paulo: Cosue & Naify (First edition in).

Rolim, Ana Luisa and Isabella Leite Trindade (2016), 'Arquitetura moderna no cinema pós guerra', *Docomomo*, http://docomomo.org.br/wp-content/uploads/2016/01/153R.pdf (accessed 20 April 2019).
Saraceni, Paulo César (1993), *Por dentro do cinema novo – minha viagem*, Rio de Janeiro: Nova Fronteira.
Shohat, Ella and Robert Stam (1994), *Unthinking Eurocentrism*, New York: Routledge.
Solanas, Fernando and Octavio Getino (1969), 'Hacia un tercer cine', *Tricontinental*, 14 (October): 107–32.
Stam, Robert (1989), *Subversive Pleasures*, Baltimore and London: Johns Hopkins University Press.
Tate Modern (2017), 'Tropicalia and Beyond: Dialogues in Brazilian Film', https://www.tate.org.uk/whats-on/tate-modern/film/tropicalia-and-beyond-dialogues-brazilian-film-history (accessed 12 March 2019).
*Terra em transe/Landmp in Amguish* (1967), [Film] Dir. Glauber Rocha, Brazil, Rio de Janeiro: Mapa Films.
White, Erdmute Wenzel (1977), *Les Années vingt au Brésil: Le modernisme et l'avant-garde international*, Paris: Editions Hispaniques.
Williams, Bruce (1999), 'To Serve Godard: Anthropophagical Processes in Brazilian Cinema', *Film/Literature Quarterly*, 27 (3): 202–9.
Williams, Bruce (2003), 'Julie Christie Down Argentine Way: Reading Repression Cross-Nationally in Bemberg's *Miss Mary*', *Journal of Film and Video*, 55 (4): 15–29.

# 3

# 'Unreal city': The aesthetics of commitment in *Pratidwandi* and *Interview*

## Koel Banerjee
## (Carnegie Mellon University)

*This is not a time for political art, but politics has migrated into autonomous art, and nowhere more so than where it seems to be politically dead.*

(ADORNO 1980: 194)

### A cinema of troubled times

The debate over realism remains an abiding one in Indian cinema.[1] Commenting on reproduction of reality in cinema, Satyajit Ray points out:

---

[1]While realism as an aesthetic practice has been a contested subject in film theory, the debate takes a slightly different form in Indian cinema. In Indian film theory, the classic realist text, Ravi Vasudevan notes, 'has been aligned with the development of a culture of modernity with certain political ramifications. These comprise the understanding that realist cinema addresses, indeed seeks to constitute a modern spectator invested in the cognitive practice of individualised perception central to the development of a civil society of freely associating individuals' (Vasudevan 2001: 55). In a similar vein, Sumita S Chakravarty points out the anomalies of realist aesthetics in popular Indian cinema: 'the concept itself is alien to Indian philosophic and aesthetic traditions (not to speak of Bombay filmmaking practices generally) and certainly owed some of its impetus to the international climate favouring neorealism but was taken as a transparent means whereby "Indian reality" could be revealed. In other words, the West provided the frame whereby Indians could view themselves' (Chakravarty 1989: 34). 'Realist', a term often used to distinguish the social film from other genres like the mythological and fantasy, came to signify a wide range of cinematic practices ranging from verisimilitude to the desire to represent the 'authentic' India.

The sharpest revelations of the truth in cinema come from the details perceived through the eyes of artists. It is the sensitive artist's subjective approach to reality that ultimately matters, and this is true as much as documentaries as of fiction films. Details can make both of them real, in the same way and to the same degree, while lack of details can turn both into dead matter in spite of all the verisimilitude that camera and microphone can impart. I like Sukhdev's *India '67*, but not for the broad percussive contrast between poverty and affluence, beauty and squalor, modernity and primitivity – however well shot and cut they may be. I like it for its details – for the black beetle that crawls along the hot sand, for the street dog that pees on the parked cycle, for the bead of perspiration that dangles on the nose-tip of the begrimed musician. (Ray 2011: 38)

It is significant that Ray, in his exploration of the status of reality in cinema, mobilizes as his example S. Sukhdev's documentary *India '67*. The reference sheds light on Ray's own position on reality in cinema, which, as he clarifies, is not to be confused with verisimilitude. Furthermore, Ray's example illustrates his stance on the subjective aspect of representation of reality, a constant in both documentary and fiction films. In his reading, the representation of reality, in both fiction and non-fiction films, has a subjective aspect that ultimately determines the film's success or lack thereof in animating its subject matter.

In many ways, *India '67* was a radical departure from the then-prevalent trends in Indian documentary cinema. Filmed twenty years after Indian independence from British colonialism, it chronicles the tensions between rural and urban India, highlights the incongruity of poverty and affluence, and depicts the co-existence of the modern and the pre-modern in postcolonial India. Funded by the Government of India's Films Division, *India '67* departs from conventional exercises in nation-building as it does not pay the customary homage to the postcolonial state; instead, it documents the inherent contradictions of the Nehruvian vision of the postcolonial nation as it captures the political unrest that marked the decade of the 1960s in India. With its careful manipulation of the visual montage, further underscored by its use of political Urdu poems by Kaifi Azmi, S. Sukhdev's documentary, arguably, takes a political stance. Furthermore, in a marked departure from the conventions of the-then contemporary documentary films in India, S. Sukhdev introduces an auto-telic moment, when the filmmaker visits his ancestral home. However, for Ray, the film's appeal does not lie in its political subtext or self-reflexivity. Instead, Ray singles out moments in the film that, according to him, not only make the film more 'real' but, more importantly, bear testimony to the filmmaker's subjective approach to a far greater degree than his appearance in his film could ever achieve. Ray points out that in the absence of such moments, all cinema, whether fiction or documentary, despite all protestations of verisimilitude attained by technological means, would be dead matter. Although such moments are not essential to the socialist-realist aesthetics towards which many of his contemporaries aspired, they are, Ray argues, capable of truth-claims that exceed those made with the manipulation of technological verisimilitude. In this reading, it is the filmmaker's subjectivity that alone can forge the cinematic idiom that best speaks to and about times of political and social turmoil.

However, this view of the nature of reality in cinema, which involves a fine distinction between reality and verisimilitude, coupled with an emphasis on artistic subjectivity, was not shared by his contemporary Mrinal Sen. In a stark contrast to Ray's valorization of artistic subjectivity in filmmaking, Sen, in a characteristic polemical fashion, posited that the filmmaker's role was that of an 'agent-provocateur'. For Sen, filmmaking and film-viewing were, in equal measure, a call to political action:

> Film, like literature and other art media, has a certain role in our society. It creates a certain climate. It may also provoke a certain kind of debate. My job is to provide information from a point of view which is clearly not neutral... My intention is to communicate as effectively as I can, to provoke the audience. The filmmaker has to be an *agent-provocateur* – one who disturbs the spectator and moves him to action. (Hood 1993: 22)

For Sen, the task of cinema, like that of other narrative arts, was to provoke its viewers into political action. Although Sen leans towards a more political cinematic idiom than Ray, he shared some of Ray's suspicion of realism as he was well aware of the limits of a realist aesthetic. While Ray's reservation about the realist aesthetic in cinema hinged on the possible absence of artistic subjectivity, to be simply 'realistic' was not political enough for Sen. For Sen, cinema was meant to be politically 'partisan' in its depiction of reality:

> It is not enough, to my mind, to be just 'realistic'. The point is to give it direction. Which means, one needs to develop a partisan attitude as one gets to the analysis of reality. This, of course, calls for commitments, political and social... I, for one, believe in involvement. I stand by commitment. (Hood 1993: 21)

Realism as a cinematic goal was, thus, already in the balance even before Ray and Sen started filming the first instalment of their Calcutta trilogies. While the subjective aspect of cinema that Ray emphasizes requires involvement, in Sen's view, the involvement of the filmmaker has to be at the level of politics. The views held by Ray and Sen on the stakes and status of realism in cinema shape, as this chapter will argue, their own cinematic takes on the political turmoil of the 1960s. Focusing on the first instalments of their respective city trilogies – *Pratidwandi* (*The Adversary*, Ray 1970) and *Interview* (Sen 1971) – the chapter charts how the turmoil of the 1960s became the crucible in which two very distinct cinematic idioms were formed. The protagonists of both films are young men who are interviewing for jobs at a time of political unrest and a steadily worsening unemployment crisis. And yet, despite the similarity of story and the shared political milieu, the films present two different tales of a city.

The polemic between Ray and Sen about the status of reality and commitment in art resonates with a long-standing debate in Marxist theory about commitment as an aesthetic strategy. Ray's views on the reproduction of reality in cinema, an opinion not shared by Sen, echo Theodor Adorno's reservations towards committed art. For Adorno, it is art's autonomy that makes it truly radical. Art, when burdened with philistine moralism, ceases to be art and degenerates into ideology, and in being so reduced, it loses its political potential.

Adorno writes,

> When a work is merely itself and no other thing, as in a pure pseudoscientific construction, it becomes bad art – literally pre-artistic. The moment of true volition, however, is mediated through nothing other than the form of the work itself, whose crystallization becomes an analogy of that other condition which should be. As eminently constructed and produced objects, works of art, even literary ones, point to a practice from which they abstain: the creation of a just life. The mediation is not a compromise between commitment and autonomy, nor a sort of mixture of advanced formal elements with an intellectual content inspired by genuinely or supposedly progressive politics. The content of works of art is never the amount of intellect pumped into them: if anything, it is the opposite. (Adorno 1980: 194)

Art, in this reading, is at once real and an indictment of reality. Responding as much to Brecht as to Sartre, Adorno notes that the radical possibility of art is not in its enunciation of politics or didacticism; rather, it resides in its autonomy. In a similar vein, Herbert Marcuse locates autonomous art's political potential in its dialectical relationship with reality. Marcuse notes: 'The truth of art lies in its power to break the monopoly of established reality (i.e. of those who established it) to define what is real. In this rupture, which is the achievement of the aesthetic form, the fictitious world of art appears as true reality' (Marcuse 1978: 9). For this reason, only autonomous art, which both Adorno and Marcuse distinguish from art which has 'intellect pumped into them', has the ability to change consciousness. Ray's own evaluation of S. Sukhdev's film, which he praises not for its politics or technical mastery but for the details that animate it, thus resonates with Adorno's and Marcuse's insistence on the radical potential of art's autonomy.

In a manner quite dissimilar to Ray, Sen emphasizes commitment as aesthetic practice. In so doing, he echoes what Fernando Solanas and Octavio Getino claimed was the primary task of the revolutionary filmmaker in an alienated world. Solanas and Getino argue that artists and intellectuals in dependent nations have to choose between relegating all intellectual and artistic production to a political agenda, on the one hand, and a separation of politics and art, on the other. In the latter case, the artist or the intellectual demonstrate their political commitment by signing manifestoes while, at the same time, ensuring that their politics does not intertwine with the aesthetics of artistic production. For Solanas and Getino, this antonymy between politics and aesthetics, in essence, is a false one for it rests on two significant elisions, the most notable being that it fails to take into cognizance that

> the revolution does not begin with the taking of political power from imperialism and the bourgeoisie, but rather begins at the moment when the masses sense the need for change and their intellectual vanguards begin to study and carry out this change through activities on different fronts. (Solanas and Getino 1970: 1)

And cinema, because of the nature of the medium and its mass appeal and reach, can often be a far more effective rallying point than political rhetoric. Taking their cue from Marx's final thesis from his *Theses on Feuerbach*, they argue that decolonization has to be coterminous with the decolonization of culture (Solanas and Getino 1970: 6). For Solanas and Getino, in a world where 'the unreal rules', films cannot limit themselves to an apologetic view of reality (Solanas and Getino 1970: 6). The movie camera is no longer the impassive *caméra-stylo*; rather, in the hands of revolutionary filmmakers, it is no less effective than a rifle in 'contributing to the downfall of capitalist society' (Solanas and Getino 1970: 1).

# Calcutta of the 1960s

The conflicting attitudes towards the aesthetics and politics of filmmaking of Ray and Sen make their way into their respective Calcutta trilogies: Ray's *Pratidwandi* (The Adversary, 1970), *Seemabaddha* (The Company Limited, 1971) and *Jana Aranya* (The Middleman, 1975); and Sen's *Interview* (1971), *Calcutta 71* (1972) and *Padatik* (The Guerrilla Fighter, 1973). When the filmmakers started filming the first instalments of their city trilogies, their debate about the relationship of cinema and politics became all the more immediate because of the political milieu of the times. The 1960s were a turbulent period in India. India's defeat in its war against China, rising unemployment, stagnation of growth, food shortage, and the failure of the

Nehruvian welfare state to fulfil its mandate created a politically volatile situation. The situation in Bengal was further exacerbated by fissures in the Communist Party of India–Marxist (CPI-M) in 1969 when a group of radicals known as the Naxalites, under the leadership of Charu Majumdar, Kanu Sanyal and Saroj Dutta, left the CPI-M to form the Communist Party of India–Marxist Leninist (CPI-ML). The newly formed party tried to mobilize landless peasants into armed conflicts with landlords, moneylenders and government officials. The urban youth, who went to the villages to participate in and lead armed struggles, formed a significant part of the Naxalites. The situation in Calcutta was particularly tense as student rebellion spread to colleges and universities. The response of the state government was a reign of police repression and indiscriminate hunting down of suspected Naxalites. By the 1970s, that is, when Ray and Sen were gearing up to film the first films of their respective trilogies, the situation in Calcutta had further worsened. The Bangladesh Liberation War in 1971 led to large-scale immigration and displacement of people. The food shortage crisis continued to worsen, and jobs became even more scarce, leading to widespread social unrest.

When Ray and Sen were filming *The Adversary* and *Interview* respectively, the terror spread by the Naxalites was at its peak. And equally terrible were the police atrocities on the Naxalites, their sympathizers and on people suspected as revolutionaries. Ray, perhaps more than the more politically vocal Sen, felt the need to respond to the political turmoil in his city. Andrew Robinson notes that Ray's attitude was one of 'sympathy for those trying to change post-independence Bengali society, but not for their violent methods' (Robinson 2004: 216). Ray's reluctance to take part in public rallies – being 'too much of an individualist to be a Communist' – is well-documented (Robinson 2004: 216). Calcutta of the late 1960s was a nightmare city, and Ray was acutely aware of the political requirements of a film set in the city: 'You felt certain changes taking place, almost in day-to-day existence. You felt that without reflecting those changes, you couldn't make a film' (Robinson 2004: 217).

While Ray had reservations about making a city film, he was also well aware that his films were being criticized for not being political enough. The 1970s was the decade when the anti-Ray sentiments were at a peak. For instance, Chidananda Das Gupta scathingly observed that the 'Calcutta of the burning trams, the communal riots, refugees, unemployment, rising prices and food shortages does not exist in Ray's films (Das Gupta 1980: 46). However, despite his declaration that he failed to understand what motivated the politically active youth in these tempestuous times, Ray's film, like Sen's, pivots on the unemployment crisis that the youth were facing at the time. Ray not only returned to Calcutta to make political trilogy; he also made his protagonists members of the generation that he, failed to completely understand. While *The Adversary*, by his own admission, is his most political film, *The Company Limited* has a distinct allegorical quality, and the final film of his trilogy, *The Middleman*, is uncharacteristically farcical world of pimps and middlemen.

## *The Adversary*: A failed dialogue

Ray, who was sceptical about the possibility of an Indian New Wave, was well aware that in order to make a Calcutta-centric film in the 1970s, he would have to forgo his usual cinematic style. That is not to say that Ray did not think that his film was not pro-revolution film:

> I'm pretty tense about the possible reaction to my new film – certainly the first truly contemporary film made here – and basically though not blatantly – pro-revolution – because I feel nothing else can set the country up on its feet. (Robinson 2004: 217)

Ray here makes the case that pro-revolution films do not have to be blatant. Elsewhere, he has commented that while a degree of commitment was inevitable for the filmmaker, there remains a fine distinction between committed art and propaganda.

The protagonist of Ray's film, Siddhartha, a young man who belongs to the generation that Ray claimed he was unable to comprehend, comes to represent the auteur's own sense of alienation from the city and its increasingly violent politics. Siddhartha emerges as one of Ray's most complex protagonists whose feeling of estrangement is reflected by the film's idiom. Siddhartha, once a medical student, had to abandon his studies in order to provide for his family after his father's death. In many ways, Siddhartha's political views reflect Ray's own. While he is acutely aware of the politically charged climate of the times, he remains somewhat of a passive onlooker unlike his brother, Tunu, who is a Naxalite. The tension between Siddhartha's political awareness, coupled with his perceived passivity (in that he does not take an active part in the political struggle), manifests in his alienation from the city and from his family, a recurring theme in Ray's trilogy. Ray himself shared some of the estrangement felt by his protagonist, and the film evokes Siddhartha's dilemma and interiority with the use of flashbacks and imaginary scenes of wish fulfilment. It is notable that *The Adversary*, an adaptation of the eponymous novel by Sunil Gangopadhyay, deviates from its source text whose protagonist was nineteen years old. Ray, instead, makes his Siddhartha much older and considerably more mature. After failing to get a job in the city, having confused a question of general knowledge as a question of political know-how, Siddhartha finally is exiled from the city to a small town. Closure is finally achieved when Siddhartha, now banished from the city to a small town, hears a bird call, a recurrent theme in the film, symbolic of his childhood. The film's ending, which takes place outside the city and has aural resonances (in the form of the bird song) with a time that was politically less turbulent, signifies the protagonist's and his creator's inability to completely come to terms with the city in its time.

Of the three films in Ray's trilogy, *The Adversary* shows the most stylistic experiments. It opens with Siddhartha's father's funeral. The mourning relatives and the final rites are shown in film negative, as is the first shot of Siddhartha standing by his father's pyre. The rest of the film follows in positive film stock. The use of negative re-occurs in two later scenes in the film – first, when a nurse bends to light a cigarette, and second, in Siddhartha's dream where both positive and negative film stock are used. Ray justified the use of negative film stock in the former instance by pointing out that the use of film negative toned down the fact that the nurse (who moonlights as a prostitute) is undressing. Later in the film, negative film stock is used in Siddhartha's dream sequence. The dream is a collage of the day's events overlapping with Siddhartha's inner monologue, and the use of negative serves a stylistic purpose as the film negative and film positive are juxtaposed to give the dream sequence a surreal quality. The use of negative film stock, an uncharacteristic foregrounding of the apparatus in Ray's oeuvre, adds to the feeling of uncertainty that permeates the film and haunts its protagonist. Through a careful deployment of style and manipulation of the sights and sounds of cinema, Siddhartha emerges as the most complex of Ray's protagonists. The breakdown of Ray's earlier seamless narrative style highlights his and his protagonist's political ambivalence.

Ray was aware that *The Adversary* marked a departure from his earlier films not only in terms of subject but also in terms of the filmic idiom that it employed. Ray's treatment of his protagonists is markedly different in the Calcutta trilogy. Whereas there was a sense of identification with his earlier protagonists, here, in the trilogy, it is replaced by his need to understand the post-independence generation and a growing sense of frustration at his inability to do so. In this manner, Ray's attitude towards his protagonists in the trilogy shifts from sympathetic to satirical. What Ray achieves is a narrative of interiority and alienation, visually accentuated by quick zoom-outs and use of negative film stock, fast cutting, top-angle shots and crepuscular lighting. Ray's art in his trilogy becomes more self-conscious in the face of the troubled political climate that it seeks to capture. Moinak Biswas argues that *The Adversary* inaugurates the stage in Ray's career when, his art seems to suffer a kind of decomposition, something that looks symptomatic now. The unemployed protagonist appears in the film as an unanchored, floating being. Limbs, faces, fleeting gestures connected to the street, the crowded bus, the random assembly, cafes and terraces – the narrative is nothing but a record of a wandering through moments of suspension. (Biswas 2007: 78)

*The Adversary*, with its stylistic experiments, however, is not a standalone film in Ray's career. He abandons his 'classical style' altogether in the later instalments of his Calcutta trilogy. Although Ray's early narratives are marked by an almost 'classical' seamlessness, Ravi Vasudevan locates elements that are antithetical to that seamlessness even in Ray's early films (2006). His early films, Vasudevan argues, had undercurrents of a dialogue with the modern that ruptured the flow of the narrative and distanced the audience from the diegetic world via a self-conscious cinematic idiom. Vasudevan points out the famous train sequence in *Pather Panchali* (Song of the Little Road, 1955), where the swish-pan disturbs the realist aesthetics of the film, and for a brief moment, Ray strays from character-focalized narration. There are other notable instances in Ray's early films where the invisibility of his narration is disrupted, including self-conscious uses of the camera, for example, travelling shots, zooms, symbolic use of the frame. However, his Calcutta trilogy displays to a far greater degree the foregrounding of cinematic apparatus and an abandonment of his classical realist aesthetics. Ray's inability to understand his protagonist's generation is echoed in the style he adopts for his most political film.

If Ray's visual style marks his inability to represent the Calcutta of the 1970s without abandoning his classical realism, then the dissonance between the visual and the aural elements highlights Ray's ultimate inability to strike a dialogue with the generation he seeks to portray. In a scene set at a restaurant, Siddhartha is nursing a headache after his unsuccessful job interview when he runs into an old acquaintance, Naresh-da, who sits down at his table, saying he has been watching Siddhartha for some time. However, it is not shown how and from where Naresh-da has kept keeping an eye on Siddhartha. This scene is notable for two reasons. First, the spectator does not see the face of Naresh-da; she only hears his voice. Ray himself lent his voice to this faceless character, a communist ideologue. Second, the scene marks the failure of a dialogue between Ray's disembodied voice and his protagonist. Even as Naresh-da continues to talk to him, Siddhartha's mind drifts off in an interior monologue to which the audience is privy. Like Siddhartha had been presented as an assortment of limbs in earlier scenes, in this scene Naresh-da is synecdochally replaced by hand gestures. Naresh-da's presence, therefore, is entirely aural. Ray's decision to dub for Naresh-da is significant here. It signals both Ray's failed attempt at a dialogue with the younger generation and also the younger generation's unwillingness to participate in an exchange.

The failure of the dialogue is heightened further by Siddhartha's interior monologue 'Ar gyaan deben na... ' ('please do not lecture'), which overlaps with and finally overpowers the ideologue's voice in the almost one-sided conversation. Ray discards the convention of lip-sync in this scene. The absence of the body (at least the source of articulation) places the sequence as a go-between to synchronous and asynchronous sound. It prevents recognition/identification of the spectator with the speaker (i.e. Naresh-da) as the source of the voice is both inside the frame and yet remains out of focus because the camera continues to focus on Siddhartha. Whereas Siddhartha can hear Naresh-da, Siddhartha's monologue remains unheard by Naresh-da, thereby indicating a failed dialogue between the two generations that these characters represent. The voice of Ray is unable to engage in a conversation with his protagonist. The absence of lip-sync further underscores the alienation and estrangement that permeates the film. Even by lending his voice to a faceless and almost choric character, the directorial voice does not gain the authority of a third person omniscient narrator as his own protagonist mutes his voice with his inner monologue.

If the foregrounding of the cinematic apparatus, coupled with the fractures of the visual and the aural that mark the cinematic idiom of *The Adversary* seem to point to an abandonment of Ray's classic realist style, Ray's reading of Sukhdev's film might offer us an insight into the style adopted by Ray in this instance. For Ray, it was the 'sensitive artist's subjective approach to reality' that animated cinema. In parting ways with his usual seamless narratives, Ray opens up *The Adversary* to another kind of realism, which Raymond Williams called social realism. Writing about the plays of Arthur Miller, Williams laments the decay of the 'magnificent realism' of the nineteenth century – one that highlighted the mutual constitution of personal life and society (Williams 1959: 140). Social realism, according to Williams,

> lies in a particular conception of the relationship of the individual to society, in which neither is the individual seen as a unit nor the society as an aggregate, but both are seen as belonging to a continuous and in real terms inseparable process. (Williams 1959: 141)

Approaching the plays of Arthur Miller in the light of this tradition, one that has been overtaken by the 'personal' and the 'sociological', Williams argues that the expressionism that Miller employs embodies the alienation of his characters to a far greater degree than naturalism. The style adopted by Ray in *The Adversary* could be read in a similar vein. The film, one that sees Ray abandon the classical realism of his earlier films, gravitates towards what Williams terms 'a magnificent realism', its style reflecting its narrative of alienation.

Darius Cooper reads Siddhartha's dilemma, 'a convincing exhibit offered by Ray as a contemporary display of male dislocation', as a 'lack' (Cooper 2000:135). However, this 'lack' that marks the narrative and the formal aesthetic of *The Adversary* is in itself a political stance. If Sen, by claiming the role of the filmmaker to be that of an *agent-provocateur*, shares Solanas and Getino's views on the revolutionary praxis of Third Cinema, then Ray's position, one that emphasizes artistic subjectivity over technical perfection, resonates with Julio Garcia Espinosa's call for an 'imperfect cinema' (Espinosa 1979: 24). Espinosa equates 'perfect cinema', one that is both 'technically and artistically masterful' with reactionary cinema (Espinosa 1979: 24). For Espinosa, as long as elitism of class society remains a reality, art cannot be impartial. In this reading, imperfection is a political device as art cannot be perfect as long as society is not. Keya Ganguly locates in Ray's films the same vein of imperfection, reading his films as 'an experiment in conjoining technical and aesthetic "mastery" while questioning the form of life enabling it' (Ganguly 2010: 177). Ray's city trilogy was compared to Sen's more political films by their contemporaries and was found lacking. However, this seeming lack or imperfection, Ganguly suggests, is in itself no less of a political statement as it highlights the impossibility of offering a 'perfect critique of imperfect life' (Ganguly 2010: 177).

## *Interview*: Commitment as aesthetic practice

If Ray's voice failed to start a dialogue with his protagonist, Sen's voice in *Interview* rouses his protagonist into action. *Interview*, like *The Adversary*, is based on the subject of an unsuccessful job interview. Ranjit, the film's protagonist, wants a better paying job at a commercial firm. The camera follows Ranjit all day long as he tries to procure a suit, an attire crucial to his success in the interview. The series of adventures and misadventures that mark Ranjit's day is the subject matter of the film and not the actual job interview, despite its suggestive title. The film, using a handheld camera, tracks Ranjit's futile efforts to get a suit (the preferred attire for the interview). Failing to procure one, Ranjit is unable to get the job. While Ranjit's many failed attempts throughout the day to acquire a suit for the interview had a comical element, his failure to get the job because of his sartorial choice lends the film a satirical quality. The suit now comes to represent something more than the desire and precondition for class mobility; it stands for the incompleteness of the processes of decolonization and a protracted imperial hangover.

While Ray introduced his protagonist by contrasting negative film stock with positive film stock, Sen introduces his protagonist in a more dramatic manner. Ranjit's introduction takes place in a tram – Calcutta's most identifiable public transport, another legacy of the British Raj. The hanging limbs are reminiscent of a similar scene in a crowded bus in Ray's *The Adversary*. Ranjit is seen standing in the overcrowded tram while the camera zooms in on a young woman reading a film magazine. She flips pages and comes to a page where Ranjit's photograph is prominently displayed. Ranjit looks into the camera and addresses the audience directly:

> I am not a star – by no means. My name is Ranjit Mallik, I live in Bhawanipur, and work for a weekly magazine. I go to the press, correct proofs, run for advertisements and odd errands. (There is a cut to Ranjit in the press). I have a very uneventful life.
>
> But somehow attracted Mrinal Sen – the filmmaker. He told me. 'My camera will follow you from morning to evening.'(The camera shows K.K. Mahajan shooting the sequence)
>
> I am not supposed to do anything special, I have to be just I am. I have also told Mrinal Sen that today is something special. I have the interview to get a better job. He said, great! it will be really dramatic –

(Again, we see Mahajan with his handheld camera)

> But let me tell you – whatever you have seen till now is not entirely true. I am real, this journey is real, and today's interview is also very real. You, the passengers, are real. But the lady who is supposed to be my mother is not my real mother – in fact she is an actress.

A shot from Ray's *Song of the Little Road* with Karuna Banerjee as Sarbojaya follows. Following this, Ranjit's fellow traveller looks directly at the camera and addresses the audience:

> Do you think that this is cinema? It is my story – (pointing a finger at the audience) – your story.

This self-reflexivity, Ananda Mitra notes,

> ... provides an area of congruence where the audience of the period could begin to see the ways in which the protagonist was a representation of the audience's lived experiences, which were closely tied to the city that plays a central role in these films. (Mitra 2000: 42)

While *The Adversary* highlights the alienation of its protagonist through stylistic experiments, *Interview* strikes a Brechtian note whereby its protagonist becomes everybody. By incorporating the scene from *Song of the Little Road*, *Interview* is no longer a world unto itself but opens itself up to multiple diegeses. It echoes other worlds from other films, not just as intertextual references, but to create a textual polyphony that challenges a singular reading of the film. Cinema forms a part of the narrative world of *Interview*, but Sen strives to make the cinematic experience not an exception but the norm by juxtaposing the reel and the real and by insisting that the everyday is a worthy cinematic subject. For example, when a pickpocket is caught, the camera zooms in on the face of the pickpocket and this close-up is then juxtaposed with a close-up of a face in a film poster, evidently of a villainous character.

*Interview*, in a tongue-in-cheek manner, also references *The Adversary*, which was being shot around the same time. Deepankar Mukhopadhyay notes that while shooting Ranjit's interview scene, Sen found out that Ray had shot a similar scene where his protagonist Siddhartha was asked what the most important event of the decade was. Siddhartha's answer was the Vietnam War – an answer that cost him his job. Sen asked the board members to ask Ranjit what the most important event of the day was. Ranjit's prompt answer was 'My interview, Sir!' (Mukhopadhyay 1995: 87). While intertextuality is now a common occurrence in popular Indian cinema (including Bollywood films), it was not a widely used cinematic device when Sen was filming *Interview*. In addition to the references to Ray's films and to popular Hindi and Bengali cinema, Sen also used footage from foreign films, including Fernando Solanas's *La Hora de Los Hornos* (The Hour of the Furnaces, 1968) and Joris Ivens's *Le 17e parallèle: La guerre du peuple* (17th Parallel: Vietnam in War, 1968). Besides opening up the film for multiple readings, these intertextual elements place *Interview* in conversation with political unrest all over the world.

Another cinematic style that Sen adopts throughout *Interview* is the cinema verité style of filmmaking by using handheld cameras. The effect is sometimes shaky and jerky – flouting the rules of seamless editing and smooth camerawork of classic cinematic realism by foregrounding the cinematic medium and its mediations. The camera movement prevent spectatorial identification with the fictional world of the narrative. Sen often used documentary-like images of Calcutta, such as cranes lifting the statues of the colonial era, the images of rallies, protests and bomb blasts, the images of the lower and the lower middle classes in the city, and pavement dwellers and office goers jostling for space in overcrowded public transports. Later in the film when Ranjit comes home after his unsuccessful interview, the images of the city, vignettes of the day, even the faces of the people he encountered, fill the screen. Camera movement throughout the film is slow and Sen keeps narrative cinema techniques like eye-line matches, continuity editing, and shot-reverse-shots to a minimum. As Sen noted in an interview:

The establishment always uses its machinery to tell you and also to convince itself that for anything you do, there are set principles, set norms, set laws. The Establishment manifests itself everywhere, at different levels of social phenomena... When the camera refuses to behave in a copybook manner, it is an unmistakable act of defiance. When the cutting of shots and juxtaposition of sequences are erratic, quite possible they are serving as a slap in the Establishment's face. (quoted in Sarkar 2000: 102)

However, despite its Brechtian underpinnings and its self-reflexive style, *Interview* is almost 'easy-going' till the last few minutes. Other than the pre-credit scenes depicting the dismantling of colonial statues, the film does not articulate a definite political stance against imperialism and the colonial hangover of the Indian elite. While Sen's deployment of style, camera movement, use of Brechtian tropes and foregrounding of the cinematic apparatus are motivated by his politics, the film's final sequence takes a more direct stance on decolonization and imperialism. After his frustrating day, Ranjit is sitting in the dark when an unseen person offers him a light for his cigarette. This person introduces himself as someone who has been observing him all day. The faceless voice is joined by another voice that taunts Ranjit about his failure to land the job. A rattled Ranjit finally loses his calm and throws a stone at a mannequin displayed in a storefront, ruining its impeccable suit. This charged scene is followed by newsreels of the Vietnam War, Civil rights movements. With this visual juxtaposition, Sen equates Ranjit's case with that of other victims of imperialism all over the world. The authorial voice here is different from the voice of Ray in the restaurant scene in *The Adversary*. Whereas in *The Adversary*, Ray's voice failed to start a dialogue with his protagonist, in *Interview*, the unseen speaker not only manages to strike a conversation with Ranjit but also plays the catalyst to the violence (i.e. the disrobing the mannequin) in which the film culminates.

## The aesthetics of commitment

In *Interview*, particularly in the final sequence, Sen adopts a distinctly Brechtian stance, while Ray carefully treads the fine line between ham-fisted propaganda and puerile aestheticism throughout *The Adversary*. Both films offer their viewers an occasion to rethink the relationship between art and political engagement and also query if there is a measure of adequate political commitment that art can or *should* demonstrate without losing its status as art. At this juncture, Adorno and Marcuse's caution against committed art merits a revisit. While Sartre's utilitarian stance on prose was the occasion for Adorno's polemic against committed art, he is equally critical of Brecht's didactic style. This didacticism, Adorno claims, reduces art to ideology. And in so doing, it destroys what makes art truly radical, its autonomy. On similar lines as Adorno, Marcuse argues that aligning art with politics makes art less subversive. Marcuse too takes Brecht's didacticism to task when he writes:

> The political potential of art lies only in its own aesthetic dimension. Its relation to praxis is inexorably indirect, mediated, and frustrating. The more immediately political the work of art, the more it reduces the power of estrangement and the radical, transcendent goals of change. In this sense, there may be more subversive potential in the poetry of Baudelaire and Rimbaud than in the didactic plays of Brecht. (Marcuse 1978: xiii)

Art's radical potential, for Adorno and Marcuse, lies in its opposition to society while remaining a part of it. It is because of this dialectical relationship with society that art needs to take on the mantle of autonomy in order to perform its task of social criticism. Reduced to propaganda, art too becomes one dimensional and is thus cut off from the society that it seeks to rectify. In this light, perhaps the most radical claim of Ray's political cinema is that it challenges the false binary of aestheticism and propaganda through its deployment of the cinematic idiom, while Sen's film, despite its overt political leanings, remains firmly fixed in, what Adorno calls, art's 'manifest social content'.

# Bibliography

Adorno, Theodor (1980), 'Commitment', in *Aesthetics and Politics*, 177–95, London: Verso.
Biswas, Moinak (2007), 'Speaking through Troubled Times', *Journal of the Moving Image*, 6: 72–85.
Biswas, Moinak (ed.) (2006), *Apu and After: Re-visiting Ray's Cinema*, London: Seagull Books.
Chakravarty, Sumita S. (1989), 'National Identity and the Realist Aesthetic: Indian Cinema of the Fifties', *Quarterly Review of Film & Video*, 11 (3): 31–48.
Chaudhury, Supriya (2006), 'In the City', in Moinak Biswas (ed.), *Apu and After: Re-visiting Ray's Cinema*, 251–76, Calcutta: Seagull Books.
Cooper, Darius (2000), *Cinema of Satyajit Ray: Between Tradition and Modernity*, Cambridge: Cambridge University Press.
Das Gupta, Chidananda (1980), *The Cinema of Satyajit Ray*, New Delhi: Vikas Publishing House.
Das Gupta, Chidananda (1981), *Talking about Cinema*, Calcutta: Orient Longman.
Espinosa, J. G. (1979), 'For an Imperfect Cinema', *Jump Cut*, 20: 24–6.
Ganguly, Keya (2010), *Cinema, Emergence, and the Films of Satyajit Ray*, Berkeley: University of California Press.

Hood, John W. (1993), *Chasing the Truth: The Films of Mrinal Sen*, Calcutta: Seagull Books.

Marcuse, Herbert (1978), *The Aesthetic Dimension: Toward a Critique of Marxist Aesthetics*, Boston: Beacon Press.

Mitra, Ananda (2000), 'Imaging of the 1970s: Calcutta and West Bengal', in Sumita S. Charkavarty (ed.), *The Enemy Within: The Films of Mrinal Sen*, 37–66, London: Flicks Books.

Mukhopadhyay, Deepankar (1995), *The Maverick Maestro, Mrinal Sen*, New Delhi: Indus.

Ray, Satyajit (2006), *Our Films Their Films*, Kolkata: Orient Longman.

Robinson, Andrew (2004), *Satyajit Ray: The Inner Eye: The Biography of a Master Film-Maker*, London: I.B. Tauris.

Sarkar, Bhaskar (2000), 'The Inward Look: Self-Reflexivity in Mrinal Sen's Films', in Sumita Chakravarty (ed.), *Mrinal Sen: The Cinema of Politics, the Politics of Cinema*, 98–130, London: Flick Books.

Sartre, J. P. and S. Ungar (1988), *"What Is literature?" and Other Essays*, Boston: Harvard University Press.

Seton, Marie (2003), *Portrait of a Director: Satyajit Ray*, New Delhi: Penguin Books.

Solanas, Fernando and Octavio Getino (1970), 'Toward a Third Cinema', *Cineaste*, 4 (3): 1–10.

Vasudevan, Ravi (2001), 'Nationhood, Authenticity and Realism in Indian Cinema: The Double Take of Modernism in the Work of Satyajit Ray', *Journal of the Moving Image*, 2: 52–76.

Williams, Raymond (1959), 'The Realism of Arthur Miller', *Critical Quarterly*, 1 (2): 140–9.

# 4

# The Peruvian Kuntur group: A Marxist-Indigenist filmmaking practice

*Isabel Seguí*
*(University of St Andrews)*

While I finish writing this chapter (October 2019), I learn about the enormous commercial success of the recently premiered documentary *La revolución y la tierra* (*Revolution and Land*, Gonzalo Benavente, 2019). The theme of the film is the agrarian reform decreed in Peru, in 1969, by the government of General Juan Velasco Alvarado, head of the military-revolutionary regime between 1968 and 1975. Although Benavente's work was awarded in the last edition of Lima International Film Festival, the box-office results have come as a surprise. It has sold over 55,000 tickets in six cities (Lima, Cusco, Chiclayo, Arequipa, Huancayo and Trujillo) during its first three weeks, and it is already considered the highest-grossing Peruvian documentary in history. In my view, the success among critics and general audiences of this film indicates that the Peruvian public feels a need to return to the subject of the land struggles and the agrarian reform, which had been eclipsed, indeed, by the subsequent twenty hard years of bloody internal conflict between the State and Shining Path (1980–2000).

As contemporary audiences are re-discovering, the agrarian reform initiated in 1969 through a Decree-law promulgated by General Velasco, just one year after his rise to power after a military coup, led to a radical transformation of the Peruvian society.¹ Until that time, the masses of indigenous peasants – especially in the southern highlands, the scenario of this chapter – lived and worked in semi-slavery conditions on the *haciendas* (agricultural states). This situation was fought back through periodic rebellions that went back to colonial times, but in the second half of the twentieth century, these struggles intensified substantially. The military knew first-hand the situation in which the peasantry was stuck because, until that moment, they had actively participated in the repression of the peasant masses. However, in a spectacular U-turn, they declared themselves a revolutionary government aligned with the people. This move facilitated the historical demand of the indigenous movements of the south of the country: the end of the *latifundium* (concentration of land) through the expropriation of landowners.

The peasant-indigenous agenda stemmed from two different traditions: on the one hand, various currents of Marxist thought and, on the other, from the communal tradition prior to the conquest of America that had been preserved in the Andes (García Hurtado 1965; Neira 1968; Blanco 1972). Acting as an unlikely supporter of these demands, General Velasco's military government encouraged a system of communal tenure, as well as the creation of agricultural cooperatives.² This plan had a modernizing component and one of historical justice. Velasco, in his message to the nation on the occasion of the promulgation of the Agrarian Reform Law, stated:

> From now on, the peasant of Peru will no longer be the outcast or the disinherited who lived in poverty from the cradle to the grave, and who looked helplessly at an equally bleak future for his children. As of this successful June 24, he will truly be a free citizen to whom the country finally recognizes the right to the fruits of the land he works and a place of justice within a society of which he will never be, like until today, diminished citizen, man to be exploited by another man. (Velasco 197–:40)³

---

¹The previous government headed by Fernando Belaúnde Terry had already carried out a tepid agrarian reform in response to peasant uprisings, but nothing comparable to Velasco's decree.
²Full text of the decree available online: http://www2.congreso.gob.pe/sicr/cendocbib/con4_uibd.nsf/428255957E3E495805257DD5006CCBCC/ $FILE/DecretoLey_17716_LeyReformaAgrar%C3%ADa.pdf
³All translations are mine unless indicated otherwise. Enrique Mayer states that Velasco's speeches, like the one mentioned above, were written by Carlos Delgado (Mayer 2009: 35), an anthropologist trained in the United States, who had the idea of creating a government department that would serve to spread the ideas of the regime, in a spectrum of action between awareness and propaganda. For this purpose, both visual arts and cinema were used profusely. For an in-depth reflection on the use of visual propaganda during Velasco's governement (see Roca-Rey 2016).

But this was not only the agenda of the disenfranchised populations – and in this odd occasion, the military. The indigenous peasant movements relied on key allies such as young urban organic intellectuals of Marxist background (organic in the Gramscian sense, that is counter-hegemonic intellectuals aligned with the subaltern classes),[4] who developed a growing interest in the peasant struggles in the southern region of Peru, somehow actualizing the Indigenist tradition present in the cultural élite circles throughout the century.[5] Hugo Neira candidly summarizes the motivations of his likes in a text written in 1968:

> by an implacable dialectic, the irrationality of the ancient [indigenous] cults will be integrated into the revolutionary rationality. In a time of 'rebirths', like that of third world cultures, these historical alchemies are everyday events. And I do not see why the Indian America will be exempted from them. On the contrary, the resistant Andean myths can play among us a role similar to that played by, for example, Islam in the resurgence of the Arabs against European colonialism. Or an inspirational role like that of the ancient Chinese culture in the adaptation of Marxism in Asia, in a quick, urgent, 'indigenisation' of Marxism in the Andes. (Neira 1968: 18)

These young intellectuals – mostly white and middle or upper class – perceived a messianic element in the indigenous cosmogony that appealed to them straightforwardly because it mirrored their own messianic approach to the liberation struggles in the continent. Leftist filmmakers in the Andes were among those organic intellectuals that felt the urge of incorporating indigenous subjects and narratives into their work, and for that established strategic alliances with peasant communities, organizations and leaders.

Probably the most remarkable case of participation of an indigenous union leader in revolutionary filmic projects is that of Saturnino Huillca, who in only four years, between 1973 and 1977, starred in four films. His first participation was in *Runan Caycu* (*I Am a Man*, Nora de Izcue, 1973), a testimonial documentary on the agrarian reform, commissioned by the above-mentioned Hugo Neira, who at the time was head of diffusion at the National System for Social Mobilization (SINAMOS) – the propaganda body of the military-revolutionary regime. This film was post-produced at the Cuban Film Institute (ICAIC). Huillca's second participation in a film was in *El enemigo principal* (*The Principal Enemy*, Ukamau Group, 1974),

---

[4] Term coined by the Italian Marxist Antonio Gramsci in his *Prison Notebooks*.
[5] In Peru, it is known as *indigenismo*, a cultural movement that flourished in literature and the visual arts (painting, sculpture, engraving, photography, film) from the second decade of the twentieth century onwards. The aim of these broad variety of cultural manifestations was to incorporate the indigenous topics and imagery into the mainstream criollo public sphere. This movement was mostly led by white middle-class intellectuals and artists.

a feature film loosely based on Héctor Béjar's book *Peru 1965: Notes on a Guerrilla Experience*, and in which Huillca plays the traditional Quechua role of storyteller.[6] Soon after, he is invited to film *Si esas puertas no se abren* (*If Those Doors Do Not Open*, Mario Arrieta and María Barea, 1975), a short documentary now lost. Finally, he plays his own character in the fictionalized docu-drama *Kuntur Wachana* (*Where the Condors Are Born*, Federico García, 1977), a feature film which is analysed in this chapter. He will also appear as an extra in another film by Federico García, *Tupac Amaru* (1984), a bio-pic on the legendary indigenous leader.[7]

Some scholarly attention has been given to the films produced by Nora de Izcue and the Ukamau Group. However, a rigorous approximation to the contribution to Peruvian and Latin American film history of two professed *velasquistas*, the director Federico García and the producer Pilar Roca – core members of the Kuntur Group – it is long overdue. The aim of this chapter is to redress this situation by analysing their Marxist-Indigenist filmmaking practice. To that end, I focus on a captivating trilogy produced by them, at the end of the 1970s, in collaboration with different indigenous Quechua-speaking rural communities. These early works are *Kuntur Wachana* (1977), *Laulico* (1980) and *El caso Huayanay: Testimonio de parte* (*The Huayanay Case: Part Testimony*, 1981).

## The Kuntur (Condor) group: Serendipitous beginnings

Firstly, a clarification, García and Roca have not openly declared themselves in favour of a collective cinematic practice as other Andean groups, such as the Bolivian Ukamau or the Peruvian Chaski, have done. However, their collectivist praxis is similar to the aforementioned cases, meaning that in addition to the core team composed by Roca and García, different crews, related to them by friendship, kinship or political affinity, were summoned on occasion of the different stages of production. These similarities include all the problematic aspects and contradictions, such as de facto vertical power structures and sexual division of labour, that are often found in supposedly emancipatory cultural formations, including militant cinema groups.[8]

García and Roca were working as well as sentimental partners. The director was born in Cusco, the ancient capital of the Inca empire, in 1937.

---

[6]Héctor Béjar was also part of SINAMOS.
[7]For a complete analysis of the films participated by Saturnino Huillca, see Seguí 2016.
[8]For a further analysis and problematization of the concept 'group' in Andean oppositional cinema practices, see Seguí 2018 and Aimaretti and Seguí 2020.

He was a fluent Quechua speaker, a common feature of the urban middle classes of the region. This characteristic differentiates him from other organic intellectuals and mediators of the voice of the indigenous born in the Hispanic capital of the country, Lima. García was also a member of the Communist Youth movement and a poet. He trained to be a guerrilla fighter in Cuba, but, he never engaged in combat. He had also participated in the land struggles of the mid-1960s and even published a book on the Peruvian agrarian reform, the foreword of which was written by the Peruvian economist Hilda Gadea, the first wife of Ernesto 'Che' Guevara.

Pilar Roca, younger than García, was born in Lima in 1948 from a white middle-class conservative background and studied sociology in the university of San Marcos. As I have developed extensively in other place, the prolongation of traditional domestic roles to the film production process was very common in the precarious mode of production of Latin American political cinema. The labour structure was often sexually divided, with the husband playing the creative role of the director/auteur and the wife the invisible role of producer of 'his' films (for an in-depth reflection on the role of the producer-wife in Andean third cinema, see Seguí 2018).

In this particular case, it is worthy to note that Roca facilitated García's incursion in the cinematic medium. Both were young *velasquistas* working for the state when she, a sociologist, was commissioned to write a report on media strategy by the regime. Roca concluded that, in Peru, cinema had the potential to be one of the most effective tools of communication for a target audience consisting of isolated peasant masses, only after radio. This was because, among other things, the state had seventeen mobile film units, equipped with projectors, screens and electric generators, and a staff of drivers (Roca and García 2015). To her surprise, she was then invited to make a film by the board of SINAMOS. García – who was an amateur photographer and film lover – was working at the time at the publicity office of the Ministry of Energy and Mines headed by General Jorge Fernández Maldonado (Bedoya 1992: 208). Roca, who was not very interested in filmmaking, invited her partner to work with her in this project. Soon after, García asked to be moved to SINAMOS and ended up directing the film section of this propaganda body.

Roca and García had at the time neither training in filmmaking nor connection with the precarious *Limeño* film world, a small group of women and men united by inextricable personal and professional relationships, who although being politicized were not necessarily fully aligned with the military government. According to García and Roca, due to their unorthodox and partisan initiation in filmmaking, they were always regarded as opportunistic outsiders by Peruvian film circles (Roca and García 2015). However, they were only partially supported by the state in their first production, *Kuntur Wachana* (1977), which stands as the cinematic swan song of Velasco's military-revolutionary regime. That work – post-produced during the second, conservative, period of the military rule – caused innumerable problems to García and Roca, from political prosecution by the new authorities (who witch-hunted those radical elements of the so-called 'first phase' of the military rule)[9] to judicial problems with the indigenous leaders of the community protagonist of the film, who accused them of scam. Moreover, many of the members of the Peruvian union of film workers, SITEIC, supported the members of the cooperative of Huarán in their claims against García and Roca.[10] Feeling prosecuted in Peru, they sought to coproduce with the Cuban ICAIC from their second film onwards.

Although their beginnings were serendipitous – and the path followed by their first docu-fiction film probably too eventful – Federico García and Pilar Roca persevered and developed a career that spans over forty years and includes fourteen movies.[11] Due to lack of space and to stick to the scope of this volume, I am going to focus only on their films produced in the late 1970s. All of them are heavily staged political docu-fictions with the participation of different indigenous communities and peasant union leaders.

Beyond showcasing the work of the Kuntur group, this chapter aims to raise some issues about why these films and filmmaking processes have been so far excluded from the canon of Latin American Third Cinema.[12] I argue that certain gatekeeping practices (mechanisms of exclusion) resulted in the disregard of García and Roca's work in the national sphere and, as a consequence, their work has not had enough resonance outside

---

[9]The military rule is divided into two phases. The first one, led by the progressive General Velasco, lasted from the 1968 coup until 1975. The second phase, led by General Francisco Morales Bermúdez and characterized by a turn to the right, lasted until 1980, when democracy returned to Peru.

[10]A group of forty-five filmmakers wrote a statement in solidarity with the claims of the cooperative against Federico García. This statement was published in the newspaper *La Prensa* of Lima on 30 April 1980.

[11]Besides the films studied in this article filmography of Federico García includes *La leyenda de Melgar el poeta insurgente* (1982), *Tupac Amaru* (1984), *El socio de Dios* (1986), *La manzanita del diablo* (1990), *La montaña sagrada* (1991), *La yunta brava* (2000), *El forastero* (2002), *Alfredo Torero cuatro estaciones de un hombre total* (2011) and *Venezuela, país en trance* (2013).

[12]García and Roca's films are not early manifestations of Latin American third cinema because they started their career in the 1970s, releasing their first feature in 1977. However, they are not included or even collaterally named in those texts that, willingly or not, canonised the field such as Julianne Burton's *Cinema and Social Change in Latin America: Conversations with Filmmakers* (Burton 1986). The only example of a very timid attempt of incorporation of their cinema to the canon is John King's chapter 'Andean Images: Bolivia, Ecuador and Peru' in *Magical Reels: A History of Cinema in Latin America*(King 1990: 189–206). This piece addresses in passing the cinema of García and Roca. Later in the decade it was included in the second volume of Michael T. Martin's comprehensive compilation *New Latin American Cinema* (Martin 1997: 483–504).

the Peruvian borders. For instance, they have been incorporated into the canonical histories of Peruvian cinema, mostly under the contemptuous label of 'peasant cinema' (*cine campesino*), coined by the editors of the very influential journal *Hablemos de cine* (Bedoya 1992; Huayhuaca 2017). For the Westernized critics of this journal – who lately, and dangerously, became film historians – only those highly aestheticized film products able to be marketed as second cinema/auteur films deserved recognition. Yet, for them, the so-called *campesino* filmmakers, scrutinized under a purely formalist magnifying glass, never seemed to achieve enough linguistic correction. To counteract this conventional approach, I offer a feminist production studies perspective that ascribes value not only to the product but also to the process and re-inscribes the praxis and material conditions of production in cinema history. In doing so, I also vindicate Third Cinema theory – García Espinosa's imperfect cinema (García Espinosa 1997), Sanjinés' cinema with the people (Sanjinés 1979) and Solanas and Getino's decolonizing approach (Solanas and Getino 1979) – as pertinent theoretical frameworks unjustifiably underused by oppositional film historians.

# The filmic swan song of Velasco's project: *Kuntur Wachana* (Where the Condors Are Born, 1977)

In the middle of the 1970s, SINAMOS commissioned Pilar Roca and Federico García a series of short films, such as *Huando: tierra sin patrones* (*Huando, Land without Landlords*), *Socavón y tajo abierto* (*Underground and Open Pit*) and *De la colonia a la cooperativa* (*From the Settlement to the Cooperative*), among others. None of these survives. In 1977, they released their first feature docu-fiction, *Kuntur Wachana* (Quechua for *Where the Condors Are Born*). This film was produced in association with the indigenous community of Huarán, organized for agricultural production as the Agricultural Production Cooperative n°001 José Zuñiga Letona Huarán (Calca, Cusco), and the support of the Tupac Amaru Revolutionary Agrarian Federation of Cusco (Federación Agraria Revolucionaria Tupac Amaru del Cusco, FARTAC).

When still working for SINAMOS, Roca designed an audio-visual communication project, with activities such as training workshops on film, serigraphy and journalism, to be developed at the cooperative José Zuñiga Letona, in the region of the Sacred Valley of the Incas, near Cusco. The state contributed 1,200,000 soles to the project, but this amount was insufficient to make a movie about the struggle of this peasant community to become a cooperative, which was the hidden aim of the project. Therefore, the communards set up a film cooperative and asked the Industrial Bank for a loan (García et al. 1982: 17).[13] García convinced the communards that this experience could turn into an inspiring long-term project: a film production coop in the countryside led by the indigenous people of the Sacred Valley. This over-ambitious approach was the source of all future problems.

Regarding the resultant film, *Kuntur Wachana*, it is an example of cinematic recovery of popular memory, a trend in Latin America in the 1970s and 1980s. It is also an example of Marxist-Indigenist filmmaking because it tells the story of the peasant community of Huarán from a dialectical materialist point of view. The film focuses on a very specific class struggle, which led a collective of peasants living under an Andean type of feudalism to develop a class consciousness that allowed them to revolt against their landlords and the colonial order. As a consequence of this revolutionary project, endorsed by the national authorities through the decree law of agrarian reform, the land was expropriated, and a cooperative was created where before stood a *hacienda*. Consequently, the relations and the mode of production were changed forever, paving the way to a socialist future.

The script was based on the oral testimonies of the members of the cooperative, who wanted to tell their story in their language, Quechua. In addition, in the film, other peasant union leaders from the countryside and the city self-represent themselves, among whom stand out Saturnino Huillca, Aparicio Masías and Rubén Ascue. The action is divided into two parts. The first part takes place between 1958 and 1962. Saturnino Huillca arrives in the community with the purpose of organizing a union, a subsidiary of the FARTAC, in order to prepare the farmers to recover their lands. To do this, he contacts Mariano Quispe, an old shepherd and a figure of authority in the community. The local *hacendado* (landowner) is notified by his godson (who is a communard but maintains a relationship of *compadrazgo* [patronage] with the landlord) that the communards and the serfs of the *hacienda* are trying to organize a union. The old Quispe is imprisoned, but, when he is released, he flees and becomes a clandestine leader. Alongside Huillca, he dedicates himself to touring the sacred valley organizing the communities. Later (*c.* 1962) he dies poisoned by order of the landowner. Taking advantage of the terror that invades the peasants and the lack of leadership, the local oligarchy – formed by landowners, police, judges and other authorities – unleashes repression and the union is annihilated.

This type of repression is the one that resulted in a historical wave of land invasions that in the film is addressed through an ellipsis. The second part of the movie begins in 1968, just at the time of the rise to power of Velasco after a coup d'etat. In this new political situation, the young community

---

[13]The payment of this loan was afterwards one of the sources of conflict between García and the leaders of the cooperative José Zuñiga Letona.

members who participated in the invasions in recent years, such as José Zúñiga Letona and Rubén Ascue, are granted amnesty and leave prison. They return to the community and restart the struggle that concludes in the conversion of the *hacienda* into an agricultural cooperative thanks to the agrarian reform law of 1969 promoted by the Velasco government, which gives legal legitimacy to the peasant struggles. Shortly before the creation of the cooperative, José Zúñiga Letona is killed in a confusing incident, in which somehow the peasants see the black hand of the landowner. The cooperative decides to homage him by bearing his name.

The film accounts for three distinct periods: (1) the organization of revolutionary peasant unions in the late 1950s and early 1960s; (2) the time of violent land invasions (mid-1960s), which is not directly represented but referred to through its background and consequences; and (3) the agrarian reform, starting in 1969, that was not exempt from complexity because, although the law was on the part of the peasants, the landowners were up to the last moment urging tricks to prevent its application. The film ends with documentary images of a FARTAC rally in the *Plaza de Armas* of Cusco (the main square filled to capacity on this occasion) in which the charismatic leader Saturnino Huillca is haranguing the masses.

The film is a fictionalized collective testimony, which uses freely any expressive resource available without clearly subscribing to a genre. It has superb documentary and ethnographic scenes, such as representations of traditional Andean festivals and dances. It also performs powerful re-enactments in which hundreds of peasants of all ages take part, such as a sequence in the church where the mass of Indians is threatened by the priest (represented by Federico García making a convincing sermon in Quechua) that they should denounce the agitators who are trying to set up a union or a procession of children asking for the rain. There are also remarkable re-enactments of political activities, such as a meeting at the headquarters of FARTAC or the burial of Zuñiga Letona (figure 4.1), which turns into a demonstration. All these scenes attest to the way of life and political actions of organized peasant communities.

The tone of the re-enactments performed by nonprofessional actors contrasts sharply with the highly staged scenes portraying the upper classes starred by professional actors, with a completely different method. The costumes and period sets, in addition to the affected performance, seem stiffened in comparison to the scenes in which the peasants self-represent themselves outdoors or in humble peasant houses wearing their traditional attire. Those two records, the nonfiction and the purely fictional, in some ways collide. Or so was considered by Peruvian film critics, who accused García of formal eclecticism and narrative weakness (León Frías 2014: 54–5). Especially redundant was for them the music, a cantata composed by Celso Garrido Lecca with lyrics written by García (Bedoya 1992: 210).

FIGURE 4.1 Meeting at the headquarters of the Tupac Amaru Revolutionary Agrarian Federation of Cusco (FARTAC). On the wall, portraits of Lenin and José Carlos Mariátegui, an influential Peruvian Marxist public intellectual.

In spite of the cold critical reception, the film was favourably embraced by the Peruvian public, especially the peasant-indigenous audiences, always eager to see their image on the big screen. Thus, it circulated in the commercial theatrical circuit, with remarkable success, as well as in television and in the alternative circuits. It was also well received internationally. It won the critics award in the festival of Moscow and participated in European festivals specialized in the exhibition of Third Cinema like Pesaro (Italy) and Benalmádena (Spain).

## A Marxist-Indigenist Western: *Laulico* (1980)

After the failure of the cooperative project in Huarán and in order to take advantage from the new Law for the Promotion of the Film Industry (Decree Law No. 19327), implemented by Velasco – which among other things, guaranteed the mandatory exhibition of Peruvian cinema – Pilar Roca and Federico García created the film company Kausachum Perú (Long Live Peru). The first project of this company, in coproduction with the ICAIC, is *Laulico*, a film dedicated to the eminent indigenist intellectual José María Arguedas.

The film was shot in Quechua in 1978, in collaboration with the indigenous communities of Chumpe Poques and Fuerabamba and premiered in 1980 after several problems with censorship. The initiative was taken this time by the filmmakers who had to gain the trust of these communities which, according to Pilar Roca, distrusted them and felt threatened, because they were perceived as *gringos* who wanted to 'take pictures' and learn about their history (Roca and García 2015). Finally, the film was shot with the participation of community members, and another filmic testimony was made by the Kuntur group, in this case a more allegoric one. The most striking part of this collaboration are the sequences of cattle theft that, according to the directors, were shot with the participation of authentic cattle thieves or *abigeos*, expert horsemen who show off their skills in astonishing equestrian scenes ('Auténticos' 1980, 'Abigeos' 1980).

The film seeks to write the hagiography of the Andean popular hero Laulico, a legendary cattle rustler, belonging to the community of Fuerabamba. According to a legend, the people of this place were doomed to become cattle thieves when their pre-Columbian guardian deity, Apu Wamani, was defeated by Spanish *encomenderos* and locked in the jail of the *hacienda* Pamparqui. As a result of the kidnapping of their god the springs dried up, taking away the fertility of the earth and people alike. The only way out the *Fuerabambinos* found was to become thieves. The communards had tried unsuccessfully for generations to free Apu Wamani from his prison in the *hacienda*, until Laulico – in another example of the fusion between Marxist and Indigenist narrative traditions developed by Kuntur – manages to understand that the deity is only a symbol of the collective force of the people and leads his countrymen on the road to liberation.

The role of Laulico is performed by Honorato Ascue, a peasant from Calca, who had already participated in *Kuntur Wachana* (Ramos 1978). At one point, the press takes him for an authentic *abigeo* ('Abigeo convertido' 1980, 'Abigeo actor'1980), a confusion that worked as a publicity stunt (figure 4.2). In the film also stars Aparicio Masías, who in *Kuntur Wachana* had played the character of Quispe, the murdered old leader and who in this film represents the role of *altomisayoq* (Andean priest).

Nelson García Miranda, writing for *Hablemos de Cine* in 1980, affirms that what led Federico García to make this film is 'the metaphorical projection of the class struggle in the Peruvian inner land, based on the realistic and metaphorical materials that [the legend of] Laulico provides' (García Miranda 2017: 139); this idea resonates with the words of Hugo Neira, quoted in the introduction of this chapter: the Andean myths could play a key role in the cultural adaptation or indigenization of Marxism (Neira 1968: 18). However, García Miranda considers that this is a failed film, where the lack of a well-structured storytelling turns the events narrated into a series of incohesive and folkloric anecdotes. Despite this generally negative approach, García Miranda appreciates some virtues in the movie, such as the selection of landscapes and settings, like the stone prison of Haquira, a spectacular construction dating from colonial times (García Miranda 2017: 140).

FIGURE 4.2 *Newspaper publicity 'Laulico Wanted Dead or Alive'.*

In my view, the result is stunning not only due to the natural beauty of the portrayed Andean landscape, or the opportunity of recycling an old legend for current political use, bridging two seemly antagonistic cultures, but also because this Robin Hood-esque hagiography is made using narrative tropes stemming from genres such as Western and action films. For these scenes the filmmakers counted on the key participation of dozens of local horsemen, actual cattle rustlers, who show off their equestrian skills delivering a sensational performance. This cinematic collaboration allows the filmmakers to represent a marginalized community in full agency in a way unseen until that moment in Andean-Peruvian cinema. Far from painting a miserabilist picture, Laulico shows an irredentist indigenous collective undefeated by the colonial rule.

Probably because of the stance taken by the film, it had many problems to be approved for exhibition by the censorship board. When finally passed, it was rated for audiences over eighteen ('Autorizan' 1980; Kato 1980; 'Laulico' 1980). The film was successful at home and abroad, especially in the Second World. It participated in Tashkent Film Festival (USSR) and inaugurated the first Havana Film Festival in 1979 (Galiano 1979).

## Taking sides in the postcolonial conflict: *El caso Huayanay: testimonio de parte* (1981)

The production of this remarkable film was almost improvised – made with some leftover film stock that the ICAIC sent for the production of *Laulico* and a bit of money granted by an NGO (Roca and García 2015). The idea of the film was suggested by the lawyer Laura Caller, a militant of the Worker Peasant Student and Popular Front (Frente Obrero Campesino, Estudiantil y Popular, FOCEP). Caller was part of the defendant team of the imprisoned members of the peasant community of Huayanay (Huancavelica), who were accused of the murder of Matías Escobar, a minion of the local *hacendado*. The communards fed up with the impunity enjoyed by this serial rapist and thief condemned and killed him following procedures of community justice. After the events, the police intervened, and, although over 200 communards declared themselves guilty of murder, only a handful of them ended up in jail.

The so-called 'Huayanay Case', which gives name to the film, was thoroughly covered by the press at the time because it exemplified the conflict between two cosmogonies: on the one hand, the law system of Western origin that was systematically used to beneficiate the local oligarchy, and on the other, the rural communal justice, which was considered brutal and unlawful by the city inhabitants. As the title indicates, with this film, García and Roca tell the story taking the side of the indigenous community. Again, this is a dialectic film, in the Marxist sense, which shows the particular class struggle of a community against the landowners but emphasizing the Indigenist element of this conflict and showcasing the vernacular modes of resistance to the colonial order that are on the basis of the revolutionary practice of the peasants.

The docu-fiction starts showing on-screen six articles of the Universal Declaration of the Rights of Peoples – the Algiers Charter – and reminding the spectators that Peru has signed this declaration. The aim is to signal the hypocrisy of a state that does not abide by the international law it subscribes, while enforcing the law on its subjects. The next scene shows a group of communards at the town square advancing towards the camera holding a banner that reads: 'Ama Llulla, Ama Quella, Ama Sua' (do not be

FIGURE 4.3 *In the banner, the three basic Inca moral principles,* Ama Llulla, Ama Quella, Ama Sua *(do not be a liar, do not be idle, do not be a thief).*

a liar, do not be idle, do not be a thief), the three basic Inca moral principles (figure 4.3). This party, composed by the communards of Huayanay, is bringing the body of Escobar to the police. When the commander asks who is responsible of the murder they respond: 'Us, sir. The communal mass!' (*la masa comuna*). After this introduction come the initial credits.

The narration of the facts is done through a voiceover that imitates the testimonial register although it is scripted and read by an actor, who plays the role of one of the imprisoned communards. This is a typical example of testimonial mediation conducted by educated urban intellectuals, in possession of the means of production and cultural capital, who created cultural products in collaboration with disenfranchised groups under shared authorship. As a consequence, the vast majority of Latin American testimonies of this era (written or filmic) show a bidirectional type of ventriloquism. The intellectual mediators give voice to the subaltern subjects, using them to create cultural products that foster their agenda, while, at the same time, they are used by the subaltern groups to convey their message and reach distant audiences.

## Neo-colonial bias in film criticism

In 1982, after the release of these three films, the editorial board of the journal *Hablemos de Cine* decided that the work of the Kuntur group was significant enough to devote a space in their issue number 75 to Federico García's cinema (note the, by default, auteurist approach). This dossier is divided into two sections: a long interview conducted by the editorial board (Ricardo Bedoya, Federico de Cárdenas, José Carlos Huayhuaca, Reynaldo Legard and Isaac León) and an article by José Carlos Huayhuaca entitled 'El dilema del lenguaje o el compromiso: el cine de Federico García' (The dilemma between language or commitment: Federico García's cinema). Both pieces are openly hostile. In the interview, the journal's editorial team, in a clear numerical majority, submits Federico García to something similar to an interrogation, where the film critics act as judges that have issued the sentence before listening to the accused. Pilar Roca, who was present, only intervenes once, interestingly, to refer to the tasks of circulation of films through the alternative circuit (García et al. 1982: 18). Maybe she participated more extensively and her voice has been edited out, although it is very likely that she let Federico García act as the spokesperson, because as she recognizes, it took her many years to realize the gender inequality present in her work relationship with García (Roca and García 2015; Roca 2019).

The main accusation of the *hablemistas* to García is related to the eclecticism, unbalance and formal contradictions in which the movies allegedly incur. For instance, they question the legitimacy of the hybridization of melodramatic and testimonial expressive forms in *Kuntur Wachana*. The critics perceive as an incongruity the use of these antagonist modes of representation (García et al. 1982: 20). Another accusation is of Manichaeism (in Spanish a quite common word to refer to a type of dogmatic and schematic dualist approach to reality). García does not try to defend himself against either of these recriminations. He admits that his cinema presents a Manichaean political scheme (García et al. 1982: 21), because he does not aim to be equidistant but aligned with the participant peasant movements. Furthermore, he does not see himself primarily as a filmmaker, in the sense that, for him, cinema is not an end but a means (García et al. 1982: 24). He understands that critics consider his cinema unsophisticated and admits that probably they are right, noting:

> My agenda is not cinematographic. My concern is not fundamentally that of language, that of dramatic development, that of form, that of shots or frames, which is all that has to do with film architecture. My concern in the first place is to tell a clear story, extremely clear because it is aimed at an audience that will not understand circumlocutions or the cinematic artifice. (García et al. 1982: 23)

Roca and García were self-taught filmmakers that advocated for an imperfect cinema. The ascription of value to García and Roca's filmmaking practice could have been facilitated by the vernacular theoretical approach provided by García Espinosa – who affirms that imperfect cinema is no longer interested in quality, technique or taste[14] – but this perspective is ignored by the prosecution team formed by the members of *Hablemos de*

---

[14] Julio García Espinosa, in 1969, in his groundbreaking manifesto 'For an Imperfect Cinema' affirms: Imperfect cinema is no longer interested in quality or technique (...) is no longer interested in 'good taste.' (...) The only thing it is interested in is how an artist responds to the following question: What are you doing in order to overcome the barrier of the 'cultured' elite audience which up to now has conditioned the form of your work? The filmmaker who subscribes to this new poetics should not have self-realisation as their object (García Espinosa 1997: 82).

*Cine*, who prefer to stick to pre-68 *Cahierist* principles. In Jeffrey Middents words, for the critics of *Hablemos de cine* 'to talk about cinema (hablar de cine)... meant to privilege the formal structural elements intrinsic to cinema – the mise-en-scène – over all other aspects referenced by a particular film' (Middents 2009: 1). Consequently, their verdict is consummated through the article by José Carlos Huayhuaca, who – after reclaiming the distinction between a urban and a *campesino* divide among Peruvian films (which I argue has proved to be not only superficial but misleading) – develops a thesis on what he calls 'the imperative of formal coherence' between the different levels that make up a cinematographic text – both denotative and connotative – and whose ultimate objective is the difficult 'poetic unity' (Huayhuaca 2017: 175). As a result of the application of these doctrinaire formalist principles, the work of the Kuntur group is overall dismissed.

# Conclusion: Towards a comprehensive canonization of Latin American Third Cinema

The clash between the critics of *Hablemos de Cine* and García is an excellent case study on how poor gatekeeping and canon-making practices have affected the historization of Latin American Third Cinema. For too long, it has been left in the hands of white middle-class men (critics who follow Western cinephilic precepts) the ascription of value to political cinema. This has led to a current situation in which a rewriting is needed because many emancipatory political-cinematographic processes – remarkable in terms of what Julianne Burton calls 'use value' (Burton 1997: 180) – have not been effectively incorporated into the canon(s) and therefore languish ignored.

We can begin by asking ourselves if it is necessary to have canons – lists of valuable films – in place, because canonization of any kind is a cultural practice of exclusion. In any event, aesthetic or artistic value should not be the only element indicative of whether a film resulting from a political process enters or not a given canon. Furthermore, in the concrete case of Latin American Third Cinema, the use of purely formalistic approaches demonstrates disregard for the renewed value hierarchies expressed by Latin American Third Cinema theorists and practitioners: the notion of imperfect cinema (García Espinosa 1997), the ultimate decolonial aim (Solanas and Getino 1979) and the methodology of a cinema 'with' the people, and not 'about' or 'for' them (Sanjinés 1979), among others. Ignoring these developments by applying pre-eminently imported formalistic criteria is an irresponsible praxis, especially if it results in the expunction of history of valuable cultural/political products.

A rigorous film history and criticism would focus on the valuable aspects of the Kuntur group's filmography. Their formal eclecticism should be further investigated and not dismissed as impure or ineffective because these cultural products are striking examples of the mediation of the voice, image and memory of the Peruvian popular classes carried out by committed organic intellectuals in a very specific context. García and Roca were unapologetic *Velasquistas*. Thus, their lyrical and magical agitprop films were competent instruments of transmission of a clearly situated ideology. A neutral or equidistant position was never intended. They were trying to indigenize Marxism through cinema and this effort represents, at the very least, a valuable early phase in the long road to cultural decolonization – a process in which we are still collectively engaged.

# Bibliography

'Abigeo actor presente en la premier de Laulico' (1980), *La Crónica* 46, Lima, March.
'Abigeo convertido en actor principal' (1980), *Diario* 80, Lima, 22 February.
'Abigeos actúan en Laulico' (1980), *Expreso*, Lima, 13 February.
Aimaretti, María and Isabel Seguí (2020), 'Ukamau Abigarrado: Nuevas nuevas miradas críticas y fuentes de investigación', *Secuencias. Revista de Historia del Cine*, n°49: pags.
'Auténticos Abigeos en Laulico' (1980), *La Prensa*, Lima, 10 February.
'Autorizan filme peruano Laulico' (1980), *Correo*, Lima, 31 January.
Bedoya, Ricardo (1992), *100 años de cine en el Perú: una historia crítica*, Lima: Universidad de Lima.
Bedoya, Ricardo (2009), *El cine sonoro en el Perú*, Lima: Universidad de Lima.
Blanco, Hugo (1972), *Land or Death: The Peasant Struggle in Peru*, New York: Pathfinder Press.
Burton, Julianne (1986), *Cinema and Social Change in Latin America: Conversations with Filmmakers*, Austin: University of Texas Press.
Burton, Julianne (1997), 'Film Artisans and Film Industries in Latin America, 1956–1980: Theoretical and Critical Implications of Variations in Modes of Filmic Production and Consumption', in Michael T. Martin (ed.), *New Latin American Cinema*, vol. 1, 157–84, Detroit: Wayne University Press.
*El caso Huayanay: testimonio de parte* (1981), [Film] Dir. Federico García, Peru-Cuba, Available online: https://www.youtube.com/watch?v=UtNADvNSzHM
Galiano, Carlos (1979), 'Inaugura el Festival Nuevo Cine Latinoamericano', *Granma*, La Habana, December 1979.
García Espinosa, Julio (1997), 'For an Imperfect Cinema', in Michael T. Martin (ed.), *New Latin American Cinema*, vol.1, 71–82, Detroit: Wayne State University Press.
García Hurtado, Federico (1965), *Tierra o Muerte: La Revolución Agraria del Perú*, Havana: Centro de documentación Juan F. Noyola, Casa de las Américas.

García Hurtado, Federico and Ricardo Bedoya, Federico de Cárdenas, José Carlos Huayhuaca, Reynaldo Lagard e Isaac León (1982), 'El cine peruano entre la realidad y el deseo (II): Encuentro con Federico García', *Hablemos de Cine*, 75: 16–25.

García Miranda, Nelson (2017), '*Laulico* de Federico García', in León Frías, Isaac y Federico de Cárdenas (eds), *Hablemos de Cine. Antología*, vol. 1, 139–41, Lima: PUCP.

Gramsci, Antonio (1975), *Prison Notebooks*, New York: Columbia University Press.

Huayhuaca, José Carlos (2017), 'El dilema del lenguaje o el compromiso: el cine de Federico García', in León Frías, Isaac y Federico de Cárdenas (eds), *Hablemos de Cine. Antología*, vol. 1, 173–9, Lima: PUCP (Originally published in *Hablemos de Cine* 75 (1982): 26–9).

Kato, Alfredo (1980), 'Detrás de la pantalla', *La Prensa*, Lima, 30 January.

King, John (1990), *Magical Reels: A History of Cinema in Latin America*, London: Verso.

*Kuntur Wachana* (1977), [Film] Dir. Federico García, Peru, Available online: https://www.youtube.com/watch?v=157PC-ZA3HE&t=2s

*Laulico* (1980), [Film] Dir. Federico García, Peru-Cuba, Available online: https://www.youtube.com/watch?v=Le7eqiCW4JU

'Laulico superó la censura' (1980), *Caretas*, no. 585, 28 January.

León Frías, Isaac (2014), *Tierras Bravas: Cine Peruano y Latinoamericano*, Lima: Universidad de Lima.

Mayer, Enrique (2009), *Ugly Stories of the Peruvian Agrarian Reform*, Durham/London: Duke University Press.

Martin, Michael T. (1997), *New Latin American Cinema*, vol. 2, Detroit: Wayne University Press.

Middents, Jeffrey (2009), *Writing National Cinema. Film Journals and Film Culture in Peru*, Lebanon: University Press of New England.

Neira, Hugo (1968), *Los Andes, Tierra o Muerte*, Madrid/Santigo de Chile: ZYX.

Neira, Hugo (1974), *Huillca: Habla un campesino peruano*, Havana: Casa de las Américas.

Ramos, Pilar (1978), 'Cine', *Tercera Edición*, Lima, 19 December.

'Responsabilizan a trabajadores del fracaso de 'Kuntur Wachana' (1980), *La Prensa*, Lima, 30 April.

Roca-Rey, Christabelle (2016), *La propaganda visual durante el gobierno de Juan Velasco Alvarado (1968–1975)*, Lima: Instituto Francés de Estudios Andinos and Instituto de Estudios Peruanos.

Sanjinés, Jorge and Grupo Ukamau (1979), *Teoría y práctica de un cine junto al pueblo*, Mexico: Siglo XXI editores.

Seguí, Isabel (2016), 'Cine-Testimonio: Saturnino Huillca, estrella del documental revolucionario peruano', *Cine Documental*, 13: 54–87.

Seguí, Isabel (2018), 'Auteurism, *Machismo-Leninismo*, and Other Issues: Women's Labor in Andean Oppositional Film Production', *Feminist Media Histories*, 4 (1): 11–36.

Solanas, Fernando and Octavio Getino (1979), *Cine, Cultura y Descolonización*, 3rd edition. Mexico: Siglo XXI.
Velasco Alvarado, Juan (1970), *Velasco: La voz de la revolución. Discursos del presidente de la república general de división Juan Velasco Alvarado (1968–1970)*, Lima: Ediciones Peisa. Consulted in University of Florida Digital Collections: https://ufdc.ufl.edu/UF00087193/00001/1

# PART TWO

# Comparative readings

# 5

# The legacy of the furnaces: The twenty-first century documentaries of Fernando Solanas

## *Mariano Paz*
## *(University of Limerick)*

The Argentine film *La hora de los hornos* (*The Hour of the Furnaces*), directed by Fernando 'Pino' Solanas and released in 1968, is a combination of documentary, essay film and agitprop work that became a landmark of Latin American cinema and one of the foundational texts of Third Cinema. Its global impact was increased by the publication, in 1969, of the manifesto 'Towards a Third Cinema', authored by Solanas and Octavio Getino. As part of a radical cinematic project produced by peripheral or the so-called Third World countries, Solanas and Getino wanted to create, through both the film and the manifesto, an alternative to dominant Hollywood Cinema (First Cinema) and auteur-driven, art cinema from Europe (Second Cinema). Most importantly, *The Hour* was conceived as militant cinema, a cultural tool in the fight against imperialism, and its authors saw the film as a tool in the search for radical political change in Argentina, moulded along the lines of the Cuban revolution (the film presents, in fact, an extended homage to Ernesto Che Guevara at the end of its first part). One of the foremost experts on the film, Mariano Mestman, writes that 'militant cinema was conceived as the most advanced category of Third Cinema' (Mestman 2003: 127).

*The Hour* became the emblem of the cinema of resistance and social commitment in Argentina, in Latin America and beyond, and it gained widespread recognition by academics, political activists and filmmakers alike. There are several ways in which Marxist theory and Marxist-inflected thinking have informed the film (Stam 1998; Mestman 2003; Oubiña 2016; Campo 2018). The political ideology of dependency that underlies the film's discourse, for example, derives from decolonial Latin American theory. As Paul A Shroeder argues, the film 'rearticulates violence not only as a Marxist would – that is, as a symptom of the changes in modes of production – but also as a Leninist and especially a Maoist would: as a tool to be actively wielded against an oppressive status quo in order to overthrow it' (Shroeder 2007). However, as Campo (2018) notes, rivers of ink have been used to write about *The Hour* (2009), so it is not necessary to explore it further in this chapter, which is concerned instead with the series of nine documentaries that Solanas produced since the turn of the century.

After shooting two additional documentaries in 1971, in collaboration with Getino, Solanas's career took a different path. Professionally, he concentrated on fiction films for the remaining of the twentieth century. Personally, after living in exile in France during the Argentine dictatorship of 1976–1983, he returned to the country and launched a career as a politician that saw him elected to the Argentine Congress and Senate. Following the severe economic crisis of 2001 in Argentina, however, Solanas returned to documentary filmmaking. In fact, the new century would see Solanas's most prolific period as a director. If in the thirty-five years between 1968 and 2003 Solanas released eight feature-length films (three documentaries and five fiction works), in the fourteen years between 2004 and 2018, he released nine feature-length films as sole director, all of them documentaries.[1] The list includes: *Memoria del saqueo* (*Social Genocide*, 2004), *La diginidad de los nadies* (*The Dignity of the Nobodies*, 2005), *Argentina latente* (*Latent Argentina*, 2007), *La próxima estación* (*The Next Station*, 2008), *Tierra sublevada: oro impuro* (*Rebelled Land: Impure Gold*, 2009), *Tierra sublevada: oro negro* (*Rebelled Land: Black Gold*, 2011), *La guerra del fracking* (*The War on Fracking*, 2013), *El legado estratégico de Juan Perón* (*The Strategic Legacy of Juan Perón*, 2016) and *Viaje a los pueblos fumigados* (*Voyage to the Fumigated Towns*, 2018).[2] This series of nine works, or nonology, has received very limited academic attention. The aim of this chapter is to trace the legacy of *The Hour* within Solanas's new

---

[1] Solanas has stated that he intends to make a series totalling ten documentaries (Otra vuelta de tuerka 2016). At the time of writing (2019), nine films have been released.

[2] Of the new documentary series, *Memoria del saqueo* is the only one that was released internationally with English subtitles and an English title: *Social Genocide* (a literal translation in Spanish would read 'memories of the plundering'). I will refer to the other films using my translation of the titles, provided here.

documentaries as a way to introduce these films, while at the same time exploring continuities and departures between the Marxist-informed, radical opus and the political ideology conveyed in the new films. In particular, drawing on the utopian and dystopian bents that can be found in Marxist theory, I will address how concerns about politics, national identity and globalization play out in the corpus of Solanas's post-2000 films.

## The twenty-first-century films of Fernando Solanas

In the words of Gonzalo Aguilar (2011), Argentinean cinema in the 1980s and early 1990s was characterized by the presence of two main imperatives or demands: the political one (what to do in political terms) and the identitarian one (what is the meaning of *argentinidad*; i.e. what is it that defines Argentinean identity). Although more recent films in the 1990s and 2000s rejected the call to answer these two demands, the films of Solanas have continued to engage with them. They seek to offer a very clear, univocal answer as to what should be done in political terms for the country to reach a future defined by progress, social justice and emancipation from foreign powers and, in addition, to construct an idea of what the Argentinean people is like. Such model was already present, to an extent, in *The Hour*, with its combination of left-wing, revolutionary ideals and the political mandate of Peronism – the Argentinean political movement that emerged in the 1940s with the rise to power of General Juan Domingo Perón. Peronism, a matrix that has informed, structured and conditioned the Argentinean political field since 1946 until the present, has multiple, and conflicting, ideological currents and phases, including right-wing and left-wing nationalisms, a neoliberal, globalizing side, expressed by the Menem administration in the 1990s, and the radical, socialist left, expressed by several Peronist groups in the 1970s, including the guerrilla organization Montoneros. Argentine cultural critic Beatriz Sarlo (2011) uses the term 'revolutionary Peronism' to refer to the radical-left Peronist followers, who saw in Ernesto Che Guevara a standard bearer for the policies of Juan Perón and, in particular, his wife Eva.

Analysing *The Hour*, Robert Stam has argued that the film was at the forefront of two spheres: one related to art (the formal one), the other to politics. The film 'marks one of the high points of their convergence' and fuses 'Third-World radicalism with artistic innovation' (Stam 1998: 271). None of this can be said of Solanas's post-2000 documentaries. This is perhaps understandable, given that thirty-six years elapsed between the release of *The Hour* and *Social Genocide*, the first work in Solanas's nonology. None of the recent films could be described as belonging to an aesthetical avant-garde. Although they draw on some of the techniques used in *The Hour* (the expanding intertitles, the ways in which archive footage is used, the asynchronous montage of image and sound), formally they still fall within the parameters of conventional documentary. In the well-known typology formulated by Bill Nichols, documentary films can be classified according to six modes: poetic, expository, observational, participatory, reflexive and performative (Nichols 2001). Although several scholars, such as Bruzzi (2006), have criticized this system, it can still serve as a guide to orient the viewer in identifying documentary styles and tropes. Accepting that the boundary that separates the modes is not a clear-cut one, and that they often overlap each other, it is still possible to map the dominant aesthetic strategies employed by these modes to the documentaries discussed here. Arguably the most common technique is the use of the voice-over narration, which dominates the expository mode of documentary. The 'voice of God' narrator is used to carefully construct an argument and to guide the viewer, often in a didactic way, through the images being portrayed, explaining their meaning and the way in which they are to be read. This technique is extensively used by Solanas in all nine documentaries. Also typical of the expository mode is the use of interviews, either with relevant experts in the fields being discussed or with ordinary citizens, interviewed on location by Solanas. However, as the series progresses, the films become more personal and incorporate tropes that characterize other types of documentary – in particular, the observational and the performative modes. For example, in the tradition of the former, the frequent use of footage shot on location throughout Argentina should be mentioned. Images of social protests and demonstrations, recording what is happening on the streets, in real time and captured by Solanas himself with a lightweight digital camera, are used extensively in the first two films. Moreover, in the most recent films Solanas himself has an increasingly prevalent role in them – a role that corresponds to the participant documentary, characterized by the presence of the author within the diegesis. In *Social Genocide* and *Dignity* the presence of Solanas is evident indirectly, through the voice narration, a few minutes of TV footage from the 1990s or occasionally when Solanas's back appears on screen. However, in *The War on Fracking* and *The Strategic Legacy of Juan Perón*, the on-screen figure of Solanas becomes crucial to the main narrative. The former, for example, contains scenes in which Solanas is shown carefully editing footage for the final cut and questioning the government's energy policy in Congress. In the latter, scenes of Solanas, situated at the centre of a small group of people, lecturing them about Peronism, are intercut with the other narrative strands of the film.[3] Clara Garavelli is right when pointing that, in these documentaries, Solanas has become himself a cinematic character (2014: 36).

---

[3] A stylistic choice situated within the boundaries between the participant and the performative modes.

It is true that some of the visual and narrative techniques mentioned above were also employed in *The Hour*. For example, the intertitles that zoom out on a black screen are used in all of the new documentaries, deliberately establishing an association with Solanas's magnus opus. But the more radical editing, narrative and sound aesthetics are absent. The new documentaries, thus, avoid the avant-garde formal aspects and enter the realm of conventional cinema in relation to editing, narrative, cinematography and sound, as Mariano and Zarini point out (2018: 200). To some extent it could even be said that, on a formal level, the films are at times rather conservative. This can be seen in the obviously ominous music that, in *Social Genocide*, accompanies shots of social protest amid the collapse of the Argentine economy and in the sad, non-diegetic string and piano scores during the interview scenes in *Digntity of the Nobodies* – particularly when interviewees recall traumatic events and are visibly distressed. These techniques would not be out of place in news programmes from conservative broadcasters such as Fox and Sky. In a less negative reading, Andermann describes the many shots showing people, often young children, living in poverty as 'well-meaning clichés' (2012: 100) – which is still far from enthusiastic praise.

It would be misguided, however, to demand of Solanas, who was almost seventy years old when *Social Genocide* was released, and eighty-two when *Voyage to the Fumigated Lands* was shot, a radical renovation of the language of documentary cinema for a second time. A simpler, more conventional style could be considered an artistic evolution on the part of Solanas, or perhaps a deliberate attempt to ensure the films reach a wider audience. However, Andermann puts this in a critical light when he states that the films (the first four in the series) simply become 'extended election spots for the political party [Solanas] now leads' (2012: 100). It is important, therefore, to further explore the ideological and political discourse of the films and to consider if the new documentaries are still part of a left-wing avant-garde. Before engaging with this point, however, it is necessary to briefly summarize what the films are about – since for the most part they have had very limited releases in Argentina and have not been released commercially in abroad.

If *The Hour* was a three-part documentary with a duration in excess of four hours, the new documentaries, taken together, have a total running time of 942 minutes (an average of 105 minutes per film), making this a significant film corpus. The first film, *Social Genocide*, released in 2004, is an examination of the causes that led to the Argentine socio-economic crisis of 2001. In particular, the film is focused on the decade of 1990 and the policies of the Carlos Menem administration (1989–99). A Peronist politician, Menem implemented widespread neoliberal reforms that included the systematic privatization of national companies (telecommunications, including telephone services and radio and TV broadcasters; electricity, gas and water providers; the administration of rail and motorway networks; the national airline; and YPF, the company in charge of oil exploration and production), deregulating the job market, sharply reducing tariffs on imported goods and borrowing extensively from the IMF and the World Bank. The outcome of these policies, continued by Fernando de la Rúa from 1999, produced massive unemployment, a sharp increase in inequality and the multiplication of the number of citizens living below the poverty line. *Social Genocide* offers a revisionist history of this period, at the same time recording how Argentinean society erupted in episodes of social unrest and violent protests that forced de la Rúa to resign at the end of 2001, when the economy collapsed. The film denounces not just the national governments but the globalization processes and the multinational organizations that pressured them into adopting the neoliberal policies they recommended.

The following film, *Dignity of the Nobodies*, could be considered a companion piece to *Social Genocide*. This time the narrative shifts from a macropolitical overview to a focus on the personal histories of ordinary citizens (the 'nobodies') engaged in work of social value that seeks to alleviate, in different ways, the dire conditions in which millions of Argentineans find themselves. Solanas presents the stories of a few men and women who 'resist' the neoliberal reforms and try to counteract its effects among the more relegated sectors of society. They include, among others, the story of Toba, a former Peronist militant who runs a *comedor infantil* (a soup kitchen for children); Margarita, a *cartonera* (a person who collects recyclable elements from garbage containers, mostly cardboard, to be sold to recyclers) who struggles to make a living by wandering on a horse-drawn cart along the streets of the Buenos Aires periphery; Carola and Silvia, two determined doctors working in a critically underfunded public hospital; and Claudia, the girlfriend of the late Darío Santillán, an activist in his early twenties who was killed by police forces in June 2002 during a violent social protest.

The third film takes a very different turn (it is arguably the most original work in the series): *Latent Argentina* is both an historical examination and a celebration of Argentinean scientific and technological achievements. Although to an extent the film is also a denunciation of the effects of the neoliberal decade (in particular the lack of funding for scientific research and the neglect of state technology companies that produced ships, light aircraft, cars and other complex machinery), *Latent Argentina* highlights past and present accomplishments in the areas of science, technology and engineering. These include discussions of (and visits to) the Río Santiago Shipyard (founded by Juan Perón in 1953), aeronautics and aerospace companies, the Conycet (the Argentinean public agency in charge of funding scientific and academic research within all disciplines), the National Commission for Atomic Energy (Conea) and the Instituto Balseiro (a prestigious higher education institute in Patagonia focused on the fields of physics and nuclear engineering). Despite the now familiar political and economic critique, the film also contains a highly optimistic message about the quality of the human resources available in Argentina in the areas of scientific and technological development – areas that, if exploited and funded coherently and systematically, would lead to social progress and the creation of a more advanced, more prosperous and more independent Argentina.

The fourth film, *The Next Station*, provides a detailed examination of the vicissitudes of the Argentinean rail network. One of the most advanced rail systems in the Americas during the early twentieth century, it was built by British investors, nationalized by Perón in 1948, privatized by Menem during the 1990s and nationalized once again by the Kirchner administration, but after this film was released. At the end of the nineteenth century, the rail network was seen as a sign of modernity, promising industrial and technological progress. The film provides a close look at the fortunes, and misfortunes, of the national train service. Dismantled by the companies that bought it in the 1990s, which closed unprofitable lines in a measure that cost hundreds of jobs and left entire towns disconnected from urban centres), the network is considered a symbol of national decay and, once again, an arena where the forces of globalized capital and national interests clash.

The three films that followed all dealt with the problem of natural resources and extractive industries. In *Rebelled Land: Impure Gold* (2009), *Rebelled Land: Black Gold* (2011) and *The War on Fracking* (2013), Solanas denounces the lack of a proper national plan for managing the exploitation of minerals, oil, gas, shale oil and shale gas that are available in deposits throughout the country, denouncing at the same time the foreign companies that extract them, with little government regulation, and the environmental damage that such companies produce. The films add a new dimension to the usual preoccupations of Solanas: the environment. Condemning the neoliberal policies that allowed foreign companies to easily gain ownership of mines and oil fields, plundering Argentina for their own private profit, the films also criticize the ways in which they pollute the land and call for a firmer protection of nature. The national government, Solanas demonstrates, lacks a solid legal framework for protecting the environment and has allowed foreign companies to reap the large profits made out of the exploitation of hydrocarbons and minerals – profits that should instead be going to the Argentinean state. *The War*, in particular, is a critique of fracking – the controversial hydraulic fracturing technique for extracting shale oil and shale gas from the *Vaca Muerta* reserve in northern Patagonia. Solanas criticizes this highly polluting practice, as well as the agreement that the nationalized oil company YPF signed with Chevron in 2013 in order to exploit the Vaca Muerta deposits.

Solanas's eighth film, *The Strategic Legacy of Juan Perón*, goes back to the founding figure of Peronism. As Boetti (2016) notes, of all his documentaries, this is the one that is most removed from the political conjuncture of the time. Closer to the essay film and the performative documentary, it rescues footage shot in 1971 for the two films Solanas and Getino made at the time (based on interviews with Perón in Madrid) but did not include in their final cut. This footage is edited alongside scenes of Solanas elaborating on his own interpretation of Peronism (a changing and multi-faceted movement) in front of a group of young listeners.

Finally, for his latest work at the time of writing, Solanas returns to ecological concerns in *Voyage to the Fumigated Lands*, tackling the problem of the widespread use of agrochemicals in national crops, the deforestation in the north of Argentina by landowners who want to clear the land in order to grow soy, the situation of indigenous natives who have been displaced from their lands due to deforestation and conflicts with the Monsanto Company over licenses for the use of genetically modified seeds.

In terms of production, all nine films have been funded by Solanas's own company *Cinesur* and the collaboration of the Argentinean film institute, the INCAA. Additionally, seven of the films are international co-productions with European companies and public agencies. The French production company *Les Films du Sud* is credited in *Rebelled Land: Black Gold*, *The Next Station*, *Latent Argentina*, *The Dignity of the Nobodies* and *Social Genocide*. Spanish producers (TVE, the Ibermedia programme) are credited in *Latent Argentina* and *Dignity*. Swiss and German companies contributed to the production of *Social Genocide* and *Dignity*, and the Venezuelan *Villa del Cine* co-produced the two *Rebelled Lands*. This is an indicator of the prestige of Solanas and the appeal that his film projects generate among European producers and of the extent to which Latin American cinema has come to rely on international partners for film production. It is also clear now that Argentina has become a consolidated democracy, Solanas can apply for and receive funding for his films, even when they are critical of the party in power at the time.

The above point leads to the issue of distribution and exhibition. *The Hour* was shot clandestinely under a dictatorial government and was screened in equally secret or semi-secret circumstances in private houses, clubs, trade unions and similar venues. For this reason, as Mestman (2011) argues, it is extremely difficult to calculate box-office earnings or number of viewers. This is not the case with the post-2000 films, all of which were commercially released in Argentina and exhibited in cinema theatres in major cities around the country. However, records by the INCAA show that the films have been watched in theatres by very low numbers of people. For example, the most recent film, *Voyage to the Fumigated Towns*, sold 6,679 tickets in 2018. To put this in perspective, the top ten highest-grossing films in Argentina that year were seen by more than a million spectators each. *Voyage* is located in the 231th spot out of 450 films released that year – or 42 out of 238 if we only count national films (INCAA n.d.). The worst numbers overall are for *The War on Fracking*, released in October 2013, and seen by only 303 people – that is, the 365th spot in 392 releases overall (INCAA n.d.). Conversely, *The Next Station* was seen by 49,882 films in 2008, putting it in the 125th place out of 304 releases, and 15th out of 83 national films (INCAA n.d.).

Overall, it is clear that the numbers are quite low, even for the films that did relatively better within the series. This should not be surprising: like most countries in the region, Argentine box office is dominated by Hollywood blockbusters, a hegemony occasionally broken by one or two national films that tend to be examples of popular genres not too dissimilar, in aesthetical terms, from the American films they compete with. At the same time, it must be noted that all of these films (except, at the time of writing, *The Strategic Legacy*) are freely available on YouTube. Free online distribution has not been blocked by Solanas or the producing companies – in fact, in some cases the films have been uploaded by Proyecto Sur and Cinesur (Solanas's political party and producing company).

Online distribution reveals an open attitude on the part of the filmmakers towards exhibition, particularly since other YouTube users and channels have been allowed to upload the films. This might also demonstrate that changing patterns in audio-visual consumption is one of the factors responsible for the low box-office numbers. It is interesting to note that *The War on Fracking*, which had 303 viewers in theatres, has been viewed 278,940 times at the time of writing ('HD – La Guerra' 2013). *Next Station* has 106,489 views from only one user, but there are several others that show either the entire film or a selection of scenes. Similarly, *Social Genocide* has been viewed over 385,000 times, but it is available through different channels, so the total number is much higher ('La próxima estación' 2012). This shows there is a significant interest in Solanas's documentaries that is not captured by standard box-office figures and, furthermore, that viewing practices for these films follow, like those for *The Hour*, less conventional routes that are not entirely subject to completely capitalist practices of distribution networks and streaming platforms.

# Peronism and Marxism in the films of Solanas

The plot summaries offered above leave no doubt that Solanas is a tireless documentarian, a person with an extensive knowledge of Argentina and a politician deeply committed to a political project that rejects foreign capital and emphasizes national growth through better management of its resources, human and natural. In order to make his case, Solanas has, over the last fifteen years or so, travelled back and forth along the country, visiting large cities and small towns, factories and plantations, oil fields and forests, key engineering sites such as dams and bridges and public organizations such as ministries, universities and research centres. All of this has been recorded in his films. The main narrative around which all of them are structured is based on an interpretation of national history that draws extensively on the theory of dependency, as formulated by thinkers such as Fernando Cardoso and Enzo Faletto (1979), which already informed *The Hour*, as Olivera (2008: 251–2) has demonstrated. According to dependency theory, peripheral countries such as Argentina are directly prevented from achieving higher levels of economic growth and development by the deliberate action of central countries, who want to reduce Third World countries to producers of cheap raw materials. Furthermore, true independence for peripheral countries can be reached not only politically and economically but also culturally. In this sense, American culture and Hollywood cinema would be another tool of domination that must be rejected.

In addition to the main arguments of dependency theory, Solanas's films are informed by his own personal interpretation of the ideology of Peronism. This was already evident in the second part of *The Hour* – perhaps the section of the film which had less international appeal, since it is closely focused on Peronism and the Peronist resistance in the late 1950s and early 1960s Argentina. But the version of Peronism that Solanas upholds is arguably based on myth as much as historical fact. As Aguilar (2016) argues in relation to *The Strategic Legacy*: 'Solanas chose to give us another monument, another idealisation, another rosy legacy that does not allow us to reflect – through cinema – about the blood spilled.'[4] That is to say, Solanas gives an account that is uninterested in exploring any critical views of Peronism.[5] Although there would be no obligation to do this, Aguilar is right when adding that the film's premise, of searching for the authentic legacy of Peronism, is in itself impossible: 'there is no true, authentic, definitive Perón, and this contradicts the main concept that structures the Peronist legacy: loyalty' (Aguilar 2016). In fact, the recent films are laden with the vocabulary of Peronism: terms such as *loyalty*, *traitor*, *strategy* and *comrade* (compañero) are loaded signifiers within the semiotics of Peronism (and also show the militaristic undertone of this language).

At the same time, despite Andermann's claim (cited above) that the films could be considered election ads for the Proyecto Sur campaigns, it should not be forgotten that, although Solanas has been, for the past two decades, both a filmmaker and politician, he never considered these two activities as separate. For him, being a filmmaker means being a politically active

---

[4] 'Solanas prefirió entregarnos otro monumento más, otra idealización, otro legado rosa que no permite reflexionar – con el cine – sobre la sangre derramada.'
[5] The film poster itself is revealing: it features photographs of Perón and Solanas superimposed onto a living room. Peron's figure, sitting on a sofa, is about three times larger than Solanas, who is standing on his feet and looking up at Peron, as he holds a digital camera. Peron, in black-and-white while everything else in the image is in colour, clearly resembles a monument.

and engaged individual. Alternatively, as a politician he has sought to better understand, represent and engage with national reality through the practice of filmmaking. *The Hour* was intended to be a call for political action; as militant cinema, it cannot be separated from political action. The new documentaries are less focused on mobilizing people, and distanced from the idea of Frantz Fanon, quoted in *The Hour*, that spectators can only be traitors or cowards. Now that Argentina is living in democratic times, Solanas may well consider that social change should be sought through legal demonstrations and by participating on elections, and not through political violence. Would this mean, however, that the new documentaries undermine the original premise of Third Cinema and are no longer interested in the interpellation of the audience, and in fight for emancipatory change?

In 1980, referring to the political discourse of *The Hour*, Stam wrote that 'events subsequent to 1968 have if not wholly discredited at least relativized the film's analysis' (Stam 1998 [1980]: 272). However, though some of the political problems addressed in *The Hour* have been overcome by Argentine society (no longer ruled by military juntas that rose to power unconstitutionally; no political parties are proscribed from elections), it must be recognized that many of the social problems that Solanas denounces have in fact become much worse. As Prividera (2016: 152) argues, the levels of poverty and inequality in Argentina are much higher today than they were in 1968. Therefore, at least in this sense Solanas is right when he commented, on occasion of the *The Hour*'s fiftieth anniversary screening at the Cannes Film Festival in 2018, that that film's message is more relevant today than it was at the time of its release (Duarte 2018).

From a Marxist perspective, many of the enemies (of the working classes, of the nation) identified in the recent documentaries would be familiar: they include multinational companies such as Chevron and Monsanto; the banking system; supranational organizations such as the IMF; local elites whose worldview, culture and values respond only to foreign interests; corrupt politicians; and industry bosses who, to cut losses, are happy to close their factories at the first sign of economic trouble and transfer their savings to off-shore bank accounts while workers are fired. Moreover, and against Stam's belief that historical events have discredited the radical view offered by *The Hour*, Yanis Varoufakis (2018) claims that true globalized, unrestricted capitalism only came into being after 1991, with the collapse of the communist regimes in Eastern Europe and the gradual incorporation of China to the market economy. According to Varoufakis, 'unbearable inequality, brazen greed, climate change, and the hijacking of our parliamentary democracies by bankers and the ultra-rich' are among the effects of globalised capital (2018). All of the post-2000 documentaries by Solanas offer evidence of this thesis. Varoufakis adds that the mainstream response to such disadvantage consists of 'issuing fiery condemnations of the symptoms (income inequality) while ignoring the causes (exploitation resulting from the unequal property rights over machines, land, resources)' (2018) – a point that is also illustrated by Solanas' documentaries, which strongly denounce the causes of these symptoms.

How these issues are to be tackled constitutes one important difference between *The Hour*, influenced by historical events such as the Cuban revolution and by theoretical writings such as Fanon's *The Wretched of the Earth* and the new films. If the former emphasized struggle and political violence as a means to overthrow the dictatorial Argentine government of 1968, Solanas is now in favour of democratic solutions that avoid violence (although he praises activists who voice concerns and protest against the neoliberal administrations of Menem and De la Rúa). This does not necessarily imply a rejection of a Marxist view of political action, since there are few calls to political violence within Marx's own writings. Although later revolutionaries would draw on Marxism as the basis for programmes that involved accessing power through a violent takeover of the State apparatus, an autocratic and repressive government is, for Marx, at odds with the emancipated communist society that he envisaged (Eagleton 2011: 19–20). Further links with Marxism can also be found in the eutopian and dystopian trends conveyed in Solanas' series.

## Eutopia and dystopia in Solanas's post-2000 documentaries

Discussing popular genre cinema, Carl Freedman speaks of deflationary and inflationary bents of Marxist theory:

> The deflationary dimension is represented by the attempt to destroy all illusions necessary or useful to the preservation of class society in general and of capitalism in particular. Such demystification is perhaps most familiar in the form of ideology-critique-that is, the exposure of those networks of habit and belief that capitalist societies generate and that in turn help to sustain capitalism's oppressive practices by inhibiting the development of socialist ideas and attitudes. (Freedman 2009: 72)

That is to say, the deflationary dimension is to be found in Marx's thorough and accurate revelations about the dynamics and effects of capitalism. To cite Marx's own words in his letter to Arnold Ruge in 1843: 'it is all the more clear what we have to accomplish at present: I am referring to ruthless criticism of all that exists, ruthless both in the sense of not being afraid of the results it arrives at and in the sense of being just as little afraid of conflict with the powers that be' (Marx 1843). But in addition to a ruthless critique, and criticism, of capitalism, Marxist theory also has a positive, inflationary side. According to Freedman:

> But Marxism ultimately aims at the positive project of human liberation and self-realisation, rather than only at the negative task of destroying capitalism ... Marxism is inflationary as well, insisting that, despite the fact that class oppression is essentially coterminous with the history of the human race, it need not always be so. The overthrow of capitalism... can instead be the prelude to the radically democratic self-organisation of the human race. (Freedman 2009: 72–3)

These two bents, I propose, can also be mapped onto the documentaries made by Solanas. Rather than using the terms 'inflationary' and 'deflationary', it is my opinion that the terms 'eutopian' and 'dystopian' would be instead more appropriate. The first term is related to the positive utopia: the imagination of a social alternative that is empirically better than the society in which it has been conceived (Tower Sargent 1994). Dystopia represents the opposite of eutopia: an imagined society that is significantly worse than the actual one. If the eutopia is optimistic, dystopia is informed by pessimism. According to Varghese, Marx predicted that 'capitalism's internal logic would over time lead to rising inequality, chronic unemployment and underemployment, stagnant wages, the dominance of large, powerful firms, and the creation of an entrenched elite whose power would act as a barrier to social progress' (Varghese 2018: 34). If we add environmental destruction to this list, we are left with a fully fledged dystopian scenario that has been anticipated by Marx, which also represents the targets of Solanas's criticism in his documentaries.

It is true that in the central works by Marx, such as *Capital* and *The Communist Manifesto*, more pages are devoted to the analysis of the workings and contradictions of capitalism than to describing the society, free of class struggles, alienation and exploitation that would emerge after the advent of communism. Marx does offer a few glimpses of what the future may entail, and it is clear that such an order would resolve the problems and inequalities produced by capitalism, leading to a much better society than the one in which Marx lived. Marx's utopian bent has been extensively discussed and often levelled as a critique that blamed Marx for the crimes of Stalinism and Maoism (Geoghegan 2008; Eagleton 2011; Claeys 2018). It is not possible to elaborate this point here, but, as Freedman has noted, Marxism imagines an emancipated society where contradictions and inequality have been resolved, making it possible to speak of dystopian and utopian bents in Marxist theory.

Along these lines, the documentaries described above dwell on the criticism of the dramatic effects that unrestricted neoliberal policies produced on Argentina's population and territory. But they also contain elements of celebration and optimism: the protesters who defy the police to complain against foreign banks moving their assets abroad, medics and workers who, against the odds and through hard work and solidarity manage to keep neglected hospitals and factories afloat, and so on. This reasoning finds its ultimate expression in two specific films that reflect the inflationary, or eutopian, side of a Marxist social critique, and the deflationary or dystopian bent. The first film is *Latent Argentina*; the second one is *The Next Station* (neither film is either totally dystopian or totally eutopian, as they respectively contain both pessimistic and optimist elements, but each of them presents a narrative in which one of the two bents has a dominant position).

Focused on the accomplishments carried out in Argentina by scientists, engineers and industrial designers, the eutopian core of *Latent Argentina* is explicit. The film's underlying premise is that, if the country was able to attain important technoscientific achievements in the past, under governments that pursued an agenda focused on national development, the same can be done in the future, if neoliberal policies are reverted and a strong developmental system is put in place. A revitalization of national science and technology would lead to social progress, as the national industry will be able to satisfy the internal demand for technological products and also export them, increasing the GDP and allowing the government to redistribute surplus. Visually, these ideas are conveyed by the use of long shots and aerial shots of shipyards, factories and industries, underlining the size of these locations, and connoting the grandeur and scale of these sites. Solanas's faith in science and industrial development is here much in line with the Marxist perspective that considered this a necessary precondition for progress and with Marx's positivist conception of science.

*Latent Argentina* is not calling for a radical revolution, and Che Guevara is not feted here. Is the film implying that the original project of the Latin American left has failed, and calling for a more pragmatic and achievable project that still aims to improve the life of citizens? Or could it be read as underlining that an essential first step in the path towards an emancipated society should be based on a strong, independent state and an advanced industrial sector? Ultimately, the film makes a strong case arguing that, despite the fierce crisis of 2001, social progress in Argentina is possible, and not merely as an abstract idea awaiting in an unspecified future: the material bases on which this society can be constructed are all outlined by Solanas. The potential for transformation already exists: all it needs is a further push.

Conversely, *Next Station* is pervaded by a pessimistic undertone. The film chronicles the history and, particularly, the collapse of the Argentine rail network – an exemplary system in Latin America that had been at the centre of Argentina's economic model based on agricultural exports. Cereals, fruits and beef would be transported by rail, from the plains and fields in the interior of the country to the Buenos Aires port, to be shipped onwards to European markets. Privatization, lack of investment and the closure of several lines degraded and destroyed the network. Visually, the film often gives the impression of drawing on the conventions of postapocalyptic science fiction cinema: a variety of shots dwell on deserted train stations that have not been used in years, abandoned locomotives and coaches rusting in the middle of nowhere, dilapidated train depots and workshops. If *Latent Argentina* emphasized, through cinematography and mise-en-scéne, state-of-the-art industry and technology, *Next Station* revels in post-industrial decay and technological decline. Given that the rail network fulfilled not only an economic function but a social one (transporting mostly working-class people cheaply and efficiently, uniting the lives of citizens living across the country), then the film can act, beyond the level of denotation, as an allegory of Argentinean society as a whole.

In narrative terms, *Next Station* follows the political debate on the nature of public and private enterprise: Should rail transport be driven only by profit? Or should it also be a public service? If so, does it matter that some lines do generate a profit? The film sharply criticizes the transport policy of not only the Menem administration but also the Kirchner ones (much closer to Solanas ideologically). Public prosecutors who showed no interest in investigating irregularities in the privatization process, trade unions that were complicit with the privatizations and the new owners and civil servants who do not fulfil the task of controlling the private train operators are also the target of Solanas critique, who paints a very bleak portrait here. Tragically, four years after *Next Station* was released, a terrible accident took place in Buenos Aires, involving the busy line that connects the city centre with its Western suburbs ('Argentina train crash' 2012). On 22 February, at peak time, a train on the Sarmiento line was unable to stop upon arriving the terminal station. Once, crashing at speed against the buffers. The train brakes and emergency brakes did not work. The accident, with a final toll of 51 passengers dead and over 700 injured (1,000 people were on board), was the product of multiple errors whose ultimate cause is the general state of degradation involving the network: lack of investment, lack of appropriate maintenance and lack of state control and regulations. This demonstrates the prescience and urgency that Solanas's film had. If transport ministers had paid attention to the message *Next Station* was conveying, perhaps this tragedy could have been avoided.

Although *Latent Argentina* and *Next Station* are almost totalizing case studies in their respective expression of eutopian and dystopian bents, the dialectics between these two categories are played out in all of the documentaries by Solanas discussed here. The negative appraisal of neoliberal capitalism, and the dramatic effects of its implementation in Argentinean society, also contains a way out, a call for action to reverse its effects and build a better society. However, this does not mean that the ideology that Solanas conveys in his works is fully aligned with Marxism. There is, in my opinion, a contradiction that arises of the position that Solanas embraces: that of custodian of the Peronist legacy.

## Nationalism and Marxism in the films of Solanas

Despite some points of contact (particularly in the left-wing interpretation of Peronism that Solanas favours), it is not easy to consider Peronism as compatible with a Marxist political project, one that is close to the writings of Marx and Engels, as far as this is possible, rather than one of the historical instances in which Marxism was claimed as the basis for the construction of a political system, such as Stalinism and Maoism. One evident contradiction, in my opinion, is Solanas's nationalist stance, which rejects the possibility of a supranational order and global cooperation among countries and workers. Nationalism in the writings of Marx and Engels is, several experts have argued, one of the least adequately discussed notions (Avineri 1991; Schwartzmantel 2012; del Palacio Martín 2013). Marx and Engels are clear in their defence of national unification in Europe, such as in the cases of Italy, Germany and Poland, as a precondition for the creation of a strong socialist party, the development of capitalism and the subsequent transition into socialism. Marx and Engels also discussed the universalizing nature of capitalism, which should be matched by socialism. As they write in *The Communist Manifesto*:

> In place of the old local and national seclusion and self-sufficiency, we have intercourse in every direction, universal inter-dependence of nations. And as in material, so also in intellectual production. The intellectual creations of individual nations become common property. National onesidedness and narrow-mindedness become more and more impossible. (Marx and Engels [1848] 2018: 27)

A variety of Marxist thinkers have discussed the universalizing aspect of Marxism. According to Slavoj Žižek, for example, 'Marx was fascinated by the revolutionary "deterritorializing" impact of capitalism which, in its inexorable dynamics, undermines all stable traditional forms of human interaction; what he reproached capitalism with is that its "deterritorialization" was not thorough enough, that it generated new "reterritorializations"' (2001). That is to say, for Marx a truly revolutionary form of socialism should be globalized and cannot be contained within a single country (although a national emergence of socialism could be a first step in this direction).

A sense of unity across Latin American and African nations is an ideal that informed *The Hour* – nations united by its subaltern position and deliberately relegated by a postcolonial logic of economic, political and even military relegation. The recent documentaries place the focus on the Argentinean nation as main site in which a project of social emancipation can be constructed. The problem with this logic can be illustrated by the following example: on 20th September 2019 Solanas tweeted a negative opinion on a deal signed between YPF (the Argentine oil-company, renationalized by the Kirchner administration) and the shipping company Horamar (Solanas 2019). The deal entailed the purchase, by YPF, of small cargo boats manufactured in Paraguay. Why, Solanas asks, can YPF not buy nationally made boats? The issue here is not only that Paraguay is a neighbouring Latin American country that may be in an even worse economic situation than Argentina but that, in *Latent Argentina*, Solanas celebrated the Río Santiago Shipyard and the fact that, at the time of shooting the film, the company was building a huge bulk carrier ship for a German company. The contradiction is obvious: if Germany had acted in the way Solanas is advocating, the contract with the Argentinean Río Santiago would never have been signed. If an Argentinean company can produce ships to be exported, should it not be fair that Paraguay is also allowed to do the same? Cooperation should not be limited to citizens or organizations within the same nation – at least, Solanas should not reject cooperation between Latin American countries struggling in the same postcolonial world-order.

Another important contradiction can be found in Solanas' attitude towards the administrations of Néstor Kirchner and his wife Cristina Fernández: the former was president of Argentina between 2003 and 2007 and the latter was president between 2007 and 2015. Solanas is highly critical, in all of his documentaries, of the policies implemented by Kirchner and Fernández in relation to the areas discussed in the films (natural resources, privatization, regulation of the privatized companies, and so on). Yet, in October 2019, Solanas not only endorsed the candidacy of Alberto Fernández for president – with Cristina Fernández (no relation) as the running partner – but he run for the office of senator as the leader of Proyecto Sur under the same coalition ticket. Solanas has justified the contradiction by stating that defeating the centre-right candidate, Mauricio Macri, was a priority. One may well agree with Solanas on this point, or perhaps argue that the realities of politics involve pragmatic negotiations and compromises in order to form working alliances. The realm of cultural production may follow a different dynamic, and an independent and renowned filmmaker will not be subject to the same constraints than in the political arena. Nonetheless, there remains an important contradiction in the actions of Solanas the politician and Solanas the filmmaker, which is made worse by the clarity and effectiveness of the cinematic critiques contained in such films as *Next Station*, *Rebelled Land* and *The War on Fracking*, critiques that have been endorsed by the national justice system and the wide number of judicial processes and convictions for cases of corruption in many public offices (particularly during the Kirchner and Fernández administrations).

On the other hand, the above should not be read as an agreement with Andermann's dismissal (cited earlier) of Solanas's recent films as election spots for his party. As demonstrated above, the corpus of nine documentaries he produced since the year 2000 are part of a highly elaborate and coherent political discourse that is deeply concerned with something much more important than a prosaic public job in parliament. It is, arguably, a flawed corpus that relies on a univocal and uncritical, as well as highly personal, interpretation of the legacy of Peronism, that is often Manichean, dogmatic and in some cases outdated. It is also deeply committed to the defence of the underprivileged and marginalized citizens of Argentina, the victims of unbridled neoliberalism and political corruption and of the natural resources that are essential for the country. One could imagine the same films built around a more consistent Marxist framework, more faithful to the legacy of Che Guevara as celebrated in *The Hour*, and less situated within a Peronist framework that cannot be seen as aligned with a socialist national project. It is true that these films express a coherent commitment to national development by processes that underline collective action, cooperation between different social sectors, respect for the rights of minorities and indigenous peoples, technoscientific development and sustainability. At the same time, they reject the pressures of global institutions and governments to an unrestricted opening of the economy and an alignment with the policies recommended by the IMF.

Moreover, it is also true that the consistency and the novelty of such a comprehensive cinematic series have not been recognized by critics, who have mostly dismissed or ignored these films. It is my opinion, however, that a conceptual framework that was less preoccupied with the Peronist network of loyalties, treasons and legacies, and more focused on the problems identified by Marx and Engels in their writings (alienation, exploitation, the lumpenproletariat, the unemployed and internationalization) would lead to a more accurate understanding of the situations that Solanas is chronicling and describing. From this perspective, the criticism that can be made of these films is that they do not follow Marxist theory too closely, despite sharing a common diagnostic about the issues that afflict Western societies in the new millennium. In this light, the new documentaries could have been closer to the original spirit of third cinema, a properly radical look at contemporary society that sought not simply to represent the world but also to transform it, combining the dystopian descriptive bent with the eutopian possibilities implicit in Marxist thinking.

# Bibliography

Aguilar, Gonzalo (2011), *Other Worlds: New Argentine Cinema*, Basingstoke and New York: Palgrave Macmillan.
Aguilar, Gonzalo (2016), 'El tótem de la lealtad todavía persiste', *Clarín*, 4 March. https://www.clarin.com/rn/ideas/totem-lealtad-todavia-persiste_0_rJgJbaODmx.html (accessed 1 September 2019).

Andermann, Jens (2012), *New Argentine Cinema*, London and New York: I.B. Tauris.
'Argentina Train Crash in Buenos Aires Kills 49' (2012), *BBC*, 23 February, https://www.bbc.com/news/world-latin-america-17129858 (accessed 30 May 2019).
Avineri, Shlomo (1991), 'Marxism and Nationalism', *Journal of Contemporary History*, 26 (3): 637–57.
Boetti, Ezequiel (2016), 'El legado de Pino', *Otros Cines*, 23 February, https://www.otroscines.com/nota-10642-el-legado-de-pino (accessed 14 September 2019).
Bruzzi, Stella (2006), *New Documentary*, London and New York: Routledge.
Campo, Javier (2018), 'To Invent Our Revolution: An Aesthetic-Political Analysis of *The Hour of the Furnaces*', in Javier Campo and Hugo Pérez-Blanco (eds), *A Trail of Fire for Political Cinema: The Hour of the Furnaces Fifty Years Later*, 25–46, Bristol: Intellect.
Cardoso, Fernando Henrique and Enzo Faletto (1979), *Dependency and Development in Latin America*, Berkeley and Los Angeles: University of California Press.
Claeys, Gregory (2018), *Marx and Marxism*, London: Pelican.
del Palacio Martín, Jorge (2013), 'Marx y Engels frente a la "cuestión nacional"', *Marx desde Cero*, https://kmarx.wordpress.com/2013/11/18/marx-y-engels-frente-a-la-cuestion-nacional/ (accessed 16 October 2019).
Duarte, Rodrigo (2018), 'Pino Solanas y los 50 años de *La hora de los hornos*: "Es cada vez más actual"', *Infobae*, 10 June, https://www.infobae.com/cultura/2018/06/10/pino-solanas-sobre-los-50-anos-de-la-hora-de-los-hornos-es-cada-vez-mas-actual/ (accessed 1 October 2019).
Eagleton, Terry (2011), *Why Marx Was Right*, New Haven: Yale University Press.
Freedman, Carl (2009), 'Marxism, Cinema and Some Dialectics of Science Fiction and Film Noir', in Mark Bould and China Miéville (eds), *Red Planets: Marxism and Science Fiction*, 66–82, Middletown, CT: Wesleyan University Press.
Freedman, Carl (2012), 'Marxism, Cinema, and Some Dialectics of Science Fiction and Film Noir', in Mark Bould and China Mieville (eds), *Red Planets: Marxism and Science Fiction*, 66–82, Middletown, Connecticut: Wesleyan University Press.
Garavelli, Clara (2014), 'Fernando E. Solanas', in Beatriz Urraca and Gary M. Kramer (eds), *Directory of World Cinema: Argentina*, 32–6, Bristol: Intellect.
Geoghegan, Vincent (2008), *Utopianism and Marxism*, Bern: Peter Lang.
'HD – La Guerra del Fracking de Pino Solanas' (2013), [broadcast] YouTube, https://www.youtube.com/watch?v=YA6Xp1WDQq4&t=177s (accessed 29 September 2019).
INCAA (no date), http://fiscalizacion.incaa.gov.ar/index_estadisticas_peliculas.php (accessed 1 October 2019).
'La próxima estación pino solanas 2008' (2012), [broadcast] YouTube, https://www.youtube.com/watch?v=fcRwa2srWIQ&t=63s (accessed 29 September 2019).
Mariano, Magalí and María Emilia Zarini (2018), 'Solanas' recent documentaries', in Javier Campo and Hugo Pérez-Blanco (eds), *A Trail of Fire for Political Cinema: The Hour of the Furnaces Fifty Years Later*, 191–210, Bristol: Intellect.
Marx, Karl (1843), 'Letter to Arnold Ruge', https://www.marxists.org/archive/marx/works/1843/letters/43_09.htm (accessed 29 September 2019).

Marx, Karl and Friedrich Engels ([1848] 2018), *The Communist Manifesto*, London: Vintage Classics.
Mestman, Mariano (2003), 'The Hour of the Furnaces', in Alberto Elena and Marina Díaz López (eds.), *The Cinema of Latin America*, 119–30, London and New York: Wallflower Press.
Mestman, Mariano (2011), 'Third Cinema/Militant Cinema: At the Origins of the Argentinian Experience (1968–1971)', *Third Text*, 25 (1): 29–40.
Nichols, Bill (2001), *Introduction to Documentary*, Bloomington and Indianapolis: Indiana University Press.
Olivera, Guillermo (2008), 'Dependency Theory and the Aesthetics of Contrast in Fernando Solanas's *La hora de los hornos* and *Memoria del saqueo*', *Hispanic Research Journal*, 9 (3): 247–60.
'Otra Vuelta de Tuerka: Pablo Iglesias con Pino Solanas' (2016), [broadcast] YouTube, https://www.youtube.com/watch?v=ZKOyVExYu2Y (accessed 1 September 2019).
Oubiña, David (2016), 'Argentina: El profano llamado del mundo', in Mariano Mestman (ed.), *Las rupturas del '68 en el cine de América Latina*, 63–122, Madrid: Akal.
Prividera, Nicolás (2016), *El país del cine: para una historia política del nuevo cine argentino*, Córdoba: Los Ríos Editorial.
Sarlo, Beatriz (2011), 'El peronismo es tan indispensable como Borges', *La Nación*, 30 April 2011. https://www.lanacion.com.ar/opinion/el-peronismo-es-tan-indispensable-como-borges-nid1369124 (accessed 27 August 2019).
Schroeder, Paul A. (2007), 'Violence and Liberation in the Hour of the Furnaces', *Senses of Cinema*, 45, November 2007, http://sensesofcinema.com/2007/cteq/hour-furnaces/ (accessed 11 June 2019).
Schwarzmantel, John (2012), 'Rethinking Marxism and Nationalism in an Age of Globalization', *Rethinking Marxism: A Journal of Economics, Culture & Society*, 24 (1): 144–61.
Solanas, Fernando (2019), 'Repudiamos el contrato entre YPF y la empresa Horamar, subsidiarias de la multinacional Navios, para construir barcos y barcazas en Paraguay…' 20 September 2019, 7:22AM. Tweet (@fsolanas), https://twitter.com/fernandosolanas/status/1175052613714419714 (accessed 3 October 2019).
Stam, Robert (1998), 'The Two Avant-Gardes: Solanas and Getino's *The Hour of the Furnaces*', in Barry Keith Grant and Jeannette Sloniowski (eds), *Documenting the Documentary: Close Readings of Documentary Film and Video*, 271–86, Detroit: Wayne State University Press.
Tower Sargent, Lyman (1994), 'The Three Faces of Utopianism Revisited', *Utopian Studies*, 5 (1): 1–37.
Varghese, Robin (2018), 'Marxist World: What Did You Expect from Capitalism?', *Foreign Affairs*, 97 (4): 34–42.
Varoufakis, Yanis (2018), 'Marx Predicted Our Present Crisis – and Points the way Out', *The Guardian*, 20 April, https://www.theguardian.com/news/2018/apr/20/yanis-varoufakis-marx-crisis-communist-manifesto (accessed 27 July 2019).
Žižek, Slavoj (2001), 'Repeating Lenin', *Lacan.com*, https://www.lacan.com/replenin.htm (accessed 4 August 2019).

# 6

# Third Cinema after the turn of the millennium: Reification of the sign and the possibility of transformation

*Paulina Aroch Fugellie and André Dorcé*

Third Cinema cannot be reduced to a specific set of films, to certain modes of production or distribution, to the audiences it targets nor to its contemporaneous modes of reception and not even to the ideological programme it follows. 'Third Cinema', understood as the name given to a particular – yet dynamic – constellation of all of the above in the 1960s and 1970s, is a pre-eminently political project. It refers to films consciously produced in resistance to the Hollywood hegemony in Asia, Africa and, especially, Latin America during that period. Third Cinema is, perhaps more than any other, a *context-specific* political, aesthetic and ideological device. With historical contextuality at the very core of the Third Cinema project, the question of its existence, uses and misuses today becomes urgent.

Revisiting past and present instances of films within the Third Cinema tradition, in this chapter we set out to investigate to what degree and in what ways the critical potential of the 1960s and 1970s persists today or to what degree and in what ways it has been depoliticized, its critical edge converted into reified signs of emancipation. We will concentrate on a comparison between two films made by Chilean film director Patricio Guzmán. One of them is his 1975 film *La insurrección de la burguesía* (*The Insurrection of the Bourgeoisie*, first in the trilogy *La batalla de Chile* [*The Battle of Chile*]). The film documents Chilean political history in the making during Salvador Allende's democratically elected socialist government and up until the coup d'état, orchestrated by national and international private interest, the Chilean military and the CIA.

The documentary engages in a realistic or matter-of-fact narrative style delivered in the present continuous and focuses on the Chilean bourgeoisie's actions against Allende's government. The second film we will engage with is Guzman's 2004 film, *Salvador Allende*. Filmed in a much more evocative, almost lyrical style, this film revisits the events registered in *The Battle of Chile* but, rather than recording and reporting historical events as the former does, it provides a platform from which to reflect on Allende, the man; on the generation of Chileans in Chile and in exile whose lives were affected by the 1973 coup; and, especially, on questions of memory as a political performative and on artistic modes of representation. Since both films are made by the same author, both are documentaries and both focus on the same subject matter, while being three decades apart, the comparison offers us an 'all other things being equal' scenario, a ground from which to explore Third Cinema before and after the full implementation of neoliberalism around the globe.

In the spirit of Third Cinema itself, our analysis is not limited to formal exegesis. We are interested in the relationality between the films, their modes of production and reception and their participation in a wider discursive network, co-constitutive of broader economic, social and cultural circuits around the globe. With the tools of decolonial critique and cultural analysis, we implicitly interpellate the meanings that are put in and out of circulation by the concept and reality of Third Cinema in the era of 'cognitive capitalism' (Moulier-Boutang 2011). Above all, we are interested in exploring how Third Cinema as a semiotic, aesthetic and socio-political object withholds or liberates the possibility of *transformation* of the world around it, because, as Getino and Solanas (1970) wrote in the manifesto in which the term was coined, it is only through its own praxis that the militant cinematographic artwork may be appreciated.

# Transformative and conservative modalities of melodrama

*The Battle of Chile* trilogy was filmed while the events leading up to the 1973 coup d'état in Chile took place, recording the events as they happened.

Separated by neither time nor place from its object of investigation, this documentary is emphatically not an archival record, unlike *Salvador Allende*, Guzmán's lesser-known 2004 film. If the distinguishing trait of *The Battle of Chile* is its direct participation and enmeshment in 'real time' politics, its piercing presence in the middle of the unravelling of history, in the case of *Salvador Allende* the obstinate pursuit of that ever-fleeting past is what takes centre stage – an attempt, perhaps, at exploring the political potential of memory, the 'felicity' of which, to borrow J. L. Austin's term (1962), is to be explored here.

Both films attend – effective and affectively – to different and contrasting aesthetic strategies, while at the same time positioning themselves comfortably within the limits of the documentary realm. They do so by revisiting the same subject matter: the violently interrupted Chilean socialist revolution, some of its causes and repercussions as they unfold through different temporalities. We argue that the contrasting aesthetics of the films are not only the outcome of formal singularities but also the result of a complex set of relations between two different conjunctures: the socio-political configurations of the 1960s and 1970s, in the one case, and the early twenty-first century, in the other.

These divergent historical formations dialectically structure two singular contexts of production and reception, which in turn materialize in two different modalities of representational and decodifying practices. One of these modalities activates a series of potentially emancipatory readings (the transformative modality) and another one obfuscates such forms of decoding by means of a merely rhetorical mobilization of nostalgia (the conservative modality). We contend that both modalities can be read as articulating affective frameworks that display particular forms of melodrama that work differently in each (con)textual instance.

We understand melodrama as an episteme that tends to reduce and simplify (in a moralistic and emotional fashion) power struggles to a Manichean 'binarism', often disavowing complex causal relationships between processes, agents and contexts (Dorcé 2005). Yet 'melodrama' – as an umbrella term for particular modes of mobilizing affect across different media – is a device that, in itself, has no inherent transformative or conservative quality but a particular range of potentials that may be realized, or not, with particular uses and for particular aims in specific historical contexts. To borrow Raymond Williams's (1977) terminology, it may operate as a residual, dominant or emergent form at different times and according to the different uses to which it is put and the particular ways in which this is done. The category of melodrama will allow us to discern the activation of either conservative or transformative modalities of the two films before and after the neoliberal turn in world history, emblematically marked by the 11th September 1973 coup d'état in Chile.

## The transformative modality and *La insurrección de la burguesía*

Let us introduce Guzmán's 1975 film by way of a verbatim quote, using what Jonathan Gray (2010) would refer to as a *paratext* that, in its circulation, consolidates certain types of preferred readings of the text it refers to. Film critic Zuzana Pick writes in 1980:

> *The Insurrection of the Bourgeoise*, deals with the bourgeoisie's strategic change of policy at the moment when the people had reached the peak of their political involvement with Popular Unity [*Unidad Popular* – henceforth UP]. Guzmán illustrates the different battle fronts with concrete cases: the hoarding of basic necessities, the systematic interference by the bourgeois parties in Congress and their sabotage of the parliamentary process, the violence and social chaos stirred up by extreme rightist groups, such as *Patria y Libertad*, the offensive by the 'gremios' and the 76 days of the copper strike. The class struggle in Chile in 1973 is seen as cutting across the economic struggle, the political struggle, and the ideological struggle. After the people's victory in the miners' conflict, the bourgeoisie prepares itself for a coup d'état: the *Regimiento Blindado no. 2* with its armed tanks attacks *La Moneda* [The presidential house] and downtown Santiago [Chile's capital city]. While the *Tancazo* only lasts a few hours, an Argentinian cameraman, Leonardo Henricksen, finds himself on Agustinas Street and films his own death, along with 'the true face of Chilean fascism'. (Pick 1980: 24)

Pick's synopsis, written for a specialized international Anglophone audience on the left, in the times of Prime Minister Margaret Thatcher and President Elect Ronald Regan, is a fairly standard account of the generalized impression of what the film's most significant elements were in such circles in the 1980s. Pick's deployment of time as a grammatical and diegetic variable is particularly interesting. Her usage of the simple present tense (when narrating the 'action' scenes that precipitate towards the film's ending with Leonardo Henricksen's death) contributes a sense of immediacy, as if pointing to the facticity of the documentary itself, to the illusion it conveys of witnessing events as they occur in the here and now. This is reinforced by Pick's constant flow of authenticating detail, such as referring to the military attack as the '*Tancazo*' or specifying that Henricksen's death occurred 'on Agustinas Street'. Yet her choice of vocabulary ('the true face of Chilean fascism'), her superimposition of the mundane ('hoarding', 'strikes') with the abstract ('class struggle', 'ideological struggle') in a very quick succession and her closing metaphoric turn – which gives the filming of a fact and the filming of an idea equal standing – all speak about the retrospective, differed, nostalgic quality of Pick's gaze, as she shares it with an audience perhaps equally in need of recovering from that specific past which no longer has a place in the neoliberal regime of the 1980s.

From our own standpoint, today, we consider that *The Insurrection of the Bourgeoisie* – itself a form of representation – offers a modality to read the events it registered that differs from that by which it has been read and overwritten for three decades. As a reading device of the events it registers, the film neither seeks to hide its own mediation to create an illusion of immediacy nor does it channel the audience's affectivity towards nostalgia. More than working towards the recovery of a past potential or of presenting the past – in the sense of both exposing it and of making it present – *The Insurrection of the Bourgeoisie* does the work of dialectically allowing the viewer to engage with the immediacy of the recorded events, while also taking a strategic non-impartial distance from the diegetic events through the critical highlighting of its own symbolic and political mediation, conforming to what could be characterized as a Third Cinema ethos.

Guzmán's own reflexive approach to his mediation in the documentary is to be read in context. The class war in Chile that led to the institution of the first socialist president in world history to be elected via bourgeois democratic means also drove forward a revolutionary cultural project that gave an important role to the documentation of everyday life. The years leading up to Allende's electoral triumph were key to the development and implementation of cultural and communicational policies by the left, which sought to open up the space for documenting and revealing the ideological tropes that were set against the emancipation of the people. Bowen Silva (2008) has characterized this rational criticism of ideological illusion in Chile at the time as 'immunological', which also gives a sense of the urgency there was to record events as they were happening.[1] But while the unveiling of the opponent's ideological strategies through rational means – such as that which the documentary form promises – was of vital importance, the affective bond of the UP (the collective subject that brought Allende to power) and its utopian desire were equally important. Guzmán comments:

*The first year*, my opera prima, exposed – in an enthusiastic and celebratory way – the first twelve months of Allende's government, which in my country were lived as a true popular festivity. But in October 1972 the first bus owners' strike broke out. It was there that I perceived that the party was over. (Guzmán 1976)

---

[1]Peter Schumann refers to the cultural climate of that time in terms of a shared necessity to politicize and popularize cinema 'as a medium at the service of social transformation' (cited in Zarowsky 2008).

In an interview with Brazilian film critic José Carlos Avellar, Guzmán described his reaction to the events leading up to the establishment of Allende's government as a 'falling in love' which motivated him to abandon his original plans to direct fiction and change to documenting the situation around him; he also refers to that surrounding atmosphere at the time among Chileans as 'a collective being in love' (Avellar 2009). This libidinal energy at the heart of UP is not a decorative element but indivisible from its emergence as a grassroots movement and its unique condition as a socialist revolution through peaceful means. Jyostna Kapur in fact ventures the thesis that the reason why the United States – and the CIA in particular – decided to kill the UP's project was the enormous traction and attraction it would have for populations worldwide and the great difficulty to discredit it if allowed to live on, as opposed to Stalinism, to name the most contrasting example on the left (Kapur 2017).

The third part of *The Battle of Chile*, entitled *El poder popular [Popular Power]*, centres on spontaneous social actions at the time which sought to resist the boycott on Allende's government coming from the national and transnational right and, in that way, hinges on that 'collective being in love', whereas *The Insurrection of the Bourgeoisie*, centring on the attack from the right, does not. Nonetheless, *The Insurrection of the Bourgeoisie* does capture – and seems to be itself propelled by – that sense of driven social cohesion, vitality and mobility, which is reproduced in its accelerated rhythm and saturation of action, the quick and intense succession of scenes and the agitation of the shots. It is no coincidence that while the filming of the whole trilogy lasted only a year, its editing process (taking place in exile in Cuba) lasted six. The long editing process speaks – besides the difficulty of the conditions of exile in which it took place – of the importance that a thorough procedure of selection and organization of the material had for the director. Yet, such self-reflection – that is, the film's incursion into the sphere of the *meta* – is not merely a formalist exercise but the very core of its political dimension, as we shall analyse further below.

While exhibited in movie theatres in 34 countries worldwide and receiving an avalanche of prestigious awards abroad, in Chile itself the 1970s trilogy was shelved by censors for decades. It was the coup itself which put an end to the actual filming: Guzmán's small team 'started working on the 15th of October, 1972 and ended on the 11th of September, 1973 (the day of the coup)' (Guzmán 1976). Such is the imbrication of the film in the political sphere that the cameraman, Jorge Müller, was abducted by Pinochet's military police and is now counted among the 3,200 'disappeared' by Pinochet's government. In addition, Federico Elton, head of production, was detained for 24 hours at military facilities in Chile's capital city of Santiago, while Guzmán himself was detained for two weeks at the National Stadium in 1973, then used as a concentration camp by the Pinochet regime, with thousands of people imprisoned there, many of them tortured and killed.

Furthermore, as Pauline Kael has suggested, there is a sense in which it is not only the outward political events that shape the film's form and content but also the other way around: the film itself would appear to intervene in the unravelling of the events around it:

> Patricio Guzmán... has said, in an interview with Julianne Burton (in the magazine *Socialist Revolution*), that during the street battles he could anticipate what was going to happen and, standing next to the cameraman, tell him when to pan or lower the camera or raise it. That is, he was so attuned to the possibilities in the situation that it was almost as if he were directing the action. (Kael 1980: 387)

Another film critic, Louis Marcorelles, writing for *Le Monde* in the 1970s, grounds this idea in terms of the conditions of production of the documentary:

> Guzmán and four of his friends organized to follow, day to day, the Chilean political actuality with an almost military discipline... The field of actuality will be swept every morning, before going out to film, in such or such other precise place, guided by word of mouth: 'One must be present in every place where the political process unravels its most important phases, the most significant ones'. But, to his great concern, Guzmán, who had enthusiastically filmed the first two years of the Unidad Popular, is realizing, in his own words, that he is filming 'not only the revolution but the counterrevolution'. Events advance at such a vertiginous speed that the team, at a certain point, has the sense of desperately running after an unreachable reality. (Marcorrelles 1976a)

The degree and type of claim that this documentary makes on reality is different from that of emergent documentary film forms in the North Atlantic around the 1960s, such as Direct Cinema and *cinema vérité*. Thematically, it coincides with those tendencies in its concern with the social; stylistically, there also are similarities, for example, the handheld camera or the strong reliance on editing work. In the case of *The Battle of Chile*, this style is directly correlative with conditions of production and scarcity of means: a team of six with no experience in filming, a 16mm camera, a sound recorder, a microphone, a tripod, two chassis and three camera batteries, besides 44,000 feet of film and 134 virgin sound tapes donated to the Chilean team by the French documentarian Chris Marker.

The greatest contrast of this documentary with most films of Direct Cinema is its decided intent not to obscure its own mediation. The film has no pretence of accessing an ontological dimension of truth or reality, while at the same time it certainly does not operate in an ideological vacuum. Guzmán reflects:

It is not about making a film based exclusively on interviews: Direct Cinema – with its exaggerations – has imposed this on us many times. It is about the possibility of being present in the face of an event and filming it in all its audio-visual richness. I think that, in this sense, there is an opening up of something which is interesting to follow up and which can take us further beyond. (Guzmán cited in Marcorrelles 1976b)

This 'further beyond' is opened up, because the cinematographer's immersion in the audio-visual richness allows him to rediscover himself in the face of history. Lacking a pretence of 'objectivity', understood as an ontological truth, does not mean that the film is not positioned and radically so: it could more accurately be described as the glimpse of a subjective encounter in and with history as it unfolds, an attempt at a dialectical deployment of different sides of the events from a very grounded and recognized place of its own.

To illustrate, we may take Ignacio Rodríguez's observation that the sequence that covers the copper mineworkers' strike is overdetermined by the guidance of a *voiceover*: the images end up working as the 'incontestable proof' of what the voice is conveying. Rodríguez contends that 'the omniscient narrator expresses a partiality that guides an exclusive understanding of the facts exposed in the film. This does not nullify the validity of the argumentation, but suggests that the access to the real is not transparent' (Rodríguez 2010: 5). While Rodríguez considers *The Insurrection of the Bourgeoisie* overtly didactic, he reads Guzmán's oeuvre as becoming increasingly reflexive, poetic and subjective as the years go by; he thus finds in Guzmán's latter films greater space for transformative interpretations than in his earlier work.[2]

The degree of poetic abstraction of some of Guzmán's later films – such as *Nostalgia de la luz* (*Nostalgia for the Light*, 2010) or *El botón de nácar* (*The Pearl Button*, 2015) – has led most critics to partake in Rodríguez's view. Unlike that generalized reading of the Chilean director's oeuvre, we argue that this subjective turn corresponds with the advent of a relativizing epistemic regime that challenges all truth claims available in the public sphere as questionable (what could be seen as a neoliberal take on postmodernism). This is to say that Guzmán's position of assuming a non-ambiguous political stance through the deployment of an expositive and didactic voice was indeed far more potentially transformative in relation to its historical context of enunciation and social reception than a relativizing voice may be in the context of postmodernism or, more to the point, in the context of what Zygmunt Bauman (2000) calls liquid modernity.

---

[2]For instance, Rodríguez praises the transformation of the authoritative narrator's voice in *The Insurrection of the Bourgeoisie* to a 'group of subjective and individual voices that create a sense of community' in *Salvador Allende* (2010: 6).

Because form alone does not hold a transhistorical political value, but holds a series of potentials that may only be realized in a particular way in the dialectics it holds with particular contexts, to deem *The Insurrection of the Bourgeoisie*, Manichean speaks more of the present context of reception than of the film itself, understood as constituted by the producer-work-contemporary receptor triad. In this sense, there seems to be a gradual loss of socio-political effervescence and effectiveness in the reception contexts of Third Cinema films today, as the individuation techniques of neoliberalism increasingly colonize subjectivities worldwide. Third Cinema as a phenomenon of its time – and *The Insurrection of the Bourgeoisie* as paradigmatic of it – is today overdetermined by our nostalgic gaze, which it reflects back at us, as we reduce films to banners of times lost or look condescendingly at their pre-post-Enlightened discursive modes, reducing their representational styles to a sign of themselves rather than exploring, in context, their performative and transformative effects.

*The Insurrection of the Bourgeoisie* had a transformative effect in its contemporary context of reception – not in Chilean public space, which had been paralyzed by the bloody repression of Pinochet's military regime – but in mobilizing support for the resistance worldwide. This was partly possible because of how its aesthetic construction of political binaries channelled affect:

> What is characteristic of this film is its sociological perspective, in which individual actors are not the main focus... The film shows the struggle between the bourgeoisie and the proletariat, the *momios* and the people, the rich and the poor... the selected testimonies account for the joy and faith poor people on the streets have in the process [of the UP's imminent electoral triumph]. (Rodríguez 2010: 8)

The film includes testimonies from the opposition; there are steep socio-economic differences between interviewees. We hear testimony from the upper class, convinced that the right-wing liberal front will win the elections. Some of them candidly and passionately assert that the only way to revert the Chilean path to socialism is through the rule of democratic law. An angry woman shouts at the camera:

> They should impeach the president... and throw him out on May 21st. He's destroyed the country, ruined it! This is a corrupt, degenerate government. Degenerate, corrupt, filthy! All those dirty communists should get out of Chile!! On May 21st, thank God, we'll have the cleanest, finest government we've ever had! Democracy will win and we'll get rid of those rotten Marxist communists! Damn them!

The film thus creates a dramatic tension that relies on the derivative *pathos* produced by exhibiting the criminal violation of the socio-democratic pact by the right, the very same people that championed the primacy of the rule of law as the only legitimate path to political change. This is one of the most characteristic *modi operandi* of melodrama: displaying fundamental ideological differences as irreconcilable. In this way, the film articulates what we could define as 'tactical Manicheism', a way of leading emotional realism up to a moral and political disjunctive.

In such 'tactical Manicheism' we observe a performative use of representational tools which is not dissimilar from what postcolonial theorist Gayatri Spivak has termed 'strategic essentialism' (1993). In order to elaborate further on how Guzmán's 1975 film operates in what we have termed a transformative modality of representation, in the next section we will introduce his 2004 film and engage in a comparative contrast of both films, while revisiting Spivak's take on representation as a transformative action.

## The conservative modality and *Salvador Allende*

In a review for *the New York Times*, Manohla Dargis writes:

> *Salvador Allende* is the Chilean filmmaker Patricio Guzmán's plaintive look back at the rise and violent fall of the world's first democratically elected Marxist president. Mr. Guzmán's... passion informs the filmmaking in this documentary dirge, a memento mori about 'the other Sept. 11' that's drenched in revolutionary tears but lacking much in the way of historical and political insight. In the movie's eloquent opener, Mr. Guzmán speaks in voice-over while he rifles through a battered wallet. This, he explains, is almost all that remains of Allende. In the scenes that follow, the documentarian restlessly circles back to Allende, envisioning him as a structuring absence that hovers over the country like a ghost, shaping even its troubling silence about the past. For Mr. Guzmán the present, which he shoots in serviceable colour with some nice detail, holds little evident appeal. What gives the film a pulse, enlivening both it and his actual voice, are the black-and-white archival images of cheering workers and youth on the march, visuals that melt into a blur of placards, fists and smiles. (Dargis 2007)

Earlier, we introduced *The Insurrection of the Bourgeoisie* by way of another long quotation denoting the textual configurations of the film that were privileged in conventional readings. With this synopsis of *Salvador Allende*

(2004), however, we aim at rescuing an unusual take on the film that found its way into mainstream media. Against the prevalent view of the film as a political performative – by way of its voguish excursus into memory – Dargis's tongue-in-cheek comments point to how the film's retrospective gaze actually depoliticizes the events of 11th September 1973. Not only does nostalgia determine the formal stylistics of Guzmán's 2004 film but memory itself is thematized as the main labour that the film exerts; and, centrally, there is a will to characterize this labour as the place of the political 'real'. To assess the form of claim made on reality by each of the films, we now return to the question of the conservative versus the transformative modality of representation at different points in Guzmán's personal history, in Chilean history and in world history.

The closing scene of *The Insurrection of the Bourgeoisie*, repeated as the opening scene of *El golpe de estado* (*The Coup d'Etat*, 1976; part 2 of *The Battle of Chile*), is footage of the assassination of Argentinean cameraman, Leonardo Henricksen by the military as he recorded the failed coup on Allende on 29th June 1973 (figure 6.1). We will examine this scene in order to explore the relation between representative and transformative modalities of the film at the moment of the Chilean coup – paradigmatically known as the inaugural moment of neoliberalism worldwide – in comparison with the film tracing the 1973 events, thirty years later. To do so, we first take a detour to the problem of representation via Spivak's classic 'Can the Subaltern Speak' (1994).

**FIGURE 6.1** *Cameraman Leonardo Henricksen is shot by the military as he recorded the failed coup on Allende.*

Building on a strategic re-reading of Karl Marx's *Eighteenth Brumaiere of Louis Napoleon* ([1897] 2005), Spivak distinguishes two categories: 'representation as "speaking for," as in politics, and representation as mimesis' (Spivak 1994: 70). These two forms may be distinguished by the German words *Vertretung* and *Darstellung*, respectively. The first refers to representation as an act of persuasion, which is transformative; the second to representation as a trope, descriptive rather than transformative (Spivak 1994: 72). Therefore, Spivak argues, contrary to common opinion, Karl Marx discusses a social subject whose consciousness – that is, his self-representation (*Darstellung*), which grants him a subject status – and the political representation (*Vertretung*) of whom are dislocated (Spivak 1994: 74–5). In this way, not only is the subject in Marx a dislocated entity but 'class' also emerges as a non-essentialist category, since it is defined relationally (in relation to other classes). Hence, to analyse class agency or class transformation is only to propose the replacement of something that is always already conceived as artificial (Spivak 1994: 71, 74).

In Spivak's view, the work of poststructuralist authors, operating outside the Marxist tradition, such as Gilles Deleuze, is only pseudo-radical because in it acts of *Darstellung* (e.g. the representative acts of an author writing about subaltern subjects) are often claimed to be acts of political *Vertretung*. Spivak affirms that as long as these two forms of representation are conflated, in the sense that the descriptive takes the place of the transformative to simulate its existence while in fact foreclosing the possibility, there can be no true transformation in critical consciousness (Spivak 1994: 70–3). When *Darstellung* and *Vertretung* are conflated, transformation is foreclosed and hegemony reinforced since a rhetorical gesture towards representing the other dissimulates and thus perpetuates the lack of a *de facto* representation of his or her class interests (Spivak 1994: 70–5). More than enabling emancipatory change, representation of this kind forecloses transformation by emulating and emptying out emancipatory discourse.

The last and most paradigmatic part of Spivak's text is an inquiry into the problem of representation through the drama of Bhuvaneswari Bhaduri, the subaltern who, for reasons of class, race and gender, is excluded from any form of participation in the symbolic order which, for Spivak, is identical to the hegemonic order. Spivak analyses a subaltern group associated to *sati* (widow self-immolation) in the context of colonial India (Spivak 1994: 94–103). She explores three representations of sati – by the Hindi patriarchy, by the British imperialists and by Bhaduri – and how none of them are able to represent the subaltern.

Bhaduri is a young revolutionary woman in India's struggle for independence. She is asked to carry out a political assassination. Feeling unprepared to kill but also unwilling to commit treason, she opts for suicide. However, given that the usual reason for a young unmarried woman to commit suicide was pregnancy out of wedlock, Bhaduri waits for menstruation before committing the act. But, still, her family distorts the history of her death, attributing it to illicit pregnancy (Spivak 1994: 104). Unable to intervene in the symbolic hegemony, the only way in which Bhaduri can attempt to be heard is by killing herself and turning her body into the material support of discourse. Without access to the chain of signifiers that constitutes the symbolic order, Bhaduri cannot be heard; that is to say, she cannot access the subject position of enunciation.

We have proposed elsewhere (Aroch Fugellie 2015) that another political suicide – Salvador Allende's – the content matter of both of Guzmán's films, but particularly *Salvador Allende*, holds an interesting comparison to Bhaduri's suicide, under Spivak's interpretation. Surrounded by the Chilean military forces, led by Pinochet and supported by the CIA, Allende chose to sacrifice his life rather than surrender, arguing that he had given his word to those he represented to fulfil their mandate, of which he was only the representative. Similarly to Spivak's subaltern, Allende is reduced to a position in which the hegemonic text (of transnational capital, in this case) can only be rewritten with the body, with blood and at the cost of one's life. As in the case of Bhaduri's suicide, Allende's self-sacrifice will be rewritten by hegemony.

Nonetheless, an important difference between the two figures persists. Bhaduri is in a position of absolute subalternity; Allende is head of state. In the case of Bhaduri, the word that is not heard is her own, and she must sacrifice her life in the hope of being heard. Allende is in a position of access to the symbolic order. Yet he is also a subject that represents a collective subaltern other. With his last act, Allende validates that collective subaltern other as a subject of enunciation and takes his own life to reduce himself to being the material support for the enunciation of that collective to prevail. In other words, Allende privileges his role as representative standing in for the Unidad Popular over his own life, over his role as an individual subject. His last action traces the profound political and ontological implications of the act of representation. Taken, under the circumstances, to the ultimate limit, this act of representation, in order to be fulfilled felicitously, requires that Allende reduce himself to a signifier, in order for the Unidad Popular project as signified to live on and in order to felicitously and radically represent those who voted him into office.

This potent sacrificial gesture is also intelligible in both films when read through the optics of melodrama, which works here in two layers. First, it guides the affective compass of the films towards an identification with Allende and the UP as the positive element of a Manichean equation. In *Salvador Allende*, this identification is elicited from the very first scene when we are confronted with Allende's remaining possessions – namely, his glasses – that trace of the subject that was and is no longer, the glasses that were so characteristic of how the man looked, but which also point to the idea

FIGURE 6.2 *Salvador Allende's broken glasses*.

of how Allende saw the world (figure 6.2). In the case of *The Insurrection of the Bourgeoisie*, we can think of how Allende's supporters, glorified in scenes of celebratory enthusiasm, elicit the audience's empathy, while the anti-democratic, interventionist impetus of the opposition generates a pathos which, for the audience, is linked to the unfortunate outcome of the events the documentary narrates. Such moral topology – notwithstanding its ethical assertiveness – works by rendering the narrative of a unique historical conjuncture where the conflation of progressive class interests (those of the subaltern peasants and workers aligned with those of middle-class professionals) antagonize in an emotional affective *pathos* with the pro-capitalist interests of the mighty oligarchy.[3]

As in many other audiovisual instances analysed across diverse cultural contexts, melodrama builds up much of its symbolic effectiveness by portraying victimhood as a legitimate transitional position towards moral superiority, especially when associated with conventional forms of realism, as in the case of the documentary genre, where the notion of 'modified melodrama' operates. As Ravi Vasudevan puts it:

---

[3]Of course, we do not consider the melodramatic mode as an essentially regressive or excessive cultural form but as a constitutive matrix of popular culture (thus subjectification) with a particular history in Latin America (see Dorcé 2005).

I group this problem of modified melodrama, melodrama's (culturally verisimilar) calibration to realism, and melodrama as a system for integrating *pathos* and action to highlight a particular way in which melodrama, rather than being a system of excess, increasingly appears to acquire the status of a highly adaptable normative system. In my reading, to remain a productive analytical category, melodrama has to enact a large-scale gesture towards the moral domain based on its engagement with a situation of victimhood. (Vasudevan 2010: 23)

Subalternity, characterized both in a conservative and in a transformative modality in the case of Guzmán's films analysed here, operates under the melodramatic ethos.

Second, the revelatory gesture of Allende's suicide – as a way of becoming a signifier but also a martyr – unveils Allende's real identity to the eyes of those who questioned the extent of his political commitment to the subaltern cause. It also reinforces his followers' impression of him as the key articulating figure for the whole movement. Using Martín Barbero's (1993) notion, the 'drama of recognition' is constitutive here of the UP's potential future in the people's sociological imagination to the extent of feeding the transformative potential of *The Battle of Chile* in its contemporaneous context of reception.

As its title suggests, *Salvador Allende* focuses on the figure of the Chilean president, yet the drama of recognition here operates complementarily as a sort of melodramatic reconstitution of Guzmán's audiovisual *memoire*. Thus, producing an alternate point of entry to the actual recognition of Allende's pivotal role as a political signifier in the 1960s and 1970s and as an object of longing, loss and impossibility (in its utopian potential) within the neoliberal context of the first decade of the twenty-first century in Chile.

The cinematographic act of representation that *Salvador Allende* entails operates in an almost opposite way to Allende's last act. The truth that Allende makes real through his suicide is that he is nothing but a signifier. He may only operate as meaningful sign when dialectically attached to his signified – the historical subject for which he stands. Moreover, his last performative statement, from the perspective of pragmatic semiotics to which we adhere, can only produce its intended meaning in the historical context in which it took place. Guzmán's 2004 film reads like an attempt to capture the forcefulness and meaning that signifier 'Allende' potentially holds in an era in which the UP project has been rampantly eliminated by the neoliberal world order and the Chilean coup as its cornerstone.

Explicitly produced as a homage to Allende, the film attaches itself not only to Allende as signifier but to a series of other signifiers, the signifieds of which seem to always escape the cinematographer's grasp. Not because certain names and images are not still attached to specific meanings but because a melancholic appreciation of the past, as well as an orthodox teleologic reading of history, does not allow for the actualization of its original meaning in the context of 2004. For instance, the sequence of a man running as he pulls a wagon filled with stuff, as he gathers momentum the wagon pushes him forward, making the man seem as if he were floating (figure 6.3). The scene conveys the idea of a man being pushed forward (to the left) by the inertia he initially created by pulling the car. Once history is given the adequate pull, it will push you progressively to the future, the allegory seems to suggest. By 2004, it was clear that history did not follow that linear path towards socialism. The sequence is further reaffirmed by an overlapping travelling shot of men being transported by a carriage pulled by a horse as they scream repeatedly: 'Workers in Power, Workers in Power! Popular Unity against criminal mummies!', 'mummies' being Chilean lingo for 'conservatives'.

A solipsistic attachment to signifiers prevails over their function, hence habilitating a potentially depoliticizing experience. Such an alleged portrayal of the past is in fact more telling of the present which, as Byung-Chul Han (2010) has observed, is characterized by a sensibility of melancholia, disorientation and reification of the lost object of desire.

Since Third Cinema's political edge is linked up to its function as a particular text in articulation with its contexts of production and reception, Guzman's 2004 film, consecrated as art cinema, with its well-established director, its high production costs, its circulation among a knowledgeable

FIGURE 6.3 *Floating wagoner.*

elite and its nostalgic embrace of a politically militant past cannot be characterized as an incursion in Third Cinema. Rather, the reification – and sublimation – of politics as memory, as a labour limited to the realm of the subjective, places the film decidedly outside the boundaries of Third Cinema as a political project, which is not to say that a new Third Cinema, what could be called a Fourth Cinema, re-examining the proper place of 'the political' cannot or should not be imagined. Perhaps, with the lessons learnt from the generation of the 1960s and 1970s, and taking into account the narrative and aesthetics of *Salvador Allende*, today we could put forward that subjectivity and affect, as collective, social phenomena are, in fact, the proper starting point of 'the political'.

*Salvador Allende* concentrates on memory's ideological function and on the recuperation of the realm of subjectivity, as well as on affective re-articulation – all of which it casts as central to our political selves. This certainly offers a potential for re-imagining a politically operative project in the neoliberal world: a project that privileges the coherence and integrity of the thinking, sensible, emotional (collective) subject in its political pursuits. Yet today's world, overdetermined by capital's tireless capacity to turn opposing actions and discourses into commodities, to turn films and their reception into cultural, symbolic and academic goods, makes such a task a difficult – perhaps an impossible – one. This is not to say that we should not – in the utopian spirit of Third Cinema – push for the realization of Getino and Solanas's (1970) original promise that cinema always already entails a praxis that can be leveraged for emancipatory social transformation.

# Conclusions

The closing scene of *The Insurrection of the Bourgeoisie* gives us insight to the particular relation that the documentary as a form of representation holds with the realm of reality. *The Insurrection of the Bourgeoisie* does not merely operate as a descriptive act (*Darstellung*), but as a transformative one (*Vertretung*): the assassination of the cameraman inscribes the making of the film as a political threat to certain characters in the diegesis. The act of filming the historical events alters the course of that history, as it does with external historical agents represented in it, which in turn interpellates the means of their own representation in the most violent way possible: killing the cameraman and thus putting an end to the shoot, at the same time as that action, brings him into the field of diegesis and determines its trajectory. With the soldier responding to the camera shoot with a gunshot, the scene gives depth to the semantic continuity between both understandings of what 'shooting' does. In both cases, it is an action, a political one, a life or death one.

This scene thus also gives us insight to the particular relation that the documentary as a form of representation holds to the realm of the real (in the Lacanian understanding of the term (see Lacan 1949): the realm of death as something much deeper than reality, as a hovering presence that shapes reality yet is not in it, cannot be grasped by it. For these reasons, we can say that the final shot of *The Insurrection of the Bourgeoisie* encapsulates the realm of the real at its purest. Not because it presents unmediated reality to us but precisely because of the opposite: because of its enormous degree of mediation and also because of how it points to the subjects and instruments of mediation as existing in a continuum with the subjects and events to be represented.

The cameraman is displaced from being a transparent point of observation to becoming a character in the diegesis and a traumatic point of presentation of death as the ultimate real. The soldier becomes displaced from being a character in the diegesis to becoming the structural enabler of what we can and cannot see in the shot. It reveals that signs are not a set of things outside reality, nor even a set of things in reality, but a potential *function* of *any* thing in reality. According to the Peircean principle that a sign is one thing that represents another thing for someone, the scene highlights the instability of signs which take up different functions and so bring forth as well our own roles as audience, as the 'for someone' necessary to complete the production of meaning in the pragmatic semiotic structure. If the act of representation is always already a political one, then by virtue of our participation in the completion of meaning, and as structural enables of the filming in the first place, we are interpellated as political subjects.

The shot with which the documentary ends, as mentioned earlier, is hypermediated in a number of ways. First and foremost, it is edited post-facto. It is emphatically not the cameraman of the Guzmán crew that is shot but another cameraman, and at a previous coup attempt. So, rather than indexing the reality of the filmmaking of *The Insurrection of the Bourgeoisie*, it indexes the 'real' in the Lacanian sense of the term, the real potential outcome of events as they film, the real risks and fears, that which is at stake beyond the visible and beyond factual reality in the strict sense. The inclusion of the scene is a *meta*-act of representation. It shows the director's deliberate sculpturing of a narrative and the placing of it as a closure to the film, as the crafting of a forceful emphasis on the continuity between *Vertretung* and *Darstellung*, on their alignment and on the presentation and placing of the shot as an act of *representation*: not unmediated reality but participation in it.

We have taken what we characterize as a polyptych approach to Patricio Guzmán's oeuvre that has allowed us to comparatively analyse two specific films produced and consumed in different conjunctures: the distinguishing trait of *The Insurrection of the Bourgeoisie* is its enmeshment in living politics, which highlights the importance of the present, the possibility of transformation, of forging a different future. In the case of *Salvador Allende*, its elusive persecution of memory operates as a defining characteristic. Not only does nostalgia determine its formal stylistics but also memory itself is thematized as the main labour that the film exerts. Centrally, there is a will to characterize this labour as political. But it is infelicitous in a contemporary world context where all too easily such images are converted into reified signs of emancipation. However, taken as polyptych cluster, Guzmán's work – notwithstanding some of the contradictions identified here – mobilizes many contextually determined readings that could potentially enable utopian projects. The recourse to Allende as a politically operative memory in the recent uprisings of October 2019 in Chile attests to this potential.

Understood as a context-specific phenomenon, Third Cinema does not, *cannot* operate today, because Third Cinema is not a thing but a function of and in history. Guzmán's films examined here address the moment of change from representation as a tool for liberation to representation as one of the most value-making co-optable elements of the contemporary economic system. And yet the memory of the Unidad Popular, in cinematographic representation, continues to re-emerge as a flag in the political landscape of the present, of the future in the making. In this context, Allende's last words superimposed on images of the one million Chileans taking the streets of Santiago circulated on social media, through memes, pictures and videos in October 2018, are reminiscent of Guzmán's two documentaries; the views of his oeuvre on YouTube, particularly of *The Battle of Chile*, have increased exponentially since the uprisings began. Both of Guzmán's incursions in the documentary melodramatic mode analysed here seem to continue to mobilize affect against the grain of the neoliberal project. The struggle for hegemony in the symbolic, affective and libidinal spheres goes on in the streets of Chile as we sign off these lines. The outcome of the forty-six-year-old ideological struggle is yet to be decided.

# Bibliography

Aroch Fugellie, Paulina (2015), *Promesas irrealizadas: el sujeto del discurso poscolonial y la nueva división internacional del trabajo*, Mexico City: Siglo XXI.

Austin, John L. (1962), *How to Do Things with Words*, Oxford: Clarendon.

Avellar, José Carlos and Patricio Guzmán, Interview included in the 2009 DVD set of *La batalla de Chile*, Icarus Films.

Bauman, Zygmunt (2000), *Liquid Modernity*, Cambridge: Polity Press.

Bernades, Horacio and Patricio Guzmán (2004), Interview, 'Ya en 1972 percibí que la fiesta se había terminado' *Pagina 12*, 22 June. Available online: https://www.pagina12.com.ar/diario/espectaculos/6-37051-2004-06-22.html (accessed 19 September 2019).

Bowen Silva, Martín (2008), 'El proyecto sociocultural de la izquierda chilena durante la Unidad Popular. Crítica, verdad e inmunología política', *Nuevo Mundo. Mundos Nuevos*. Available online: https://journals.openedition.org/nuevomundo/13732 (accessed 22 October 2019).

Dargis, Manohla (2007), 'Clinging to Memories of a Ghost Who Haunts Chile', *The New York Times*, 5 September. Available online: https://www.nytimes.com/2007/09/05/movies/05salv.html (accessed 19 September 2019).

Dorcé, André (2005), 'The Politics of Melodrama: The Historical Development of the Mexican Telenovela, and the Representation of Politics in the Telenovela "Nada Personal," in the Context of Transition to Democracy in Mexico', Ph.D. diss., London: Goldsmiths College, University of London.

Getino, Octavio and Fernando Solanas (1970), 'Toward a Third Cinema', *Cinéaste* 4 (3): 1–10.

Gray, J. (2010), *Show Sold Separately: Promos, Spoilers, and Other Media Paratexts*, New York: New York University Press.

Guzmán, Patricio (1976), *Interview with Louis Marcorelles*, Paris: Le Monde, Available online: https://www.patricioguzman.com/es/peliculas/la-batalla-de-chile-i-ii-iii (accessed 19 September 2019).

Guzmán, Patricio (2004), *Interview with Horacio Bernardes*, 'Ya en 1972 percibí que la fiesta se había terminado' *Pagina 12*, 22 June. Available online: https://www.pagina12.com.ar/diario/espectaculos/6-37051-2004-06-22.html (accessed 19 September 2019).

Guzmán, Patricio (2009), *Interview with José Carlos Avellar*, DVD set of *La batalla de Chile*, Icarus Films.

*El botón de nácar* (2015), [Film], Dir. Patricio Guzmán, Chile: Atacama Productions and Valdivia Films.

Han, Byung-Chul (2010), *The Burnout Society*, Stanford: Stanford University Press.

Kael, Pauline (1980), *When the Lights Go Down*, New York: Holt, Rinehart and Winston.

Kapur, Jyostna (2017), 'When Time Pauses: Patricio Guzmán and the Third Cinema's Confrontation with Neoliberalism', *Pathways Out of Neoliberalism: Dystopia and Utopia in Contemporary Latin American Documentary Sawyer Seminars: Documentary Media and Historical Transformations*, [lecture] The Center for Documentary Research and Practice, Indiana University. Available online: https://cdrp.mediaschool.indiana.edu/conference/pathways-out-of-neoliberalism/ (accessed 24 October 2019).

*La batalla de Chile: El poder popular* (1976), [Film] Dir. Patricio Guzmán, Chile-Venezuela-France-Cuba: Patricio Guzmán.

*La batalla de Chile: La insurreccion de la burguesia* (1975), [Film] Dir. Patricio Guzmán Chile-Venezuela-France-Cuba: Patricio Guzmán.

*La batalla de Chile: La lucha de un pueblo sin armas* (1979), [Film] Dir. Patricio Guzmán, Chile-Venezuela-France-Cuba: Patricio Guzmán.

Lacan, Jacques (1949), 'Le stade du miroir comme formeteur de la fonction du je, telle quelle nous est révélée dans l'expérience psychanalytique', Communication faite au XVIe Congrès international de psychanalyse, à Zurich le 17-07-1949. Première version parue dans la Revue Française de Psychanalyse 1949, vol. 13, n° 4: 449–55.

Marcorelles, Louis (1976a), 'La lute des classes filmée comme un paysage', Paris: Le Monde.
Marcorelles, Louis (1976b), 'La mise en images des contradictions del Unite populaire', Paris: Le Monde, 20 May.
Martín Barbero, Jesús (1993), *Communication, Culture and Hegemony: From the Media to Mediations*, Elizabeth Fox and Robert A. White (trans.), London: Sage.
Marx, Karl ([1897] 2005), *The Eighteenth Brumaire of Louis Bonaparte*, D.D.L. (translator). Berlin and New York: Mondial.
Moulier-Boutang, Yann (2011), *Cognitive Capitalism*, Cambridge: Polity Press.
*Nostalgia de la luz* (2010), [Film], Dir. Patrico Guzmán, Chile: Atacama Productions.
Pick, Zuzana M. (1980), 'A Special Section on Chilean Cinema', *Ciné Tracts. A Journal of Films and Cultural Studies*, 3 (1): 18–34.
Rodríguez, Ignacio (2010), 'Giro subjetivo en el documental latinoamericano: el caso de Patricio Guzmán', *Revista Imagofagia. Asociación Argentina de Estudios de Cine y Audiovisual*, 2. Available online: www.asaeca.org/imagofagia
Spivak, Gayatri Chakravorty (1993), *Outside in the Teaching Machine*, Nueva York: Routledge.
Spivak, Gayatri Chakravorty (1994), 'Can the Subaltern Speak?', in Patrick Williams and Laura Chrisman (eds), *Colonial Discourse and Post-Colonial Theory. A Reader*, 66–111, New York: Columbia University Press.
Vasudevan, Ravi (2010), *The Melodramatic Public: Film Form and Spectatorship in Indian Cinema*, Ranikhet: Permanent Black.
Williams, Raymond (1977), *Marxism and Literature*, New York: Oxford University Press.
Zarowsky, Mariano (2008), 'Cine, política e intelectuales. En torno a La Spirale de Armand Mattelart', *Cuadernos Críticos de Comunicación y Cultura*, 4, Buenos Aires. Available online: https://www.pagina12.com.ar/diario/espectaculos/6-37051-2004-06-22.html (accessed 21 October 2019).

# 7

# We have never been transnational: The female condition in socialist realism, postsocialism and Third Cinema

## *Lucian Tion*
## *(National University of Singapore)*

In the 1960s, during a time when the world was still divided in three ideological camps that roughly represented the capitalist, socialist and postcolonial worlds, cinema played an important part in forging ties between the spheres considered in the jargon of the time as 'in development' and 'underdeveloped', the rough equivalent of the Second and the Third Worlds coined by Alfred Sauvy in 1952.

In this chapter I look at what I consider are the interweaving connections between postcolonial and socialist cultures, which led, I argue, to aesthetic borrowings that deeply impacted the themes and look of the cinemas of Asia and Eastern Europe but also that of the postcolonial world. More specifically, I argue that the themes, style and goals of socialist realism, the cultural arm of state socialism in the Eastern bloc and China, influenced Third Cinema despite the current slippage of socialist realism into disrepute. I further posit that the hybrid of anti-imperialist filmmaking which was personified in the mutual affinity between postcolonial and socialist cinemas in turn influenced the postsocialist one.

To highlight the similarities in methodological approach between these styles, I look at four apparently disconnected films: *Bai Mao Nu* (*The White

Haired Girl) produced in 1950 in China representing a solid paradigm of socialist realism; Humberto Solas's *Lucia* of 1968, which is a defining work of Third Cinema despite its being released a year before the manifesto written by Fernando Solanas and Octavio Getino ([1969] 2000); Zhang Yimou's *Hong Gaoliang (Red Sorghum)* of 1988, which reprises in post-Mao Reform and Opening Up China the feminist motifs used abundantly in the so-called worker-peasant-soldier films of the socialist period; and finally, one of the flagships of the Romanian New Wave, *4 luni, 3 săptămâni și 2 zile (4 Months, 3 Weeks and 2 Days)*, directed by Cristian Mungiu and released in 2007.

In this comparative approach I focus on the theme of women's empowerment and how this was handled by postcolonial, socialist and postsocialist cineastes in order to show the resemblances in aesthetics and content that defined these eras and movements. I start by outlining the theoretical approach of contemporary film theorists who attempt to disengage Romanian and Chinese cinema (maybe the foremost representatives of postsocialism in what used to be the 'Eastern bloc') from the erstwhile Marxist theories which birthed socialist realism by maintaining that postsocialist films have been hybridized with First Cinema to achieve a transnational state. For this reason they claim that Chinese and Romanian New Wave films should be regarded as integral part of World Cinema, a Western-designated category that was allegedly enriched after the collapse of socialism in 1989 by the addition of the former Second World to the postcolonial project. I then move on to discuss *Lucia*, which should be seen, despite arguments criticizing revolutionary Cuban cinema for its inability to transcend local gender issues, as incorporating motifs present in socialist cinema, which in turn influenced filmmaking in the postcolonial world. In conclusion, against scholarly positions trying to integrate what used to be anti-imperialist filmmaking to World Cinema, I argue that in the forcibly neoliberal world of the twenty-first century, films from the postsocialist and postcolonial countries still make up a loose, yet common 'bloc', whose aesthetic starkly differentiates them from the corpus of First Cinema. Finally, I posit that the 'coalition' between the 'posts' of colonialism and socialism, as Katherine Verdery referred to it, continues in the age of omnipresent neoliberalism to counter through its inheritance, aesthetics and narratology the First Cinema model personified by the otherwise unstoppable proliferation of Hollywood, as well as that of World Cinema, to which these films have been forcefully and wrongly assimilated.

## Westernizing Chinese cinema

Academics of varied research backgrounds have recently tried to identify a transnational turn in the neoliberal consensus that seems to have taken over the postsocialist world after the demise of state socialism in the early 1990s. In her book *From Tian'anmen to Times Square*, Gina Marchetti makes the case that fifth-generation Chinese cinema has finally entered the hall of fame of high culture, and therefore World Cinema, through the work of Zhang Yimou, who, in his female-centred trilogy *Red Sorghum*, *Ju Dou* and *Da Hong Denglong Gaogao Gua* (*Raise the Red Lantern*), produced in 1988, 1990 and 1991, respectively, has ensured that themes which have been up until then accessible only to Chinese audiences have not only been made available to the world at large but they also led to a liberation of Chinese women. Passionate about this shift from local to global exposure, Marchetti states that 'Zhang Yimou's films cross borders because of their ability to shift gears as they circulate on different screens globally' (Marchetti 2006: 4) by which the American scholar intimates that these films approach female sexuality from a point of view that makes this topic assimiliable to the more general condition of the woman in capitalist societies. Marchetti goes on to quote another theorist of Chineseness and Chinese language cinema, Rey Chow, who, writing on the same subject, states that Yimou's films 'wish to liberate Chinese women, which seems to be the content shift into the liberation of China which shifts into the liberation of the image of China on film, which shifts into the liberation of China on film in the international culture market, and so on' (Marchetti 2006: 4).

The first problem with this statement is that, without probably intending to do so, the two theorists commit an apology for globalization and promote a universalized rather than localized way of understanding feminism. The second problem is that the theme of female liberation has been a mainstay of Maoist cinema since at least the nationalization of the film industry in 1949. If we are to take a cursory look at some earlier examples of film from the Mao era, we will immediately come to the conclusion that Yimou's films do not liberate either women or the 'Chinese image', as claimed by Chow, because, put very simply, the Chinese woman and the Chinese image, inasmuch as onscreen feminism goes, have never been imprisoned, particularly if we employ in this analysis a Marxian prism of class struggle in understanding social relations.

Finally, what is immanently problematic with the argument cited above is the fact that the two theorists in fact put a Western spin on Chinese feminism, and Chinese society at large. This is a postcolonial attitude that has been observed by many critics of Western feminism in Asia. Writing about the Middle East, Deepa Kumar calls the actions of contemporary feminists 'imperialist'. Noticing that the Western NGO sector in some countries has become more powerful than the state, Kumar sees 'imperialist feminism simply as liberation at gunpoint' (Kumar 2019). Furthermore, in *Do Eastern Women Need Saving?* Egyptian activist Lila Abu-Lughod writes: 'Generalizing about cultures prevents us from appreciating or even accounting for people's experiences and the contingencies with which we all live' (Abu-Lughod 2013: 6). Observing that Western feminism is projecting

Western problems onto Eastern landscapes, she further warns that the valuable work of many local Middle-Eastern feminists was subverted and their power erased by Western feminists pushing onto their territory and replacing local activism with Western-bred goals and tactics, an action which, given the local context, cannot be seen in any other way but imperialist.

It would not be an exaggeration to equate the criticism of these theorists of the Middle East with those of Marchetti and Chow, who, even though eminent scholars of China, fail to ascertain the connection between the progressive programme of Mao's Chinese cinema and its postsocialist aftermath. To establish this connection, we need only take a comparative look at Zhang Yimou's *Red Sorghum* released in 1988 and *The White Haired Girl*, an eminently feminist film directed by Wang Bin and Choui Khoua, who belonged to the first generation of Communist directors in China, and was produced in 1950. While the former represents Yimou's breakthrough on the global market and was sanctioned by a majority of critics and scholars for bringing into the open the plight of women under hard labour conditions and oppressing patriarchy, the latter film is currently seen as nothing but a typical product of the Party propaganda that ultimately led to the enslavement of women despite the film's otherwise emancipatory battle cry.

In *Red Sorghum*, Zhang Yimou focuses sympathetically on his female lead, who at an early age is forced, following ancestral traditions, into an arranged marriage. As bad luck would have it, her future husband is not only far from her choice in consort but also a leper and an owner of a sorghum distillery. After endless tribulations caused by bandits who add to the dramatics of the situation, the unnamed female character becomes the de facto head of the household, which, after years of intense labour and ingenuity, she manages to turn financially successful. An adaptation of an earlier novel written in the post-Mao Reform and Opening Up years of the 1980s by Nobel Prize laureate Mo Yan, *Red Sorghum* is cleverly shot in a warm-tinted palette by Changwei Gu, who would go on to act as cinematographer on *Ju Dou* and *Baweng Bie Ji (Farewell My Concubine)*. The warm colours and the meditative pace of the story melodramatically told in flashback by the heroine's grandson contrasted sharply in 1988, when the film came out, with the previous era black-and-white, unidimensional heroes of Mao's gritty cinema. This has also made Western critics embrace Zhang Yimou as 'the auteur [who] burst onto the international stage with a stunning debut that would help usher in a new era for China's nascent film industry' (Kerr 2019).

If one would take a closer look at the apparent rupture between China's by then eighty-year-old 'nascent industry' and what would become the postsocialist era, one would quickly notice, however, that what appeared in *Red Sorghum* as the female character's celebrated transformation from semi-slave into business owner, in all its emancipatory intent, was not as groundbreaking as the international press made it out to be. Put side-by-side with Mao's feminist sagas of the 1950s, one would observe that Yimou's film is in fact developed out of the very motifs that stood at the centre of the CPR's Marxist philosophy, in which the abolition of feudal relations took centre stage. Unsurprisingly, so did the condemnation of arranged marriage and the liberation of women from their enslaved condition, which characterized these relations during the Qing dynasty.

This is in fact the central plotline of earlier films of similar nature, of which *The White Haired Girl* is but one of many. A socialist realist drama if there ever was one, *The White Haired Girl*, modelled on an influential Chinese folktale and later developed into a ballet under Jiang Qing's vilified cultural policy of the late 1960s, which came to be known as the Cultural Revolution, tells the story of the daughter of a poor famer who, unable to pay his debts to his feudal landlord, is forced to sell her into indentured servitude. The girl, suffering abuse and finally rape at the hand of the landlord, runs away in hope of finding her one-time lover who had in the meantime turned to the emancipatory ranks of the People's Liberation Army. Pregnant and homeless, she roams the Chinese mountainside for years on end, only to lose the child and have her hair turn grey from, as she puts it in a revealing line, 'the grudge that kept her alive'. Feared by the natives as a grey-haired goddess who lives in abandoned temples, she is finally found by her lover, and in time comes to discover the emancipatory mission of the Communist Party. The film was well received in the 1950s both domestically and internationally (it got an honorary prize at the prestigious Karlovy Vary International Film Festival in 1951) and was perceived as popular despite its favouring an ideological story line. Wang Bin's and Choui Khoua's dexterity consisted in flaunting the film's progressive philosophy while simultaneously employing the melodramatic Asian tradition popular with the masses. This helped the visual illustration of a well-known legend quickly become popular entertainment. Despite this, the film (along with its ballet version and other revolutionary 'model operas' of the Cultural Revolution period, such as *Hongse Niangzi Jun (The Red Detachment of Women)* of 1961) would later be considered part and parcel of the so-called propagandist cultural works that the Party allegedly churned out to indoctrinate and oppress its people. Moreover, the film was later surprisingly seen as endorsing the very opposite of its gender-liberatory message. Of *The White Haired Girl*, Rosemary Roberts writes in 2010:

> The argument that gender was progressively erased from culture of the Maoist era was first made prominent by Meng Yue's examination of socialist fiction, and has been strongly supported by work including Mayfair Mei-hui Yang's analysis of 'gender erasure' from public space and Cui Shuqin's study of modern film in which she argues that Maoist heroines have been 'erased of anything that is feminine.' Studies of the

Cultural Revolution yangbanxi (model works) have labelled their central heroines as 'emptied of female signifiers' and 'genderless revolutionaries'. (Roberts 2010: 17)

Interestingly, in the 1950 version of the film, the heroine is anything but genderless, since the driving force of the story is her forced enslavement and rape by the feudal landlord, something which motivates her revenge in the final act against her oppressor in a public trial held by the mass of peasants and soldier-revolutionaries to whom her one-time lover belongs. Even if the final scenes of the film demonstratively show, in typical socialist realist style, the women and the men working the fields under the banner of the red flag with a hammer and sickle, the finale amounts to nothing less than an improved condition for a heroine who, up until then, has been the subject of continuous abuse and hardship at the hands of her oppressors. As propagandistic as this may appear to the post-ideological eyes of a transnational audience unwilling to admit the oppressing power of feudalism in pre-Maoist China, it is hard to believe audiences in 1950 would interpret the ending as anything but liberatory for a social class that endured the poverty and subjugation of civil war for twenty years. Indeed, as Yingjin Zhang writes, '[c]onsidering the fact that many filmmakers as well as military and rural audiences had lived through years of battles and that the Korean War was raging on, it is not surprising to see the immense popularity of the war or military genre during this period' (Zhang 2004: 192). Furthermore, Paul Clark writes that '[m]aking opera films was also a useful way to popularize the reform and modernization of the traditional sung dramas that continued after 1949' (Clark 2012: 50). Wang Bin capitalizes on both these tendencies popular in the early fifties, the modernization drive and the war, to ensure that *The White Haired Girl* would be met with large popular appeal (figure 7.1). Furthermore, the film underscored the Party's genuine dedication to changing the old social order and championing the liberation of women, themes that would later lead to the fulminating excesses of both the Great Leap Forward and the Cultural Revolution.

*The White Haired Girl* is an example of the many films produced in the 1950s and 1960s under the Party's leadership, whose themes and motifs were later re-used and re-modelled by fifth generation directors in the 1990s. Of these jump to mind *Nong nu* (*Serfs*, 1963), directed by Jun Li, which tells the story of a Tibetan slave liberated by the PLA; *Zhu Fu* (*New Year Sacrifice*, 1956), an adaptation of a Lu Shun story about the struggles of a widow with her feudal lord; *Dang de nu er* (*Daughters of the Party*), produced in 1958, whose plot is centred on a woman finding her calling as a soldier in the Communist army after enduring years of self-sacrifice, and many others. Whereas these original films are currently thought to be contaminated by the oppressive communist ideology of Mao's cultural workers, films belonging to the New Chinese Cinema movement of the 1990s are considered to be,

FIGURE 7.1 *Tian Hua in her first role as the white haired girl.*

as Rey Chow best put it, for neoliberalism, freeing of social conditions oppressed under communism, especially the condition of women. Films like Yimou's *Raise the Red Lantern* and *Ju Dou*, as well as Tian Zhuangzhuang's *Dao Ma Zei* (*Horse Thief*), the latter of which literally reprises the story of *Serfs* in the minimalist tradition of the Chinese New Wave, prove that rather than advancing the themes of female and social emancipation on global screens, the fifth generation merely repositioned these themes in the flux of international competition of the global film market, thus making them palatable to world audiences, which in turn won them the acclaim of the international press. Indeed, if a film like *The White Haired Girl* used the now disparaged conventions of socialist realism, which, given the time the film was made, were only natural, it appears that Zhang Yimou's technique, and that of the fifth-generation directors at large, is to adapt rather than create from scratch the themes, motifs and plots that won the hearts and minds of Western audiences during postsocialism.

In fact, Chris Berry and Mary Farquhar are duly aware of this when, in their referential study of Chinese language cinema, *China on Screen*, they assert that the fight for emancipation from patriarchy that Yimou stages in his films through the figure of his beloved choice of heroine, the arresting Gong Li, is not particularly original: 'In fact, there is nothing new at all in this rebelliousness itself, and by the late twentieth century the trope that Gong Li cites here was already hackneyed' (Berry and Farquhar 2006: 125). We could safely take their observation a step further to note that it is not so much the emancipatory trope that made foreign audiences aware of the Chinese female condition, as much as Gong Li's luscious acting, which, exotic as female representations onscreen have been since Laura Mulvey drew our attention to them, succeeded in making Chinese films profitable for the first time on the world market.

In spite of these facts, when discussing Zhang Yimou's film, Rey Chow and Gina Marchetti praise precisely the alleged disconnect between the Chinese New Wave and its Maoist sources of inspiration, effectively glorifying the movement's new style as representing China's promotion into the World Cinema league. This is in fact a criticism that ignores the historical conditions that birthed socialist realism and an argument that whitewashes the dominance of world capitalism. However well-intended the two scholars' interpretation of *Red Sorghum* as an ideological triumph of the forces of change over authoritarian socialism is, they fail to see the progressive side of Chinese socialist cinema. Furthermore, they equally ignore the visible changes this cinema adduced for both Chinese feminism and the self-image of China as a country no longer identifiable with an economic colony of the West or a dominion of the corrupt Qing dynasty in the latter half of the twentieth century.

## The socialist–Third Cinema connection

It is the contemporaneous ideology of World Cinema, deeply suspicious of socialist values, and not ideological indoctrination *per se*, that deems the previous models on which Yimou's films were based indoctrinating. What we as scholars need to remind ourselves is the fact that socialist realist films like *The White Haired Girl* had as much in common with Third Cinema as Yimou's films now have with Maoist filmmaking.

Even though socialist realism was redacted by Stalin in the 1930s in a cultural space that has little apparently to do with postcolonialism, this should not stop us from seeing the mission of socialist filmmakers as intimately connected with that of South American auteurs. The themes espoused by socialist realism from the early 1930s onwards, such as preaching the utopia of a better society, promoting national sovereignty in contrast to foreign exploitation and encouraging self-management of national resources went hand in hand with opposing imperialism and creating an egalitarian society. Chinese cinema, even more so than Soviet or Eastern European cinemas, followed this principle so religiously that audiences dubbed the films churned out by Chinese studios in the 1950s and 1960s 'worker-peasant-soldier' dramas for the obsessive attention they paid to these three types captured in a perpetual struggle for social justice. Indeed, if there was a cinema that adhered closely, albeit anachronistically, to Solanas and Getino's creed, it was the cinema of the Mao era *par excellence*.

What is even more striking is that social justice and female emancipation were themes that have been promoted by Chinese films as early as the mid-1930s, when few national cinemas in the Third World, let alone the First, were interested in the subject. A few titles from this period worth mentioning are *Shen Nu* (*The Goddess*, dir. Wu Yonggang, 1934), *Da Lu* (*The Big Road*, dir. Yu Sun, 1934), *Malu Tianshi* (*Street Angel*, dir. Yuan Muzhi, 1937), *Shizi Jietou* (*Crossroads*, dir. Shen Xiling, 1937) and finally *Wuya Yu Maque* (*Crows and Sparrows*, dir. Zheng Junli, 1949). Furthermore, while all these films forefronted issues such as workers' exploitation, unemployment, the housing crisis and so on, *The Goddess* and *Street Angel* focused exclusively on the condition of disempowered women. These films were produced by directors working in the so-called Shanghai Island, which is a part of the cinema industry with leftist inclinations that had not yet been besieged by either the Kuomintang or the invading Japanese armies. The Chinese directors working there were thus able to continue producing socially conscious–themed films even though the twenty-year-old civil war that the Kuomintang fought with the Communists since 1927 and the resistance war against Japanese forces were draining artistic creation elsewhere in the country.

Naturally, these themes would continue to be employed after Mao's hold on power, when propagating social justice became as important as glorifying the sacrifices made by the People's Liberation Army in the two wars. It is therefore important that, when researching the origins of Third Cinema in Latin America, we take a look at influences that came from other parts of the world. A country like China did not only have extensive experience with circulating leftist themes by the mid-1960s but it is safe to say that almost its entire cinematic industry was built around them. To underline what I think is the under-researched connection between Chinese and Third Cinema, let us follow the way in which Humberto Solas's *Lucia* handles the topic of female emancipation in what is one of the most powerful iterations of feminism in New Latin American Cinema and compare it to the already discussed *The White Haired Girl*.

Although he has been viewed exclusively as representative of the New Latin American Cinema movement of the 1960s, Humberto Solas should be incorporated, I argue, into the wider ideological scope of anti-imperialist cinema that has been practiced in the socialist world and was at the time finding a new voice in postcolonial countries. If Solas's *Lucia* belongs to a line of progressive works made by Cuban filmmakers, such as that of Tomás Gutiérrez Alea, Santiago Alvarez and, via the Cuban-Soviet connection, Mikhail Kalatozov, the history of female oppression, which the film discusses, as well as the socialist revolutionary goals from which Solas's entire work hails also make *Lucia* a prototype of early Third Cinema.

Unlike his Cuban predecessors who tackled topics of social injustice and attacked the opulence of capitalism, Solas, in *Lucia*, focuses exclusively on the condition of women before and after the Cuban Revolution. Produced in the same year as Solanas's and Getino's paradigmatic *La hora de los hornos* and released only a year before their famous manifesto, *Lucia* is divided into three parts set in different historical periods: the revolutionary turmoil of 1895 that ultimately led to independence from Spain; the anti-governmental uprising of 1933 that overthrew Cuba's first dictator, Gerardo Machado y Morales; and the post-revolutionary, socialist Cuba of the 1960s. As Anna Marie Taylor aptly puts it in her 1975 review, *Lucia* is a film 'which magnificently shows three stages in a process of historical transition in a country which, within the space of seventy-five years, has moved from European colony through socialist revolution' (Taylor 1975: 58). The motif that links the segments is the presence of a character named Lucia in all three periods. John Mraz argues that this is Solas's attempt to show that 'the individual in history contrasts sharply with films of the West which, rarely *explicitly* reflective of history, instead reinforce the dominant liberal ideology of an abstract and universal humanism' (Mraz 1975: 9, emphasis in original).

Despite their identical name, the women represent radically different characters. In the first segment, Lucia is an upper-class Europeanized woman involved with a Cuban aristocrat who leads a regiment of Spanish troops against rebelling locals. Shot in oneiric black-and-white with tinges of magical realism (figure 7.2), the scenes help raise the heroine's consciousness about the oppression the colonial government enacts on black plantation workers and locals alike. Lucia lives on one of these plantations and witnesses the atrocities committed by the Spaniards. Unfazed by the intimidating figure

FIGURE 7.2 *Raquel Revuelta playing the first of the three Lucias.*

of her lover and made conscious of the injustices wrought on the local population, Lucia resorts to the upmost act of rebelliousness and decides to kill her lover.

The Lucia of 1933 is the idealist brought up in the climate of burgeoning capitalism that follows Cuba's liberation. When a new dictator rises from the rabble in the guise of Gerardo Machado, an underground anarchist movement plans to assassinate him. Lucia works in a cigar factory in which her boyfriend, Aldo, is one of the conspirators. Although the couple join the anti-dictatorial movement, the segment ends with Aldo's murder at the hand of government forces, thus rendering their opposition to injustice futile. As Taylor puts it, the point of the second segment is to show, despite the political confusion that reigns onscreen, that any movement framed by individualistic idealism and a lack of political programme is doomed to fail (Taylor 1975: 57).

For the third, contemporaneous segment, Solas changes pace to turn his film into an almost satirical comedy. This new Lucia is the wife of a macho labourer who, incapacitated by jealousy, does not want Lucia to work and refuses her the chance to find a job despite her continuous efforts to persuade him to the contrary. Tomas's intransigence costs him dearly in the eyes of his wife as well as the community, as both regard his machismo as excessive. It is the same machismo that ultimately leads to the unravelling of the marriage. A moralistic tale of sorts, this segment represents Solas's commentary against the re-emerging traditionalism that begins to endanger social relations in the victorious, post-revolutionary environment.

Teshome Gabriel was among the first scholars of Third Cinema to draw ideological parallels between anti-imperialist filmmaking produced in disconnected parts of the world. Grouping together *Dongfang Hong (The East Is Red)* made in China with the Pakistani-made *Towers of Silence* and the Bolivian *Yawar Mallku (Blood of the Condor)*, Gabriel stated: 'These films made in Africa, Asia and Latin America, isolate imperialism as the enemy, identify the masses as the true hero and the only force capable of defeating the class enemies in their home fronts' (Gabriel 1979: 5). However, when discussing *Lucia* as a paragon for the 'unity of Third World texts', Gabriel drew criticism from Julianne Burton, who claimed that the critics' lack of consensus in reaching a common conclusion regarding *Lucia*'s feminism stands proof that this cinematic text failed to coalesce the Third World around the notion of gender (Guneratne 2003: 13).

Despite Burton's finding a lack of consensus around its message, *Lucia* won the golden prize at the Moscow Film Festival in 1969. We can only speculate to what degree it went on to influence feminist filmmaking in the Eastern bloc. What is easier to speculate is the way in which Eastern bloc and Chinese filmmaking in their turn influenced and modelled the themes employed by postcolonial and Latin American filmmakers. The circulation of postcolonial films such as Mexican and Indian in China, as Li Jing shows in his thesis (Li 2010), as well as the screening of Chinese, Soviet and Eastern European films at festivals held in other socialist and postcolonial countries in the 1950s and 1960s, ensured that ideological cooperation was not an empty slogan. This is particularly so at a time when tri-continentalism and the non-aligned movement were making the Third and the Second World aware of their commonalities. The three main themes present in *Lucia*– that is the importance of history for development, the oppression of the peasant and the working class and the raising of consciousness in rapport with the condition of women – all are forefronted in *The White Haired Girl*. Even though Solas employs in parts a magical realist style by overexposing film to create a hallow effect that references the surreal conditions pervading class divisions in pre-revolutionary Cuba, the overall mission of the Cuban director is to raise social awareness about the plight of women, and in that way it matches the goals of socialist realism, those of *The White Haired Girl* included.

It is hard not to notice that Solas shares many of the themes, ideals and even style of his socialist filmmaker counterparts. In an interview he gave in 2002, the Cuban director explained to Amanda Rueda the context in which he produced his first films. According to his testimony, Solas did not know personally the work of other South American filmmakers like Pereira Dos Santos and Glauber Rocha, who were almost contemporaneously setting the foundation stones for the New Latin American Cinema movement. Indeed, when speaking of these directors he stated that although 'there was no interaction between us, we were like mushrooms that exploded in all regions at once. It was a continental act. It was a historically necessary movement' (Rueda 2004: 139, my translation). Solas dubs the continent-wide anti-colonial filmmaking that erupted in Latin America in the 1960s as the fateful finding of a common voice of otherwise disparate directors: 'Historically, with the perspective that the years give you, [the films] were a group of coincidences. It was like an immanent event, which was developed and articulated theoretically as a result of the authors' work' (Rueda 2004). However, drawing parallels to 1968 globally, he also places his work within the bounds of a global anti-establishment sentiment through which underprivileged nations demanded change, a sentiment that covered the world from Cuba to South America but also from Eastern Europe to India and the Congo (Rueda 2004).

While it is easy to see how Santos was an exponent of this sentiment, we have to acquiesce for the fact that a similar sentiment, as the Cuban director intimated, had been burgeoning in other parts of the world. It so happens that in China (and, of course, in Soviet Russia and Eastern Europe) this sentiment was present ever since the days of the civil war. As such, progressive Chinese filmmakers promoted not only women's liberation but, in films like *The Goddess* and *Street Angel*, they even demanded social justice for females forced into prostitution, which for 1934 was a progressive topic indeed. The circulation of these films ultimately raised consciousness about female subjugation and social injustice, which were continuing to plague not only China but various Third World and socialist countries.

It is in this common awareness of one another (as cultures, as nations and as shared universal conditions) that we should ultimately place the manifesto of Getino and Solanas. As Solas makes clear, although Third Cinema developed topically in South America, it drew its voice from a communal affect shared across wildly varied cultures. It is for this reason that it would be incorrect to erase the socialist heritage of fifth-generation filmmakers in China, as well as the undeniable connection between Third Cinema and postsocialist cinema. Seeing Yimou's films as sole expression of universal cognitivism as Marchetti does is therefore to ignore the way in which the global leftist currents of the mid-twentieth century interpenetrated each other and fed off one another while spurring a veritable revolution.

# From socialism to transnationalism: The case of Romania

As in the case of Marchetti's writings on mainland Chinese cinema, a re-accentuation of modernism is now taking place in Romanian film studies in the detriment of other influences, such as socialist realism. In this vein, Doru Pop argues that postsocialist Romanian cinema is indebted to both Italian neorealism and the theatrical tradition of the British 'kitchen sink' (Pop 2014), while Dominique Nasta claims that the Romanian New Wave is successful in the West because its films 'break from the past, striving to express themselves in a universally recognisable language' (Nasta 2013: 140).

A member of the Eastern Bloc since 1949, Romania developed, like most other countries in the bloc, a socialist realist trend in the 1950s and early 1960s, which came to be replaced by the 1980s with a somewhat more ambivalent filmmaking style that favoured metaphor and stylistic innovation over the simplicity of early utopian collectivization dramas. A decade after the collapse of socialism, this in turn developed into the so-called 'New Wave', which, criticism has it, was able to reveal the horrors of communist indoctrination while finally catching up with the liberal and much-coveted values of the West (Nasta 2013: 231). This is at least the most frequent reading of a film like Cristian Mungiu's *4 Months, 3 Weeks and 2 Days* (2007). Purportedly made to show the disastrous effects of Romanian dictator Nicolae Ceaușescu's aberrant abortion policy of the late 1960s, the film follows a female university student who, with the help of her best friend and roommate, endeavours to rid herself of an unwanted pregnancy. The overall atmosphere that permeates the film is one of destitution and despair,

FIGURE 7.3 *The brooding universe of socialist oppression.*

which is only matched by the low-key lighting and the drab colours of the surroundings of a provincial Romanian town of the 1980s (figure 7.3).

Like many such towns, this was built by the Communist government to meet a looming housing crisis spurred by the fast industrialization of the country, following a Second World tendency to liberate postcolonial enterprise from the dependency on capitalist indebtedness. Not unlike Maoist reforms meant to liberate China from feudal encroachments on a mostly destitute rural population, the policies of socialist Romania were aimed at boosting national sovereignty at the expense of consumption. It is the same policies, however, that significantly raised the standard of living in a mostly agrarian country, in which literacy during the monarchic period was placed at roughly 30 per cent.

Dominique Nasta, a theorist of New Romanian Cinema, praises the work of directors like Mungiu for showing the harsh living conditions that Romanians endured throughout much of the socialist period, while vituperatively condemning the economic policies of the Communist Party. However, she also unknowingly endorses a Third Cinema reading of postsocialist cinema and the Romanian New Wave at large. In frequent occasions, she describes the landscape favoured by postsocialist directors like Cristian Mungiu as 'miserable'. While her choice of words is not always fortunate (she even calls a garbage dumpster 'miserable' in one occasion), the reference to garbage and insalubrious living conditions in Mungiu's work validates in Nasta's view the above-mentioned preference of postsocialist directors to reveal the underbelly of the Communist project, warts and all. It is true that, following this aesthetic, Cristian Mungiu lingers his camera on dilapidated apartment buildings and the sometimes dirty tenement yards of the urban environment in which his drama takes place. Indeed, the result, as Nasta claims, is that '[e]verything looks quite miserable, revealing an economic situation Ceaușescu sought to hide and minimise for Western observers' (Nasta 2013: 45).

What is interesting is that Nasta's well-observed miserabilism of *4 Months, 3 Weeks and 2 Days* and, quite literally, the garbage that she associates with failed socialist policy in the film can alternatively be seen as personifying the very aesthetics promoted by Third Cinema theorists. In their manifesto *Toward a Third Cinema*, Solanas and Getino discuss several advisable methods which the Third World could employ to valorise the disadvantages created by imperialist oppression and capitalism in the colonized countries. These include, in the interpretation of film theorist Robert Stam, the fashioning of a certain 'aesthetics of garbage' meant to turn into positives the negatives of colonial domination. 'That garbage pile' that surrounds the colonized and the postcolonial subject, writes Stam taking his cue from the South American theorists, 'can be seen as an archeological treasure trove precisely because of its concentrated, synecdochic, compressed character. As congealed history, garbage reveals a checkered past. As time materialized in space, it becomes coagulated sociality, a gooey distillation of society's contradictions' (Stam 2003: 41).

Although she understands that the very focus on garbage is what makes the Romanian New Wave unique, Nasta attributes the success of the film to its employment of 'Western' narratology and Western standards: 'After difficult beginnings, uneven improvements, sparse moments of accomplishment during a short thaw, Stalinist-inspired state censorship control over all aspects of the film industry, and post-Communist difficulties in catching up with western standards, several encouraging conditions marked a twenty-first-century revival of Romanian cinema' (Nasta 2013: 231). The obsessive focus on economic conditions and the West betrays Nasta's tendentious reading of the film: by employing numerous references to the film's reception by Western critics, and repeatedly focusing on its winning the Palme D'Or at Cannes among many other prizes, Nasta enacts a simplistic, Western reading of a story that in her view is only about 'the terror of everyday life during the last days of one of the most oppressive dictatorships in Eastern Europe' (Nasta 2013: 187). She backs this up with similar interpretations of the film by Western critics: 'Mungiu's achievement is to have made a film both accurate to a specific place and time and a timeless illustration of the DNA-level damage such repression can wreak' (Megan Ratner qtd in Nasta 2013: 197). Or: 'I can't think of a film that has shown life in the Eastern Bloc more fiercely than this... It was from wretchedness and rage such as this that bred the uprising that changed Romania and the world' (Peter Bradshaw quoted in Nasta 2013: 197).

In her quintessential study *Imagining the Balkans*, Maria Todorova has warned that deprecatory Western views of Eastern Europe had become the norm for Western intellectuals ever since at least the age of the Enlightenment (Todorova 2009). Larry Wolff has similarly shown that Eastern Europe was created out of the pens of such universalists like Voltaire, who, while not promoting humanist values at home, in his correspondence with the Russian empress Catherine the Great would advise his much-admired penpal to hurry and spread civilization and empire among the barbarian tribes that still inhabited the Crimea, Tartary and other territories situated in the vicinity of the Black Sea (Wolff 1994). Alex Drace-Francis similarly talks of 'traditions of invention', which, according to the Dutch theorist, created Eastern peasants in the shape of benevolent savages. These inventions were based on accounts sent to their readers in the West by travellers to Eastern Europe who revelled in describing the region as backward and savage (Drace-Francis 2013).

Endorsing the reading of postsocialist films like *4 Months, 3 Weeks and 2 Days* as faithfully portraying the lives of a whole postsocialist generation, especially when this generation is seen as damaged at the DNA-level by what Nasta calls the 'lies of Communism', is akin to perpetuating the same self-orientalizing image of the East 200 years later. Such a reading blames the socialist period for having allegedly damaged Eastern Europe more than the writings of Enlightenment philosophers, while in fact endorsing a neo-colonial view of the East.

In this light a film like *4 Months, 3 Weeks and 2 Days*, which sells, so to speak, the effects of failed socialist policy to the West, could be seen not only as a literal accumulation of garbage in the yards of the socialist apartment blocks but also as an accumulation, as Stam suggests, of socio-historical garbage. Since Romania was before 1918, a successive dominion of either the Tsarist, the Ottoman or the Habsburg Empires, and before the Communist takeover an economic colony of the West, as Mira and Antonin Liehm put it, a postcolonial view of the region would warrant such a reading. Far from being the result of failed socialism alone, this particular garbage could therefore be seen as one fostered by the colonial conditions predating socialism, those which state socialist policies were not able to fully eradicate, namely rural poverty, economic dependence on the Empire or the West and squandered natural resources. A richer reading of the film, one that would put *4 Months, 3 Weeks and 2 Days* in the right historical context, would admit therefore that Mungiu indeed flaunts the garbage wrought by socialism in the face of the West, but he does not do so to evoke sympathy but to show the dramatic underpinnings of the condition of the subaltern in a postcolonial, postsocialist world.

Mungiu, in fact, not unlike the Chinese fifth-generation directors, who merely re-emphasized the theses of Maoism, builds upon a previous heritage of contestation of government policies that was present during the socialist era proper. In 1977, over a decade after the ban on abortion instituted by Ceaușescu's decree, Andrei Blaier, a Romanian director with a solid artistic reputation, turned his attention to the unthinkable topic of abortion in *Ilustrate cu flori de câmp* (*Postcards with Wildflowers*) in full Communist dictatorship. In a somewhat similar setup with Mungiu's, the film tells the story of a woman who decides to get rid of an unwanted pregnancy by appealing to a small-town shopkeeper who doubles as illegal abortion doctor. Both moralistic and multi-layered, the film resolves to show the tragic consequences of performing an unsanitary abortion by having the female protagonist die at the end while the 'doctor' is forced to face the legal repercussions. Even if there is a dose of preaching in Blaier's work, through the actions of his only slightly unidimensional characters, the director succeeds not only to bring into public debate the soundness of an ill-conceived political decision but to articulate concerns that were hugely important for women living in a full-blown totalitarian regime.

If Mungiu adds something to the debate on abortion that goes beyond *Postcards with Wildflowers*, this is not so much an effective condemnation of Ceaușescu's abortion decree but a focus on the complex inner life of the female protagonist faced with such a dramatic choice as abortion. I would argue that the emphasis of the story is not on the existence of political oppression or lack thereof (ultimately the action could take place just as well in a liberal society) but on ethical questions raised by the protagonist's choices. Moreover, rather than directly discrediting socialism, Mungiu is interested in showing the type of human relationships that socialism forced people to form with each other. If the portrait of the abortion doctor (as in Blaier's film) is not particularly flattering, it is the friendship between the two female roommates that receives, so to speak, the most praise. What comes across is that authoritative Communism, by limiting the access of ordinary citizens to power, brings people facing gargantuan decisions, such as Mungiu's protagonists, closer together and on the whole forces people to turn towards each other, which constitutes in itself an act of contestation. Indeed, when looked at from the current neoliberal perspective marked by the spectre of individualism, which also characterized the time of transition in which the film was made, the troubled friendship between the two females in the film acquires an almost holy quality that contrasts with both the obtuseness of the socialist regime but also the cruel indifference of capitalism.

Mungiu's camera is thus eager to record the metaphorical garbage of Romanian socialist life, but it is also interested in profiling the positive side-effects this garbage had on an essentially impoverished society in which humans found in each other the most valuable resource. Unsurprisingly, this comes close to Stam's reading of Solanas's and Getino's manifesto. In his film, Mungiu shows that despite the socio-political 'garbage', as in the obstacles posed by both the regime and the shady characters this regime spawned (such as the abortion doctor), women could ultimately decide the fate of their lives even if this came (as in *The White Haired Girl*) with huge sacrifices to their personal well-being. Ultimately, this is the very mission of Third Cinema filmmaking. In this light, the film becomes about moral choices in an authoritative milieu whose effect is to highlight the importance of contestation, responsibility and maturity. It is through these acquired qualities that the female protagonist in the end discovers her agency, the agency to take control of her body while accepting the nefarious consequences of her actions. Finally, these qualities also make the female subject-of-the-regime realize her altogether powerful agency to contest the supremacy of that very regime and of the authoritative-paternalistic-totalitarian state.

Nasta's West-filtered interpretation could therefore be turned on its head. Instead of placing exclusive importance on the reception of Romanian films in the West, and thus reconfirming the archaic belief that Romanian cinema (not unlike Romanian culture in general) lacks the necessary self-confidence to stand on its own two feet without the propping arm of Western moral support, we could see the Romanian New Wave as an extension of Third Cinema philosophy. Hanging on to the good reception of Romanian New Wave films in the West, as Nasta does, represents the unfortunate confirmation of the fact that the narratology imposed by First Cinema on the postcolonial world ultimately made World Cinema the winner of its own aesthetic Cold War with socialist-era filmmaking. To make this even clearer, let us briefly analyse in closing another Romanian film critic's laconic framing of Mungiu's film in the history of Romanian cinema:

> In discussing the impact of *4 Months, 3 Weeks and 2 Days*, it is important to note that Romanian cinema did not have a New Wave in the 1960s or 70s. The 2000s, with 2000 being the 'year zero' when no film was produced in Romania, are this country's moment in the history of cinema. It is significant that this revival – which extends the legacy both of the 1970s feminist project and of the deeply humanist Italian and Czech schools – is happening in a country that had been saturated with official discourse, which was imposed on its citizens from above. (Uricaru 2008: 12)

What we have here is another Nastaesque rupture imposed from the top on the history of Romanian film as well as the history of gender equality in Romania. Correctly judging Mungiu's film as being feminist for its ability to speak for the subjects of an oppressive regime – even if the film does so through the silence of the female characters – Uricaru endows Mungiu with the apostolic quality of not only revealing the horrors of an oppressive past but lifting a taboo of sorts: that of allowing talk about abortion and female choice to rise to the forefront of public space. We only have to consider the existence of Blaier's film here to understand how incorrect this assessment is, and how purposefully divisive Uricaru is when treating the history of Romanian cinema. By separating cinema history into the 'before and after' moments set around the *anno mirabilis* 1989, despite the presence of a contestatory discourse in both periods, Uricaru perpetuates the clichés popularized by World Cinema which accept as 'worthy' or 'qualitative' only those discourses produced in a full-blown liberal democracy.

While there is no contention that Ceaușescu's decree making abortion illegal represented an infringement on the universal rights of women, what proponents focusing exclusively on this political act forget is that feminist themes and female-centred cinema, as seen from Blaier's film among others, was equally a mainstay of the socialist era. When discussing feminism in the Eastern context, particularly in Romania, we should be careful to distinguish between two facets of socialism: the programmatic goals of socialism, which included, as Katherine Verdery notes, equal pay for women (Verdery 1996: 4), but also a larger inclusion of women in the workforce, drastically improved educational opportunities for women in comparison with the monarchical period and advancement of women into leading functions in professional environments, on the one hand, and the nationalistic (and thus contradictory) goals of the same socialist governments, on the other. As Verdery makes clear, Romania's particularly ambiguous mixture of the erstwhile goals of Marxism-Leninism and the post-1960s promotion of nationalistic policies ensured that the country was nominally managed by a Communist Party while both the intelligentsia and the population supported a dramatic version of Romanian nationalism: 'Nearly all Romanians I have met, regardless of social position, are deeply attached to the values of the Nation, whereas the values of Marxism-Leninism have enjoyed the respect of almost none' (Verdery 1991: 139). It is the same nationalism, of course, in contradistinction with the goals of socialism, that ultimately used the female body as a generative matrix for the coveted enlargement of national population. However, inasmuch as socialist-era cinema is concerned, we should give directors like Blaier their due for using their films to critically engage with issues such as abortion and women's rights.

If Blaier and other directors of his generation did not speak in the language of World Cinema recognizable today, as Nasta claims, this does not detract from the quality of their films or the courage of the themes they skirted in full dictatorship. Moreover, the fact that Romania did not have its Italian neorealist or Czech New Wave moments in the 1970s, as Uricaru suggests, does not preclude the cinema of the era from being seen as emancipatory or critical of the regime in its own right. Rather than allowing that the only influences for Mungiu's feminism are the 1970s Western feminist movement and the humanist Czech and Italian schools, we should pay closer attention to films like Blaier's and, overall, to the ontology of feminism in Romanian cinema. Shouldn't we ask, in view of this ontology, moreover, whether the very allowance of progressive female-themed films under the Communist dictatorship didn't perchance influence the lightness with which Mungiu treated such themes in postsocialism, not to mention the look and style of his film?

Instead of accusing the socialist government of instrumentalizing film for the use of political propaganda, as Nasta does, one could therefore see socialist policies as a source of inspiration for a movement that continues to champion the rights of the disempowered today as it did during socialism, and in this case, particularly the condition of disempowered women. A more careful reading of Mungiu further underlines the complex connections between postsocialist Romanian film and its antecessor socialist cinema, the vilified style of socialist realism included. According to this reading, New Romanian Cinema appears as highly indebted to the so-called propaganda of women liberation and social justice championed by the socialist realists. To erase the influence of this movement on postsocialism by only highlighting the importance of aesthetics and forms of storytelling made famous by World Cinema is to neglect the impact that early progressive movements created for the Romanian New Wave.

## Conclusion

In this chapter I wanted to show that one can draw a number of parallels between the apparently unrelated cultural currents of socialist realism and the goals of Third Cinema, which makes these disparate movements appear in retrospect in closer relationship with one another. Although occurring at different times and in widely dissimilar circumstances, films promoting the emancipation of women in the Communist China of the 1950s and the post-revolutionary Cuba of the 1960s are tied to each other not only by a common social agenda but by the influences of a style of filmmaking created from opposition to and an active struggle against the bourgeois values of First Cinema. Moreover, despite current criticism equating socialist realism with the suppression of creativity in socialist countries before the downfall of Communism, we need to allow that socialist realism promoted a genuine struggle for social emancipation and anti-imperialism, which are equally the values that birthed Third Cinema.

If we want to engage critically with the history of cinema, we should make certain to differentiate between the local condition of women under socialism in Chinese, Romanian and Cuban films of the era and the drastically different conditions adduced by transnationalism, multiculturalism or cosmopolitanism today. It is problematic to expect that the economic conditions now subsumed to the capitalist project personified by World Cinema could speak retroactively for the condition of women under socialism without projecting the neoliberal desiderata of the capitalist project over socialist realities of the 1970s and the 1980s. By allowing such interpretations as Nasta's, Uricaru's and even Marchetti's to dominate the world of postsocialist film studies, we allow transnationalism to become the uncritical porte-parole of a capitalist type of ideatic encroachment on local postsocialist and postcolonial values that previously had nothing to do with capitalism.

As flashed out by the above-mentioned scholars, the crux of the argument promoting World Cinema is that, by virtue of its predication on fluid, uncentred and anti-essentialistic identities, transnationalism represents a progressive movement, both in academia and geopolitics. Identity politics alone, in other words, is meant to resolve the multiple setbacks created by both globalization and the postcolonial impasse, while the more complex relations between socialism and nationalism, as in the Second World, or internationalism and anti-imperialism, as in the postcolonial world, are wilfully relegated to the dustbin of history.

Even though transnationalism is equally supposed to erase borders, create bridges, combat inequality and so on, the problem with its ideology, and that of its sister practice, World Cinema, is that they seek to promote egalitarianism by imposing a monologic similarity between postsocialist and postcolonial countries, which is one that is predicated solely on the spirit of capitalism. Although the method of World Cinema consists in ignoring differences and promoting allegedly universal values that makes us all the same, this method, not unlike that of the similar Enlightenment project, is a potential ideological trap. Just as the Enlightenment was ultimately an instrument for popularizing and imposing Western values on colonial and semi-colonial peoples, those of multiculturalism and transnationalism not only ignore but ultimately destroy the local histories of the cultures that have been called without history in order to impose a universal, white and Western history in its stead.

What both Marchetti and Nasta ultimately celebrate by integrating the Romanian and Chinese New Waves to World Cinema is merely their own euphoria for an alleged ending of these cinemas' inferior status in relation to First Cinema. This is, however, a double-edged sword which signals not the becoming equal of Eastern and Western cinemas but the ultimate acknowledgement of the East's defeat by Western hegemony or the moment when the East's colonization by the West, not only economic but also cultural, is unreservedly complete.

# Bibliography

Abu-Lughod, Lila (2013), *Do Eastern Women Need Saving?*, Cambridge, MA and London: Harvard University Press.

Berry, Chris and Mary Farquhar (2006), *China on Screen: Cinema and Nation*, New York: Columbia University Press.

Bordwell, David (1996), 'Contemporary Film Studies and the Vicissitudes of Grand Theory', in David Bordwell and Noel Carroll (eds), *Post-Theory: Reconstructing Film Studies*, 3–36, Madison: The University of Wisconsin Press.

Clark, Paul (2012), 'Artists, Cadres, and Audiences: Chinese Socialist Cinema, 1949–1978', in Yingjin Zhang (ed.), *A Companion to Chinese Cinema*, 42–57, Chichester: Wiley-Blackwell.

Drace-Francis, Alex (2013), *Traditions of Invention: Romanian Ethnic and Social Stereotypes in Historical Context*, New York: Brill.

Gabriel, Teshome (1979), 'Third Cinema in Third World: The Dynamics of Style and Ideology', PhD Thesis, University of California, Los Angeles.

Guneratne, R. Anthony (2003), 'Introduction: Rethinking Third Cinema', in Anthony R. Guneratne and Wimal Dissanayake (eds), *Rethinking Third Cinema*, 1–27, London: Routledge.

Kerr, Elizabeth (2019), 'Hong Kong Flashback: Zhang Yimou Put China on Art House Map with Period Epic "Red Sorghum"', *Hollywood Reporter*, 18 March. https://www.hollywoodreporter.com/news/zhang-yimou-put-china-art-house-map-period-epic-red-sorghum-1194629 (accessed 27 October 2019).

Kumar, Deepa (2019), 'Imperialist Feminism', *International Socialist Review*, 102, 2 May, https://isreview.org/issue/102/imperialist-feminism (accessed 28 October 2019).

Li, Jing (2010), 'Xin shiqi tizhi yanbian zhong de dianying jinkou yanjiu (The Study of Film Imports with the System Evolution in the New Era)', PhD dissertation, Shandong University.

Liehm, Antonin and Mira Liehm (1977), *The Most Important Art: East European Film after 1945*, Berkeley: University of California Press.

Lu, Sheldon (2007), *Chinese Modernity and Global Biopolitics: Studies in Literature and Visual* Culture, Honolulu: University of Hawai'i Press.

Marchetti, Gina (2006), *From Tian'anmen to Times Square: Transnational China and the Chinese Diaspora on Global Screens, 1989–1997*, Philadelphia, Temple University Press.

Mraz, John G (1975), '*Lucia*: History and Film in Revolutionary Cuba', *Film and History*, 5 (1): 6–16.

Nasta, Dominique (2013), *Contemporary Romanian Cinema: The History of an Unexpected Miracle*, London and New York: Wallflower Press.

Pop, Doru (2014), *Romanian New Wave Cinema: An Introduction*, Jefferson: McFarland.

Roberts, Rosemary (2010), *Maoist Model Theatre: The Semiotics of Gender and Sexuality in the Chinese Cultural Revolution (1966–1976)*, London and Boston: Brill.

Rueda, Amanda and Humberto Solas (2004), 'Encuentro con Humberto Solas', *Caravelle*, 83 (1): 137–45.

Solanas, Fernando and Octavio Getino ([1969] 2000), 'Towards a Third Cinema', in Robert Stam and Toby Miller (eds), *Film and Theory: An Anthology*, 265–86, Malden and Oxford: Blackwell.

Stam, Robert (2003), 'Beyond Third Cinema: The Aesthetics of Hybridity', in Anthony R. Guneratne and Wimal Dissanayake (eds), *Rethinking Third Cinema*, 31–50, London: Routledge.
Taylor, Anne-Marie (1975), 'Lucia', *Film Quarterly*, 28 (2): 53.
Todorova, Maria (2009), *Imagining the Balkans*, Oxford: Oxford University Press.
Uricaru, Ioana (2008), '*4 Months, 3 Weeks and 2 Days*: The Corruption of Intimacy. Ioana Uricaru Analyzes a Powerful Depiction of Life under Communism', *Film Quarterly*, 61 (4): 12–17.
Verdery, Katherine (1991), *National Ideology under Socialism: Identity and Cultural Politics in Ceauşescu's*, Romania, Berkeley: University of California Press.
Verdery, Katherine (1996), *What Was Socialism, and What Comes Next?*, Princeton, NJ: Princeton University Press.
Verdery, Katherine and Sharad Chari (2009), 'Thinking between Posts: Postcolonialism, Postsocialism, and Ethnography after the Cold War', *Comparative Studies in Society and History*, 51 (1): 6–34.
Wolff, Larry (1994), *Inventing Eastern Europe: The Map of Civilization on the Mind of the* Enlightenment, Stanford, CA: Stanford University Press.
Zhang, Yingjin (2004), *Chinese National Cinema*, London: Routledge.

PART THREE

# Third Cinema versus World Cinema

# 8

## Dialogical encounters on the cinema of revolution: *Save the Children Fund Film* and *Metalepsis in Black*

*David Archibald and*
*Finn Daniels-Yeomans*
*(University of Glasgow)*

DA: In this chapter we seek to bring aspects of Marxism into dialogue with some of Third Cinema's thematic concerns and practices by discussing two relatively unknown but, we contend, important films: *Save the Children Fund Film* (*STCFF*) (Loach, UK, 1971) and *Metalepsis in Black* (*Metalepsis*) (Kaganof, South Africa, 2016). In dispensing with the conventional monological essay form, we embrace dialogical openness rather than dialectical synthesis, rejecting the need to present a closed and seemingly coherent argument. Although we analyse both films in detail, we also allow the dialogue to drift into the broader aesthetic, intellectual and political concerns that emerge. As such, we allow the conversations and contradictions to flow, as the struggle for emancipation, be it in terms of class, gender, race or nation, itself continues to flow.[1]

---

[1] Since 2016 I have been developing a series of performed dialogues with Carl Lavery. In Glasgow Glam Rock Dialogues, which we have described as 'Machines for Thinking', we

FDY: The dialogical is intrinsic to Third Cinema, and I think for the very refusal of certainty, or finality, that you have touched upon. In their influential manifesto, 'Towards a Third Cinema', Fernando Solanas and Octavio Getino speak of film as a means of instigating an 'open-ended' dialogue (1970: 10) and note that revolutionary cinema is 'inconceivable' without experimentation, embracing failure and placing oneself 'on the outside limits of the familiar' (1970: 7). Following the Third Cinema approach, then, we could see this chapter as an experiment in academic form, in keeping with Solanos and Getino, when they write of 'an unfinished work, open in order to incorporate dialogue and for the meeting of revolutionary wills' (in Chanan 1997: 373).

DA: Rather than viewing Third Cinema as an historical movement whose time has passed, if we view Third Cinema itself as unfinished, perhaps we can, in a modest way, breathe some life into its spirit. Our dialogue, then, is not an engagement with the past; rather, we suggest that the movement provides progressive models for how film scholars, in the Global South and the Global North, might operate, in terms of form and method, in the present and, indeed, the future. We seek not to explain or to close down an understanding of what Third Cinema is or might have been but to explore what affordances might emerge from dialogical encounters with it, with Marxism and with the two films we discuss below. As with Solanas and Getino: 'Our time is one of hypothesis rather than of thesis' (1970: 7).

FDY: I also see an engagement with Third Cinema as enabling the process that Priyamvada Gopal in *Insurgent Empire: Anticolonial Resistance and British Dissent* terms 'reverse tutelage' (2019: 8), of academics/citizens in the metropole being the subjects of political/anticolonial tutelage, of learning from those who were and are colonied.

DA: Absolutely: the 'reverse tutelage' that Gopal describes is dialogical. Part of this colonization process must involve questioning the need for the monological certainty so often advanced in conventional academic thinking, and form. Third Cinema suggests we should be more open to embracing doubt, uncertainty, provisional knowledge. I'm reminded of Bertolt Brecht's poem 'In Praise of Doubt', not as an injunction to inaction but one to considered action. Of course, Brecht's own practice was informed by an engagement with Chinese theatre and opera, and, in turn, Brecht's theatrical practice was a major influence on Third Cinema (Wayne 2001). This dialogue between artists on and of emancipatory culture, which Mikhail Bakhtin (1981) might have referred to as a 'chain of dialogues', has a long, and unfinished, trajectory.

---

address aesthetic and political concerns, often from conflicting perspectives, but always refusing resolution. In one of our regular dialogues about contemporary concerns in the university, Carl suggested that decolonizing the academy is not simply a question of content but also a question of form. I concur; however, as we propose in this chapter, it is also a question of method.

FDY: I agree that academics should be exploring other ways of thinking, and writing. I found the work of Paolo Freire ([1970] 1996) to be particularly instructive in this sense. Freire writes of education as needing to be 'dialogical and problem-posing' ([1970] 1996: 22). Although working in a different context, he suggests that people suffer from an 'absence of doubt' and that this doubt keeps them prisoners of a 'circuit of certainty' ([1970] 1996: 21). In practice, learning to embrace the free-flowing and more speculative dimensions of a dialogical approach, without sacrificing academic rigour and analytical depth, can be both liberatory and generative in developing ideas and getting them on the page.

DA: Perhaps a dialogical encounter might be a better model for how white academics operating in the Global North might write about filmmaking in Africa. We're fully aware of our own position as two white, male academics, based at the University of Glasgow, writing about two white, male film directors – one from the UK, one from South Africa – making films exploring the politics of class and race on the African continent. The dialogical allows for the distance between ourselves and our subject matter, both geographically and historically, to be factored in.

FDY: Positionality is central to decolonial thinking, a particularly important element of which is Standpoint Theory and its relation to the concept of epistemological ignorance. Described by Alison Wylie as an 'inversion thesis' in which epistemic tables are turned (2003: 29), Standpoint Theory foregrounds that those who face structural oppression may be epistemically advantaged over those who occupy a comparatively privileged position in what decolonial scholars refer to as the 'modern/colonial capitalist/patriarchal world-system' (Grosfoguel 2007: 213). To summarize: oppression may afford epistemic insight and privilege may produce ignorance. In reversing – in the sense that Gopal refers – traditional notions of Western superiority, when we – two white, British men – engage with films that grapple with, among other thorny questions, black consciousness and racial capitalism, and that we do so from the geo-and socio-politically privileged position *and* location that we occupy, we need to be aware of the epistemic ignorance that this position may afford; there will most likely be key issues that emerge in these films that we do not know, that we miss or misread, inadvertently ignore or even deny.

DA: Yes, in striving to develop a critical solidarity, we need to recognize our position and location as you say. I might baulk at the British label, but that's another discussion. Gopal argues for what she terms 'shared ground', whilst aware of the dangers of erasing difference, in search of what she describes as 'something like a reconfigured critical humanism and an expansive universalism' (Gopal 2019: 23). For me, and this relates to theory *and* praxis, there is still value in the concept of universal humanism, even if I am well aware that this might be derided as naïve.

## Marxism and Third Cinema

DA: In relation to Marxism, as I see it, with the collapse of the Soviet Union and its satellite states *c.* 1989, Marxism as a political project appeared, for some, to be finished. In the wake of the 2007/8 financial crash, however, Marxism as a theory for explaining capitalism in crisis had something of a re-birth and Marxism as a political movement, or a strain of thought within broader political movements appears to be back. Contra the notion of the dominance of capitalism as a system in Mark Fisher's 2009 book, *Capitalist Realism: Is There No Alternative?*, perhaps we are back, once more, to imagining possible large-scale transformations as we desperately seek out new ways of living to avert the cataclysmic future which capitalist-fuelled climate change heralds. The dialectic at work here is that Marxism, communism even, which should have been buried with the collapse of the USSR and the Soviet-controlled states, has enabled the birth of a new Marxism, one untainted by these regimes' histories.

FDY: How might this new Marxism respond to long-standing critiques of a certain Eurocentrism in Marxist ideas, and particularly the accusation that they downplay questions of race? Kehinde Andrews argues that 'Marxism's central problem is its relegation of the question of racism' (2018: 183): how it overlooks racialized unevenness in the world-system. He notes that the admittedly terrible conditions faced by Europe's working class were 'a luxury compared to the enslavement of African peoples' (2018: 187), thus making any sense of global solidarity – or the shared ground you mentioned above – something of a myth.

DA: Firstly, it is important to recall the contribution to Marxism from theorists such as C. L. R. James and José-Carlos Mariátegui, born in Trinidad and Peru, respectively, and the many other Marxist thinkers and artists working in the Global South, from Frida Kahlo in Mexico to Ousmane Sembène in Senegal. Moreover, in a study of his later writings in *Marx at the Margins*, Kevin S. Anderson suggests that 'Marx developed a dialectical theory of social change that was neither unilinear nor exclusively class-based. Just as his theory of social development evolved in a more multilinear direction, so his theory of revolution began over time to concentrate increasingly on the intersectionality of class with ethnicity, race and nationalism' (2010: 244). So, a nuanced Marxist approach would be absolutely concerned with the particularities of racial and other forms of oppression. An activist Marxism perhaps too readily erases these differences in the interests of building practical solidarity and its focus on class can exclude other forms of oppression. The advantage of an intersectional approach, as developed by Kimberlé Crenshaw (1991), is that it brings the question of totality back to the discussion. The advantage of a Marxist intersectional approach, for instance as advanced by Ashley J. Bohrer

(2018), is that it forces reflection on the relationship between these forms of oppression within the framework of capitalism. Marxism itself is not set in stone but always being developed. I wonder that with the return of Marxism, are we also witnessing a return to Third Cinema?

FDY: Third Cinema certainly has had something of a resurgence in the past few years, at least in Western academic film studies, and this parallels the calls to decolonize this disciplinary field.[2] A key text here is Anthony R. Guneratne and Wimal Dissanayake's *Rethinking Third Cinema* (2002). In his introduction, Guneratne notes that Third Cinema theory is 'the only branch of film theory that did not originate within a specifically Euro-American context' and thereby offers an alternative to the dominant Eurocentric film studies model, which Guneratne suggests operates from an exclusively Anglo-Francophone perspective (Guneratne 2003: 9–10). The alternative approach outlined here has been used in revisionist theories of World Cinema. For example Lucia Nagib and her co-authors (2012) draw on the 'Thirdness' of Third Cinema theory to move beyond binary models of film studies that continue to frame non-Western cinema and cinema scholarship as variously peripheral to film studies' Euro-American centre (as the moniker 'world cinema' has sometimes been taken to imply). Third Cinema features here as a key harbinger in their call for a 'polycentric approach to Film Studies', paralleling Ella Shohat and Robert Stam's earlier articulation of a 'polycentric multiculturalism' in *Unthinking Eurocentrism: Multiculturalism and the Media* (1994). Saër Maty Bâ and Will Higbee draw attention to much of this in *De-Westernising Film Studies*, referring to Third Cinema in terms of a 'de-westernising gesture' (Bâ and Higbee 2012: 3). They echo Guneratne's emphasis on the need to provincialize film theory in championing a break from 'the Euro-American dominance of theoretical models' (2012: 12). Third Cinema is not only a key component of contemporary Film Studies, then, but has also been – and remains – central to the project of provincializing – unthinking, de-Westernizing, decolonizing – the Eurocentrism that persists within the discipline. Third Cinema's advocation of film as a de-territorialized form of anticolonial pedagogy has been influential to the re-emerging debates around decolonizing the academy, which has in turn breathed new life into the Third Cinema project.

DA: The Third Cinema manifesto states that it represented 'the decolonization of culture', so it does seem particularly relevant. Decolonizing the academy involves rejecting the post-imperial-like

---

[2]See, for example, the 'African Screen Worlds: Decolonising Film and Screen Studies' (2019–2024) project run out of the School of African and Oriental Studies by Lindiwe Dovey (https://screenworlds.org/). See also Beschara Karam's 'An-Other'-Centred Film Curricula: Decolonising Film Studies in Africa' (2018).

scramble to claim new territory as one's own, refusing the urge to invent illusory disciplinary 'turns', breaking free of often-arbitrary institutional boundaries and kicking back against the notion of fields that are often imposed by regulatory and institutional academic frameworks. There is a moment in *Metalepsis* when one of the academics (Angelo Fick) talks of categories that 'order the world but they do not describe it'. This is certainly true of many educational structures in which academics conjure an illusion of mastery and control over a world which is more in keeping with Deleuze and Guattari's concept of rhizomatic fields (2013). As Marx himself transcended disciplines, perhaps what is needed is to move beyond the current drive to be interdisciplinary or transdisciplinary and strive for what Jacques Rancière describes as being 'indisciplinary'. As he puts it, 'It is not only a matter of going besides the disciplines but of breaking them' (in Baronian and Rosello 2008). Third Cinema was no stranger to breaking convention, and one of the small but important practices that I have utilized in my own pedagogical practice is the interrupted screening which Italian scholar Elena Boschi introduced to the 2016 Radical Film Network Unconference in Glasgow. There is much work to be done in decolonizing the academy; however, interrupted screenings can help break down some of the barriers that have been erected.

FDY: Screenings were indeed conceived of as politicized pedagogical events, wherein the film's importance is as a pretext, or what Solonas and Getino (1970: 9) refer to as a 'detonator', for a debate or dialogue that would politicize the film's spectators, calling upon them to become active participants critically engaged with their oppressive social situations. Screenings were 'essentially a way of learning' (1970: 10), a learning that was influenced by the consciousness-raising critical pedagogy advocated for by Freire. Third Cinema's conceptualization of film screenings as expanded, politicized classrooms expresses a subversive desire to break away from the institutionalized educational environments that Freire derided, and a similar impulse is animating the move to decolonize film studies.

DA: Yes. Third Cinema also provides a different model for how film scholars might operate in rejecting the dominant neoliberal individualism which dominates the higher education system. Miguel Errazu and Alejandro Pedregal (2019) suggest that Third Cinema 'can be understood as a call to rethink the possibilities of modern academia to radically resist and dispute, through research and praxis, the social order established from top-down, and all the naturalised assumptions that derive from it'. Their position reinforces the view that an engagement with Third Cinema is not simply for the past but for the present and future of film culture, in the academy and beyond, one which champions a diverse and emancipatory pedagogical practice.

FDY: We've set up a few lines of flight; maybe we should get to the films.

## Save the Children Fund Film

DA: For sure. In 1969, the Save the Children Fund charity commissioned Kestrel Films, established by director Ken Loach and producer Tony Garnett, to make a documentary to celebrate the charity's fiftieth anniversary. The film they made, however, was perhaps not what the funders had in mind. Shifting from footage of the charity's work from the UK to Africa, the film's socialist politics are evident in the polemical narration which heavily critiques charity as a concept and in a series of interviews with prominent African revolutionary figures. This progressive content, however, is in stark contrast to several racist commentaries from some of the charity's staff. Originally scheduled to be screened by London Weekend Television, when the charity's leadership watched a rough-cut, they were appalled and, after extensive legal disputes, the unfinished 16mm fifty-three-minute film – the sound is not mixed and there are no credits or title page – was consigned to a vault in the British Film Institute's archive. It was only in 2011 that the Save the Children Fund agreed to a screening as part of a British Film Institute retrospective on Loach, and I had the honour of organizing the film's Scottish premiere at a May Day screening the following year.[3]

FDY: What do you think is specifically Marxist, or socialist, about this film?

DA: Although Loach's output is understood primarily within the context of British social realism, there has always been a socialist and internationalist dimension to his work, particularly in the historical films. For instance, *Land and Freedom/Tierra y Libertad* 1995, which deals with the revolutionary heart of the Spanish Civil War, and *The Wind that Shakes the Barley* (2006), which is set during the Irish War of Independence and foregrounds the socialist ideas within it. Loach's position as an anti-imperialist filmmaker emerges most clearly when he focuses on Ireland, which features regularly in his work: *Hidden Agenda* (1990) deals with state collusion with loyalist death squads in the north of Ireland, and *Days of Hope* (BBC 1975) contains a rendition of Peadar Kearney's Irish Rebel song 'Down by the Glenside (The Bold Fenian Men)' before a contemplative troupe of British soldiers in 1916. This anti-imperialist position is in keeping with the perspective of Marx ([1868–1870] 2010: 475), who wrote that the task of the communist movement was to champion Irish independence and 'to awaken the consciousness of the English working class that, *for them, the national emancipation of Ireland* is not a question of abstract justice or humanitarian sentiment, but *the first condition of their own social emancipation*'. In *STCFF*, however, Loach turns his attention to a broader examination of

---

[3]There is no major academic literature on the film written from a Film or Television Studies' perspective but see Hilton (2015) for background.

British imperialism, interrogating the role of NGOs in Africa and creating a platform for African revolutionaries to communicate their idea into millions of British living rooms. For instance, the film includes testimony from Jaramogi Oginga Odinga (Figure 8.1), whose political affiliations are identified in interview when he states, 'we in the KPU', a reference to the Kenya People's Union, a socialist breakaway from the Kenya African National Union that had come to power with the advent of independence in 1963. Loach's method here, evidenced in the *STCFF* and across the body of his work, is to highlight the socialist dimension of international conflicts and amplify the voices resisting capitalism and imperialism. Consigned for so long to the BFI vaults, this chapter brings their ideas, as expressed in the film, into dialogue with the present.

FDY: Another presence in the film is that of the writer Ngũgĩ wa Thiong'o (Figure 8.2), whose *Decolonising the Mind* (1986) became a highly influential book in relation to debates on postcolonial literature and politics, and indeed Ngũgĩ's ideas remain central to the decolonizing university initiatives in *Metalepsis* (Mbembe 2016: 34–6). It is a quite remarkable moment when the young Ngũgĩ first appears on screen, framed in close-up so that the smoke from his cigarette rises across his face. Without forewarning or an introduction, here we have one of the most significant figures in postcolonial

FIGURE 8.1 Jaramogi Oginga Odinga in *Save the Children Fund Film*.

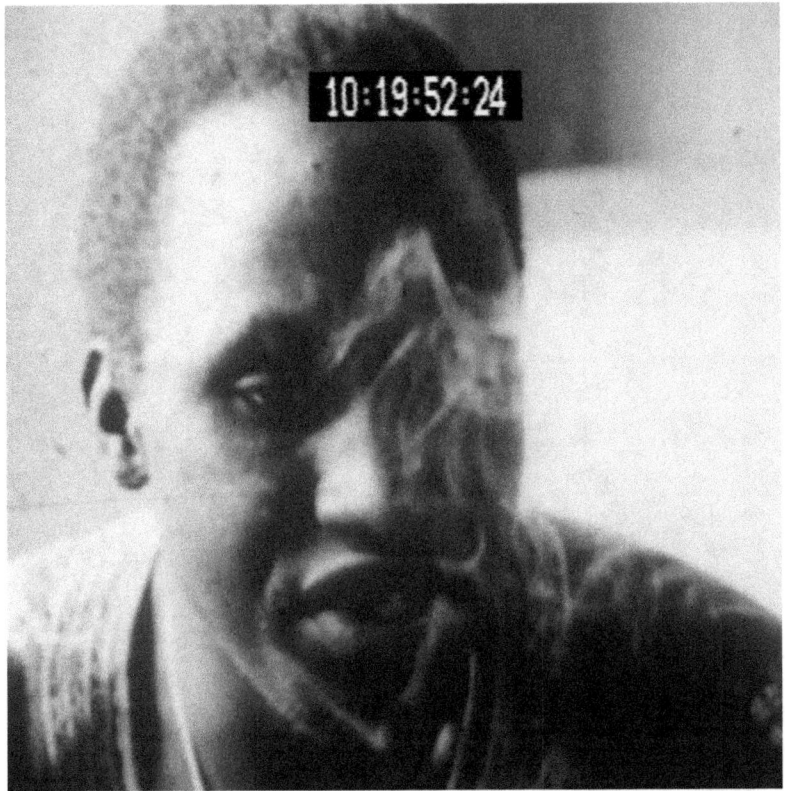

FIGURE 8.2 Ngũgĩ wa Thiong'o in *Save the Children Fund Film*.

criticism at a time before he has reached the kind of recognition he would go on to receive, reflecting – in a quiet, nonchalant manner – on some of the Marxist ideas that would come to characterize not only his later work but also the postcolonial thinking that was in vogue at the time. When he first speaks, Ngũgĩ indeed locates Kenya's struggle for independence within a class framework, suggesting that independence had created two categories of people: 'There are of course the middle class who are only really fighting to assume the shoes formerly worn by their colonial rulers.' And, he goes on, 'the masses, the large peasantry in the countryside and a few workers in towns. Those who were really expecting different things: expecting enough food, expecting educational opportunities, expecting a standard of living that would lift them above the breadline'. While the middle classes have 'attained their independence' – they have cars and houses – the masses 'have not yet got anything out of independence. They are still living in the same conditions as they used to live under their colonial rulers'. Ngũgĩ is offering

FIGURE 8.3 Ben Kantai in Save the Children Fund Film.

something similar to Fanon's critique of the false decolonization of newly independent states, in which a self-serving native elite replaces the colonial elite while the masses suffer. The 'vocation' of the national bourgeoisie, Fanon writes, 'is not to transform the nation but prosaically serve as a conveyor belt for capitalism' ([1963] 2004: 101). It is in this moment that the film – via Ngũgĩ – signals its Marxist leanings, denouncing colonialism and capitalism in the same breath.

DA: Yes, these points are developed further when the academic Ben Kantai (Figure 8.3) states, 'There are people who are becoming fantastically wealthy… and yet you find the direst poverty in the same square mile.' As the film depicts this poverty through shots of sprawling shack settlements, it brings to mind the work of one of Third Cinema's most prominent filmmakers, Ousmane Sembene, in particular, *Xala* (Senegal, 1975). Adopting a similar Marxist perspective, *Xala* suggests that even when the colonial rulers have been overthrown, without social change the native bourgeoisie will occupy the seats of power.

FDY: Ngũgĩ and Kentai go on to discuss the specificities of imperial economic control, with Ngũgĩ voicing that it is the 'job' of Western countries to create conditions where 'African countries will always need aid'. They argue that conditions for loans/aid are routinely that African countries spend the money on what the loaner specifies – their own exports – so that the money never materializes in localized development even while they will have to pay back the loan. Aid is thus a 'form of investment' for the countries in the Global North, employed as a means of forcing African states to become economically dependent on and indebted to the countries supposedly supporting them. The significance of this is that the film – again via Ngũgĩ – provides an account of Africa's place in the world-system at the moment of the downturn of the late 1960s post-war boom, and is a premonition of sorts of what was to happen to the postcolonial world in the final quarter of the twentieth century: by the 1980s growing Third World debt was managed via the introduction of the Structural Adjustment Plans, these being the favoured means of imposing a neoliberal restructuring of postcolonial states in the efforts to render them 'subservient to the needs of the global market' (Lazarus 2011a: 9). It also ensured the development of underdevelopment; that the world-system remained combined and uneven.

DA: Ngũgĩ's thinking chimes with Trotsky's theory of uneven and combined development (UCD), which underpins his broader theory of Permanent Revolution ([1930] 2010). This theory has had something of a renaissance in recent years: Marxist geographers, notably Doreen Massey and David Harvey, have deployed UCD in their work, but it has also had some purchase in literary studies with the 2015 publication of the Warwick Research Collective's *Combined and Uneven Development: Towards a New Theory of World-Literature* (2015). I would suggest that there might be some fruitful work to be done in film studies in analysing cinema history in general, and Third Cinema in particular, through the lens of UCD. Paradoxically, with the demise of Trotskyism as a political force with any significant agency, one might see an academic engagement with some of his ideas. I have always thought that the existence of the Trotskyist groups discourages academics from examining his writing on politics and culture for fear of association. Loach and Jim Allen, the writer with whom he worked regularly and from whom we hear in *STCFF*, were heavily influenced by Trotsky's ideas in the 1960s and they would not be strangers to UCD.[4]

FDY: Although the body of *STCFF* takes place in Kenya, and much of the screen time is taken up by Kenyan academics/activists, the film both begins and ends in Britain. Moreover, near the start, there is a quote from Engels's *The Condition of the Working Class in England* (1845), and the film clearly invites parallels to be drawn between Britain and its former colony, especially in its

---

[4] As there are no credits on the film, Allen is not credited; however, his working-class, Mancunian accent is quite distinctive and in an interview Loach confirmed that it is his voice that we hear. Interview partially published as 'Reeling from injustice', *Financial Times* (Archibald 2011)

representation of the 'reeking' outlays of Manchester and the impoverished Kenyan settlements – both of which are captured via sweeping pans – in ways that Kehinde Andrews would probably find suspicious. Andrews argues that the Western working class 'has benefitted from imperialism and forged political movements that mostly aim to distribute the wealth gained from the exploitation of darker people more equitably between whites' (2018: 189). His example here is how imperial profit and the labour of Britain's colonial subjects made possible Britain's post-war welfare state, even while the left imagines this as the product of tireless working-class campaigning.

DA: Well, I think Andrews is half-right, but I also think he's half-wrong. As Frederick Douglas notes, 'Power concedes nothing without a demand', and the British welfare state was, of course, achieved through working-class struggle of people of all colours and certainly not handed down with the benevolence of the British state. However, imperial plunder has ensured that there has been a greater amount of wealth to be distributed in the UK. If we take the city of Glasgow, where we are based, often described as the Second City of the Empire, as an example, there were undoubtedly intolerable working and housing conditions in the city. For instance, in the 1840s there were serious outbreaks of typhoid and cholera; however, the municipal authorities were able to respond by arranging the supply of clean drinking water. The material benefits of Empire helped enable such reforms to be introduced. To downplay the specificities of Empire to develop working-class unity is a mistake: this is another instance in which we need a nuanced approach, one that recognizes the particularity of oppression within the totality.

That said, remember that London Weekend Television commissioned the film for a UK television broadcast. The visit to Africa is framed from an English perspective; however, on a visual level, the haunting, agonizing images of emaciated, hospitalized, black children that we see make explicit that the misery is qualitatively different to that experienced in England. There are, however, problems with how the film deals with the shift between England and Africa. Towards the end Allen states,

> it isn't a question of black power or white power but of workers' power because this is a class issue. In the labour market, the colour of a man's skin is of no more importance than the hair colouring on cattle bred for the knacker's yard. Black sweated labour supplied raw cotton for the same employers who hire white sweated labour to work in the cotton mills of Lancashire. And the solution to the problem does not exist within the framework of capitalism.

Then as the film shifts between still images of Africa and England, he continues, 'First we must change the property relationship of society, then we change man [sic]. That's the only real, honest solution and all the rest is propaganda.' As the narration concludes, in an unsettling fourth wall-breaking moment, it is accompanied by a still image of a young, working-class white boy who gazes direct to camera. By returning the focus to England, I do not think that the framing device is Eurocentric, but there is a problem with collapsing difference.

FDY: The critique here might be that while the film places class as a common point of exploitation, pointing to an abstract capitalism's colour blindness, it erases the conditions facing black workers in actually existing capitalist countries in Africa and England, who face real discrimination on the basis of their colour.

DA: Yes; while the sentiment is admirable, the desire to find a commonality of experience is achieved through a degree of erasure of difference when, in fact, a commonality of experience, and a solidarity, can only be achieved when both similarity and difference are factored into the equation. One can absolutely remain committed to a Marxist analysis that prioritizes class, both as a category of exploitation and as a category for advancing political struggle, without downplaying other forms of oppression. Of course, Marx was not blind to race. He famously wrote in relation to slavery in the United States: 'Labour in a white skin cannot emancipate itself where it is branded in a black skin' ([1867] 1990): 414).

FDY: But perhaps we also need an intersectional lens when discussing whiteness. To collapse the class chasm between the white colonialist discussing the development of the Kenyan economy and the white boy who gazes direct to camera at the end would also be somewhat misjudged.

DA: Absolutely. The concluding scene invites reflection on Loach's film form. His earlier work, as evidenced in the television dramas *Up the Junction* (BBC, 1964) and to a lesser degree, *Cathy Come Home* (BBC, 1965), is marked by a Brechtian-inspired level of experimentation. What is noteworthy, however, is that as leftist filmmakers tended to adopt more radical film forms in the heady political days of the late 1960s, Loach moved in the opposite direction, producing work that was overtly political in content but more conventional in form. Allen had worked on the early years of the British soap opera *Coronation Street* (ITV, 1960 – present) utilizing popular forms to 'smuggle' in radical ideas. In the 1970s the film form utilized by Loach was the focus of an extended debate in *Screen* about its seemingly reformist nature. Working within the confines of what was described as the 'Classic Realist Text', Loach was critiqued for utilizing a form that did not represent contradiction, as was in favour with the academic film critics who championed a more overtly Brechtian or Godardian cinematic practice.[5] Formally, then, Loach's practice was removed from Third Cinema in terms of

---

[5] For an excellent overview of these debates, see John Caughie 'The Rush of the Real: An Aesthetic of Immediacy' in *Television Drama* (2000: 88–124).

its style and its desire to work within the mainstream. Yet, I'm always struck by the fact that, despite Loach's supposedly conservative form, the content of the work and the success with which it meets ensure that it regularly invites his opponents' wrath – the *STCFF* being a perfect example. Loach's style contrasts with Third Cinema's radical form, of which *Metalepsis* is exemplary.

## Metalepsis in Black

FDY: *Metalepsis* is what I would term a 'conference film' that chronicles the three-day 'Thinking Africa' symposium held at the University of the Free State, South Africa, on 4–6 October 2016. Entitled '#MustFall: Understanding the Moment', the conference aimed to provide a space for reflection on the radical turmoil facing South African universities since the eruption of mass student protests eighteen months earlier. In March of 2015, students at the University of Cape Town (UCT) demanded the removal of the statue of Southern Africa's apex colonialist, Cecil John Rhodes, which had occupied a prestigious place of honour atop UCT's campus since 1934. The #RhodesMustFall initiative, as it came to be known, and which coalesced as #FeesMustFall later that year, set out a vocal and violent challenge to the resilient forms of colonialism that continue to structure South Africa's universities two decades after the official end of apartheid – a challenge that has reverberated well beyond the university's walls and the country's borders, and indeed continues to do so.[6]

The bulk of the film consists of monochrome footage of conference delegates discussing the ideology, methods and significance of the student protests. Issues addressed include the turbulent context in which the protests emerged; the movement's decolonial philosophy, which draws on a mixture of Steve Biko, Black Consciousness, Frantz Fanon, Pan-Africanism, Black radical feminism and intersectionality; its strategic mobilization of disruption (vandalism, occupying); and the relative absence, or 'disappearance' in the film's terms, of established academics supporting the students' central demand for free and decolonized university education (Mabasa 2017). The conference footage, which has been edited together with recordings of the protests themselves, has been arranged in accordance with director Aryan Kaganof's experimental 'remix' or 'mashup' editing philosophy, which is

---

[6]These demands encompass not only access to university education for the countries black majority but also a thorough rethinking of what Achille Mbembe terms the 'dominant Eurocentric academic model' (2016: 36), which includes the introduction of Afrocentric curriculum, more diverse and representative teaching bodies, less alienating institutional cultures, and a halt to the endless reproduction of Eurocentric epistemic and critical canons, pedagogical practices and traditions of knowledge formation across South African universities.

characterized by a disregard for formal coherence and narrative linearity and a related iconoclastic treatment of the visual. The film, for example, begins with the intertitle 'THIS IS NOT THE BEGINNING' and ends with one that reads 'THIS IS NOT THE END', major audio-visual juxtapositions permeate the film, and throughout the recordings of the conference, speakers are deformed through a series of experimental cinematic devices, including jump-cuts, image inversions and croppings. Far from a mere documentation of the conference, then, *Metalepsis* is an aesthetically discordant film that is challenging both in terms of the intellectual content of the conference presentations and in Kaganof's highly stylized treatment of them.

DA: For all their formal differences, there are some broad and quite striking similarities between these films: in dealing with questions of societal transformation and oppression, both frame education as a key site of decolonial struggle; *Metalepsis* thematizes inconclusivity while *STCFF* is unfinished; Kaganof, like Loach, is no stranger to controversy and censorship.[7]

FDY: Most remarkable, for me, is the parallels in the type of postcolonial thinking that both films present. The Marxist-inflected postcolonialism of Ngũgĩ, Kentai and Odinga critiques imperialism and capitalism in a manner akin to the liberationist ideology of what Neil Lazarus describes as the 'Bandung era' of postcolonial thought (*c.* 1945–75); an 'era of Third World insurgency' (2011b: 5) characterized by anticolonial, liberational nationalism. Despite emerging nearly half a century after the end of this era, the Fallists share some of its core ideas. The 'new form of militancy' that Achille Mbembe (2015) associates with the Fallists resonates with the insurgent energies of the Bandung period, as does the movement's re-investment in Fanon. While not a Marxist initiative, moreover, their decolonial agenda has a materialist bent. The Fallists are largely made up of the 'born-free' generation, a youth raised under conditions of democracy in what after the 1994 fall of apartheid was heralded as the 'Rainbow Nation'. Against the ideals of equality and reconciliation that Rainbowism promised belies the fact that as post-apartheid South Africa embraced neoliberalism, it left the black majority significantly worse off than during apartheid, with the born frees, somewhat ironically, constituting 'the core of the socio-

---

[7]Kaganof experienced censorship with *Night Is Coming: A Threnody for the Victims of Marikana* (2014), a conference film that documents the 'Hearing Landscape Critically: Music, Place and the Spaces of Sound' conference (Stellenbosch University, 2013). The film, which is formally more experimental, and indeed challenging, than *Metalepsis*, was considered so offensive to its commissioners (the conference organisers) that they cancelled a scheduled screening at Harvard University in 2014, the decision a response to the film's almost sole focus on the noticeable absence of the Marikana massacre (where 134 striking miners were killed at the hands of the South African Police Service) from a conference centred on landscapes held in South Africa a year after the massacre took place. As with *Metalepsis*, a key theme is the academy's disconnect from South Africa's socio-political reality.

economically marginalized' (Mabasa 2017: 99). Hence their demand for free *and* decolonized education, which foregrounds a commitment to both economic-material as well as ideational-political freedom.[8]

Significantly, the Bandung era ended as the world-system stumbled into economic recession in the 1970s. The prevailing political sentiment (in the West) was to turn against the radical liberationist frameworks that had dominated to this point, and it is against the backdrop of this shift that postcolonial studies emerged. Over the next two decades a poststructuralist, postmodern and 'constitutively anti-Marxist' (Lazarus 2011a: 12) mode of postcolonial analysis reigned (*à la* Homi K. Bhabha and Gayatri Spivak), one that prioritized notions of cultural difference and epistemic subjugation over the anti-capitalist, anti-colonial energies of the Bandung-era. Writing in response to *The New Imperialism* (Harvey 2003) of the twenty-first century, such as that witnessed in the US-led invasion of Iraq, Lazarus (2011a) voices something of an imperative to return to the Bandung era and its Marxist-materialist underpinnings. The Fallist movement, as I have suggested, is in some ways embodying this shift. Despite the half-century between these films, then, there are some quite striking parallels, not least in the post-or decolonial ideas that both present. The real value in bringing them into conversation in the way that we have done here is that, when apprehended, they index, or gesture towards, certain macro transformations

**FIGURE 8.4** *Graffiti on unspecified university campus in South Africa. Screen grab from* Metalepsis in Black.

---

[8]For various discussions of the Fallist movements see Mbembe (2015; 2016); Booysen (2016); Mabasa (2017); wa Bofelo (2017); Chikane (2018); Bhambra et al. (2018); Kotze (2018).

in decolonial and postcolonial thought, with the materialist militancy espoused by the Fallists in *Metalepsis* resonating with the overt Marxist position laid out by the African revolutionaries in *STCFF*, although never naming it as such.

DA: It is worth noting that in the 1980s, some of the more radical voices in South Africa viewed apartheid and capitalism as 'two sides of the same bloody coin'. The film *Mapantsula* (Scmitz, South Africa, 1988), which has been heralded as the first anti-apartheid feature film by, for and about black South Africans, is a radical film that deals with the intersecting issues of class, racism and liberation. In contrast, socialism and class politics seem very much in the background of *Metalepsis*. Steve Biko (Figure 8.4) is referenced repeatedly – one might argue that his spectre haunts the film; however, his socialist politics are never made explicit. Is this 'absence' an absence in the film or in the movement more broadly?

FDY: This is an issue that John S. Saul and Patrick Bond discuss at length in *South Africa: The Present as History* (2014). In a chapter called 'Liberating Liberation', they note that Biko's Black Consciousness movement 'clearly underestimated' the degree to which South Africa's racial capitalist system was to be transformed into a 'relatively colour-blind' system structured around 'a hierarchy of class and corporate power', and which was 'locked into place by means of a continual recruitment... of the local, largely black, political elite, notably those within the upper echelons of the ANC' (Saul and Bond 2014: 246) – the false decolonization that I mentioned earlier. If Biko's Black Consciousness, which is the *lingua franca* of the Fallist movement, promotes a politics of black self-assertion, this is at a time when the life chances of many South Africans confront an oppressive class hierarchy determined by 'an indirect, profit driven, and dependency-deepening mode of global and local capitalist control' (Saul and Bond 2014: 246). While class 'remains substantially raced' in the country, Bond and Saul do suggest that race and class are no longer equals in determining the inequality of today's South Africa. Elelwani Ramugondo raises this issue in *Metalepsis* when she suggests that 'where colonisation used race as a marker to dictate who has access to social goods, fees in the age of austerity become that marker and a way of reintroducing segregation'. This all suggests that the next liberation struggle needs to be waged along class and not principally racial lines (and gender, environmental and all other lines), which is perhaps why the Fallist movement grounds itself within an intersectional framework, the details and indeed failures of which are addressed by a number of speakers throughout the film.

DA: The intersectionality of race and class does emerge in the drone shots of the townships, which are reminiscent of the shots of the townships in *STCFF*. Kaganof introduces a split screen during one of these shots, so that a young black protestor, pictured singing on the left of the screen, is presented alongside the footage of the townships, thus simultaneously visualizing – and tying together – the experience of racial oppression *and* the material poverty of the township. While class here is not being relegated to race, more generally the film does seem to be prioritizing race; it is called *Metalepsis in Black*, refers to itself as 'a film about whiteness' and much of the discussions centre on Black Consciousness, black pain and on unpacking race as a category of difference.

FDY: Rekgotsofetse Chikane, himself a Fallist, notes that the movement 'created a veil of secrecy over a black person's class difference to place focus on the broader struggle of black people' (2018: location 2271). If we follow Chikane's assessment, class politics is less prominent – in the movement and in the film – precisely because it served the interests of the movement's class-privileged black members (Chikane refers to these within the critical category of 'Coconuts'), inasmuch as it allowed them to climb the ranks of the movement's supposedly non-hierarchal structure. So, a false decolonization of sorts was potentially happening in the movement itself, hence the first chapter of Chikane's book being the Fanonion question: 'Can Coconuts be Trusted with the Revolution?' (Chikane 2018: location 37). The movement's deliberate relegation of class to race – a reversal of the politics of *STCFF* – may explain why the issue of class, or indeed socialism, is not explicitly addressed in the film, even though this omission would certainly contradict the movement's intersectional framework.

DA: In addition to discussing the false decolonization that you are mentioning, Ngũgĩ makes the point that the West wanted the state to be indebted. In charting the shift from the Foucauldian 'disciplinary society' to the Deleuzian 'control society', Maurizio Lazzarato suggests that '[d]ebt constitutes the most deterritorialized and the most general power relation through which the neoliberal power bloc institutes its class struggle' (2012: 90). So, is this focus on fees in *Metalepsis* much more than an economic demand; could we see it representing a desire not simply to afford education but to escape the shackles of debt, which capitalism seeks to secure?

FDY: The demand for free, de-commodified education is a challenge to the neoliberal logic structuring post-apartheid South Africa. '[T]o win free education', Patrick Bond writes, 'fossilised neoliberalism must fall' (in Booysen 2016: 192). At the same time the question of fees is also a question of access. Universities in South Africa, as elsewhere, are strategically positioned at the centre of not only knowledge but also skills production, and uneven access to these skills clearly has societal ramifications. This is why, as Sizwe Mpofu-Walsh argues in the film, 'you cannot speak about a country without speaking about its higher education system'. The racial and class disparities in South Africa are thus not merely reflected in but are indeed produced by the differential access to the country's higher education system. The financially brutal fee structure reproduces this, hence the university being a key site of struggle; it is 'fundamental... to inequality', as Walsh states. If the debt trap that *STCFF* narrates works as a means of ensuring the development of underdevelopment, unaffordable fees preserve societal inequality, as Elelwani Ramugondo so lucidly argues.

DA: I found it quite striking that, whereas *STCFF* is explicit in its calls for socialist solutions to these problems, here the struggle is located as more localized. Do you think this is representative of a wider tendency away from demanding large-scale social transformation to more localized solutions, or the move to the 'totemic activism' that Walsh also mentions in the film?

FDY: I guess this depends on what one means by large-scale. Totemic activism, as Walsh describes it, is about condensing structural issues into more tangible, visible symbols so that they become easier to rally around and against; the Rhodes statue is a symbol for white supremacy so the call for Rhodes to fall is a call for white supremacy to end. As with the movement itself, totemic activism is societal and structural in scope. Having said that, *Metalepsis* certainly has a more localized focus than *STCFF* – the film does not leave South Africa – and does not seem interested in the kind of international socialism that we see at the end of *STCFF*.

DA: This brings up the question of screening the film outside of South Africa, as I know you did, and how the film's more localized focality was taken up by audiences perhaps less familiar with these debates. In addition to the film's radical aesthetics, Kaganof does not help to orientate viewers by providing the contextual detail that more conventional documentaries provide, and there is indeed no narrator or narration as we have in *STCFF*.

FDY: The event's co-organizer, Rebecca Duncan, and myself were concerned that the issues in the film may be unfamiliar to audiences here in Glasgow, and so Rebecca, in her introduction to the film, provided a comprehensive account of the context within which the Fallist movement emerged. At the same time, we were confident that the film's decolonial themes would resonate with UK audiences – indeed that this is a film that academics in the UK, in particular, need to see. Although the film does not itself leave South Africa, the issues it addresses – not least British colonialism – quite clearly stretch beyond the country's borders. We screened the film at the University of Glasgow as it had announced a report into this institution's historical links with the slave trade (Mullen and Newman 2018), so the film's focus on decolonizing the academy was something of a *zeitgeist* issue within the university at the time.

DA: At that screening I was struck by the repeated references to Guy Debord and the Situationist International. The film is described as a 'Situationist Message in a Bottle', Debord himself is credited as André Keet in the film, and when Keet suggests that 'the project of critique... has been usurped into the spectacle', he references Debord's 1967 book *La société du spectacle/The Society of the Spectacle*, which he adapted to the screen in the film of the same name in 1973. There seems something quite situationist in breaking up the linearity of the film – opening with, as you've noted, a statement that says 'THIS IS NOT THE BEGINNING', and concluding with

'THIS IS NOT THE END', while running the credits in the middle. What is at stake in Kaganof importing Debordian sensibilities into the South African context?

FDY: I think there is a certain tension in the way that Kaganof – who spent years in exile in Europe – grafts European aesthetic principles onto a movement that not only insists that it is generating its own theory but also one that takes very seriously the issue of decolonizing, or provincializing, the intellectual hegemony of the Eurocentric canon. There is no need to 'run to your Western theorists', Walsh suggests in the film, because 'theory is being generated here'. The issue, then, is not whether one should or should not use such and such a framework, but rather which framework is the most appropriate and generative. Having said that, Debord is writing about the commodification of life at roughly the time when *STCFF* was made, and if we earlier suggested that *Metalepsis* indexes a return to some of the ideas that emerged in the socio-political or world-historical climate of *STCFF*, then perhaps this is part of that return. The Paris-based student protests of 1968, for example, weigh heavy on Debord's thinking, and the scenes in *Metalepsis* in which the students shut down university campuses in South Africa invite parallels with similar actions in Europe five decades previously.

DA: I am reluctant to continually frame *Metalepsis* within a European framework; yet, comparisons with the rhythmic disruptions of Debord's cinema are difficult to avoid. In his 'On the Concept of History', Walter Benjamin discusses revolution in terms of the interruption of the continuity of linear progress, the Benjaminian 'flash' creating 'a revolutionary chance in the fight for the oppressed past' ([1940] 2003: 396). We might view the aesthetic practice of *Metalepsis* as a continuation of the 'chain of dialogues' that we discussed earlier – in this instance linking the politics of film form with the development of historical consciousness, something which is common to Third Cinema and the cinema of Debord.

FDY: The key point for me is that this 'chain of dialogues' needs to include the voices – and theoretical insights – of those that emerge from the place under consideration. Our analysis of *Metalepsis* should therefore take account of the Fallist's own theoretical or philosophical framework, one significant component of which happens to be a creative employment of disruption. Achille Mbembe (2015) writes of a Fanonian 'politics of... disruption' that the movement ushered in. Chikane also dwells on this in his *Breaking a Rainbow, Building a Nation* (2018), noting that the movement's adoption of 'disruption as its method' (location 1504), while often excessively violent, is motivated by 'the creation rather than destruction of the social infrastructure in South Africa' (2018: location 1508); the Fallist philosophy, as the title of Chikane's book attests, is as much concerned with building as it is breaking. The cinematic 'disruption as method', including narrative discontinuity, image mirrorings, extreme close-ups (Figure 8.5)

FIGURE 8.5 Extreme close-up on conference delegates in Metalepsis in Black. Screen grab from Metalepsis in Black.

and audio-visual dislocations, are discordantly arranged, resulting in the fragmented, almost schizophrenic ordering of the conference speakers, and of the film.

DA: These disruptions do conjure the ideas of Debordian and Benjaminan.

FDY: Yes, but I do think it is important – and more in keeping with the film's decolonial thematics – to adopt a more localized interpretive grid, one located in the movement itself. *Metalepsis* can be said to be embodying, if unintentionally, the Fallist philosophy of creative disruption, of breaking to build – something that I have tentatively coined Cinematic Fallism. The paradox here is that as an academic from the Global North writing on African film, I am acutely aware of the need to avoid a proprietary relation to this critical concept. Yet, simultaneously, the academic system within which I operate demands of researchers to be original or innovative, with the associations with the imperial trope of discovery that this demand encompasses. I'm not sure how to resolve this contradiction, if indeed it is resolvable. Perhaps it needs more dialogue, with filmmakers and with academics working in Africa.

DA: It is probably best, then, not to not conclude anything too neatly. Kaganof forcibly refuses to provide any closure, and much of our thinking around the dialogue has been concerned with opening instead of closing ideas.

FDY: The film's final images picture student activist Jodi Williams berating academics who write about the movement 'from a very comfortable distance', while her fellow activists encounter police violence. Addressing church figures and academics, she exclaims, 'your silence has been painful; your silence has been painful'; these are the last words we hear.

DA: And yet, there is evidently a lot more to say about these two films, whether approached individually or as a pair. Moreover, discussion and debate on Third Cinema, Marxism, reverse tutelage, positionality, intersectionality, the nature of academic work and the other ideas which we have discussed will be ongoing, both within the academy and beyond. This dialogue has sought to be a provocation to thought rather than a forum for conclusivity. In keeping with the dialogical spirit of Third Cinema, the ongoing political struggle and the open-ended nature of both films, the work continues. As with the final scene in *Metalepsis*, 'THIS IS NOT THE END'.

## Bibliography

*Africa, Thinking in Motion/Afrique La Pensée en Mouvement* (2017), [Film] dir. Bekolo, Senegal/Cameroon.

Anderson, Kevin S. (2010), *Marx at the Margins: On Nationalism, Ethnicity, and Non-Western Societies*, Chicago & London: The University of Chicago Press.

Andrews, Kehinde (2018), *Back to Black: Retelling Black Radicalism for the 21st Century*, London: Zed Books.

Archibald, David. (2011), 'Reeling from Injustice', *Financial Times*, 26 August.

Bâ, Saer Maty and Will Higbee (eds) (2012), *De-westernising Film Studies*, Abingdon: Routledge.

Bakhtin, Mikhail (1981), *The Dialogic Imagination: Four Essays*, Austin: University of Texas Press.

Baronian, M. A. and M. Rosello (2008), 'Jacques Rancière and indisciplinarity', *Art & Research*, 2 (1). Available at http://www.artandresearch.org.uk/v2n1/jrinterview.html (accessed 7 July 2019).

Benjamin, Walter ([1940] 2003), 'On the Concept of History', in Howard Eiland and Michael W. Jennings (eds), *Selected Writings, Vol. 4*, trans. Edmund Jephcott et. al., Cambridge: Harvard University Press.

Bhambra, Gurminder, Dalia Gebrial and Karem Nişancıoğlu (eds) (2018), *Decolonising the University*, London: Pluto Press.

Bohrer, Ashley J. (2018), 'Intersectionality and Marxism: A Critical Historiography', *Historical Materialism*, 26 (2): 46–74.

Booysen, Susan (ed.) (2016), *Fees Must Fall: Student Revolt, Decolonisation and Governance in South Africa*, Johannesburg: Wits University Press.

Caughie, John. (2000), *Television Drama: Realism, Modernism, and British Culture*, Oxford: Oxford University Press.

Chanan, Michael. (1997), 'The Changing Geography of Third Cinema', *Screen*, 38 (4): 372–88.

Chikane, Rekgotsofetse (2018), *Breaking a Rainbow, Building a Nation: The Politics behind #MustFall Movements*, Johannesburg: Picador Africa (Kindle edition).

Crenshaw, Kimberlé (1991), 'Mapping the Margins: Intersectionality, Identity Politics, and Violence against Women of Color', *Stanford Law Review*, 43 (6): 1241–99.

*Days of Hope* (1975), [Film] dir. Loach, UK.
Debord, Guy ([1967] 1995), *The Society of the Spectacle*, trans. Donald Nicholson-Smith, New York: Zone Books.
Deleuze, Gilles and Félix Guattari (2013), *A Thousand Plateaus: Capitalism and Schizophrenia*, transl. Brian Massumi, London: Bloomsbury Academic.
Errazu, Miguel and Alejandro Pedregal (2019), 'Future Experiments from the Past: Third Cinema and Artistic Research from Below', *Alphaville: Journal of Film and Screen Media*, 17: 38–63.
Fanon, Frantz ([1963] 2004), *The Wretched of the Earth*, trans. Richard Philcox, New York: Grove Press.
Fisher, Mark (2009), *Capitalist Realism: Is There No Alternative?*, London: Zero Books.
Freire, Paolo ([1970] 1996), *Pedagogy of the Oppressed*, trans. Myra Bergman Ramos, London: Penguin Books.
Gopal, Priyamvada (2019), *Insurgent Empire: Anticolonial Resistance and British Dissent*, London & New York: Verso.
Grosfoguel, Ramon (2007), 'The Epistemic Decolonial Turn', *Cultural Studies*, 21 (2-3): 211–23.
Guneratne, Anthony R. and Wimal Dissanayake (eds) (2003), *Rethinking Third Cinema*, London: Routledge.
Harvey, David. (2003), *The New Imperialism*, Oxford: Oxford University Press.
*Hidden Agenda* (1990), [Film] dir. Loach, UK.
Hilton, Matthew (2015), 'Ken Loach and the Save the Children Film: Humanitarianism, Imperialism, and the Changing Role of Charity in Postwar Britain', *The Journal of Modern History*, 87 (2): 357–94.
Karam, Beschara (2018), '"An-Other"-Centred Film Curricula: Decolonising Film Studies in Africa', in Bruce Mutsvairo (eds), *The Palgrave Handbook of Media and Communication Research in Africa*, 111–27, Basingstoke: Palgrave Macmillan.
Kotze, Joleen S. (2018), 'On Decolonisation and Revolution: A Kristevan Reading on the Hashtags Student Movements and Fallism', *Politikon*, 45 (1): 112–27.
*Land and Freedom/Tierra y Libertad* (1995), [Film] dir. Loach, UK & Spain.
Lazarus, Neil (2011a), *The Postcolonial Unconscious*, Cambridge: Cambridge University Press.
Lazarus, Neil (2011b), 'What Postcolonial Theory Doesn't Say', *Race and Class*, 53 (1): 3–27.
Lazzarato, Maurizio (2012), *The Making of the Indebted Man: An Essay on the Neoliberal Condition*, trans. Joshua David Jordan, Los Angeles: Semiotext(e).
Mabasa, Khwezi (2017), 'The rebellion of the Born Unfrees: Fallism and the Neocolonial Corporate University', *Strategic Review for Southern Africa*, 39 (2): 94–116.
*Mapantsula* (1988), [Film] dir. Scmitz, South Africa.
Marx, Karl ([1867] 1990), *Capital: A Critique of Political Economy*, trans. Ben Fowles, London: Penguin Classics.
Marx, Karl ([1868–1870] 2010), 'Letter to Sigfrid Meyer and August Vogt (April 1870)', in Karl Marx and Frederick Engels (eds), *Collected Works, vol. 43, Letters 1868–70*, 471–6, London: Lawrence and Wishart.

Mbembe, Achille J. (2015), 'Achille Mbembe on the State of South African Political Life', *Africa in a Country* https://africasacountry.com/2015/09/achille-mbembe-on-the-state-of-south-african-politics (accessed 15 July 2019).

Mbembe, Achille J. (2016), 'Decolonizing the University: New Directions', *Arts & Humanities in Higher Education*, 15 (1): 29–45.

*Metalepsis in Black* (2016), [Film] dir. Kaganof, South Africa.

Mullen, Steven and Simon Newman (2018), *Slavery, Abolition and the University of Glasgow: Report and Recommendations of the University of Glasgow History of Slavery Steering Committee*, [Report: History of Slavery Steering Committee] University of Glasgow. https://www.gla.ac.uk/media/Media_607547_smxx.pdf.

Nagib, Lucy, Chris Perriam and Rajinder Dudrah (eds) (2012), *Theorizing World Cinema*, London and New York: I.B. Taurus.

*Night Is Coming: A Threnody for the Victims of Marikana* (2014), [Film] dir. Kaganof, South African

*Save the Children Fund Film* (1971), [Film] dir. Loach, UK.

Saul, John S. and Patrick Bond (2014), *South Africa – The Present as History: From Mrs Ples to Mandela and Marikana*, Woodbridge: James Currey.

Shohat, Ella and Robert Stam (1994), *Unthinking Eurocentrism: Multiculturalism and the Media*, London and New York: Routledge.

Solanas, Fernando and Octavio Getino (1970), 'Towards a Third Cinema', *Cinéaste*, 4 (3): 1–10.

Trotsky, Leon ([1930] 2010). *Permanent Revolution & Results and Prospects* (Seattle: Red Letter Press).

Wa Bofelo, Mphutlane (2017), 'Fallism and the Dialectics of Spontaneity and Organization: Disrupting Tradition to Reconstruct Tradition', *Pambazuka News*. https://www.pambazuka.org/democracy-governance/fallism-and-dialectics-spontaneity-and-organization-disrupting-tradition (accessed 6 July 2019).

Warwick Research Collective (2015), *Combined and Uneven Development: Towards a New Theory of World Literature*, Liverpool: Liverpool University Press.

Wayne, Mike (2001), *Political Film: The Dialectics of Third Cinema*, London: Pluto Press.

Wa Thiong'o, Ngũgĩ ([1986] 2005), *Decolonising the Mind: The Politics of Language in African Literature*, Woodridge and Rochester, NY: James Currey.

Wylie, Alison (2003), 'Why Standpoint Matters', in Robert Figueroa and Sandra Harding (eds), *Science and Other Cultures: Issues in Philosophies of Science and Technology*, 26–48, New York: Routledge.

# 9

# Newsreel Front: A revived vision of Third Cinema in Slovenia

## Andrej Šprah
## (Slovenian Cinematheque, Ljubljana)

After the disintegration of the Socialist Federal Republic of Yugoslavia, its film landscape changed drastically. In Slovenia, this amounted to wild privatization of distribution and screening circuits, on the one hand, and the attempt of the state to regulate film creativity, on the other. The new situation dealt a great blow to all forms of film production, especially independent filmmaking. After a short period of seeming prosperity, the expansion of the market economy and ruthless capitalism, the economic crisis and political instability led to the rise of rebellious energies culminating in the great social unrest of the so-called 'uprising movements' at the end of 2012. In the aggravated conditions of social struggles, guerrilla film strivings gained new momentum and, in a practically budgetless production (a consequence of them operating outside the Slovenian Film Centre's system of allocating state funds earmarked for cinema and the audiovisual field), provided an enviable level of quality and quantity of radical political films on the borderline between documentary and experimental filmmaking.

In light of the rise of resistant filmmaking, it was important that in 2009 the Slovenian translation of one of the fundamental texts of Third Cinema, the celebrated 'manifesto' by Fernando Solanas and Octavio Getino,

'Towards a Third Cinema', was published. The new forms of politically committed films in Slovenia strive to operate in accordance with some of the fundamental postulates of Third Cinema – the demand for creativity that the 'system finds indigestible' and cannot assimilate, and the necessity of a committed film reception that considers the viewer as an active co-participant in the film event.

> Third Cinema is a political cinema about much more than politics in the narrow sense. It is a cinema of social and cultural emancipation... [which] needs fundamental and pervasive transformation, and if cinema is to make its own, relatively modest contribution, it too must feel the heat of such transformations, not only as films, but in its modes of production and reception. Third Cinema is such a cinema, or at least it is as close as we can get to such a cinema *this* side of such profound transformations. (Wayne 2001: 1)

On the basis of the binding ideal platform of Third Cinema, the experiences of militant film collectives from the end of the 1960s (in Latin America, the United States, France, Italy, Germany, Japan etc.) and the heritage of the political cinema of former Yugoslavia ('black wave', 'black documentary'), an independent film collective named Newsreel Front was established, bringing together filmmakers, artists and theoreticians. The collective strives towards a revitalization of a specific form of the anti-newsreel as a film practice of counter-informing, which is characterized by its 'immediate relationship to current events and struggles, with which they call for action; documenting facts or situations ignored, concealed or falsified by the dominant media; expressing critical perspectives largely absent in the dominant media; reflecting *in situ* on the role of images and their depiction in history' (Brenez 2017: 58). With this form, the collective follows the tradition of those precious cinematic strivings that throughout the history of moving images drove cineastes to the world's hotspots where they combined their visions with the oppositional and resistant endeavours. It also belongs to the current initiatives for the revival and revitalization of the 'forgotten' or 'obsolete' non-fiction genres (film pamphlets, film leaflets, agitprop films, polemical films etc.) characteristic of the avant-garde of contemporary political filmmaking all over the world. It thus joins the tendencies of raising awareness, which has, with their disclosed provenience and a defined vision, persistently resisted indoctrination – the basic tool of politico-cultural imperialism. The activities of Newsreel Front thus prove that the anti-newsreel and several other forms of committed films are exceptionally tenacious genres of progressive creativity that, receiving the impulses from the extra-filmic reality of social conflicts and class struggle, keep being revolutionized and keep inventing new forms of articulating resistance with moving images.

The purpose of this chapter is to analyse the creativity of the Newsreel Front and thereby show how, with the new forms of drawing on the original ideas of Third Cinema, its liberatory tendencies can be realized anywhere in the world. Persistence in the struggle against the inequalities resulting from capital accumulation brings images of emancipation, evidencing that Third Cinema is far from being a thing of the past; rather, it is still a breakthrough and vital film-theoretical factor. It is not only tenacious but also exceptionally responsive to the changes required by the new environments and the new socio-political formations in which it operates. Its fundamental programme orientations can still – or again and again – be detected everywhere where the subjugated, endangered, suppressed and marginalized communities are fighting for freedom. What is at stake here is not only the pointing out of the intolerability of certain situations but a direct breaking of the frameworks of the established social and cultural conventions. Thus, a consciousness is generated that, regardless of its geo-strategic placement and socio-political circumstances, recognizes its current position as a site of resistance. Such cinema represents a specific 'dialectical synthesis, that is, the critical sifting and reconfiguration of First and Second Cinema according to the needs of contemporary struggles' (Wayne 2016: 26). All this shows how justified Mike Wayne was in his belief in the persistence and the tenaciousness of the practice and theory of Third Cinema: 'It will continue to emerge in new and changing forms, tied to the specificities of the struggles it is exploring, as long as the political-ethical imperative for those struggles exists: that is as long as capitalism and its offshoots in imperialism continue to exist' (Wayne 2016).

## Constellation

One of the key creative strategies of Newsreel Front is the attempt at establishing a specific connection with the audience. The collective devotes special attention to the final, reproductive phases of the cinema event – the distribution, projection and presentation of the works. In line with the principles of alternative modes of production, the reproduction of films also takes place in a number of possible or accessible ways. In Slovenia and abroad, the films have been presented at cinemas, art galleries, film festivals, cultural and youth clubs, alternative culture squats, havens of the excluded and the marginalized, but also schools, universities and, of course, on various web platforms. What comes most to the fore in the exhibition processes is the principle of collective operation and the commitment to the tradition of Third Cinema. In the production phases, the films are made according to various working principles – from completely individual to tandem or group creation. The presentation itself, however, is always a collective act, with the co-operators addressing the audience at the projections and encouraging reflection, discussion and reaction in ways that encapsulate the principles of the cinema event of Third Cinema: 'The "cine-acción" or "cinema event" was theorised as an encounter capable of catalysing the latent potentialities of the spectator, presumed passive, into the active "protagonist" of cine-event; this protagonist bore the same relationship to cinema as the militant actor to political process' (Eshun and Gray 2011: 5). Film projections are thus combinations of a series of different strategies that Kodwo Eshun and Ros Gray point out in the editorial of the special issue of *Third Text*: 'The Militant Image: A Ciné-Geography' – which is a concept that defines the processes and activities of the current international situation of Third Cinema.

The new geography of world cinema includes activities that, as forms of afterlives of the militant image, are involved in current social struggles or intensively deal with the past. Eshun and Gray's answer to the question of how to understand the militant image in the current geostrategic cinema situation centres, especially on inclusivity:

> Expansively, capaciously, exorbitantly: the militant image comprises any form of image or sound – from essay film to fiction feature, from observational documentary to found-footage ciné-pamphlet, from newsreel to agitational reworkings of colonial film production – produced in and through film-making practices dedicated to the liberation struggles and revolutions of the late twentieth century. (Eshun and Gray 2011: 1)

The formal heterogeneity of adopting a series of mentioned practices that is characteristic of Newsreel Front's creativity is an additional motivation for its direct communication with the audience. The production process is far from professional – original images are shot and edited with cheap, unprofessional equipment, while the gathered and found footage comes from everywhere; it is taken from a range of formats and carriers and is (most often) of poor quality and resolution (figure 9.1).

This material is best characterized by the mentioned concept of a 'poor image', which, as Steyerl argues, 'initiates another chapter in the historical genealogy of nonconformist information circuits' (2009: 8). The discussed strategies reflect the specific quality of filmic counter-informing and awareness raising, which, on the one hand, has a rich history but, on the other, demands the invention of new approaches for new emancipatory endeavours. Even though the newsreel format is essentially informative and like a reportage, it can also be subversive in its innovative approaches, especially in searching for non-consensual images, revealing the areas of invisibility or interpreting a certain liminal state. Showing uncapturable, undeterminable and unstageable images is synonymous with representing subjects that express themselves and become other precisely through the

FIGURE 9.1 Karl Marx Among Us, 2013, black & white, sound, videostill. Copyright: Jurij Meden & Newsreel Front.

very processes of liberation. The commitment of Newsreel Front to new forms and subjects of social struggle is thus in accordance with the tasks of contemporary political cinema pointed out by Ewa Mazierska and Lars Kristensen:

> the task of modern political filmmaking is not to address itself to a predetermined people but to recognize its absence and contribute to its invention. Such attempts already exist; examples are concepts such as 'multitude' and 'precariat', which largely replaced the old term of 'working class'. It could be argued that a large proportion of contemporary political cinema addresses these new subjects rather than the proletariat in the old sense. (Mazierska and Kristensen 2015: 14)

But even though the protagonists of Newsreel Front's films are rightless, excluded, silenced, exploited and so on, they are not treated as helpless victims caught in the vicious circle of hopelessness but as active bearers of the struggle for justice.

One of the conceptual orientations of Newsreel Front is to establish an audiovisual relation between the current and the past liberatory initiatives. Their activities are directed towards the crisis points of Slovenian reality (from popular uprisings to advocating the rights of rightless workers, asylum seekers, overlooked and silenced communities). At the same time, they focus on the flows of energy that take place through the connection of current creativity with the historical stages of filmmakers participating in the class struggle. Such connections are evident primarily in two determinations. On the one hand, in the use of the connecting elements with which they combine archival and found footage and the originally filmed images, and, on the other hand, in the direct foregrounding of and reflection on the correlations themselves. So, the substantive focus on the underprivileged members of society, who maintain their dignity precisely through various forms of resistance, is always accompanied by a reflection on the legitimacy of the images of their endeavours. In line with what is an important factor of Third Cinema, that is, the use of a wide range of forms, approaches and methods, the creative spectrum of Newsreel Front is also heterogeneous. The production range thus includes thirteen film titles and countless related projects (unique cinema events). Such a variety does not allow us to strictly categorize the works of Newsreel Front according to their formal determinations. Nevertheless, based on their basic principles and predominant characteristics, we can distinguish between three groups of works: documentary, experimental and newsreel, among which we will focus mostly on the latest two.

## Experimental principle

The earliest work in the experimental group is Jurij Meden's *1717 km poletja* (*1717 Km of Summer*, 2009). This medium-length experimental road movie shot on Super 8mm film documents a journey through the part of the Balkans that had not long before been part of the same country – in a frenetic montage similar with images of a film diary, without any differentiation between the important and the unimportant, between the real, the sensuous and the symbolic, between the concrete and the abstract. A simple composition conceived on the experience of unstoppable time becomes a film of pure experience, which nevertheless suggests that such journeys also testify to the weight of everything that has caused new nationalisms, new borders, new limitations and new stratifications (figure 9.2).

Nika Autor's *Solidarnost* (*Solidarity*, 2011) is a remake of Joyce Wieland's 1973 minimalist avant-garde newsreel of the same title. The film documents the workers' protest in Ljubljana in 2011 in the same way that, in the 1970s, Wieland filmed the strike at Dare Foods factory in Kitchener, Ontario, which lasted for more than a year. The two films do not show the protestors in their entirety but focus merely on their feet or footwear and the ground on which they walk. The only significant difference in an otherwise faithful pastiche

FIGURE 9.2 1717 Km of Summer, 2009, black & white and colour, sound, videostill. Copyright: Jurij Meden & Newsreel Front.

of Wieland is the insertion of a title card with the lines taken from Bertolt Brecht's poem 'German War Primer', written during the early years of the Second World War. Despite the time gap, both filmmakers remind us that 'worker struggles form a long unbroken continuum in capitalist and post-capitalist history and art, from Daumier to Bertolucci, and that movement and effort – by feet, mouths and bodies in general – constitute the true index of solidarity, whether in Kitchener or Ljubljana' (Waugh 2017: 35). Autor raises questions such as: What is solidarity today? Who is solidary? With whom? When are we solidary? The reshot of the movie was motivated by the current situation of mass unemployment, horrifyingly exploitative work conditions and ever-more exploitative restructuring of the labour market when the question of solidarity is undermined by structures of domination.

The above works were followed by three short films: Nika Autor's *General* (2012) and Jurij Meden's *Normalen film* (*A Normal Film*, 2012) and *Viharni vrh: Ljubezenska pesem* (*A Love Poem: Wuthering Heights Redux*, 2012). All three are didactical leaflets, unique visualizations of their main point foregrounded as a (spoken or graphically represented) quotation on the topics of class struggle and film history. *General* is a film interpretation of Bertolt Brecht's poem 'General, Your Tank Is a Powerful Vehicle', which alludes to the war commanders on the territory of former Yugoslavia. *A Normal Film* documents the view of Peter Kubelka, the godfather of twentieth-century avant-garde cinema, about the misplaced use of the designation 'experimental film' for the works he and likeminded filmmakers are making. Kubelka thus emphasizes: 'I always say I make normal films'. Based on the ascertainment of the *Communist Manifesto* that 'the history of all hitherto existing society is the history of class struggles', *A Love Poem* is a visualization of the eponymous poem by Miklavž Komelj, one of the most prominent Slovenian contemporary committed poets, which begins with the following line: 'I would like to talk to you, as a communist to a communist.'

The distinct tendency towards raising awareness and using film expression that can best articulate it is most directly conveyed in Meden's medium-length *Karl Marx med nami* (*Karl Marx Among Us*, 2013). With its telling title and unambiguous subtitle ('Agitprop Video'), the experimental collage expressly points out its orientation, with which it continues in the tradition of those strivings with filmic means that, throughout history, have driven cineastes to the world's hot spots where they combined their visions with resistance endeavours. It refers directly to a 'film pamphlet or agit cinema', which, in the vision of Third Cinema, strives towards fulfilling goals that are 'specifically related to concrete circumstances' (Getino 2015: 67). It thus joins the tendencies of raising awareness that, with a clearly foregrounded provenience and a defined vision, have persistently resisted indoctrination and regime propaganda. The film's basic characteristic is its heterogeneity, for it plays on the registers of the various traditions, styles, concepts and genres of politically committed filmic approaches. In its complex conception, we recognize the principles of cinematic pamphlets as defined by Nicole Brenez in her discussion of the permanent invention of the cinematic pamphlet. This form, which always focuses on social injustice, invents ways of articulating injustices, both in dealing with interpersonal relations and in the conception of filmic space and time; but it above all endeavours to convey the physical dimensions, the symbolic role and the violence of exploitation and oppression.

> In order to achieve this, a way of organising images must be invented that will join the powers of *syntax* (what can be shown as a relation, in a conflictual form: class struggle) and *parataxis* (what refuses relation, generating caesurae, cracks, breaks: for instance, the workers' smiles). Thus establishing that cinema can elucidate phenomena by removing appearances and recovering social logics. (Brenez: 2005)

In the film under discussion, the syntax is reflected in the composing of different levels of images into meaningful links between the segments of the film, which consists of eight chapters or 'trials', a prologue, an epilogue and an intermezzo. Parataxis, on the other hand, can be found in the strategies of combining the heterogeneous audiovisual sections with other film elements. At the level of images, the formal determinations are characterized by ambivalence and polyvalence since the film includes abstract, concrete and indistinct images. The first type of images includes both non-figural abstraction (the chapter 'Karl Marx in Abstracto') and non-narrative abstraction (elements of Kurt Kren's type of *structural film* and *abstract (rhythmic) film* in the trials 'Karl Marx in the Sky', 'Karl Marx in the Woods' and 'Karl Marx on the Road'). Concrete images can be found in the filmmaker's original documentary footage. Indistinct images (which don't allow 'inattentive perception' but demand 'special, focused attention') are characterized especially by frenetic editing (of documentary footage), at times in consonance with the rhythm of the musical accompaniment. The determinations at the declarative level include the dimensions of picture, music and text (intertitles and comments). Most of the images are original, with a few archival additions. The music ranges over various genres: classical music, revolutionary instrumental and choral songs, alternative rock, death folk, free jazz, contemporary experimental electronics, film scores and so on. The textual level consists of chapter announcements, comments and a series of quotations from literature (William Shakespeare, Srečko Kosovel – one of the key avant-garde poets of Slovenian modernism – and Samuel Beckett), culture and politics (Young Communist League of Yugoslavia) and philosophy (Mladen Dolar and Slavoj Žižek). In this method, it is especially the use of the various levels of articulation that is in close agreement with the principles of Third Cinema. So the use of image, text and music, while the editing, which is based on the principles of carefully synchronizing the musical rhythm and the visual level, is reminiscent of such legendary works as *Now!* (1965) by Santiago Álvarez or *Me gustan los estudiantes* (*I Like Students*, 1967) by Mario Handler. An added value can be seen in certain experimental approaches, including abstraction, indeterminacy and hypotheticalness, which are in line with the strategies of underground and avant-garde cinema and go beyond representation.

The content determinations are reflected through the film's actional and conceptual aspects. The first is characteristic especially of the chapter 'Karl Marx in the Street'. This trial is a unique film-within-a-film presented as a 'Film found in the trash can', which suggests the 'garbage heap of history' and at the same time foregrounds the found footage method as one of the key creative principles of Newsreel Front. This chapter is the longest, and it also has its opening credits (K.O.S.O.V.E.L. in cooperation with the 7th International and Liberation Front 2.0). The trial documents the night action of spray painting the slogan 'To be or not to be' on the facades of establishment institutions – government facilities, the buildings of official culture, capital, religion and the bearers of other ideologies (figure 9.3).

FIGURE 9.3 Karl Marx Among Us *(To be or not to be)*, 2013, black & white, sound, videostill. Copyright: Jurij Meden & Newsreel Front.

The spray painting was carried out especially for the film and shot as a combination of a city symphony and soft guerrilla action, but it also had a real effect (for a long time, the graffiti adorned the facades of certain 'desecrated' buildings). In this part of the film, the predominant image is a special kind of an 'action image' that refers to the revitalization of the 'culture-as-a-weapon' vision (the slogan of the illegal resistance movement of the Young Communist League of Yugoslavia). It also revives the tradition of night underground actions during the Fascist occupation, whose aim was to call attention to the presence of the 'Liberation Front' as a form of a nationwide cultural, ideal and finally armed resistance. In addition to the musical motifs from the time of workers' revolutions and the partisan struggle against Fascism, the chapter also features a song by the folk death band *Los Duggans* entitled 'Rise Up You Workers!' (whose lyrics are based on the concluding part of the *Communist Manifesto*). The second found footage segment is 'Karl Marx in a Dream', the trial announced as a 'Film found in a mailbox'. This is the only part of the film that contains actual archival material, for, in addition to the staged burlesque scenes, we come across the famous motif of Lenin's simple apartment and the even more famous shot of him holding a cat in his lap. The highlighted factors meet the criteria that Thomas Waugh has set for politically engaged non-fiction filmmaking by emphasizing that what surfaces here is 'disposability, ephemerality, topicality, directness, immediacy, instrumentality, didacticism, collective or anonymous authorship, unconventional formats, non-availability, and ultimately non-evaluability' (1984: xxii).

In addition to the alternating abstract and concrete elements of the visual and sound dimensions, the film's conceptual aspects are reflected especially in its references. In addition to its direct references to the Marxist and Leninist tradition of the relation to art and class struggle in picture, words and music, the film uses a series of indirect signs indicating the consideration of new forms of exclusion, 'new forms of social apartheid – new walls and slums' (Žižek 2009: 53), especially the ones pointed out by Žižek and Dolar. 'Karl Marx and Smoking' is thus an attempt at articulating one of the new forms of exclusion through the prism of Dolar's pamphlet 'The Smoking Communism', which equates smokers with proletarians and concludes with the following belief quoted in the film: 'But against all odds and in a wild fancy I would like this statement to read: communism has a chance.' This is also the film's first concluding premise. The second is Beckett's demand featured in the Epilogue: 'Try again. Fail again. Fail better.' The third concluding point belongs to the musical motif of John Ford's *My Darling Clementine* (1946), accompanying the end credits of Meden's film. All three concluding emphases suggest attempts at calling for the conception of a new community, a becoming-people, which can be an excluded people, a minor race, the others, the mob.

## Newsreel principle

The most complex work in this group is *Filmski Obzornik 55* (*Newsreel 55*, 2013). This medium-length project by Newsreel Front, specifically Nika Autor, Marko Bratina, Ciril Oberstar and Jurij Meden, focuses on three different connections between the past and the present of class struggle in Slovenia and former Yugoslavia. The film's title originates in the fact that, between 1946 and 1951, fifty-four state-regulated newsreels were made in Slovenia. After more than sixty years, *Newsreel 55* thus informally continues and at the same time subverts this tradition. At the conceptual level, it includes several temporal dimensions and various visual elements of their articulation. It focuses on the period of the Second World War, the 1988 workers' protests in Maribor, the genocide during the disintegration of Yugoslavia and the Slovenian popular uprisings in 2012 and 2013. The visual level includes the use of archival film and television material, amateur footage, newspaper sources, current guerrilla images, documentary notes and film staging. The use of visual material is often combined with verbal commentary, quotations and writings, with which the film questions the status and the meaning of images in social conflicts. One of the main preoccupations of *Newsreel 55* is the questioning of the appropriateness of the image that could visualize the various forms of class struggle and the connections between the past and the present ways of their expression. At the same time, it belongs to the line of counter-informing, which, through the development of cinema, sought, discovered and developed various forms of providing information and news that subverted and belied the official media. These are the tendencies that are reflected both in the cinematic and the theoretic connections intensively permeating *Newsreel 55*.

The film's cinematic reference spectrum includes works that contributed to the various possibilities of filmic cooperation in the class struggle but also works that criticized the systems where the post-revolutionary reality became bureaucratized and bourgeois. Among the first are especially the works of Third Cinema in Latin America with a special emphasis on the newsreel activity of Santiago Álvarez, the activities of the Newsreel collective in the United States and the endeavours of French militant collectives such as Groupe Medvedkine, Groupe Dziga Vertov, SLON/ISKRA and so on. Among the second, we find referential connections with the area the filmmakers come from, that is, with the Yugoslav tradition of polemical 'black documentary', which boomed between the mid-1960s and the mid-1970s. More specifically: the segment of committed Yugoslav documentary filmmaking which displays certain affinities with the creative principles of newsreels, both in the regime and in the oppositional approaches. We can follow three main orientations in this development line of analysing social conditions with filmic means. The first is characterized by a direct critique of the anomalies of the socialist reality in its various segments. In the second tendency, the formal principles form the basis for an in-depth, but a poetically coloured reflection on the political, social or personal quandaries in the present or the recent past. The third tendency can be seen in works similar to the revolutionary, militant, guerrilla (either collective or individual) newsreel endeavours at the core of almost contemporaneous resistance ferments in the West and Latin America and also in the atmosphere of the 'thawing' waves in Eastern Europe (Munitić 1967; see also Munitić 1999; Žilnik 2003; Levi 2009). We can see in this an affinity with certain works from the Black Series of Polish School of Documentary Movies or certain documentaries made during the 'Prague Spring' and its brutal crackdown in Czechoslovakia.

The theoretical reference spectrum is related primarily to the questioning of the appropriateness of images as the carriers of memory, on the one hand, and their possibility of representing the traumatic episodes of recent history, on the other. The memorial potential of images is reflected in the highlighted questions on the possibility of one's visualization of the happening under consideration: 'What image would I have shot if I had had a camera in

FIGURE 9.4 Newsreel 55, 2013, black & white and colour, sound, videostill. Copyright: Nika Autor & Newsreel Front.

1989? The real image of the past whooshes by. Shattered images that not even memory or celluloid tape can wrest from oblivion.' (figure 9.4)

This commentary from the film refers directly to the aspect of Walter Benjamin's dialectical image (as a form of materialistic historiography) that represents the possibility of resurrecting the past by referring to it – a reference that is not necessarily bound to the visual value of the image but to all possible forms of legibility. This is why the quotations, writings and intertitles as used in *Newsreel 55* are a legitimate composite part of its structuring. The film thus reflects the awareness that the number one question in the revival of former visions is the question of 'political subjectification', which 'redefines the field of experience that gave to each their identity with their lot' (Rancière 1999: 40). Namely, any act of resistance is possible only as the consequence of self-awareness – both the awareness about one's current position in the world and the awareness that this position is permeated with the heritage of the past generations, which, as Deleuze and Guattari point out, is reflected in need to enter new struggles 'whenever the earlier one is betrayed' (1994: 100).

The questioning of the relation between cinema and the tragic factors of concentration camps, genocides, ethnic cleansing and other forms of annihilation is put to the fore by way of quoting and paraphrasing various thinkers who dealt with the dilemmas regarding the relation between traumatic events and the possibility of their filmic representation. Through the reflections of Benjamin, Brecht and Georges Didi-Huberman, we follow a series of controversies and confrontations that accompanied the discussions on the (non)representability of intolerable images from these horrific episodes of human history. This quandary culminates in one of the most traumatic parts of the film that focuses on the events at the Omarska concentration camp in Bosnia and Herzegovina. The commentary taking place against the abstract visual transition between the 1992 archival TV footage and present-day scenes of the 2012 commemoration ceremony in Omarska raises some key questions regarding the possibility of visually representing the Holocaust and the status of images when discussing it: 'The image became a monument. Created in a vacuum, without the air for inhalation or the space for exhalation, it roused the oblivion buried alive in the memory of the Holocaust and triggered conflict regarding its own reality.'

Meden's *Filmski obzornik 57: Vprašajmo se* (*Newsreel 57: We Should Ask Ourselves*, 2014) is a short film that re-stages the famous speech performed by actor Stevo Žigon upon the occupation of the Faculty of Arts in Belgrade during the 1968 student protests. Žigon's performance of Maximilien Robespierre's speech owes its additional fame to Želimir Žilnik's *Lipanjska gibanja* (*June Turmoil*, 1969), which is one of the most precious examples of anti-newsreels in former Yugoslavia and at the same time one of the rare film documents about the happening in Belgrade in June of 1968. Žilnik's film remains an ascetic 'report' on the protests. The filmmaker first listens to the testimonies of the victims and witnesses of police violence in the ferocious clash of the special units with the protesters at the famous Belgrade overbridge, and then, in a manner of direct observation, takes part in the meetings within the 'liberated territory of the Red University'. Žilnik refrains from any commentary and only rarely uses the devices of audiovisual interventionism, preferring to persist with direct, guerrilla images of the happening characterized by a twitchy, flitting and sometimes out-of-focus or blurred picture. Such a visualization reaches its climax in the final part of his depicting the protests in which he focuses on the performance of Žigon, whose spirited interpretation of Robespierre's speech (from Georg Büchner's revolutionary drama *Danton's Death*) evokes loud enthusiasm and ovations. Thus, the film concludes with one of Robespierre's slogans – 'No truce with the people for whom the Republic is a speculation only and the Revolution – a craft!' – which ends up floating over a frozen image of a protesting mass. Forty-five years later, the reason for revisiting this speech (the predomination of capital in all fields of social and individual life) and placing it in the here and now ('Let's ask ourselves…'), the different coordinates notwithstanding, no longer sounds so distant and different.

Like the previous two works, *Filmski obzornik 62* (*Newsreel 62*, 2015) also focuses on the questions about the (in)tolerability of the images of turbulent changes and emergency situations. It differs from the previous views in its very principle, with the absence of pictures taking the place of explicit images. The film has a two-part structure; it is divided into the examination of the archival material on the preparations and the opening of 'Peace, Humanity and Friendship among Nations', a large international exhibition mounted in Slovenj Gradec in 1966, and the position of refugees that got stuck at the Slovenian border in 2015 on the so-called Balkan route (figure 9.5).

What connects both years is the fact of two countries being 'wiped off' the geopolitical map and its tragic consequences. The film's missing images are two paintings entitled *Family* and *Worker*, which were contributed to the exhibition by Mahmoud Hamad and Akrass Gayass, Syrian modernist artists. After the exhibition closed, all traces of the paintings were lost. Thus, the crucial question posed by *Newsreel 62* is: 'What was this image of the family like? And what was the image of the worker like? What image can we imagine today, half a century after the exhibition, when Yugoslavia has been wiped off the map and Syria is being wiped off?' Although the point of *Newsreel 62* focuses on two explicitly visual elements – the absent artistic creations from the exhibition in 1966, and the brutally present documentary footage of refugees on the Croatia-Slovenia border in 2015 – the charge in vision and the visible is by no means clear or distinct. Such is also the view of Bill Nichols, who in his discussion of *Newsreel 62* emphasizes: 'This *Newsreel* uses blurry, undecipherable footage and unexpected juxtapositions

**FIGURE 9.5** Newsreel 62, 2015, *black & white and colour, sound, videostill. Copyright: Nika Autor & Newsreel Front.*

to announce its departure from didactic information. It puzzles and troubles, questions and provokes more than it informs. It is representative of the avant-garde, politically radical status that characterizes much of Newsreel Front's work' (Nichols 2017: 41).

The refusal of unequivocal informativeness and the absence of explicit images contributed to the decision for the film to place in the same order of meaning the archival images of the past, the documentary images of the present and the imagined images, so the pictures permeated with the reflective charge of both the experience of the past and the utopian vision of a new struggle. This is why we are witness to a symbolic reconstruction or reconfiguration of the missing paintings in the form of the indeterminacy of abstraction, which is counterposed to the trite images of present-day dehumanization. For the current reality of the refugee tragedy, which we face in the second part of the film, is a direct reflection of the already seen, the recognizable scenes of dehumanization conveyed by the media. What *Newsreel 62* tries to point out is the relation between the unknown images of emancipation, that is, the works by the Syrian artists, which represented the legitimate voice of the people, and the actual images of degradation, the Syrian refugees as the objects of the known, repeating scenes of oppression, silencing, annihilation, cleansing (figure 9.6).

The fifty-year gap, a period in which almost everything had changed, not only expresses the transient nature of any kind of certainty, or speaks of the vulnerability of individuals, communities and systems, but also attests to the fact that art is the very thing that can and must mirror the true 'face of reality'. However, only by not actually showing anything. What could be

**FIGURE 9.6** Newsreel 62, 2015, *black & white and colour, sound, videostill. Copyright: Nika Autor & Newsreel Front.*

stressed here is the striving to achieve a sense of the imperfection of film – as a process of 'revealing the making of problems' in the groundbreaking manifestoes of the Third Cinema movement in the 1960s and spearheaded by the eponymous manifesto by Julio García Espinosa. Or, the wager on the aesthetic and political charge of impoverished contemporary digital images, as defined by Hito Steyerl in her defence of the 'poor image' in the early outset of the twenty-first century. Such a wager also reflects another important element of incompleteness: the singularity of the relation to the audience, which becomes – through its engaged reception of such images – a necessary factor in the structuring of the meaning of an individual film event.

What is left to the viewer is therefore not to seek the answers to the questions directly expressed in the film, neither does any chance of finding an answer lie in the credibility of definitive images that are unbearable – be it due to their perfection that serves to disable the prospect of interpretation or their always being the same that prevents the possibility of our understanding. How can they appear unchanged time and time again, with no lesson learnt from the unbearable facts of history and experience? Watching the images, from the heart of oppression, restriction, prohibition, elimination and so on, when those in power systematically abuse the rights of 'inferior' members of humankind, we, the audience, are ultimately left to recapitulate, to internalize the efforts of the creative film gesture. It is a gesture of urgency, to try and do something (although what that remains unspecified and incomplete); the same gesture that is stressed, along with the worn-out images, seen countless times, of the refugee tragedy along the border by the commentary of *Newsreel 62*: 'Therefore: An attempt. /To sharpen./To fail./To resist./To get entangled. In images and language./Cut.'

The discussed films were not picked up for standard theatrical or television distribution. But this was not their intention anyway since such distribution lacks one of the key components of showing films according to the 'cinema event' principles – discussion with the audience. The discussions thus took place at special screenings in cinemas and film clubs practically all over Slovenia – from Ljubljana, Maribor and Celje to Domžale, Novo Mesto and Nova Gorica – and abroad, at Border Gaze: Grenzblick/ Dokumentarfilm aus Europas Südosten in Munich; Atlante Sentimentale del Cinema per il XXI secolo in Rome. The discussions also took place at a series of festivals where the films were screened: Slovenian Film Festival, Migrant Film Festival, Isola Cinema: International Film Festival, Pixelpoint: International Festival of Contemporary Art Practices, K3: International Short Film Festival, Independent Film Festival, Slovenian Documentary Film Festival, Ljubljana International Film Festival, Ethnographic Film Festival in Slovenia and in Prizren, Leipzig, Brest, Barcelona and Belgrade. At the exhibitions, the interaction with the visitors was carried out either at the opening or at subsequent special events at the exhibition venues in Slovenia, from Ljubljana, Celje and Piran to Maribor, Slovenj Gradec, Ribnica and Novo Mesto, the territory of former Yugoslavia, from Skopje, Trebinje and Zagreb to Novi Sad, Slavonski Brod and Belgrade and in other countries, in Vienna, Warsaw, Trieste, Graz, Ancona, Moscow, Nicosia, Plovdiv, Berlin, Villach, Wiesbaden, Mumbai, Vilnius, Cologne, Tampere, Arad and Paris. Especially important were the screenings intended for target audiences – the refugees, asylum seekers and migrant workers in squats of alternative culture and the occupied territories in Metelkova Street and Roška Street in Ljubljana; the participants of the Autumn Film School in Ljubljana, the students of the Academy of Theatre, Radio, Film and Television, University of Ljubljana, the Academy of Visual Arts, Ljubljana and Stanford University; but also the high school students and teachers endeavouring to introduce film subjects at more than twenty high schools across Slovenia. In a certain period, the films were also accessible online.

If we can judge the influence of the newsreel production based on the responses in the press, we can say it is substantial enough both in Slovenia and abroad. In Slovenia, it was covered especially by film journals *Kino!*, *Ekran* and *Kinotečnik* but also by magazines and journals covering a broader field of society and culture such as *Mladina*, *Borec* and *Likovne besede*. At the international level, let us point out *Mediantrop* from Belgrade, *Studio International* from New York and *Cinema Journal* from Austin, Texas. The newsreels also received special reflection in some of the exhibition catalogues, for example, *The News Is Ours!* (Ljubljana), *Crises and New Beginnings: Art in Slovenia 2005–2015* (Ljubljana), *Film d' actualites – l'actu est nous* (Paris) and *Resilience: Catalogue U3/7th Triennial of Contemporary Art in Slovenia* (Ljubljana). They were also discussed theoretically in the chapters of the following books: *Jolted Images, Unbound Analytic* by Pavle Levi (2017), *The News Belong to Us!*, edited by Nika Autor (et al.) and *Popularization and Populism in the Visual Arts: Attraction Images* edited by Anna Schober (2019).

# Conclusion

In relation to the practice and theory of Third Cinema, certain principles of the Newsreel Front are firmly rooted in their tradition. This is especially reflected in the choice of the film types or forms that the filmmakers of Third Cinema selected, reshaped or invented in order to participate in the class struggle. It is important to notice that, to start a resistance, one needs to recognize (one's) marginalized and underprivileged position as a site of resisting. This brings to the fore the film act as a method that includes, on the one hand, the strategies of solidarizing, informing and raising awareness but also organization and mobilization of resistance energies directed towards a transformation of society and cinema. Another characteristic is also the taking into account of one of the key demands in Getino and Solanas's manifesto that 'to a cinema made for the old kind of human being, for them, *it opposes a cinema fit for a new kind of human being, for what each one of us has the possibility of becoming*' (1997: 56). The aspects of innovation or renewal are reflected in a more intense hybridization of different (seemingly also incompatible) film forms or even aesthetics in a single work. Careful consideration of the formal aspects also encompasses certain forms of experimenting in the classical sense of the underground or avant-garde film. This also includes the use of undefined or hypothetical images, visual topology and especially abstract levels of articulation. In addition to the explicit foregrounding of the urgency of continuing the class struggle with audiovisual means, essayistically focused reflections on the relation with the past of both Third Cinema and Marxist theory are also very prominent.

All this means that, in addition to the direct forms of committedly pointing out the pressing situations of exploitation and repression and their call to resistance, the collective also questions the legitimacy, suitability and possibility of images to reveal the multiple layers and unusual causalities of repressive ideological mechanisms. They endeavour to examine both the surface and the underground of their operation as Pavle Levi also concludes when he stresses that 'there is no reason why, beyond its ability to show places, people and events, the cinema should not also insist on *actively unpacking* a wide range of ideologically underwritten spatial and temporal relations/… /figuring between various elements of representation' (Levi 2017: 123). In this process, the final goal is that both the newsreel method as a form of film documentariness that conceives a particular constellation and the agitprop vision that establishes a specific situation articulate the possibility of political action with filmic means. For both the constellation, which juxtaposes the historical and the current episodes of class struggle in Slovenia and worldwide, and the situation, which produces the germs of new non-conformist communities, foreground the vision of a specific 'new people', reflecting a concretization of the utopian possibility of radical social changes. At the same time, by directly pointing to their political provenience as one of the key preconditions of committed art, the creative principles of Newsreel Front represent a possible form of opposition to the indoctrinating tendencies of the film activity within the oppressive and greedy culture of capitalistic imperialism.

# Bibliography

Autor, Nika, Andreja Hribernik, Ciril Oberstar and Andrej Šprah (eds) (2017), *The News Belongs to Us!*, Ljubljana: Museum of Modern Art and Slovenj Gradec: Museum of Modern and Contemporary Art Koroška.

Brenez, Nicole (2005), 'À propos de Nice and the Extremely Necessary, Permanent Invention of the Cinematic Pamphlet', Rouge 7, http://www.rouge.com.au/7/propos_de_nice.html (accessed 15 February 2019).
Brenez, Nicole (2017), 'Filmic Information, Counterinformation, Ur-Information', in Nika Autor [et al.] (eds.), *The News Belongs to Us!*, 54–69, Ljubljana: Museum of Modern Art and Slovenj Gradec: Museum of Modern and Contemporary Art Koroška.
Deleuze, Gilles and Félix Guattari (1994), *What Is Philosophy?*, New York: Columbia University Press.
Eshun, Kodwo and Ros Gray (2011), 'The Militant Image: A Ciné-Geography', *Third Text*, 25 (1): 1–12.
Getino, Octavio (2015), 'Film kot politično dejstvo (odlomki)', in Nil Baskar (ed.), *Tretji film: teorija, praksa, odmevi*, 59–74, Ljubljana: Slovenska kinoteka.
Levi, Pavle (2009), 'Kino-komuna: Film kao prvostepena društveno-politička intervencija (1)', in Čurčić, Branka [et al.] (eds.), *Za ideju – Protiv stanja, Analiza i sistematizacija umetničkog stvaralaštva Želimira Žilnika*, 16–39, Novi Sad: Playground produkcija.
Levi, Pavle (2017), *Jolted Images: Unbound Analytic*, Amsterdam: Amsterdam University Press.
Mazierska, Ewa and Lars Kristensen (2015), 'Introduction', in Ewa Mazierska and Lars Kristensen (eds.), *Marxism and Film Activism: Screening Alternative Worlds*, 1–25, New York, Oxford: Berghahn.
Munitić, Ranko (1967), *Beogradska škola dokumentarnog filma*, Institut za film,
Munitić, Ranko (1999), *Srpski vek filma*, Centar film, Beograd and Prizma film, Kragujevac.
Nichols, Bill (2017), 'Now. And Then...', in Nika Autor [et al.] (eds.), *The News Belongs to Us!*, 40–3, Ljubljana: Museum of Modern Art and Slovenj Gradec: Museum of Modern and Contemporary Art Koroška.
Rancière, Jacques (1999), *Disagreement: Politics and Philosophy*, Minneapolis and London: University of Minnesota Press.
Schober, Anna (ed.) (2019), *Popularization and Populism in the Visual Arts: Attraction Images*, London and New York: Routledge.
Solanas, Fernando and Octavio Getino (1997), 'Towards a Third Cinema: Notes and Experiences for the Development of a Cinema of Liberation in the Third World', in Michael T. Martin (ed.), *New Latin American Cinema, Volume One: Theory, Practices and Transcontinental Articulations*, 33–58, Detroit: Wayne State University Press.
Steyerl, Hito (2009), 'In Defense of the Poor Image', *e-flux journal*, 10 (November): 1–9.
Waugh, Thomas (1984), 'Introduction', in Thomas Waugh (ed.), *'Show Us Life': Towards a History and Aesthetics of the Committed Documentary*, xi–xxvii, Metuchen, London: The Scarecrow Press.
Waugh, Thomas (2017), 'Meltdowns, Intertext, Ancestors, Marches, Migrations: Notes on Nika Autor and Newsreel Front', in Nika Autor [et al.] (eds), *The News Belongs to Us!*, 28–38, Ljubljana: Museum of Modern Art and Slovenj Gradec: Museum of Modern and Contemporary Art Koroška.

Wayne, Mike (2001) *Political Film: The Dialectics of Third Cinema*, London, Sterling, VA: Pluto Press.

Wayne, Mike (2016), 'The Dialectics of Third Cinema', in Yannis Tzioumakis and Claire Molloy (eds), *The Routledge Companion to Cinema and Politics*, 17–26, New York, London: Routledge.

Žilnik, Želimir (2003), *Iznad crvene prašine = Above the Red Dust*, Beograd: Institut za film.

Žižek, Slavoj (2009), 'How to Begin from the Beginning', *New Left Review*, 57: 43–55.

# 10

# Listening to the future: The film-philosophy of Abderrahmane Sissako

## *William Brown*
## *(University of Roehampton, London)*

> [T]he destiny of our planet will be played out, to a large extent, in Africa Achille Mbembe
> (2016: 323)

In this chapter, I shall analyse the films of Abderrahmane Sissako, suggesting that his work not only springs from a history of politically engaged Third Cinema but also constitutes what Gilles Deleuze (1989) might refer to as 'modern political cinema'. Drawing on Jean-Luc Nancy (2007), I shall propose that the repeated emphasis in Sissako's work on the faces of people who are listening suggests an ethical form of filmmaking absent from much 'classical' Third Cinema. Finally, I shall suggest that Sissako not only creates an African 'people to come' *à la* Deleuze but that, as per the Achille Mbembe quotation above, his films also picture the future of the whole of humanity – not least as a result of increasing water shortages and the expansion of the desert. In this way, Sissako's film-philosophy challenges eurocentrism by demonstrating that African cinema is not simply 'catching up' with the cinemas of the First and Second Worlds but is perhaps the most profound cinema in the world, helping us to visualize the very future of humanity.

## Abderrahmane Sissako: An overview

Sissako's cinema defies easy categorization – be that as an African filmmaker, as a postcolonial filmmaker, as a maker of Third Cinema or as a modern political filmmaker. For, while his films are all of these things, none quite captures their complex interweaving of politics and aesthetics, as we shall see. Born in Mauritania, raised in Mali, trained in Russia (for more on this, see Woll 2004; Gray 2012) and resident in France, Sissako himself is a transnational figure who has made films that equally transcend national borders. For example, even his early short films, such as *Le jeu/The Game* (USSR/Mauritania, 1988) and *Octobre/October* (France/Mauritania/Russia, 1993), are transnational co-productions that explore cultural displacements. Shot in Turkmenistan but featuring dialogue in both French and Arabic, the former deals with a group of boys playing at war in the desert, while the father of one of the group embarks on a secret military mission. The latter, meanwhile, depicts an unsuccessful relationship in Moscow between a Russian woman, Irina (Irina Apeksimova), and an African man, Idrissa (Wilson Buyaya).

Sissako's first feature film, *La vie sur terre/Life on Earth* (Mali/Mauritania/France, 1998), depicts life in the town of Sokolo, Mali, on the eve of the new millennium following the return to his hometown of Dramane (Sissako himself), who has been living in France for many years. *Rostov-Luanda* (Angola/Mauritania/France/Germany/Belgium, 1998) similarly features Sissako returning to Kiffa, the Mauritanian town in which he was born, before going to Russia, Angola and, finally, Germany, in search of Afonse Baribanga, an Angolan man with whom he learnt Russian in Rostov in the early 1980s. *Heremakono/Waiting for Happiness* (France/Mauritania, 2002) is about life in Nouadhibou, a coastal city in Mauritania, where a young man, Abdallah (Mohamed Mahmoud Ould Mohamed), visits his mother before hoping to continue to Europe. *Bamako* (Mali/USA/France, 2006) depicts the lives of various people who live in and around a courtyard in the Hamdallaye neighbourhood of Mali's capital, where a trial is being staged between the people of Africa and the International Monetary Fund (IMF), the World Bank and the World Trade Organisation (WTO). And *Timbuktu* (France/Mauritania, 2014) is about the seizure of the eponymous Malian city by Islamist group Ansar Dine in 2012 – although the film was shot in the town of Oualata in southeast Mauritania. In between these features, Sissako has continued to make short films, including *Sabriya* (Tunisia, 1997), a love story set in Tunisia, *Tiya's Dream* (France, 2008), which takes place at a school in Ethiopia, and *N'Dimagou/Dignity*, which involves a series of interviews with Malians about dignity for the portmanteau film, *Stories on Human Rights* (various directors, Russia/Germany, 2008).

Given the diversity of his work, especially in terms of where they are set/made, we can begin to see how Sissako is not a filmmaker who easily fits into established categories, perhaps especially national and even regional ones. That said, there seems to be a clear engagement with political concerns in his work: *October* deals with the politics of cultural difference (while in its title referencing Sergei M. Eisenstein and Grigori Aleksandrov's famous 1928 Soviet film of the same name), *Life on Earth* investigates Mali's role in a world that from the Western perspective is celebrating its new millennium, *Waiting for Happiness* looks at migration from Africa to Europe, *Bamako* looks at the issue of structural debt in contemporary Africa and *Timbuktu* explores the rise of militant Islam in West Africa. Furthermore, as we shall see later, there are repeated motifs in and consistent stylistic aspects to Sissako's cinema. In spite of the transnational dimensions of his work, then, there are enough thematic and stylistic constants in Sissako's film for him to be considered among the most important *auteurs* working in cinema today (see Gabara 2016).

However, Sissako's status as an *auteur* potentially compromises the political impact of his work, as aesthetic concerns are perceived to supersede his political message. Although I shall argue that Sissako's aesthetics in fact *reinforce* his politics, it is worth exploring this ambiguity further by situating Sissako in relation to other African cinemas, postcolonial filmmaking practices and traditions of Third Cinema.

# From African Cinema to Third Cinema

At the end of his classic study of African cinema, Manthia Diawara outlines three different types of film that African filmmakers might create. These include social realist narratives that thematize 'current sociocultural issues… oppose tradition to modernity, oral to written, agrarian and customary communities to urban and industrialised systems, and subsistence economies to highly productive economies' (Diawara 1992: 141); films of 'colonial confrontation' that position spectators 'to identify with the African people's resistance against European colonialism and imperialistic drives' (Diawara 1992: 152); and films that 'return to the source', depicting a pre-colonial Africa and which feature long takes and natural sounds, as well as close-ups that are inspired not by the plot but by a desire to 'inscribe the beauty of the characters and their tradition' (Diawara 1992: 160).

As we shall see, Abderrahmane Sissako's films fit none of these categories, even though his work combines aspects of all three. For example, all of his feature films clearly engage with socio-cultural issues, but none of them really adopts what we might call a 'social realist' style; rather than telling the story of a single character whose experiences we follow closely, each of his films instead presents a kind of collage of fragments from the lives of many different people in the places where his films take place, be that Sokolo, Luanda, Nouadhibou, Bamako or Timbuktu. Furthermore, while we might tend to think of social realism as involving a handheld camera that follows its characters, Sissako's films are characterized far more by a static camera, long shots, occasional long takes and a painterly framing style that is far more 'artistic' than 'realistic'. This style is more in keeping with Diawara's 'return to source' films, but Sissako's movies are (up until now, at any rate) set in the present (or, in the case of *Life on Earth*, in the near future) rather than exploring a pre-colonial African past. Finally, while *Bamako* perhaps most clearly engages in 'colonial confrontation' in its vociferous critique of the IMF, the World Bank and the WTO, Sissako's films nonetheless present a world that is significantly more diffuse and ambiguous than one featuring an evil colonial power and its poor, oppressed victims. In *Rostov-Luanda*, for example, Sissako is keen to point out how many Portuguese people came to and stayed in Luanda, where they continue to form an integral part of that city's fabric, especially in the Biker bar that has been run by Portuguese émigré Alberto Passos for more than forty years. Similarly, *Bamako* features not only Western advocates who themselves are engaged in the critique of the financial institutions that the film mounts but also a film-within-in-a-film called 'Death in Timbuktu', in which not only white but also black 'cowboys' are seen perpetrating violence on/towards the people of Africa.

If Sissako's work does not quite fit Diawara's 'classic' categorization of African cinema, his films can nonetheless be read through the lens of postcolonial thought. Perhaps this is most clear in the insistent references in his films to the work of Aimé Césaire, the Martiniquais poet and one of the fathers of *négritude*, or the deliberate assertion of a black identity in the face of colonial powers that sought to denigrate (de-nigr-ate) the peoples of the countries they colonized and in some senses created. *Life on Earth*, for example, is full of references to Césaire, including a radio broadcast that reads from *Discours sur le colonialisme* (1955), a voiceover that recites his poems, and an intertitle towards the end of the film that quotes Césaire's 'Les Pur-Sang' ('The Thoroughbreds'): *mon oreille collée au sol, j'entendis passer demain* ('my ear to the ground, I heard tomorrow pass'). Meanwhile, at the trial in *Bamako*, a local academic, Georges Keïta, attributes to Césaire the poem 'Prière d'un petit enfant nègre' ('Prayer for a Small Negro Child') – in fact written by Guadeloupian poet Guy Tirolien. While a misattribution, the reference nonetheless confirms the way in which Sissako locates his work in relation to Césaire (Keïta explains how Africa has known nothing but misery and that it is getting worse).

Citing Césaire, *Life on Earth* depicts a Sokolo that is 'far from the insane speed of that Europe', which 'proudly overestimates itself' in setting its own measurement of time (a new millennium) as the standard that all others should follow. While the film opens with shots of brimming supermarket shelves in Paris, Sokolo's inhabitants are facing starvation as there is no rain and as birds ruin rice crops. Furthermore, the male inhabitants have little to do but cling to the side of a house in order to remain shaded from an unforgiving sun. Finally, *Bamako* makes numerous references to the history of colonialism in Africa and the ways in which it has ravaged Mali and other countries both politically and economically – suggesting that Sissako is indeed a postcolonial filmmaker.

Nonetheless, a distinction might usefully be made between postcolonialism and the perhaps more explicit anti-colonialism of Césaire. Kenneth W. Harrow describes how 'decolonised African culture has moved from under the heavy weight of an anticolonial or antineocolonial exigency to one now defined as postcolonial', suggesting that in the process 'the controlling frames of historicism and class-based analysis have been increasingly discarded' (Harrow 2007: 20). If Sissako is more postcolonial than anti-colonial, *Bamako* surely remains anti-neocolonial in its critique of the IMF and the World Bank, which – as is argued by author and politician Aminata Dramane Traoré, one of the witnesses at the trial – have seen US$54 billion worth of loans translated into US$436 billion worth of debt.

Furthermore, *Bamako* features an extended testimony from a man, Madou Keïta, who tells of how he left Mali as a result of a lack of education, health care and so on – only to find himself ejected from Algeria and forced to return. This mirrors *Waiting for Happiness*, in which we see various attempts to migrate to Europe for economic reasons, including Abdallah's and that of Michael (Mickaël Onoimweniku), who early in the film has photos taken of himself with friends so that he has a keepsake of them before he departs for Spain – only for his body later on to be washed up on the shore in Nouadhibou. In other words, Sissako's work is clearly concerned not only with class differences but also with how the lack of employment opportunities brings about the risk of life and limb entailed in 'illegal' migration. This is not to mention the repeated emphasis in nearly all of Sissako's films on the daily struggles of ordinary people trying to subsist in the face of harsh living conditions, from the farmers in *Life on Earth* to the Portuguese electrician Senhor Silva in *Rostov-Luanda*, who prefigures the ageing electrician, Maata (Maata Ould Mohamed Abeid), and his young apprentice, Khatra (Khatra Ould Abder Kader), in *Waiting for Happiness*. Around the trial in *Bamako*, we see various characters trying to subsist, including Chaka (Tiécoura Traoré), who has no work but who is learning Hebrew in a bid to work at the Israeli embassy – even though it has not been built yet. Finally, various characters in *Timbuktu* eke out a living by bringing cattle to and/or fishing in a lake near to the film's titular city. In other words and *contra* Harrow, Sissako's work surely continues to engage in 'class-based analysis'. Even if Manthia Diawara has described Sissako's films as 'postcolonial art cinema' (Diawara 2010: 45), then, they nonetheless do not quite fit the postcolonial framework that Harrow describes.

Perhaps it is for this reason that Diawara argues that to look at Sissako's work 'through the prism of *Négritude* and colonialism' runs the risk of producing nostalgia (Diawara 2010: 104). Sissako does not romanticize Africa – as the depiction of the birds in *Life on Earth* makes clear. Whereas in many films images of birds might signal some frustrated desire for freedom, the images of birds in flight at the end of Sissako's film convey the ongoing precarity of life in Sokolo – since the birds are, as mentioned, ruining the local rice crops. Similarly, when the phone operator at the local post office (Keïta Bina Gaoussou) talks on the line to Marie, a figure who is trying to contact Dramane (from Paris?) but whom we never see, he explains that while it is indeed sunny in Sokolo (a response, presumably, to a well-intended question about the weather), the sun is in fact the greatest enemy of life there (because of droughts) – together with Marie's indifference (and by extension the indifference of all those who do nothing to help Africans get through their plight).

We shall return to the issue of the sun and drought later on, but first it will be useful to ask to what extent Sissako's work relates to another political filmmaking tradition, namely Third Cinema. First proposed by Argentine filmmakers Fernando Solanas and Octavio Getino in 1969, Third Cinema was initially part of an attempt to convert film into a medium that would do more than simply entertain (as per the First Cinema of Hollywood) or be artistic (as per the *auteur*-driven Second Cinema of Europe), but which would itself take part in revolutionary struggles around the world. Solanas and Getino use as examples of Third Cinema the Newsreel group from the United States, 'the cinegiornali of the Italian student movement, the Etats Généraux du Cinéma Français, and those of the British and Japanese student movements', whose work drew inspiration from Joris Ivens and Chris Marker (Getino and Solanas 1969: 109). Only after listing various movements in the First and Second World do they mention the work of Cuban filmmaker Santiago Alvarez. In other words, in its initial conception, Third Cinema was not confined to Third World filmmaking, but rather it provided a theoretical framework through which to understand much political filmmaking from across the globe – including Solanas and Getino's own flagship effort, *La hora de los hornos/The Hour of the Furnaces* (Argentina, 1968).

While Michael Chanan (1997) has also noted that Third Cinema is not limited to the Third World, Ethiopian film scholar Teshome Gabriel nonetheless linked Third Cinema explicitly to the Third World – as the title of his celebrated *Third Cinema in the Third World: The Aesthetics of Liberation* makes clear (see Gabriel 1982). Furthermore, while Solanas, Getino and the authors of various manifestoes related to Third Cinema 'refuse to prescribe an aesthetics' (Willemen 1991: 6), Gabriel in some senses formalized Third Cinema by saying that it should be characterized by long takes, cross-cutting, close-ups, panning shots, silence and a hero

(Gabriel 1991; see also Shaka 2004: 78). My aim is not to discuss whether Gabriel is 'correct' in his definition of Third Cinema. Nor is it to overlook subsequent theoretical engagements with the term (see, for example, Wayne 2001), or the expansion of Third Cinema to include various popular global cinemas (see Guneratne and Dissanayake 2003). Rather, I wish simply to consider Sissako's work in relation to these original, if differing, definitions of Third Cinema, which was engaged in the 'decolonisation of culture' and an emphasis on cognitive as opposed to emotional engagement with film (Shaka 2004: 78–9).

For, Sissako's work no doubt conforms in part to the style of Third Cinema as devised by Gabriel. His films feature plenty of long takes, cross-cutting, close-ups, panning shots and silence. Specifically in relation to cross-cutting, Gabriel specifies that the technique as used in Third Cinema 'shows simultaneity rather than the building of suspense' – and this is certainly the case with Sissako as he cuts between moments from the lives of the inhabitants of Sokolo, Nouadhibou, Hamdallaye and Timbuktu (see Gabriel 1991). However, Sissako's films do not really feature heroes, with the father in *The Game* being called a hero only in irony when taken prisoner and then executed by the militant group that he was supposed to spy on.

If Third Cinema decolonizes culture, then it must in some senses be self-reflexive, since cinema has itself been historically part of the colonization of culture. For example, *Hour of the Furnaces* features numerous examples of direct address to the audience, while inviting viewers to take a break and to discuss the issues raised thus far. Sissako's films are equally self-reflexive, as the 'Death in Timbuktu' sequence in *Bamako* makes clear, together with the way in which characters look directly at the camera, especially in *Life on Earth* and *Waiting for Happiness*. However, while self-conscious, Sissako's films do not quite conform to Third Cinema in the sense that they do not necessarily emphasize the cognitive aspects of cinema over the emotional ones. If Third Cinema 'need not be finely constructed technically to succeed, but must make a persuasive argument' (Zacks 1999: 7), Sissako's films are in fact very finely constructed on the technical level (sumptuous images, expressive sound, intelligent editing), and they do not necessarily seek to persuade their viewers so much as invite them to reflect, as we shall see shortly.

## Modern political cinema

If Sissako's films draw upon but do not quite fit the categories of African, postcolonial or Third cinema, then perhaps it is no surprise that his work has been considered as falling somewhere between the *auteur*-driven Second Cinema typified by European film productions and a more political Third

Cinema (see Gabara 2010). Indeed, Sissako's films are regularly compared to the work of European *auteurs* like Jean-Luc Godard (see Sicinski 2006: 16; Diawara 2010: 120).[1]

The auteurist tendency in Sissako's work (a strong sense of aesthetics; stylistic and thematic continuities) need not be a failing. Indeed, if African filmmakers have been declared as contemporary *griots*, or storytellers working in a collective, oral tradition, then today's African filmmaker – who often out of necessity must perform several roles in the making of their films (writer, director, producer, actor) – might legitimately be characterized as what David Murphy and Patrick Williams have called a hybrid *griauteur* (Murphy and Williams 2007: 9) – with Rachel Gabara directly applying the term to Sissako (Gabara 2016: 47).

If Sissako (and *griauteurs* more generally?) eludes easy categorization, then perhaps he more clearly fits into the schema of modern political cinema defined by Gilles Deleuze in his *Cinema 2: The Time-Image* (1989), and which can be seen as a development upon theories of Third Cinema. For, as Kodwo Eshun and Ros Gray suggest,

> [t]he notion of Third Cinema was reconfigured [in the 1990s] so that it now encompassed films that articulated what might be understood, in Deleuzean terms, as a 'collective utterance' expressive of the local communities in which the films were made, even though their production practices were far closer to an auteurist model of filmmaking than to the militant collectives such as Newsreel that Solanas and Getino had cited. (Eshun and Gray 2011: 4)

The appropriateness of a Deleuzian framework is implied by Murphy and Williams's suggestion that contemporary African cinema might be considered 'minor' in the sense laid out by Deleuze and Félix Guattari in their consideration of the literature of Franz Kafka (Murphy and Williams 2007: 9; see also Deleuze and Guattari 1986). Furthermore, Diawara understands that *Life on Earth* is a film 'about time: the framing of the shots and the montage reveal the image of time, its movement, rhythm and weight' (Diawara 2010: 101). Diawara describes how the film is a montage of single shots, as opposed to edited scenes, which means that each shot has its own time/tempo. This implied reference to *Cinema 2* is made explicit by Isabel Balseiro, who sees *Life on Earth* as a 'conceptual cinema… of intense

---

[1] Anecdotally, I might recount how I was hoping to include in my film, *En Attendant Godard* (UK, 2009), a scene that paid homage to the sequence in *Vent d'Est/Wind from the East* (Dziga Vertov Group, Italy/France/West Germany, 1970), where at a crossroads the filmmaker asks Brazilian director Glauber Rocha which way it is to the political cinema. This homage was to include Sissako in the Rocha role. Sissako agreed to take part, but we never found a mutually convenient date to shoot the sequence.

creation', and which is thus Deleuzian in the sense that Deleuze defined philosophy as the creation of concepts (Balseiro 2007: 444).

To establish further these links between Sissako's work and Deleuze's film-philosophy, let us look at Deleuze and Guattari's minor literature and Deleuze's modern political cinema. For Deleuze and Guattari, minor literature is a literature written in a major language (in Kafka's case, German), and yet which 'disrupts' that language, thereby revealing its limitations and biases (Kafka is a Czech Jew struggling to find his identity in a language that is not his own and from the culture of which he is in some senses excluded, or in which he, like the Gregor Samsa of *Metamorphosis*, feels like an *ungeheures Ungeziefer*, or a 'monstrous vermin').

Deleuze's modern political cinema, meanwhile, which sometimes is referred to as minor cinema, is based upon the following idea: 'the people no longer exist, or not yet... *the people are missing*' (Deleuze 1989: 216). Deleuze later refers to how 'the master, or the coloniser, proclaims, "There have never been people here"' (Deleuze 1989: 217). In other words, it is not that there are literally no people in, say, Africa. It is, rather, that the people in Africa have not been recognized as people by the colonial masters, instead being relegated to a subpersonal/inhuman condition. The task of modern political cinema, then, is to have the people recognized as such: 'the missing people are a becoming, they invent themselves, in shanty towns and camps, or in ghettos, in new conditions of struggle to which a necessarily political art must contribute' (Deleuze 1989: 217). Since modern political cinema seeks to demonstrate the personhood/humanity of its subjects, it by definition conflates the private and the political, since the recognition of personhood is political (being recognized as a legitimate member of the *polis*).

If the modern political filmmaker is invested in showing personhood, then the modern political filmmaker is invested in showing difference, in the sense that they must respect how 'there were no people, but always several peoples, an infinity of peoples, who remained to be united, or should not be united, in order for the problem to change. It is in this way that third world cinema is a cinema of minorities, because the people exist only in the condition of minority, which is why they are missing' (Deleuze 1989: 220). Modern political cinema is thus not about collecting difference under the umbrella of a singular identity but about showing a plurality of minorities. What is true of a film's contents (it shows peoples who are otherwise missing/it shows what Deleuze describes as the 'intolerable' way in which they are not considered people; see Deleuze 1989: 219) extends also to the way in which modern political cinema is made. For, as a collective medium, cinema is ripe for showing difference, and the modern political filmmaker does not dictate what happens in their film but allows their collaborators to intercede, or to become 'intercessors', resulting not in the work of a single author but in *collective utterances* (Deleuze 1989: 222). In this way, there is perhaps by definition a blurring of fiction and documentary in modern political cinema, as the filmmaker changes the film in accordance with what they find during production.

The term *griauteur* can help us to negotiate the paradox of modern political cinema being both a collective utterance and the work of a singular filmmaker. For, in their fragmented narratives, in which we follow the lives of numerous characters, Sissako's films combine the collective sensibility of the *griot* with the singular vision of the *auteur*. Films like *Rostov-Luanda*, *Life on Earth*, *Waiting for Happiness* and *Bamako* are all characterized by 'intercessors', as Sissako changes the content of his film depending on who or what crops up. As Roy Armes explains in relation to *Waiting for Happiness*, the film was basically improvised and Sissako's 'working method was to bring a mass of people into his film "by inviting them to tell their own stories as well"' (Armes 2006: 196). Sissako himself says that a screenplay is not a 'guarantee' of what the finished film will look like (see Appiah 2003), since he cannot provide in advance a road map to what will happen. Instead, each of Sissako's films takes time to look at and/or to listen to a whole host of characters, many of whom are not necessarily in agreement with each other – with the films thus straddling the boundary between fiction and documentary. Listeners turn off the radio broadcast of the trial in *Bamako*, which also is interrupted by various outbursts as characters express their views on the events unfolding, while *Timbuktu* presents characters speaking various languages (Arabic, Bambara, Tamasheq, French, English), which demonstrates a complex rather than unified West African reality.

Sissako's films also present 'intolerable' situations, in which humans are not recognized as people but instead suffer as they are understood only as economic commodities or as servants of a particular religion. The stories of dead migrants in *Waiting for Happiness* and *Bamako* suggest a capitalist machine that simply uses humans as fodder for the purposes of its own perpetuation, while Chaka in the latter film eventually takes his own life, so desperate does his situation seem to be in terms of employment opportunities (although Chaka's suicide is also in part precipitated by the threatened departure of his Senegalese wife, Melé, played by Aïssa Maïga). *October* seems to suggest that the relationship between Idrissa and Irina is impossible in a Russian society where he is quietly but forcefully excluded. And *Timbuktu* demonstrates a world in which few people can go free as long as militant Islam is in power: a local fishmonger is forced out of work because she will not wear gloves; a couple is stoned for having a relationship out of wedlock; others are arrested and beaten simply for playing music; women are forced into marriage; and Toya (Layla Walet Mohamed), the young daughter of Tuareg couple Kidane (Ibrahim Ahmed) and Satima (Toulou Kiki), is left to fend for herself in the desert, together with Issan (Mehdi A.G. Mohamed), a quasi-adopted son who looks after their small herd of cattle. Although there is silence in Sissako's films, as per Gabriel's definition of Third Cinema, they nonetheless are also desperate cries against a world that does not allow humans to exist.

## Ethical cinema

Scholars have attended to various aspects of Sissako's work, including his use of colour (Maingard 2010), his treatment of exile (Balseiro 2007; Adesokan 2010; Thackway 2014) and the roles played by language (Murray Levine 2012) and genre (Jaji 2014). Furthermore, Kenneth W. Harrow argues that *Bamako* shows Africa as being treated like 'trash' (Harrow 2013: 177–202), especially through the death of Chaka, whose body lies abandoned with the dogs on the outskirts of the city (Harrow also likens the film to the work of Kafka).

However, while Sissako clearly does show the 'intolerable' side of life in contemporary Africa, his cinema is nonetheless invested in showing faces and imbuing them with dignity (which is, as noted, the title of one of Sissako's short films). As per the French term *digne*, meaning worthy, Sissako shows that the people in his films are precisely not trash, even if the world treats them or makes them feel that way, or as if *indignado*/unworthy. For Sissako, these are people worthy of humanity – and he achieves this through his numerous close-ups. This emphasis on faces and of people listening lends to Sissako's work an ethical dimension, as Libby Saxton has noted in relation to *Bamako*. Furthermore, Saxton also suggests that the testimony of Zégué Bamba, a witness who interrupts proceedings at the trial by singing an unsubtitled lament in Senoufo, 'thwarts the desire to know, affording instead an experience of pure form and a radically disconcerting encounter with alterity, which relocates us from the realm of epistemology into the spheres of ethics and aesthetics' (Downing and Saxton 2010: 60).

The 'disconcerting encounter with alterity' is key to the ethical moment, and it is one that plays a central role in the ethical philosophy of Emmanuel Levinas, as Saxton also notes (Downing and Saxton 2010: 95–106). For Levinas, the face signifies the 'infinite alterity of the other' and inspires in us 'endless responsibility' for them (see Levinas 1979). While being responsible for others is laudable, however, Levinas has been criticized in various ways, including for elevating the other, by virtue of being 'infinite' in their otherness, to the position of God (as opposed to human), with ethics thus being general rather than something considered encounter-by-encounter. Furthermore, the 'infinity' of the other suggests a lack of anything shared between those who look upon each other (see Nagib 2011: 11, 30). In a virulent attack, Hamid Dabashi even accuses Levinas of racism, since the latter argued that '[o]nly in the European sense can the world be gathered together... humanity consists of the Bible and the Greeks. All the rest can be translated: all the rest – all the exotic – is dance' (Dabashi 2015: 256). For Dabashi, who situates himself within a tradition of anti-colonial, non-Western thought, this eurocentrism in Levinas's work is highly problematic.

Finally, Kathleen Scott and Stefanie Van de Peer have also critiqued Levinas for arguing for the radical alterity of the other. Drawing on work by Sarah Cooper and Assia Djebar, they instead propose the 'possibility of a spectatorial openness to alterity in which proximity serves as an alternative to identification. Audiences and characters are therefore... brought together in face-to-face encounters in which the space of responsibility is constructed' by both parties, as opposed to transcending the encounter itself (Scott and Van de Peer 2016: 173). In other words, rather than responsibility being based upon 'infinite' otherness, responsibility via feelings of sympathy and solidarity is developed through the two-way encounter with the other, and is based on a sense of *mitgefühl*, or 'sympathetic "feeling-with"' – as drawn from the work of Sandra Lee Bartky (Scott and Van de Peer 2016: 174).

As we look at the faces of the otherwise missing people in Sissako's films, we likewise begin to feel responsible for those others, not because of an 'infinite' alterity but because of a sympathetic connection with them. This sympathetic connection undoes the process that Césaire describes as follows: 'colonisation = chosification' ('colonisation = thing-ification'; see Césaire 1955; also Mbembe 2001: 186–7). That is, colonization sees the other become a thing or an object, meaning that the people are missing from the colonies. A post-Levinasian reading of Sissako's work highlights how his films seek to show us the people and to engender in his viewers a sense of collective responsibility for the fate of Africa.

## The touch of listening

Scott and Van de Peer draw a distinction between seeing and gazing. To gaze at the other is to see what one wants to see, and not to see the other for herself. Scott and Van de Peer suggest that this distinction is akin to that between speaking and listening: 'the postcolonial relationship between France and its ex-colonies has involved a distinct lack of reciprocity of listening and seeing – speaking and gazing at an Other have generally dominated' (Scott and Van de Peer 2016: 177). And yet, as Sissako's films regularly show characters listening to radios, to each other and to the world more generally as it passes by, so, too, might they inspire in their viewers a desire to listen – to the films themselves and to the postcolonial world that they depict more generally.

In defining *mitgefühl*, Scott and Van de Peer acknowledge that the concept has much in common with the philosophy of Jean-Luc Nancy's concept of 'being-with' (Scott and Van de Peer 2016: 169). Perhaps it comes as no surprise, then, that Nancy himself asks whether philosophy has 'superimposed upon listening, beforehand and of necessity, or else substituted for listening, something else that might be more on the order of *understanding*' (Nancy 2007: 1). For Nancy, then, philosophy is the equivalent of speaking/gazing as opposed to listening/seeing. It is not an act of spying that one does in secret (Nancy 2007: 4), nor is it simply an act of 'being-present' (Nancy 2007: 13). Rather, listening is 'presence' in the sense of an 'in the presence of' (Nancy 2007: 13). That is, listening is fundamentally an act of 'being-with' – being with the other as well as being with oneself, as is made clear by the way in which 'in a perfect condition of silence you hear your own body resonate' (Nancy 2007: 21).

Beyond understanding-as-speaking, then, 'we have to understand what sounds from a human throat without being language, which emerges from an animal gullet or from any kind of instrument, even from the wind in the branches: the rustling towards which we strain or lend an ear' (Nancy 2007: 22). In this way, Nancy is describing listening not as hearing what one wants to hear but listening as hearing the other (and the self) in a fashion that is beyond simply the meanings of words, but which also takes into account non-linguistic aspects like timbre, and by extension touch. For, Nancy explains that the German term for timbre is *Klangfarbe*, meaning 'colour of sound', which in turn lends a synesthetic aspect to listening and which may well include colour, touch and smell (Nancy 2007: 42). 'To listen, as well as to look or to contemplate', Nancy continues, 'is to touch the work in each part – or else to be touched by it, which comes to the same thing' (Nancy 2007: 65).

Sissako's films thus invite us to listen, as is clear from the unsubtitled Senoufo testimony that Zégué Bamba sings in *Bamako*. The moment involves otherness and it should indeed induce a desire to be responsible for the other. But it is not an infinite otherness in the Levinasian sense of being utterly alien. On the contrary, Sissako's film presents Zégué Bamba (and many other characters across all of his films) as an other who achieves personhood/dignity (*à la* Deleuze) as a result of touching us (Nancy) through Sissako's 'listening' and 'looking' camera that does not seek to impose 'understanding' on these people (unlike the IMF and the World Bank, which repeatedly tell Africa what it needs). This takes Sissako's work beyond the 'thing-ification' of the colonial process and into a realm of human contact.

# Africa as the future of the world/the world of the future

Nancy says that philosophy only understands and that it does not listen. Dabashi, meanwhile, critiques Levinas for saying that only a European version of life is worthy of the name. For Dabashi, philosophy is defined by a Eurocentric history that defines non-Europeans as incapable of thought, hence the title of his polemic: *Can Non-Europeans Think?* (Dabashi 2015). If non-Europeans cannot think, and if philosophy is not to listen but to understand, then can Sissako's African cinema really be philosophical if it listens and invites us to listen to the intercessors that appear in it? Surely Sissako cannot by definition be a film-philosopher, since he suffers from the double error of being non-European and of listening instead of understanding?

In *The Invention of Africa: Gnosis, Philosophy and the Order of Knowledge*, V. Y. Mudimbe famously argues that the West has since the fifteenth century submitted the rest of the world, including Africa, to its memory (Mudimbe 1988). That is, the West is superior in nothing more than imposing its own superiority on the rest of the world, as various other scholars have reminded us (see Zacks 1999: 3–4; Wynter 2000: 29, 57; Shaka 2004: 19). Tied to colonialism, this imposed superiority has also involved the erasure of how Western philosophy (which the West might claim to be 'philosophy itself') did not arise as a result of some historic split from the rest of the world but that it is deeply rooted in and remains connected to the rest of the world. Indeed, Enrique Dussel outlines in the opening section of his *Ethics of Liberation* how modernity is 'planetary' and that Western philosophy has its roots in Egyptian-Bantu philosophy, meaning that philosophy must discard its Eurocentrism and instead become global (Dussel 2013: 1–52).

Meanwhile, Matthew Holtmeier has argued how there has been a transition from the development of oppositional but singular national identities, as per the Algerian independence movement that we see depicted in a film like *La bataille d'Alger/The Battle of Algiers* (Gillo Pontecorvo, Italy/Algeria, 1966) to a more 'networked biopolitics' in the contemporary era, when another film about Algerian independence, *Hors la loi/Outside the Law* (Rachid Bouchareb, France/Algeria/Belgium/Tunisia/Italy, 2010), shows a significantly more fragmented independence movement (Holtmeier 2016). What Pontecorvo's film fails to capture is how we exist in a world of many different identities (or proliferating minorities in the language of Deleuze). These identities may well 'come together to cooperate for a shared political transformation' (Holtmeier 2016: 321), but they nonetheless remain different, or multitudinous.

What is true north of the Sahara is also true south of it. That is, Africa does not remain untouched by globalization. Indeed, not only does neoliberal free market capitalism exist in Africa but Africa can in some sense be understood as a massive experiment in neoliberalism. In this way, Africa provides an image not just of a continent trying to catch up with the rest of the world but rather of the future of the entire world should globalized neoliberal capital be allowed to continue apace (Mbembe 2016: 326). The 'structural adjustment programs' (like those devised by the IMF and the World Bank) undermine 'the postcolonial compromise, emasculating the traditional instruments of state power... bringing about a profound modification of social structures and cultural imaginations' (Mbembe 2001: 57). As Harrow explains, 'the conditions of exchange are even more powerfully controlled than under colonialism... globalisation implies a greatly expanded disequilibrium in economies throughout the world' (Harrow 2007: 36). In short, global capitalism sustains itself via the creation of money in the form of debt, with debt then undermining and even replacing traditional, political forms of government, which in turn leads to economic imbalances and even to hunger (see Olaniyan 2008).

If this process is not unique to Africa but rather global in scope (Mbembe 2001: 74), as well as part and parcel of globalization itself, then it should not be surprising that Sissako's films reflect a globalized Africa. Africans in Russia (*October*), Portuguese people in Angola (*Rostov-Luanda*), Africans in France (*Life on Earth*), Chinese people in Africa (*Waiting for Happiness*), Senegalese people in Mali (*Bamako*), Haitians and Libyans in Mali (*Timbuktu*) – Sissako's work conveys a complex network of peoples, confined neither to nation-state nor to continent. We see container ships off the coast of Mauritania (*Waiting for Happiness*), while the IMF and the World Bank are represented in Mali (*Bamako*). Harrow uses similar language to Holtmeier in arguing that Chaka's death in *Bamako* takes place not 'under the sign of tragedy, but of a biopolitical order' (Harrow 2013: 199). Under this biopolitical order, people are not seen as people (indeed, the people are missing). Instead, people are a means to perpetuate the workings of globalized capital, which is the measure, or the order, of our lives – hence life (*bios*) becoming political (biopolitics). Put differently, capitalism does not change to allow Chaka to exist – that is, capitalism does not change to fit the people; instead, Chaka must change in order to fit with capitalism – or he must perish. Now, Chaka does try to change (he learns a new language). But even this is not enough to save his marriage and his life. Sissako is thus clearly attuned to the workings of global capital, where the private is the political. As a result, his films depict not an Africa in isolation but an Africa that is entangled with the rest of the world: Africa as the world, the world as Africa.

If, after Deleuze, Sissako shows us the otherwise missing people, and thereby constructs a 'people to come', we can gain a sense of futurity in his work. Sissako is aware of this himself, as conveyed by his use of Césaire ('my ear to the ground, I heard tomorrow pass'). But Sissako is not just foreseeing a specifically African future. As befits his global outlook in this globalized era, Sissako foresees our collective future, as Africa becomes a continent not stuck in the past but the image of our planetary future.

Achille Mbembe explains how there have been great improvements in Africa with regard to the treatment of disease, improved education, getting online and even in terms of gross domestic product (Mbembe 2016: 320–6).

Nonetheless, Mbembe states that two thirds of Africa's surface area is desert or dry land (Mbembe 2016: 332), while also arguing that capitalism itself is helping to produce this dead water and dead land (think climate change; think the exploitation of land and natural resources; think the creation of scarcity; see Mbembe 2016: 335). Mbembe draws upon Robert D. Kaplan's chilling prognostications about our world as inspired by his experiences in West Africa. Looking at soaring crime in the region, Kaplan, like Mbembe, says that 'West Africa's future, eventually, will also be that of most of the rest of the world' (Kaplan 1994). He argues that violence in the region is not driven by ethnic and religious conflict so much as diminishing natural resources. The environment is, then, 'the national-security issue of the early twenty-first century', with water in particular being 'in dangerously short supply' (Kaplan 1994). No wonder, then, that the downtrodden, the hungry and the thirsty are drawn towards militant Islam – because of its militancy or its promise to bring about change (Kaplan 1994).

*The Game* is set entirely in the desert, where children play at and adults take part in war. When the boy, Ahmed (Bechim Nouriev), dreams of his absent father, we see them running towards each other in a lake (the father falls over before they can unite). Sissako's short film *Je Vous Souhaite La Pluie/I Wish You Rain* (France, 2010) also depicts a woman sitting in the desert with her child in her arms praying for water in the form of rain. *Timbuktu* likewise is set primarily in the desert, where Issan squabbles with the local fisherman Amadou (Omar Haidara) over access to a lake, and where Kidane kills Amadou as a result of the latter slaughtering one of his cattle (ironically called GPS). While Sissako imbues his characters with dignity as we see their faces and as we see them listen/listen to them, he does not romanticize the Tuareg or any other group. Even the members of Ansar Dine, while carrying out dislikeable acts, are given close-ups, and are humanized via discussions of football, scenes of dancing and more. Like *Life on Earth*, where the sun is an enemy, *Timbuktu* depicts a harsh if beautiful environment, where water has to be delivered by motorbike and where the thirsty, hungry and downtrodden turn to militant Islam as the desert, created in part by capitalism, closes in.

War and the desert are thus inherently linked in Sissako's films. Furthermore, both are linked to the era of globalized capital as the increasing siliconization of the world in the form of digital technologies (think Silicon Valley) reflects the increasing siliconization of the surface of the planet in the form of the expanding desert. The onset of the desert is perhaps what we all deserve (it is a 'just desert') if we do nothing to help our fellow humans, if we do not bring water to them, but instead leave them out to dry. As Diawara says, '[f]or Sissako, and for Césaire, we are all responsible when there is suffering in one part of the world, while the other side is wallowing in wealth' (Diawara 2010: 103).

## Conclusion

In this chapter, I have shown how the cinema of Abderrahmane Sissako draws upon but does not quite fit into existing definitions of African, postcolonial and Third Cinema. I have also shown how his work conforms in some sense to Gilles Deleuze's conception of modern political cinema, confirming his position as a *griauteur*. Considering Sissako's emphasis on faces and on listening, I have suggested that he creates an ethical cinema that touches us and which gives to his characters a sense of dignity and humanity. His films reflect not just contemporary Africa but a contemporary globalized world in which economic policy (the creation of debt) outweighs our sense of responsibility for those who are stuck in the desert (the failed migrations depicted in *Waiting for Happiness* and *Bamako*).

In an essay on Mahamat-Saleh Haroun's *Un homme qui crie/A Screaming Man* (France/Belgium/Chad, 2010), I argue that the film in some senses rejects Deleuze's idea of the passive 'seer' as elaborated in *Cinema 2*, and which he sees as characteristic of 1960s *auteur* cinema, where characters are overwhelmed by and incapable of understanding or doing anything about a world that is bigger and more complex than they can fathom. Rather than passively accept such a world, the urgent situation of the contemporary era demands active engagement (see Brown 2015). The essay was not intended as an incitement to militant engagement, although in some senses it helps us to understand the growing militancy depicted in *Timbuktu*. Haroun's film ends with a quotation from Césaire's *Notebook of a Return to My Native Land* (2001): 'Beware of assuming the sterile attitude of a spectator, for life is not a spectacle, a sea of miseries is not a proscenium, a screaming man is not a dancing bear.'

Perhaps unsurprisingly, Sissako also uses this quotation in *Life on Earth*. As we hear these lines, we see Dramane, also an exile returning to his native land, being transported in a boat with his bicycle (see Finielz 2016). The redundancy of the bicycle in particular suggests that Dramane must indeed get up and do something beyond observing his native land – like making a film about it. But more than Dramane, perhaps Sissako's viewers must equally not just sit and watch his films and then forget about them, for, to continue Césaire/Sissako's dancing metaphor, '[Serge] Daney observed that African cinema (but this applies to the whole third world) is not, as the West would like, a cinema which dances, but a cinema which talks; a cinema of the speech-act' (Deleuze 1989: 222). That is, Sissako's films are not the dancing bear that we might just watch for (cruel) entertainment; they are instead telling us something important. Furthermore, if for Levinas everything outside of Europe is just 'dance', then we must overcome our historical Eurocentrism and our contemporary globalized neoliberalism, and we must listen in order to see and hear the screaming man, rather than gaze as if at a dancing bear. For those screams are not just the screams of others as they thirst under a cruel sun. Soon enough, those screams could be our own.[2]

# Bibliography

Adesokan, Akin (2010), 'Abderrahmane Sissako and the poetics of engaged expatriation', *Screen*, 51 (2)(Summer): 143–60.
Appiah, Kwame Anthony (2003), '"A Screenplay Is Not a Guarantee": Abderrahmane Sissako with Kwame Anthony Appiah', in *Through African Eyes: Dialogues with the Directors*, 35–42, New York: African Film Festival. Available Online: http://www.africanfilmny.org/BR/through-african-eyes-dialogues-with-the-directors-excerpt-from-an-interview-with-director-abderrahmane-sissako/ accessed 10 March 2017.
Armes, Roy (2006), *African Filmmaking: North and South of the Sahara*, Edinburgh: Edinburgh University Press.
Balseiro, Isabel (2007), 'Exile and longing in Abderrahmane Sissako's *La Vie sur terre*', *Screen*, 48 (4)(Winter): 443–61.
Brown, William (2015), 'The Impossibility of Passivity: The Resurgence of Activism in Contemporary Political Cinema', in Ewa Mazierska and Lars Kristensen (eds), *Marxism and Film Activism: Screening Alternative Worlds*, 145–65, Oxford: Berghahn.
Césaire, Aimé (1955), *Discours sur le colonialisme*, Paris: Editions Présence Africaine.
Césaire, Aimé (2001), *Notebook of a Return to the Native Land* (trans. Clayton Eshleman and Annette Smith), Middletown: Wesleyan University Press.
Chanan, Michael (1997), 'The Changing Geography of Third Cinema', *Screen*, 38 (4): 372–88.
Dabashi, Hamid (2015), *Can Non-Europeans Think?*, London: Zed Books.
Deleuze, Gilles (1989), *Cinema 2: The Time-Image* (trans. Hugh Tomlinson and Robert Galeta), Minneapolis: University of Minnesota Press.
Deleuze, Gilles and Félix Guattari (1986), *Kafka: Towards a Minor Literature* (trans. Dana Polan), Minneapolis: University of Minnesota Press.
Diawara, Manthia (1992), *African Cinema: Politics and Culture*, Bloomington: Indiana University Press.
Diawara, Manthia (2010), *African Film: New Forms of Aesthetics and Politics*, London: Prestel.
Downing, Lisa, and Libby Saxton (2010), *Film and Ethics: Foreclosed Encounters*, London: Routledge.
Dussel, Enrique (2013), *Ethics of Liberation: In the Age of Globalization and Exclusion* (trans. Eduardo Mendieta, Camilo Pérez Bustillo, Yolanda Angulo and Nelson Maldonado-Torres), Durham, N.C.: Duke University Press.

---

[2] I would like to thank the British Film Institute for their help in researching this chapter.

Eshun, Kodwo and Ros Gray (2011), 'The Militant Image: A Ciné-Geography', *Third Text*, 25 (1): 1–12.
Finielz, Elisa (2016), 'Temporal subversion and political critique in Abderrahmane Sissako's *La vie sur terre*', *Jump Cut: A Review of Contemporary Media*, 57 (Summer), http://www.ejumpcut.org/currentissue/-FinielzVieSurTerre/text.html (accessed 11 March 2017).
Gabara, Rachel (2010), 'Abderrahmane Sissako: Second and Third Cinema in the First Person', in Rosalind Galt and Karl Schoonover (eds), *Global Art Cinema: New Theories and Histories*, 320–33, Oxford: Oxford University Press.
Gabara, Rachel (2016), 'Abderrahmane Sissako: On the politics of African auteurs', in Seung-hoon Jeong and Jeremi Szaniawski (eds), *The Global Auteur: The Politics of Authorship in 21st Century Cinema*, 43–60, London: Bloomsbury.
Gabriel, Teshome (1982), *Third Cinema in the Third World: The Aesthetics of Liberation*, Ann Arbor: Umi Research Press.
Gabriel, Teshome (1991), 'Towards a Critical Theory of Third World Films', in Jim Pines and Paul Willemen (eds), *Questions of Third Cinema*, 31–5, London: British Film Institute. Also available at: http://teshomegabriel.net/towards-a-critical-theory-of-third-world-films (accessed 10 March 2017).
Getino, Octavio and Fernando Solanas (1969), 'Toward a Third Cinema', *Tricontinental*, 13 (October): 107–32.
Gray, Ros (2012), '"Haven't You Heard of Internationalism?" The Socialist Friendships of Mozambican Cinema', in Lars Kristensen (ed.), *Postcommunist Film – Russian, Eastern Europe and World Culture: Moving images of postcommunism*, 53–74, London: Routledge.
Guneratne, Anthony R. and Wimal Dissanayake (eds) (2003), *Rethinking Third Cinema*, London: Routledge.
Harrow, Kenneth W. (2007), *Postcolonial African Cinema: From Political Engagement to Postmodernism*, Bloomington: Indiana University Press.
Harrow, Kenneth W. (2013), *Trash: African Cinema from Below*, Bloomington: Indiana University Press.
Holtmeier, Matthew (2016), 'The Modern Political Cinema: From Third Cinema to Contemporary Networked Biopolitics', *Film-Philosophy*, 20: 303–23.
Jaji, Tsitsi (2014), 'Cassava Westerns: Ways of Watching Abderrahmane Sissako', *Black Camera*, 6 (1): 154–77.
Kaplan, Robert D. (1994), 'The Coming Anarchy: How Scarcity, Crime, Overpopulation, Tribalism, and Disease are Rapidly Destroying the Social Fabric of Our Planet', *The Atlantic*, February, https://www.theatlantic.com/ideastour/archive/kaplan.html accessed 11 March 2017.
Levinas, Emmanuel (1979), *Totality and Infinity: An Essay on Exteriority* (trans. Alphonso Lingis), London: Martinus Nijhoff Publishers.
Maingard, Jacqueline (2010), 'Screening Africa in Colour: Abderrahmane Sissako's *Bamako*', *Screen*, 51 (4) (Winter): 397–403.
Mbembe, Achille (2001), *On the Postcolony* (trans. A. M. Berrett, Janet Roitman, Murray Last, Achille Mbembe and Steven Rendall), Berkeley: University of California Press.
Mbembe, Achille (2016), 'Africa in the New Century', in Lien Heidenrich-Seleme and Sean O'Toole (eds), *African Futures: Thinking about the Future in Word and Image*, 315–35, Berlin: Kerber.

Mudimbe, V. Y. (1988), *The Invention of Africa: Gnosis, Philosophy and the Order of Knowledge*, London: James Currey.

Murphy, David and Patrick Williams (2007), *Postcolonial African Cinema: Ten Directors*, Manchester: Manchester University Press.

Murray Levine, Alison J. (2012), 'Words on trial: Oral performance in Abderrahmane Sissako's *Bamako*', *Studies in French Cinema*, 12 (2): 151–67.

Nagib, Lúcia (2011), *World Cinema and the Ethics of Realism*, London: Continuum.

Nancy, Jean-Luc (2007), *Listening* (trans. Charlotte Mandell), New York: Fordham University Press.

Olanuyan, Tejumola (2008), 'Of Rations and Rationalities: The World Bank, African Hunger, and Abderrahmane Sissako's *Bamako*', *The Global South*, 2 (2) (Fall): 130–38.

Scott, Kathleen and Stefanie Van de Peer (2016), 'Sympathy for the Other: Female Solidarity and Postcolonial Subjectivity in Francophone Cinema', *Film-Philosophy*, 20: 168–94.

Shaka, Femi Okiremuete (2004), *Modernity and the African Cinema: A Study in Colonial Discourse, Postcoloniality, and Modern African Identities*, Trenton, NJ: Africa World Press.

Sicinski, Michael (2006), 'A Fragmented Epistemology: The Films of Abderrahmane Sissako', *Cinema Scope*, 29 (Winter): 16–19.

Thackway, Melissa (2014), 'Exile and the "Burden of Representation": Trends in Contemporary Sub-Saharan Francophone African Filmmaking', *Black Camera*, 5 (2) (Spring): 5–20.

Wayne, Mike (2001), *Political Film: The Dialectics of Third Cinema*, London: Pluto Press.

Willemen, Paul (1991), 'The Third Cinema Question: Notes and Reflections', in Jim Pines and Paul Willemen (eds), *Questions of Third Cinema*, 1–29, London: British Film Institute.

Woll, Josephine (2004), 'The Russian Connection: Soviet Cinema and the Cinema of Francophone Africa', in Françoise Pfaff (ed.), *Focus on African Films*, 223–40, Bloomington: Indiana University Press.

Wynter, Sylvia (2000), 'Africa, the West and the Analogy of Culture: The Cinematic Text after Man', in June Givanni (ed.), *Symbolic Narratives/African Cinema: Audiences, Theory and the Moving Image*, 25–76, London: British Film Institute.

Zacks, Stephen (1999), 'The Theoretical Construction of African Cinema', in Kenneth W. Harrow (ed.), *African Cinema: Post-Colonial and Feminist Readings*, 3–19, Trenton, NJ: Africa World Press.

# 11

# Class, gender and ethnicity in Alfonso Cuarón's *Roma*

## *Ewa Mazierska*
## *(University of Central Lancashire)*

*Roma* (2018) is directed by Mexican Alfonso Cuarón, set in Mexico in the early 1970s and focuses on the struggles of a disadvantaged worker during a period of political upheaval in Mexico. For this reason, one is tempted to approach it as an example of Third Cinema. Although the film has not been considered from this perspective, it was still predominantly regarded as a progressive film and this was an important reason that it was awarded an Oscar for the best film, in 2019, along with many other accolades. This award could also be seen as a snub by the Hollywood community towards Donald Trump, with his flagship policy of building a wall between the United States and Mexico, hence making the border impenetrable for potential migrants from Mexico and other South American countries, seeking employment in the United States.

In my analysis, however, I want to demonstrate that in important ways *Roma* is antithetical to Third Cinema whose goal is emancipation of the oppressed by colonialism and capitalism. Instead, it promotes preservation of the status quo, by focusing on the supposed solidarity of people from the Third World across any class or ethnic divide, and the positive role played by the wealthy in the lives of the poor, who can be easily misguided and manipulated, indirectly opposing the new movements (often dismissed as 'populist') which pit the elites against the masses.

In my analysis I will take a close look at the characters, story, and the visual and aural style of *Roma*. First, however, I will present the director and the production context of *Roma*, to account for continuities and discontinuities between this film and the earlier work by Cuarón.

## The director

Alfonso Cuarón (full name Alfonso Cuarón Orozco) was born in 1961 in a Mexican upper-middle-class family. His father was a doctor specializing in nuclear medicine, his mother a pharmaceutical biochemist. Cuarón studied philosophy and filmmaking at the National Autonomous University of Mexico (UNAM) and after a short apprenticeship in television, started to shoot his own films. His full-length fiction debut was *Sólo con tu pareja* (*Only with Your Partner*, 1991), which he made in Mexico. Then he moved to Hollywood, where he started his career with literary adaptations: *A Little Princess* (1995), based on Frances Hodgson Burnett's classic novel and *Great Expectations* (1998), an updated version of Charles Dickens's novel. These films were moderate box office and critical successes, hence did not constitute a breakthrough in Cuarón's career, prompting the director to return to Mexico and shoot *Y tu mamá también* (*And Your Mother Too*, 2001) with Mexican characters and actors, set in Mexico and engaging with Mexican history and present day. This film about two male teenagers, who take an extended road trip with an attractive married woman, turned out to be an international hit and a major success with critics. Next Cuarón made two spectacular, high-budget films, *Harry Potter and the Prisoner of Azkaban* (2004) and *Gravity* (2013), with a more modest, in terms of budget, science fiction film, *Children of Men* (2006) between them. *Roma* can be regarded as his second return to his roots and to a less spectacular and more realistic cinema, with *Y tu mamá también* being the first such return.

Does this portfolio of varied films have any traits suggesting that they came from the same hand? Critics draw attention to two such commonalities. One of them is privileging identity politics, especially the plight of women. His focus on women and female gaze is noted in relation to his early Hollywood film *Great Expectations*, where Estella resists being reduced to an object of visual pleasure and conforming to Finn's vision of her (Johnson 2005: 71). This is a remarkable achievement, as Dickens's novel is male-centred. Cuarón takes a similar approach in *Y tu mamá también*, whose female character Luisa is initially given the role of a tool of sexual maturation of two teenagers, but in the course of the film becomes a character in her own right. As Ernesto Avecedo-Muñoz puts it, 'Luisa's agency subverts classical narrative and serves as the locus for the revision and inscription of a new type of Mexican foundational fiction' (Acevedo-Muñoz 2004: 47). While Cuarón shows class differences between the men as an important factor in their self-identification, for Luisa class does not matter; she is represented as if existing outside of the class system and mediating between the two teenagers of different economic and social standing. The focus on a woman is even more obvious in *Gravity*, which the director himself described as a 'drama of a woman in space' (Masters 2014). For the reason that the film is set in space, issues about class are not included in the narrative. Ryan's plight is about surviving, not liberation of fellow human beings. Off-screen Cuarón also tends to present himself as a champion of women, including in his profession, as described by one of the journalists, who interviewed him: 'Cuarón is acutely aware of inequality, both in his industry and beyond. "This thing we are celebrating, "diversity", should have happened a century ago when cinema began". He is disappointed that no women have been nominated for Best Director at the Oscars this year' (Butter 2019).

Another trait of Cuarón's directing style is a penchant for narrative and ideological ambiguity. When discussing *Y tu mamá también* Acevedo-Muñoz, following Garcia Canclini, uses the term 'counterepic', arguing that this form is characteristic of a large part of film production coming from Chile, Argentina, Cuba and Mexico. This approach is reflected in 'choosing an interrogative or doubting relationship to the social ... If there is no longer one coherent and stable Order, and if the identity of each group is not associated with a single territory but with multiple scenarios, and history is not directed toward programmable goals, then images and texts cannot be anything but a compilation of fragments, collages' (Canclini, quoted in Acevedo-Muñoz 2004: 40). As was stated in the Introduction to this collection, ambiguity and multiplicity are privileged traits of World Cinema.

Cuarón is also revered for his visual style. Michael K. Johnson, in his analysis of *Great Expectations*, observes that reviews from this film praised Cuarón, his regular cinematographer Emmanuel Lubezki and production designer Tony Burrough for 'ravishing colour', 'luscious design' and being 'beautifully shot' and Cuarón himself for being a 'voluptuous visual stylist' (Johnson 2005: 62–3). Similar praises were bestowed on Cuarón's later films, especially *Gravity*. Bruce Isaacs observes that Cuarón

> demonstrates a fixation on the capacity of the image to display greater and more complex indices of time and space, holding shots across what would be deemed uncomfortable durations in a more conventional mode of cinema. Cuarón's films are increasingly defined by this mark of the long take, shots with durations well beyond the industry standard. Such shots are attention-grabbing spectacles, displaying the virtuosity of the filmmaker over and above the requirement of narrative unfolding. (Isaacs 2016)

I will argue that *Roma* follows in the footsteps of Cuarón's earlier films in being focused on the plight of women, counterepic approach and showing a predilection to visual excess. My aim is to show how these aspects of his film are mobilized to obfuscate the issue of class, so central to Third Cinema.

## Production and distribution context

Cuarón's trajectory makes it difficult to describe his films using the categories of First, Second and Third Cinema. His roots in Mexico and Mexican culture, which he acknowledges in *Y tu mamá también* and *Roma*, render him, if not Third Cinema, then at least a director from what used to be called Third World. However, his style aligns him both with the Second, arthouse cinema and First, Hollywood cinema, as his films are seen as both artistic and popular. Watching them one appreciates how these types merge. Cuarón can be seen as not only a World Cinema director who brings Third World histories to the attention of world audiences, but also a Hollywood director who colonizes Third World with its products. In *Roma* Cuarón does both of these things. This is reflected in the way he marketed this film, as one which 'does not follow the money' and can reach people who cannot afford going to the cinema either (Butter 2019). The budget of the film is 15,000,000 USD; this is not a high budget by Hollywood standards. By comparison, *Gravity* had budget of 100,000,000 USD. However, it is high budget for a film made in the Third World.

Yet, it was not so much the budget, as the fact that it was produced by Netflix, American media service provider, that was presented as testimony to Cuarón's artistic independence and his care for disadvantaged audiences. It should be mentioned here that since its involvement in producing cine-films, Netflix attracted much criticism from famous directors and media people, such as Steven Spielberg and Christopher Nolan, representing (especially Spielberg) older, apparently nobler times of analogue cinema. Spielberg objected to Netflix films being allowed to compete for Oscars (Nyren 2018). Nolan criticized Netflix because of its 'mindless policy of everything having to be simultaneously streamed and released, which is obviously an untenable model for theatrical presentation' (Hooton 2017). Both directors also complained about Netflix invading the cinema territory, which can be described as an aspect of postdigitalization, squeezing out the medium-sized films, which were once the staple diet of cinema theatres, a process which can be compared to the pauperization of the middle class which is characteristic of the more advanced phases of neoliberalization.

Cuarón dismissed such criticism, which can be described as deriving from the Second Cinema's tradition, pointing instead to the democratizing effect of Netflix. He said: 'Netflix brings a democratic flexibility. The combination of worlds is exciting. Yalitza, who plays Cleo, is happy because her community can see it. You need to drive for three hours [where she lives] to get to the movies and for some places outside our privileged universe the movie-going experiences is more challenging' (Butter 2019).

One can be impressed by Cuarón's concern for making his film accessible to people whom he tries to represent in his films. Read unsympathetically, however, such words can be regarded as praising a higher form of American cultural imperialism, which thanks to the development of technology managed to overcome earlier obstacles to make people from the periphery consume products coming from the centre and influence their worldviews.

## Characters and story

*Roma* is set in the early 1970s in the upper-class district of Roma in Mexico City. Its main character is Cleo, a live-in indigenous maid, working for the family of affluent doctor Antonio with four children, whose wife Sofia is a housewife. The family resembles the one in which Cuarón himself was brought up. There is a second maid in the house, named Adela. Adela introduces Cleo to Fermin, a friend of her boyfriend. When the two couples go to the cinema, Cleo and Fermin leave and they have sex in a rented room. Cleo becomes pregnant and when some time later she reveals this fact to Fermin, when they are again in the cinema, he tells Cleo that he needs to use the bathroom and never returns. Cleo thus faces the prospect of becoming a single mother. We also learn that Antonio is unfaithful to Sofia and pretends to go to medical conferences abroad, while in reality this is a pretext to spend time with his lover. Cleo's shopping trip to buy a crib for her baby coincides with a students' protest and the attempts by police and the military to extinguish it. Cleo meets Fermin in a store, when he shoots at and kills a protester. The event leads to Cleo's waters breaking and she is taken to hospital, where she gives birth to a stillborn daughter. Some time later Cleo accompanies Sofia and her children on a trip to the beach, where she rescues Sofia's daughter when she is taken by a strong current. When they return, Antonio is no longer in the family's house.

This synopsis demonstrates that *Roma* is based on parallelisms. The most important concerns the position of Cleo and Sofia. They both lose their men and have to look after their children only with the support of other women. Sofia helps Cleo during her pregnancy; Cleo looks after her children and even rescues one of them. The sense of sharing the same fate, irrespective of any differences, pertaining to class, education, age or race, is expressed openly by Sofia, who says at one point: 'No matter what they tell you – women, we are always alone.' This and similar statements also suggest that women, the way Cuarón sees them, are located on the side of nature, or at least cultural changes affect them less than changes in nature (pregnancies, births, looking after elderly relatives). Neither Sofia nor Cleo is interested in politics and view political events, such as students' protests and the burning of forests in a remote part of Mexico, where they spend New Year's celebrations, as distractions in their daily lives.

There are also important similarities between Antonio and Fermin. Both turn out to be irresponsible and selfish, thinking only about their pleasure, rather than the consequences of their actions to the women who trusted them. They are also similar because they belong to the 'external' world and cannot be domesticated. In the case of Antonio, this is demonstrated by his long absences from home due to frequent 'trips' abroad. Fermin is also never seen at home; when Cleo manages to find him, he is shown practising martial arts with a large group of other men, on the outskirts of the city. The most important difference between them is that Fermin is much rougher and more cruel than Antonio, as shown in a scene when he threatens to beat up Cleo and her unborn child, if she tries to find him again. This excess of cruelty can be attributed to Fermin being of a lower class, hence lacking good manners, which are part of the cultural capital of the higher classes.

Finally, there is a parallel between the fates of Cloe's and Sofia's children. Cloe's daughter is stillborn, possibly because of the shock of Cloe's unexpected meeting with Fermin and witnessing his brutality, as well as the difficulty to reach hospital due to demonstrations blocking roads. Sofia's daughter is also in danger of death due to not only her own reckless behaviour, but also the absence of her distracted and grieving mother. Yet, the girl survives because she is rescued by Cleo who risks her own life to save her. This incident is presented as a kind of triple salvation: of the girl, of Cleo, who following the rescue is able to express her true feelings towards her stillborn child,

FIGURE 11.1 *Cleo and Pepe. Screen grab from* Roma *(dir. Alfonso Cuarón, 2018).*

FIGURE 11.2 *Granny and Cleo being upheld.* Screen grab from Roma *(dir. Alfonso Cuarón, 2018).*

FIGURE 11.3 *Defence against the revolution.* Screen grab from Roma *(dir. Alfonso Cuarón, 2018).*

admitting that she wanted her daughter to die and feels responsible for her death. It thus appears as if Cleo is repaid for her sin of rejecting her own child. Finally, the rescuing of Sofia's daughter helps Sofia to focus on her future and appreciate her good luck of having four healthy children. The chief victors from this situation are the family of Cleo's employers, who survived the accident and made Cleo more attached to her employers than ever. The loser, or less of a winner, is Cleo, who didn't get her own child back. Most likely, she didn't even get a rise in her salary, bonus for heroism or reduction in her duties, given that after Antonio's departure, Sofia would have to get a job herself and have less time for her children. Indeed, the change of status is acknowledged by Sofia buying a smaller car – a symbol of the economic 'downsizing' of her family.

The idea that solidarity between women is more important than other types of solidarity, especially class unity, can be regarded as feminist. However, there are socialist feminists who try to merge these two positions. On this basis, Cuarón is seen as a feminist director and we can find such a reading in many reviews of *Roma*. Take these fragments:

The film thus serves as a testament to the women who raised him and populated his world. While all these frightening things were going on in the larger country around them, they kept on, choosing to rebuild after tragedies, raising children, sustaining a sense of wonder. (Wilkinson 2018)

At its heart are two women – both embattled yet resilient, and from very different backgrounds – who are left to clean up the mess after being abandoned or betrayed by the men in their lives. (Kermode 2018)

Such sentiments and attitudes dominate reviews of the film. Only a few critics, most importantly Slavoj Žižek and Richard Brody, focused on the differences between the two women. Žižek noted that while Sofia can afford to express her frustration by repeatedly scratching the family Ford Galaxie in the narrow garage area, making chunks of plaster fall down, Cleo 'cannot afford such "authentic" outbursts – even when her whole world is falling apart, the work has to go on' (Žižek 2019). Moreover, the supposed love of the family acts as a trap. He asks rhetorically: 'Can she really be reduced to the ultimate love object of a spoiled upper-middle class family, accepted (almost) as part of the family to be better exploited, physically and emotionally?' (Žižek 2019).

The film thus cannot be classified as feminist, as at the core of feminist movement is the idea of liberation. Feminism is not simply recognizing that women have a more difficult life than men and they are pushed away from political life, occupied by men, but about reversing the status quo by fighting for women's voting rights, equal pay and so on. Instead, Cuarón offers his female characters no avenue to enter polity and suggests that any effort to do so is misguided because politics consists of brutal and childish games, whose only goal is chaos and destruction.

In order to foreground the similarity between Sofia and Cleo, the story develops in a way which avoids presenting their interests as antagonistic. Inevitably, such a likely situation will be Cleo's giving birth to a living child, as it will reduce the maid's value to her employer. Curiously, there are never any discussions between Sofia and Cleo about the future of Cleo and her child: whether the maid will be dismissed, or stay in employment while her child is sent away to relatives or given for adoption, or whether she would be allowed to work as a maid while also looking after her baby. One might conjecture that neither of these scenarios is considered because the first two might reveal the cruelty of the capitalist system and Cleo's employers, who ultimately value Cleo as a worker rather than an autonomous human being. The last one, on the other hand, would come across as unrealistic, as it is next to impossible to work effectively as a maid when looking after one's own child. There are also no discussions about abortion and we never learn whether this is because abortion was forbidden in Mexico at the time or because Sofia is against abortion on moral grounds (as the large number of her own children suggests). Of course, all the options do not need to be considered either by Cleo or Sofia, given that Cleo gives birth to a stillborn baby. The death of Cleo's daughter thus not only offers a solution to Cleo's predicament, but also frees Cuarón from showing the upper-class family and by the same token his parents at the point when their interests and those of their employee at their most antagonistic.

In the cathartic scene Cleo confesses that she did not want her child to live, but the reasons for that are not revealed. It is possible that she was ashamed of giving birth to an illegitimate child and worried that without a husband she would be unable to meet the needs of her child. It is also possible that she was aware of the conflict between her role as a mother and that of as a maid.

The narrative of *Roma* is full of such omissions. We see things happening, but we rarely learn what the protagonists think about them. It feels like the director puts the viewer in the position of a child overhearing the conversations of adults and trying to put together a coherent whole out of many clues and snippets. Such narration brings to mind European arthouse cinema of the 1960s, especially those of Godard and Antonioni and their followers in Third World countries. This type of filmmaking received much praise from the critics due to the perception that it leaves viewers much scope to draw their own conclusions, even being co-creators of the film's meaning. It favours a more educated audience, because it requires from them a high level of 'cinematic literacy'. However, in their essay 'Towards a Third Cinema', Fernando Solanas and Octavio Getino are critical of filmmaking of this type, writing that 'as a rule, [Second Cinema] films only dealt with effect, never with cause; it was cinema of mystification or anti-historicism' (Solanas and Getino [1969] 2000: 265).

Such a reading, which I describe as 'Third Cinema reading', is also offered by Richard Brody, who in his review of *Roma* writes: 'In the film, politics are strictly personal, de-ideologized, dehistoricized' (Brody 2018). The effect of narrating the film this way is effacing the questions concerning class differences between Cleo and Sofia and presenting the middle-class woman as a friend and carer of the hapless maid, as opposed to putting into a sharp relief Sofia's role as exploiter of Cleo's labour, both physical and affective.

Mystification and anti-historicism also apply to the political events, depicted in *Roma*. One such event is students' demonstration, which is violently extinguished by the police and some thugs who chase the protestors to a store where Sofia's mother and Cleo are shopping for the crib. We never learn what the students' protest is about and whether it concerns their own situation or that of the entire country. Do they want to overthrow the government and if so, why? Are their interests conflicting with those of Antonio and Sofia's family? It is only by reading reviews or through familiarizing ourselves with Mexico's history that we might discover that these protests took place on 10 June 1971, the day of the Corpus Christi festival, and had a distinct left-wing character, not unlike the 1968 movements in countries such as France and Czechoslovakia. We can also learn that during their course 120 protesters lost their lives.

Finding this out from the diegesis is also obscured by making Fermin a member of the gang, which attacks the protests. This gang can be identified as Los Halcones (the Hawks), a paramilitary group made up of working-class youth, members of sports clubs and professional criminals, created and supported by the Mexican government and trained in the United States. From a Marxist perspective, Los Halcones can be described as lumpenproletariat, a rabble unaware of their class interests, exploited by the capitalist rulers in their fight against the proletariat, what Marx describes as 'the part of a bribed tool of reactionary intrigue' (Marx and Engels [1947] 2008: 49). They are also an example of an imperial (American in this case) meddling in the affairs of their less politically and economically developed neighbours, to ensure their compliance with American politics. By making Fermin a member of Los Halcones, Cuarón links working-class men with right-wing, regressive politics and brutality. We can thus conjecture that it is in Cleo's best interest to avoid such company and stay with her gentle middle-class masters.

At one point Cleo travels with Sofia and her children to the villa of Sofia's friends, where the maid meets some of her old friends. During their stay there is a fire in the forest; most likely this is a consequence of a land dispute between some wealthy landowners and poor farmers or farm hands. However, in a dialogue between Cleo and Adela it is suggested that Cleo's mother's land, in her native village, has been confiscated. Against the lack of any specifics about the political conflicts in Mexico, we can conjecture that the land dispute is about taking from the poor (as we can safely assume that Cleo's mother is poor) and giving to the wealthy, rather than other way round. Violent actions by Los Halcones are not balanced by showing in *Roma* any progressive movement of the working-class people. Politics in *Roma* is thus presented as an attack of lumpenproletariat on the progressive forces and as misguided working-class people turning against each other and as personal politics, namely good women struggling against bad men.

Even if we agree that there is something feminist in Cuarón's representation of Cleo and Sofia, as many reviewers suggest, he is certainly not Third World and Third Cinema feminist. Reina Lewis and Sara Mills observe:

Second wave Anglo-American feminist theory had generalised from Western middle-class women's experiences and developed a form of theorising – 'sisterhood is global' – which assumed that those white concerns were the concerns of women everywhere. This type of essentialising led to a silencing of Black and third-world women's interventions within early Anglo-American feminist theory. (Lewis and Mills 2003: 4)

In a similar vein, Chandra Mohanty argues that the Western feminist movement shows a tendency to lump together the many different identities of women worldwide. An example would be by using the word 'Third World Women' to describe any women who do not live in a Westernized, first-world country. She writes:

I would like to suggest that the feminist writings I analyze here discursively colonize the material and historical heterogeneities of the lives of women in the Third World, thereby producing/representing a composite, singular "Third World woman"-an image that appears arbitrarily constructed but nevertheless carries with it the authorizing signature of Western humanist discourse.' (Mohanty 1984: 335)

Likewise, Ella Shohat in her essay 'Post-Third-Worldist Culture: Gender, Nation, and the Cinema' notes:

Challenging white feminist theory and practice that emerged in a major way in the 1970s in First-World metropolises, Post-Third-Worldist feminist works have refused a Eurocentric universalizing of 'womanhood', or even of 'feminism'. Eschewing a discourse of universality, such feminisms claim a 'location', arguing for specific forms of resistance in relation to diverse forms of oppression. Aware of white women's advantageous positioning within (neo)colonialist and racist systems, feminist struggles in the Third World (including the 'third world' in the First World) have not been premised on a facile discourse of global sisterhood, and have often been made within the context of anti-colonial and anti-racist struggles. (Shohat 2003: 52)

Instead of being Post-Third-Worldist feminist work, *Roma* is premised on what Shohat describes as 'facile discourse of global sisterhood', in this case the sisterhood of an upper-class Mexican woman of European origin and the indigenous working-class woman. This idea is subtly conveyed by the title of the film, which does not refer to the name of any of the film's female protagonists, but to a district in Mexico where they lead their supposedly similar existence, both pitted against bad men.

Not only does Cuarón present Sofia and Cleo as two wronged sisters, but assigns Sofia the place of a wiser sister. If there is anything said in the film, which might be regarded as an expression of the position of a woman in Cleo's situation, it is said by Sofia, whom Brody describes as the stand-in for Cuarón's mother, to whom the director lends both voice and consciousness (Brody 2018). At the same time, as this critic observes, 'he turns the character of Cleo into a stereotype that's all too common in movies made by upper-middle-class and intellectual filmmakers about working people: a strong, silent, long-enduring, and all-tolerating type, deprived of discourse, a silent angel whose inability or unwillingness to express herself is held up as a mark of her stoic virtue' (Brody 2018). I will add that in this way Cloe not only fails to become a feminist model, but is really a patriarchal ideal of woman who silently carries her cross so that (bad) men are free to wreck the world in the knowledge that women will put up with their behaviour and try to mend the damage. Cuarón's regressive gender politics is the more dangerous as it is applied by the majority of critics not only to the world he portrays on screen, but also to the external world, namely the world populated by the actors who played in this movie as conveyed by such a fragment from a review:

> With Cleo at its center, *Roma*'s story takes on a meditative tone. Aparicio had never acted before this film, but she had worked as a domestic employee, as had her mother and other female relatives. That personal history is something she's talked about in interviews, explaining that she drew on her lived experience when portraying Cleo's life. (Wilkinson 2018)

By casting Yalitza Aparicio, an indigenous Oaxacan woman in the role of a servant, Cuarón responded to the call to cast 'minority actors' in 'minority roles' which is, again, part of a wider political movement promoting political activism along identity lines rather than class allegiance and received a lot of praise for his casting. This praise was amplified by Aparicio's expression of gratitude to the director for giving her a chance to become an actress (Tapley 2019). Although no doubt Cuarón made Aparicio a star, his casting politics suggests that there is a special fit between the actress and her role, and a wider community she represents: that of working-class indigenous people and women especially. I argue that the political message of such casting is to normalize and promote the status quo rather than lifting this stratum to a higher social position.

## Visual and aural style

The style of *Roma* can be described as a mixture of stylization and authenticity, epic and counterepic. The first pertains to the fact that the film is shot in black and white. To contemporary viewers, such a style, applied in contemporary films, signals 'arthouse-ness'. Black-and-white print is typically used for portraying past events, but not from a long distance, like antiquity or the Middle Ages, but from the past which is still remembered by somebody and whose records are available on old films and newsreels. It signifies the filmmakers' admission that they have no direct access to the people and events (re)presented, but have to rely on somebody's memory or some intermediary, such as old photos. 'arthouse-ness'.[1] Consequently, it commands respect for a recognition of one's limitations. Cuarón himself explained his stylistic choice using such arguments (Butter 2019).

Using black-and-white print might also signify the filmmaker's refusal to fully own the version displayed on screen, by suggesting that he or she has access only to its partial version and in this way pre-empt any criticism of being biased or unwilling to reveal an uncomfortable truth. I suggest that this is the case in *Roma*. The lack of answers to some difficult questions, such as how much Cleo earned, is excused by presenting her story from the perspective of Cuarón as a child, whose understanding is limited and whose subsequent memory is incomplete.

There might also be more pragmatic reasons for making use of black-and-white print.

In relation to *Roma*, Peter Bradshaw argues:

> The film is dynamically shot in a pellucid black and white, which has perhaps made it easier for the director (who is also the cinematographer) to use digital techniques for exterior shots, modifying and fabricating period details with an ecstatic, dreamlike certainty. (Bradshaw 2018)

Such statements suggest that black-and-white print offers double advantage, making the film more realistic in a sense of providing period details while also appearing more detached.

Bradshaw also points to the potential for beautification in reducing the colour palette. I will argue that this potential was exploited in *Roma*, rendering dirt, which the upper-class families are producing and with which Cleo and Adela deal on a daily basis, less menacing. Dirt, garbage, detritus are important tropes in Third Cinema. Robert Stam discusses the multiple meanings of garbage, as the position in which many colonialized people find themselves, being surrounded by garbage and reduced to garbage. Consequently, garbage becomes a resource for art of (post)colonial subjects and a tool of resistance against the aesthetic standards of the colonialists and local bourgeoisie. As Stam writes:

---

[1] One of Cuaron's competitors for Oscars, Paweł Pawlikowski, also used black-and-white print in his two recent films, *Ida* (2013) and *Zimna wojna* (*Cold War*, 2018). Conversely, Roman Polanski explained that he made *The Pianist* (2002) in colour, because his relation to the Holocaust was that of a witness rather than a browser of old photographs.

> Garbage ... becomes an ideal medium for those who themselves have been cast off, broken down, who have been 'down in the dumps', who feel, as the blues line had it, 'like a tin can on that old dumping ground'. A transformative impulse takes an object considered worthless and turns it into something of value. Here the restoration of the buried worth of cast-off object analogizes the process of restoration of the buried worth of the despised, devalued artist himself. At the same time, we witness an example of a strategy of resourcefulness in a situation of scarcity. (Stam 2003: 42)

This quote suggests that in Third Cinema garbage is or can be edified. However, in *Roma* Cuarón dismisses any aesthetic or political potential of garbage. In his film garbage is reduced to dirt and nuisance, as in a scene when Antonio's car drives through the dog's excrement in the garage area and when he subsequently complains that the house is dirty, which is a hardly veiled criticism of Cleo and Adela, who do not fulfil their duties to a high standard, and of Sofia who does not enforce such a standard.

At the same time, the lack of colour in *Roma* takes the edge from the dirt, makes it more acceptable, in the same way blood is easier to look at, when it is shown in black and white.

The most discussed aspect of Cuarón's style in *Roma*, however, was not his lack of colour, but long take, often combined with long shot. The director showed affinity to long take in his previous films, especially *Gravity* and was praised by critics for the boldness of this stylistic choice. The advantage lay in moving away from the dominant Hollywood style by creating a certain visual excess and at the same time creating a sense of realism (Isaacs 2016).

Long take, combined with the depth of field, bears positive connotations in film criticism for two principal reasons. First, since the times of André Bazin, it is seen as a more realistic style of filmmaking than one based on editing. As Bazin states in his essay, 'The Evolution of the Language of Cinema':

> (1) The depth of focus brings the spectator into a relation with the image closer to that which he enjoys with reality. Therefore it is correct to say that, independently of the contents of the image, its structure is more realistic.
>
> (2) That it implies, consequently, both a more active mental attitude on the part of the spectator and a more positive contribution on his part to the action in the progress. While analytical montage only calls for him to follow his guide, to let his attention follow along smoothly with that of the director who will choose what he should see, here it is called upon to exercise at least a minimum of personal choice. It is from his attention and his will that the meaning of the image in part derives. (Bazin 1967: 35–6)

Secondly, using long takes is seen as a measure of the artistry of filmmakers, principally the director and cinematographer, because it requires extra skill and preparation. Critics argue that only a technically proficient filmmaker is able to extract truth from the represented reality. I don't believe, however, that a long take is intrinsically more realistic or honest; this depends on the wider context in which it is deployed. A film can be built from long takes but fail to convey psychological truth and be racist or misogynistic.

Moreover, offering the viewer too much information in one shot or keeping his or her attention for too long on a particular scene might in fact prevent him or her from understanding the action. This is what happens in *Roma*. Frequently, especially in the scenes shot on the streets of Mexico City, I found myself lost, not unlike Cleo. Rather than choosing something of interest, I wanted to withdraw from the open space into the security of the Mexican apartment. Furthermore, the composition of the frame often dominates over the story. One thinks how this or that shot was made, how many extras were used and so on, rather than what happens to Cleo at a given point in the story. This problem was recognized by some reviewers. Mark Kermode in *The Guardian* observed: 'Occasionally the almost showy virtuosity of the film-making can prove a distraction, making a very personal project seem more like a technical tour de force' (Kermode 2018). Kermode also notes that such virtuosity serves the beautification of what should not be beautified: 'However frenzied or frenetic events may become (riots and earthquakes feature), these images retain an almost impassive serenity. In an echo of Emmanuel Lubezki's spiralling work on *Gravity*, Cuarón's camera seems to have a weightless quality, drifting inexorably through turbulent environments' (Kermode 2018).

It should be remembered that such virtuosity and beautification were criticized by the proponents of Third and imperfect cinema as a means to convey the values of the colonizers and the higher classes and as a distraction from the political content which the films might convey. Take, for example, the beginning of Julio García Espinosa's 'For an imperfect cinema':

> Nowadays, perfect cinema – technically and artistically masterful – is almost always reactionary cinema. The major temptation facing Cuban cinema at this time – when it is achieving its objective of becoming a cinema of quality, one which is culturally meaningful within the revolutionary process – is precisely that of transforming itself into a perfect cinema. (Espinoza 1979: 22)

What was said about Cuarón's visual style can be largely repeated in relation to the way he uses sound in his film. The sound is dense and multi-layered, encompassing house and street noises, a dog barking, as well as dialogues and music, often coming from the radio. Again, such layered sound, which brings to mind Godard's films of the 1960s, adds to the film's sense of realism, but also drowns the already weak voice of Cleo in the cacophony of noises, rendering it insignificant. Moreover, diegetic songs often replace Cleo's own voice and give a sense of fatalism, as when she hears on the radio a song with lyrics: 'But I was born poor and you will never love me.' Such a line can be seen as a premonition of her affair with Fermin, a man born poor, like her, but who left her because of her 'negative capital', caused by her poverty and pregnancy.

# Conclusions

In my discussion I argued that *Roma* tries to obliterate class issues and especially class conflict between the poor and the rich of Mexico. It does so by presenting the main character as reconciled with her position as a servant in the house of an affluent family and suggesting that changing this position will be to her disadvantage, because outside the cocooned life in the house of her masters there is danger. The main source of this danger is people of her own class who fight with each other, bringing chaos and making the situation of the vulnerable even worse. People like Cleo thus need their upper-class masters to protect them from a disorder which they are unable to resist and even comprehend.

There is a fit between Cuarón's representation of Cleo and the discourse about the poor, which dominates in the Western, particularly American and British, media, as encapsulated by articles about Donald Trump's election in 2017, the Brexit vote in the UK and the wider rise of 'populism' in the world, namely movements which pit the elites against the masses, published in newspapers such as *The Guardian* and *The New York Times*.

According to this discourse, members of the lower classes who voted for Brexit and Trump (most importantly from the rust belt in the United States and the North of England) did so as a result of misrecognition of their class interests. Hence, their political decisions would harm them.

Cuarón's film demonstrates, as Solanas and Getino argued some twenty years previously, that despite the strides made by the Second Cinema, it is still 'trapped within the conventional system of capitalism'. To put it bluntly, it supports capitalism. I will argue, however, that in contrast to the classical auteurist cinema of the 1960s, the cinema of Fellini or Antonioni, contemporary Second Cinema, as exemplified by Cuarón, is more condescending towards the working class and more sympathetic towards the bourgeoisie which it sees as its saviour. Again, to quote Solanas and Getino, the 'revolution begins at the moment when the masses sense the need for change and their intellectual vanguards begin to study and carry out this change through activities on different fronts' (Solanas and Getino 2000: 266). Indirectly, *Roma* shows that the masses need their own intellectual vanguards rather than relying on any self-appointed spokesmen from Mexico or Hollywood.

# Bibliography

Acevedo-Muñoz, Ernesto R. (2004), 'Sex, Class, and Mexico in Alfonso Cuarón's *Y tu mamá también*', *Film & History*, 34 (1): 39–48.
Bazin, André (1967), 'The Evolution of the Language of Cinema', in *What Is Cinema?*, 23–40, Berkeley: University of California Press.
Bradshaw, Peter (2018), '*Roma* – An Epic of Tearjerking Magnificence', *The Guardian*, 29 November, https://www.theguardian.com/film/2018/nov/29/roma-review-alfonso-cuaron accessed 25 May 2019.
Brody, Richard (2018), 'There's a Voice Missing in Alfonso Cuarón's "Roma"', *The New Yorker*, 18 December, https://www.newyorker.com/culture/the-front-row/theres-a-voice-missing-in-alfonso-cuarons-roma accessed 26 May 2019.
Butter, Susannah (2019), 'Roma Director Alfonso Cuarón Interview: "I Was Making Something That Came Directly from Memory"', *GoLondon*, 31 January, https://www.standard.co.uk/go/london/film/roma-director-alfonso-cuar-n-interview-oscars-a4053931.html (accessed 15 May 2019).
Espinosa, Julio García (1979), 'For an Imperfect Cinema', *Jump Cut: A Review of Contemporary Media*, 20: 24–6.
Hooton, Christopher (2017), 'Christopher Nolan Sent Netflix a Written apology for His Comments', *The Independent*, 7 November. https://www.independent.co.uk/arts-entertainment/films/news/christopher-nolan-netflix-variety-interview-film-cinemas-a8042891.html (accessed 22 November 2018).
Isaacs, Bruce (2016), 'Reality Effects: The Ideology of the Long Take in the Cinema of Alfonso Cuarón', in Denson and Leyda (eds), *Post-Cinema: Theorizing 21st-Century Film*, Falmer: REFRAME Books. Web. http://reframe.sussex.ac.uk/post-cinema/4-3-isaacs/ (accessed 17 May 2019).
Johnson, Michael K. (2005), 'Not Telling the Story the Way It Happened: Alfonso Cuarón's *Great Expectations*', *Literature/Film Quarterly*, 33 (1): 62–78.
Kermode, Mark (2018), '*Roma* review – Alfonso Cuarón's Bravura Ode to His Mexican Childhood', *The Guardian*, 2 December, https://www.theguardian.com/film/2018/dec/02/roma-review-alfonso-cuaron-ode-to-childhood-70s-mexico-city (accessed 19 May 2019).
Lewis, Reina and Sara Mills (2003), 'Introduction', in Reina Lewis and Sara Mills (eds), *Feminist Postcolonial Theory: A Reader*, 2–21, London: Routledge.
Marx, Karl and Frederick Engels ([1947] 2008), *The German Ideology, Parts I and III* New York: International Publishers.
Masters, Tim (2014), 'Oscars: *Gravity* "Not Sci-fi," Says Alfonso Cuaron', *BBC Website*, 28 February, https://www.bbc.co.uk/news/entertainment-arts-26381335 (accessed 27 May 2019).

Mohanty, Chandra Talpade (1984), 'Under Western Eyes: Feminist Scholarship and Colonial Discourses', *boundary* 2: 333–58.
Nyren, Erin (2018), 'Steven Spielberg Doesn't Think Netflix Movies Deserve Oscars', *Variety*, 25 March, https://variety.com/2018/film/news/steven-spielberg-netflix-movies-oscars-1202735959/ accessed 22 November 2018.
Shohat, Ella (2003), 'Post-Third-Worldist Culture: Gender, Nation, and the Cinema', in Anthony R. Guneratne and Wimal Dissanayake (eds), *Rethinking Third Cinema*, 51–78, London: Routledge.
Solanas, Fernando and Octavio Getino ([1969] 2000), 'Towards a Third Cinema', in Robert Stam and Toby Miller (eds), *Film and Theory: An Anthology*, 265–86, Malden and Oxford: Blackwell.
Stam, Robert (2003), 'Beyond Third Cinema: The Aesthetics of Hybridity', in Anthony R. Guneratne and Wimal Dissanayake (eds), *Rethinking Third Cinema*, 31–50, London: Routledge.
Tapley, Kristopher (2019), '"Roma" Actress Yalitza Aparicio on the Challenge of Playing Alfonso Cuarón's Real-Life Nanny', *Variety*. https://variety.com/2018/film/awards/yalitza-aparicio-interview-roma-alfonso-cuaron-nanny-1202988697/ (accessed 17 June 2019).
Wilkinson, Alissa (2018), '*Roma*, from Celebrated Director Alfonso Cuarón, Is One of the Year's Best Movies', *Vox*, 14 December, https://www.vox.com/2018/11/20/18102734/roma-review-netflix-cuaron, (accessed 19 June 2019).
Žižek, Slavoj (2019), '*Roma* Is Being Celebrated for All the Wrong Reasons, Writes Slavoj Žižek', *The Spectator*, 19 January, https://blogs.spectator.co.uk/2019/01/roma-is-being-celebrated-for-all-the-wrong-reasons-writes-slavoj-zizek/ (accessed 19 June 2019).

# 12

# 'After' or back to Third Cinema? Plebeian film, the national popular, fingernails and the resilient behemoth

*Enrique Uribe-Jongbloed*
*(Universidad Externado de Colombia)*
*and Toby Miller*
*(Universidad Autónoma*
*Metropolitana–Cuajimalpa)*

This chapter turns away from the *données* of Third Cinema, placing the concept under erasure. It challenges advocates and critics of *Tercer Cine* alike to address labour, a topic rarely discussed in detail in terms of the process whereby films are made, for all its centrality to the genre's origin myth (Solanas and Getino 2000). We do so in order to show that Third Cinema always had industrial aspects, despite its later interpretations by scholars; that the street popularity of plebeian film today represents a crucial link to that past; and that the national and regional industries sought by *Tercer Cine*'s founders are dogged by labour exploitation and Hollywood's New International Division of Cultural Labour (NICL) (Miller 2018). Our methods blend political economy with interviews.

---

Thanks to the editors for their invitation to write this piece and for their comments on it, and to George Yúdice for alerting us to *Rambo da Amazônia*.

## 'Cinema?'

The concept of 'cinema' is itself under erasure. For many years, box-office takings have largely functioned as marketing for motion pictures, with broadcast television the principal source of spectatorship and revenue, followed by physical then virtual rental and purchase. Symptomatically, Netflix is now a member of the Motion Picture Association, alongside the traditional studios,[1] and most people do not watch cinema in theatres or on film. This has been the case, really, since the televisualization of the world that began in the United States and Western Europe after the War, matched only by the spread of mobile telephony over the last decade. Cinema as a medium is at risk of disappearing under the concept of the 'audiovisual,' which is already the tendency in scholarly debate, policymaking, media discourse and everyday talk (Uribe-Jongbloed 2016).

We think 'Third Cinema' also needs to be placed under erasure, but not only in terms of money and technology. Rather, some renovation is required in order to engage a key development within cultural production in the Global South – plebeian art, undertaken by the precariat. The plebeian concept, which does not have negative connotations in its Spanish origins, relates to modes of production, textual features and audience interests. Ironically, the idea returns Third Cinema to its origins, wiping away various distortions generated across the decades by latter-day academics and polemicists; for the very concept of *Tercer Cine* soon fell prey to 'interpretation as a tactic of suspicion' (Ricoeur 1970: 26). Earnest ideological detectives lined up to identify signs of Hollywood influences, or pleasure at the cost of purity.

Third Cinema seemingly 'had its moment when it stirred its audience to action, a moment that started to pass in the 1980s, to be supplanted by the postcolonial' (Harrow and Garritano 2019: 1–2). *Tercer cine* has since been denounced for a 'proscriptive [*sic*.] tone and teleological paradigms' (de Villiers 2019: 45), allowing little room for film that is actually produced. Echoing Elizabeth Ezra and Terry Rowden (2006), Lars Kristensen wonders whether we should focus on film 'as both experimental and popular' rather than comparing it with 'what was formerly Third Cinema' (2012: 5). We are also called upon to recognize a Fourth (indigenous people living in settler colonies) (Vanstone and Winston 2019) and Fifth (refugee) Cinema (Kaur and Grassilli 2019). Perhaps the best reconceptualization is Robert Stam's proposal that Third Cinema be thought of as a hortatory marker – useful for its orientation, critique and history, but one of numerous innovations along a spectrum of alternatives to dominant norms that need not be either ordinal or cardinal (2003).

---

[1] https://www.motionpictures.org/who-we-are/.

Let's move beyond academia and return to the idea's origins for some further guidance on how to revise it.

Octavio Getino was a Spanish expat, an *arriviste Peronista* in Argentina. A supporter of national self-determination against cultural imperialism, he was no Marxist, despite the powers of imagination of his followers in the Global North. Getino was always careful to historicize *Tercer Cine*, distancing it and his own work from any refusal of pleasure, rejection of the continuity system, or requirement for revolutionary themes or narration.

Getino was ambivalent about the movement of what he and Solanas called *Cine Liberacíon* [Liberation Cinema] towards Marxism and Trotskyism and away from their own *Peronismo*, which was – and remains – a complex *mélange* of left-and right-wing nationalistic workerism. Getino was interested in national and regional alternatives to Hollywood from the beginning, and his evolution into a political economist of cultural policy should be no surprise. He became a policy wonk the better to focus on how the state could support filmmaking alternatives to Hollywood.[2]

Getino's renowned 1998 San Francisco address celebrating three decades since *La Hora de los Hornos* stressed that the emergence of *Tercer Cine* came at a very particular conjuncture in Third World and specifically Latin American history, a time of real hope in emergent progressive regimes. The filmic corollary was a search for alternatives to 'cine Americano' and 'cine de autor' [Hollywood and *auteur* film] through 'organizaciones populares' [popular organizations – popular here meaning of the working class and peasantry]. These alternatives would hew closely to the storytelling, aesthetic, and ideological norms of communities, and stress working conditions (Getino 1998). Hence our decision in this chapter to link Third Cinema to later populist tendencies and labour struggles.

## Plebeian cinema

Since Getino and Solanas' pathbreaking doctrine, what we are terming plebeian cinema has emerged across genres, nations and geopolitics, from cute cat films on YouTube to *engagés* representations of warlike conflicts (Smets and Akkaya 2016). This is how George Yúdice explains plebeian culture: 'prácticas culturales de las clases de bajos ingresos y/o de grupos racializados o subordinados que *no* se han domesticado al negociar su entrada en las esferas mediáticas nacionales o globales' [cultural practices of low-income classes and/or racialized or subordinated groups who have not been disciplined or tailored their points of entry into national or global

---

[2]We do not discern a necessary disjuncture between nationalism and Marxism; only that their relationship is complicated.

media spheres] (2016: 95). The world he investigates is neither that of an affluent élite fraction controlling the culture industries nor its gentried-poor neighbours patrolling the avant-garde. This sphere is not coopted, corporatized, valued or governmentalized.

It is some distance from Mike Wayne's desired *telos* for Third Cinema: 'social and cultural emancipation' (2001: 1). Nor is it the recently and touchingly romanticized 'amateur film' (Salazkina and Fibla-Gutierrez 2018). But it *is something*; neither hyper-commercial and fully industrialized, nor avant-garde and mysterious, it is *popular* in the Latin American sense, that is, of the working, peasant and under classes, depending on the categories one chooses.

Ghana and Nigeria have come to represent plebeian cinema via their informal, street-based networks of supply and demand (McCall 2012; Haynes 2016), although with this organic success has come a certain incorporation into the formal economy through state subvention and theatrical distribution. That said, 'Nollywood has no official institutional presence outside Nigeria, and its existence is not even acknowledged in many surveys of international cinema production' (Lobato 2013), because it is not considered 'cinema' in the classic sense (Unesco Institute for Statistics 2013: 12–13). But Nollywood's 'mobile and contingent origins' resonate (de Villiers 2019: 50), as does its 'trash' aesthetic (Harrow 2013). And the World Bank reports that Nollywood productions average just US$15,000 dollars to make (Bauer 2015). Similarly informal networks have produced 'Peruwood' (Alfaro Rotondo 2013). These tendencies diverge from the industrial mode of production typical of Hollywood and state-supported cinema.

The artisanal mode and plebeian address and popularity of such productions offer stark textual binaries and narrative simplicity. They defy the anti-realist conventions of much Third Cinema, because their project is an avowedly populist one, as per the first British punk bands in music – anyone can make culture, and we are all always already citing others, mopping up their quotations like so many tissues. Just as reactionary writers may capture the contradictory moment of epochal change from the premodern to the modern and beyond (Mazierska and Kristensen 2014: 10), so avowedly commercial yet artisanal cinema may incarnate urges, desires and difficulties both already experienced and yet to come. This is akin to the idea of the national popular.

That concept is generally associated with Antonio Gramsci. He noted that the words for 'national' and 'popular' were similar in several languages, such was their affinity, and called for a closer alignment between everyday concerns and intellectual practice to reflect that linguistic kinship and animate socialism (2000: 366). Across Latin America, the concept has been adopted by left and right, by both journalists and academics, to describe a process whereby class interests are articulated with popular culture, such that they appear to index the needs and hopes of the majority under the sign of nationalism (Massardo 1999). Latin American music represented this incorporation of popular urges into officially-sanctioned and enjoyed culture from the 1920s to the 1940s (Yúdice 2016). The process can take dialectical form: cinema has been the property and design of cultural fractions of élites seeking to recruit the population to their projects through film's sense of carnival and expressivity and its mythology of upward mobility, but brokered through multinational taste cultures of a very different kind that bring status and rewards from a cosmopolitan cultural élite. For Getino and Solanas, the struggle for the national popular *contra* those class fractions was a crucial element of *Peronismo*.

The combined force of neoliberal deregulation and technology has transformed the idea of the national popular. Carlos Monsiváis' famous 1999 essay about changes to Latin American demography and culture, *Del rancho al Internet* [*From the Farm to the Internet*], is a useful guide. It has given rise to numerous adumbrations, not the least the wee matrix below.

Monsiváis discerned major cultural shifts connected to demographic movements from the country to the city and the oral to the digital. These changes involved the complex and incomplete incorporation of rural culture into the metropole. Genres emerged to textualize such transformations, re-modelled and re-used with the proliferation of both media literacy and cheap technology.

The full genealogy of plebeian film originates much earlier, with the *melodrama*, a genre that was critically damned from its beginnings in eighteenth-century Europe because of a high-tensile emotionalism that

| DEL RANCHO | AL INTERNET |
| --- | --- |
| **THE BEFORE** | **THE AFTER** |
| Homogeneous tastes | Segmented tastes |
| Family as second site of religion | Cultural transformations |
| Fear of the city | Familiarity with urban life |
| Homage to national heroes | Sanctification of celebrities |
| Analphabetism | Multimedia literacy |
| Impact of popular film and radio | Multiple platforms and genres |
| Oral culture | Promotion of spectacle |
| Fear of technology | Consumerist style |
| Binary understandings of gender | Recognition of minorities |

SOURCE: Yúdice 2016 (trans. Toby Miller)

contrasted with latter-day naturalism and realism. But the melodrama was also a site for trying out new identities at a time of intense social disruption, when religious and monarchical power were under challenge from urbanizing capitalism and secular democracy (Merritt 1983). The genre's revolutionary referent recurred in the 1940s and 1950s, when it incarnated the fraught re-establishment of gender normativity after the War; Hollywood's melodramas and *films noirs* featured hysterical men, equally unsettled by the battlefield and their return from it (Cunningham 1981). The trajectory of Nollywood suggests a similarly traumatic reaction to the violent and progressive forces of urbanization and modernity, thematizing sex, violence, and rapturous/rapturous kinship relations, horror, magic and informal economic markets (Larkin 2008). And so do developments in Latin America. Consider the quarter-of-an hour Brazilian extravaganza *Rambo da Amazônia o Resgate da professora* [*Rambo in the Amazon and the Professor's Rescue*] (Manoel Castro Junior, 2016)[3] starring Aldenir Cóti, *guerriero da selva* [jungle warrior]. A mild-mannered ecologist is drugged and kidnapped in the field while explaining the unique qualities of her botanical findings. Cotí is dispatched to rescue her, complete with his mimesis of Sylvester Stallone's musculature, clothing, sneer and firepower. *Rambo da Amazônia* features a stereotypical *travestí* (Kulick 1998); a Jason-Voorhees figure (complete with hockey mask) from the *Friday the 13th* popular horror series (various directors, 1980–2009); and a storm trooper as per *Star Wars* (various directors, 1977–).

The film's fifteen minutes of visceral titles, graphics and editing, and its stark distinctions between good and evil, make a mimicry/mockery of Hollywood studios' costly evocations of the same masculinity, but also problematize the art-film world of festivals and theatres as national-cinema alternatives. This is story-telling right in the middle of the Amazon – not 'on location', but where people live, write, shoot, edit and watch these films, albeit now with wider availability via IAC/InterActiveCorp's Vimeo and Google's YouTube.

Director Castro Junior boasts 75,000 subscribers to his YouTube channel.[4] The artisanal nature of his work is incarnated in a promotional video: an anonymous pair of hands takes some paddle-pop sticks, lines them up, glues them together, then paints them to reveal what in static form resembled a professionally produced book prior to this speeded-up retrospective of the labour process – which takes us to our second theme.

---

[3]https://www.youtube.com/watch?v=PINGZndsOEw.
[4]https://www.youtube.com/channel/UCls3iJ5Z0TowC_TNOW9dV3g.

## The NICL

Labour, industriousness, exploitation, precariousness – these topics are routinely present in cinema as themes, as we shall see with reference to Colombia, but not in journalism or academia (Mazierska 2013: 2). Film studies looks with greater interest at cultural policies supporting national cinemas than it does at working conditions within them. And there is a wider *lacuna* here: the political economy of the media, a field supposedly driven by economic inequality and Marxism, barely interrogates the labour process, remaining instead within the safe house of a functionalist leftism where state and capital are everything and class conflict is rarely seen or sensed.

Conversely, the last four decades of Getino's professional life were largely dedicated to uncovering how to create and sustain film industries in Latin America that would provide cultural enrichment to workers and audiences alike. He coordinated the collection of data across the culture industries and wrote and edited scholarly works (Getino 2011; 'Falleció' 2012). Hollywood's use of the NICL was a major theme.

The US film industry has always imported cultural producers, such as the German Expressionists, and shot off-site. Hence Gramsci's reference to the 30,000 Italian women who sent photographs of themselves in bathing suits to Hollywood as would-be '"luxury mammals"' (1978: 306) when *Ben-Hur* (Fred Niblo and Alfred Raboch, 1925) was shot there. The movement of labour was mostly one way during the classical Hollywood era, although as early as 1938, when MGM was establishing an English studio, LA unions were expressing concern about job losses overseas, and in 1941, the Federal Government encouraged Disney to go offshore, in part to mitigate the impact of striking workers. The decade from 1946 saw increased overseas production. Once colour and wide-screen formats and portable recording technology were available, location shooting became a means of differentiating stories. Studios purchased facilities around the world to utilize cheap, docile labour. This also enabled Hollywood to avoid foreign-exchange drawbacks and local laws that prevented the expatriation of profits. The studios invested in industries overseas, simultaneously benefiting from host-state subvention of 'local' films (Miller et al. 2005).

'Runaway production' is the common journalistic and industry shorthand for the ensuing exodus from Hollywood. In 1949, there were nineteen such productions. Twenty years on, the figure was 183, mostly in Europe, while Japanese animators were drawing US cartoons from the early 1960s. Between 1950 and 1973, just 60 per cent of Hollywood films in-production began their lives in the United States, and the trend has never been bucked for long (Miller et al. 2005).

State subsidies and skilled but pliant labour proliferated across the globe. Putative alternatives to Hollywood funded under the sign of opposition to cultural imperialism frequently favoured exclusionary, art-house-centred hegemons who privileged 'talent' over blue-collar screen workers, and centralized authority over openness:

> Begun as a tool of resistance to the dominance of U.S. films, [European] film funds were initially designed to support "high quality" movies that provided an artistic voice for domestic auteurs, an outlet that could not be supported by the mass market....In the past two decades, discourse has begun to support public film policy that, instead of supporting individual local auteurs, favors the grooming of a local film industry workforce and foreign direct investment into local facilities (Miller 2011: 1019)

In reality, both tendencies led not only to public subvention of indolent national *bourgeoisies*, but permitted oleaginous Gringos to fund offshore production through the NICL via proxy locals (Miller et al. 2005; Miller 2011).

Gullible foreign governments countenance such *largesse* for a variety of reasons, such as generating precarious jobs for the duration of a film or TV shoot, stimulating tourism, transferring glamor to politicians, justifying the lives of culturecrats and meeting the needs of powerful if dependent businesspeople, from producers to hoteliers.

German money in the early twenty-first century funding Hollywood films generally came from tax breaks available to lawyers, doctors and dentists, 'raising EUR 2.3 billion in 2002, EUR 1.76 billion in 2003 and EUR 1.5 billion in 2004'. Abuse of the scheme saw it shut down in 2005 (Morawetz et al. 2007: 436). French money derived from firms with state subvention in other areas of investment, such as cable or plumbing, that then subsidized US studios. US TV shows shot in Canada relied on welfare to attract LA and New York producers as a given. Similar tales apply to New Zealand/Aotearoa, Britain, Mexico and much of Eastern Europe (Miller et al. 2005)

## Colombia's fingernails

In this next section, we consider the precarious nature of film work in Colombia, where attempts to put screen alternatives on a solid financial footing have produced the obverse of the desired results and further problematized the sector's *Tercer Cine* credentials.

Perhaps the most direct impact of Third Cinema in Colombia during the late 1960s and 1970s was seen in the work of documentary filmmakers educated in European Marxism: Martha Rodriguez, Jorge Silva, Carlos

Mayolo, Luis Ospina and Carlos Álvarez (Rivera 2019: 50). A prominent example is *Chircales* (Rodriguez and Silva, 1972), which depicts human exploitation in the brick factories that surround Bogotá. Ospina and Mayolo are well known for their short film *Agarrando Pueblo* [*The Vampires of Poverty*] (1977), a documentary parody that coined the term *pornomiseria* [poverty porn], loosely described as 'films that sold well in Europe and the US by presenting everyday scandalous stories with little research and a great deal of sensationalism' (Rivera 2019: 52). *Agarrando Pueblo*:

> unveils the triangle that makes 'misery vampirism' possible. First, social beings marginalised from the promises of development and well-being; second, the filmmakers who took advantage of the situation, and third, a European gaze hungry for validation, in which very schematic representations denote its good (fake) conscience. (Zuluaga 2018, para. 19)

A previous film by Ospina and Mayolo, *Oiga Vea!* [*Hey Look At This!*] (1971), was a short documentary about the Pan-American games in Cali:

> given the denial of an "official" permit with which to access with their camera the enclosed, guarded spaces where the Games are being held, Ospina and Mayolo resort to making their film from outside the brand new Olympic Villa, and they decide to do so aligning themselves with "the people," that vast section of the population marginalized from the event. (Goméz, n.d., Para. 13)

In the 1980s and 1990s, Colombian cinema was known for deeming quality to be a *bourgeois* pleasure that *Tercer Cine* filmmakers should strive against. The most representative films of the 1990s, *La estrategia del caracol* [*The Snail's Strategy*] (Sergio Cabrera 1993), *La gente de la Universal* [*The People of Universal*] (Felipe Aljure 1991), *Rodrigo D.* (Víctor Gaviria 1990) and *La vendedora de rosas* [*The Rose Seller*] (Víctor Gaviria 1998) exemplified the refusal of high production values.[5] *La estrategia del caracol* and *La vendedora de rosas* show the continued relevance of poverty porn. Most contemporary Colombian films criticize capitalist exploitation and its predatory nature. Such themes are present in the recent Oscar-nominated film *El abrazo de la serpiente* [*Embrace of the Serpent*] (Guerra, 2015).

*La estrategia del caracol* enjoys cult status in the country, because it defined the generation that emerged between the end of support from the state agency Focine at the end of the 1980s and the New Cinema Law in 2003. The makers thought of film as a labour of love. *La estrategia del*

---

[5] According to Jeronimo Rivera, only twenty-seven Colombian feature films were made across the decade (https://jeronimorivera.com/cinecolombiano/).

*caracol* went over budget, requiring new funding after the collapse of Focine, and finally made it to postproduction and world-wide renown thanks to support from Gabriel García Márquez.

A newspaper article commemorating twenty-five years since its release tells us a great deal about the working conditions of this cult film:

> Cabrera [the director] does not forget: "I spoke with the producers (Salvo Basile and his associates) and I decided that I would rather have half a film than no film. In preproduction we had already spent what they had given us, so we decided to film as far as it would stretch". [...] Basile laughs today with a thunder-like roar, but back then he suffered, he maxed out his credit card, Cabrera's, and the director's sister's, and still he couldn't foot the bill. He spoke with the technicians and said he had no way to pay them, and that there were still three weeks left out of the eight-week shooting schedule. (Guzmán, 2018, para. 18–19)

The fact that the highest-grossing film of a decade was short of cash to pay its technicians says a lot about the prevailing concept of cinema labour. Of course, no one could have anticipated the film's success. But the anecdotal evidence indicates a precarity that thrives thanks to myths of authorial persistence, national poverty, and, more recently, competitive advantage.

The new millennium brought with it new cultural legislation, which stimulated film production: 293 films were released between 2010 and 2019.[6] However, despite increasing employment in the audiovisual sector – something *bourgeois* media coverage assiduously emphasizes – the precariousness of such labour is not addressed. Instead, jobs 'created' are mentioned, ranging in number from 10,394 ('Cine Colombia' 2016) to 23,731 (Gómez 2019). Reporters dutifully cite data from the Ministry of Culture or Proimagenes, a quasi-autonomous non-government organization that handles money from both the New Cinema (Law 814 of 2003) and Location Colombia laws (Law 1556 of 2012).

Taking advantage of the growing number of technical and university degrees that school the willing and worthy in film and television drama, Location Colombia was enacted to lure international productions. It copied similar actions elsewhere: cash rebates and tax returns to foreign companies (AKA Hollywood) willing to relocate on an *ad hoc* basis. The lure included a new El Dorado of beautiful scenery and skilled servitude – the classic NICL. Proimagenes highlights the absence of unionized activity in Colombia as an advantage for international productions:

---

[6]https://jeronimorivera.com/cinecolombiano.

Colombian film crews are known for their enormous commitment, hard work and resourcefulness. There are no audiovisual unions at this time or fixed rates for services or labor, which makes it possible to negotiate directly with the personnel required. (Proimagenes 2019)

David Madden – then president of Fox Television Studios – said:

Le diría a cualquiera, sin reservas, que venga a Colombia. Es un sitio fantástico para filmar. La rapidez con que [los colombianos] han respondido a nuestras necesidades y deseos ha sido extraordinaria. He estado en esta industria por más de 30 años, he filmado en muchos países, y no recuerdo una mejor experiencia que la que he tenido en Colombia [I'd recommend anyone, with no reservations, to come to Colombia. It's a great place to film. The speed with which local people responded to our needs and wishes was extraordinary. I've been in this industry over thirty years and filmed in many countries and can't recall a better experience than this one]. (quoted in cduarte 2014)

Will Smith's video blog, shot during the making of *Gemini Man* (Ang Lee, 2019) in Cartagena de Indias, finds him telling us, 'If I wasn't famous, I'd live in Cartagena.'[7] No surprise, then, that the promised land of beauty and obedience has been praised by journalist after journalist, dancing to the tune of the 86 billion pesos (US$25 million) supposedly entering the country as a consequence (Carreño 2019).

There are vigorous debates and critiques about the representation of Colombia in national (Villegas and Alarcón 2017: 360–3) and international films, whether the latter were made locally (Burkhardt 2013) or abroad (Chaparro Valderrama 2013); but as per Nollywood (Obiaya 2012), almost nothing is written about working conditions.

Clearly, the cinema laws have done much for runaway productions and some local companies. It remains to be seen whether they benefit local audiovisual workers, who refer to their labour as undertaken 'con las uñas' [with their fingernails]: hard work that demands all one's effort, scraping the barrel to extend limited production budgets.

Drawing on ten interviews with film professionals who have worked under both cinema laws, we have established some critical contours of Colombia's NICL. There is a clear distinction between international and local crews when it comes to on-set safety measures. One interviewee mentioned filming on the Amazon (minus the truly plebeian Rambo):

---

[7]https://www.youtube.com/watch?v=t2sJpeL-Ars.

> A local resident approached me and said: "we need to leave". I go "What?" It's a lovely day. We are in an islet on the river. "We have to leave, the river's coming." I go to tell somebody, though I have no idea what it means. "Hey, the river's coming, we need to leave". No one cared. We were there with the stunt doubles, the DP, a bunch of us. In comes a CEO, on a CEO motorboat, and picks up all the heads [of department], takes them away. Within ten minutes we were running through the jungle because the river was coming; it was coming at us! (Interview 5, 2018)

Similar stories were told by other technicians and mid-level staff, who received lesser remuneration and accommodation than their peripatetic Californian colleagues. One interviewee spoke of:

> differences in hotel rooms, services ... organized by the Colombian production [company]. The foreign crew works along the Colombian crew, side by side. ... the foreign crew was paid way better wages. (Interview 7, 2018)

A further item of discussion was the length of the working day and overtime. Our interviewees stated that negotiations centred around a twelve-hour work day and overtime pay. They mentioned that, thanks to unionized activity, international crews had a twelve-hour-day agreement, from which the local crew benefited.

Although all interviewees agreed that lower wages attract runaway production, they also believed other areas, beyond technical or second-tier staff, should be contracted locally. One stated:

> We do not have a guild to defend us. The [Location Colombia] law allows the entry of loads of people; amongst them a director and cinematographer. They tend to work closely together, so it is hard for them to take on a local cinematographer, right? But they fill positions with outsiders that could be staffed locally. It is unfair that there is nothing protecting Colombian labour. (Interview 8, 2018)

There are also complaints that the benefits of the Location Colombia law do not extend equally to all fields, for instance postproduction. One interviewee said:

> we started meeting again with other companies and independent postproducers, to learn how to form a guild or an association and ensure that postproduction [companies] take a more active role, or are able to benefit from this law, the same way that production [companies] do. (Interview 4, 2018)

The Location Colombia law is cited by all as providing opportunities for local workers to learn from foreign crews and gain the advantages of unionization. But there is also concern over the creation of a two-tiered audiovisual industry – a primary (international) versus secondary (local) labour market. For international productions increase the quality of life for audiovisual workers in an environment that is out of reach for those employed in Colombian screen drama. One interviewee told us:

> if they call me for a telenovela, I do not even listen to the offer, because conditions in the Colombian audiovisual industry are horrifying. The wages, the hours, the treatment, everything. If we [international film workers] are battered, in television, we're destroyed. (Interview 5, 2018)

Yet they are willing to lower their standards and wages for Colombian films. Despite the lack of proper funding, these workers feel a certain commitment and loyalty to national cinema:

> Colombian films are made with one's fingernails. All stages of production are penniless. Whatever can be afforded is spent on shooting – all the effort and the money go into that. By the time people reach postproduction, they are worn out, tired of fighting for a budget, and laboring under horrible conditions (Interview 4, 2018)

Despite the increasing numbers of Colombian films – and audiences for them – the local industry remains a site of precarious work and difficult working conditions (Arias, Uribe, and Miller 2018). Runaway productions promote the exploitation of local workers by local producers, since foreign companies are required to hire Colombian firms, which profit most when expanding their overheads but reducing local costs, thereby creating and consolidating the primary and secondary labour markets that separate foreign from domestic crews. For example, Dynamo, a Colombian production company that has profited from both the 814 and 1556 laws, has done little to support local talent by producing national films (Rocha 2018: 363).

The new laws have brought a glimmer of hope to Colombian film talent through unionized activity, which had been barred for years as insurgent and communist, then avoided for fear of blacklisting. And the local television industry, controlled by an unseemly duopoly, is in the spotlight as an even worse *jefe* [boss], one that makes the troubles of film workers seem like child's play, and their precariousness a luxury.

The industry has gone full circle, from denouncing the exploitation evident in *Chircales* and *Agarrando pueblo* to its own exploitation in the interests of Hollywood; the precise opposite of Third Cinema's desires. And Colombia lacks its moment of plebeian film.

## Conclusion

The thick encrustation surrounding *Tercer Cinema*, a milky-rich crust of Marxism and post-colonialism, has obscured the realities of the concept's origins, downplayed the possibilities and realities of plebeian film, and ignored the lived experiences of screen workers. In the process, the Hollywood behemoth's exploitation of the NICL has gone unnoticed, as if leftist critics were as sanguine about – or blind to – working conditions as the celebratory Colombian journalists of our case study.

Peruwood, Nollywood and Amazonia tap into lively, urgent, exciting tendencies in the wider culture, expressions of old and new storytelling that cheerily borrow from Hollywood, adopt new technologies, foreground fun, and find audiences. They are part of how *Tercer Cine* might be re-imagined. And so are the highly trained workers who seek full-time, enriching employment in film but are stymied by the NICL's bifurcated labour markets and local state and media complicity.

In each case, as our Colombian example shows, the *bourgeois* media and academia neglect the force and experience of labour, to the cost of workers themselves, effective film policies, and an awareness of the great behemoth Hollywood's malleability as conditions and opportunities arise. Colombian workers seeking to form a national popular via the NICL lack control of the labour process.

A progressive filmic national popular could emerge in Colombia if the energies of plebeian cinema were melded with the skills of local workers, but only if their remuneration and conditions matched the way that their government supports the NICL, and if policies forwarded domestic rather than Hollywood welfare. That might make for motion pictures that could truly rival 'cine Americano' and 'cine de autor' alike.

## Works cited

'Cine Colombia' (25 June 2016), *Semana* https://www.semana.com/enfoque/articulo/balance-de-la-ley-de-filmacion-en-colombia/479201.

'Falleció Octavio Getino' (1 October 2012). *Página 12* https://www.pagina12.com.ar/diario/ultimas/20-204640-2012-10-01.html.

Alfaro Rotondo, Santiago (2013), 'Peruwood: La industria del video digital en el Perú', *Latin American Research Review*, 48: 69–99.

Arias, Oscar, Enrique Uribe and Toby Miller (2018), 'Colombia y el dilema clásico del apoyo cinematográfico', *Revista Internacional de Comunicación y Desarrollo*, 2 (9): 115–28.

Bauer, Roxanne (2015), 'Media (R)evolutions: The Epic Nollywood Machine', *World Bank Blog*, 16 September, https://blogs.worldbank.org/category/tags/nollywood.

Burkhardt, Anne (2013), 'Películas europeas filmadas en Colombia – Imaginarios de Colombia desde el "viejo" continente (1967–2009)', *Cuadernos de Cine Colombiano* (18): 52–73.

Carreño, Lucety (24 October 2019), 'Con capacitaciones en 4K, Netflix le apuesta a la industria audiovisual colombiana', *El Espectador*, https://www.elespectador.com/economia/con-capacitaciones-en-4k-netflix-le-apuesta-la-industria-audiovisual-colombiana-articulo-887563.

cduarte (24 July 2014), 'Bogotá posicionada en producción audiovisual y las industrias creativas', https://bogota.gov.co/servicios/empleo/bogota-posicionada-en-produccion-audiovisual-y-las-industrias-creativa.

Cunningham, Stuart (1981), 'The "Force-Field" of Melodrama', *Quarterly Review of Film Studies*, 6 (4): 347–64.

Chaparro Valderrama, Hugo (2013), 'Las imágenes del exotismo', *Cuadernos de Cine Colombiano* (18): 82–92.

de Villiers, Jacques (2019), 'Approaching the Uncertain Turn in African Video-Movies: Subalternity, Superfluity, and (Non-)Cinematic Time', in Kenneth W. Harrow and Carmela Garritano (eds), *A Companion to African Cinema*, 44–68, Hoboken: Wiley Blackwell.

Ezra, Elizabeth and Terry Rowden (eds) (2006). *Transnational Cinema: The Film Reader*, London and New York: Routledge.

Getino, Octavio (September 1998). 'A 30 años de "La Hora De Los Hornos"', 6th Annual Festival Cine Latino, San Francisco, https://octaviogetinocine.blogspot.com/2010/06/30-anos-de-la-hora-de-los-hornos.html.

Getino, Octavio (ed) (2011), *Producción y mercados del cine latinoamericano en la primera década del siglo XXI*, Havana: Fundación del Nuevo Cine Latinoamericano.

Gómez, Felipe (n. d.), 'Short Film and Documentary Third Cinema in Colombia: The Case of Luis Ospina', https://www.luisospina.com/sobre-su-obra/art%C3%ADculos/short-film-and-documentary-third-cinema-in-colombia-the-case-of-luis-ospina-by-felipe-g%C3%B3mez/.

Gómez, Sofía (26 October 2019), 'Asís se fortalece Colombia como escenario de película', *El Tiempo*, https://www.eltiempo.com/cultura/cine-y-tv/rodajes-en-colombia-impactan-la-economia-y-mejoran-la-imagen-del-pais-366666.

Gramsci, Antonio (1978), *Selections from the Prison Notebooks* (trans. and eds), Quintin Hoare and Geoffrey Nowell-Smith, New York: International Publishers.

Gramsci, Antonio (2000), *The Antonio Gramsci Reader: Selected Writings 1916–1935* (ed), David Forgacs, New York: New York University Press.

Guzmán, Julio César (21 October 2018), 'Los secretos de 'La estrategia del caracol"', *El Tiempo*, https://www.eltiempo.com/cultura/cine-y-tv/los-secretos-de-la-pelicula-la-estrategia-del-caracol-que-cumple-25-anos-283604.

Harrow, Kenneth W. (2013), *Trash: African Cinema from Below*, Bloomington and Indianapolis: Indiana University Press.

Harrow, Kenneth W. and Carmela Garritano (2019), 'Introduction: Critical Approaches to Africa's Cinema, from the Age of Liberation and Struggle to the Global, Popular, and Curatorial', in Kenneth W. Harrow and Carmela Garritano (eds), *A Companion to African Cinema*, 1–20, Hoboken: Wiley Blackwell.

Haynes, Jonathan (2016), *Nollywood: The Creation of Nigerian Film Genres*, Chicago and London: University of Chicago Press.

Kaur, Raminder and Mariagiulia Grassilli (2019), 'Towards a Fifth Cinema', *Third Text*, 33 (1): 1–25.

Kristensen, Lars (2012), 'Introduction', in Lars Kristensen (ed), *Postcommunist Film – Russia, Eastern Europe and World Culture: Moving Images of Postcommunism*, 1–10, London and New York: Routledge.

Kulick, Don (1998), *Travestí: Sex, Gender, and Culture among Brazilian Transgendered Prostitutes*, Chicago and London: University of Chicago Press.

Larkin, Brian (2008), *Signal and Noise: Media, Infrastructure, and Urban Culture in Nigeria*, Durham and London: Duke University Press.

Lobato, Ramon (2013), 'Informality, Development and the Creative Economy: The Case of Nollywood', in *Creative Economy Report. Widening Local Development Pathways*, 27, New York and Paris: UNDP and UNESCO.

Massardo, Jaime (1999), 'La recepción de Gramsci en América Latina: Cuestiones de orden teórico y político', *International Gramsci Society Newsletter*, 9, electronic supplement 3 http://www.internationalgramscisociety.org/igsn/articles/a09_s3.shtml.

Mazierska, Ewa (2013), 'Introduction', in Ewa Mazierska (ed), *Work in Cinema: Labor and the Human Condition*, 1–25, Houndmills and New York: Palgrave Macmillan.

Mazierska, Ewa and Lars Kristensen (2014), 'Introduction', in Ewa Mazierska and Lars Kristensen (eds), *Marx at the Movies: Revisiting History, Theory and Practice*, 1–26, Houndmills and New York: Palgrave Macmillan.

McCall, John C. (2012), 'The Capital Gap: Nollywood and the Limits of Informal Trade', *Journal of African Cinema*, 4 (2): 9–23.

Merritt, Russell (1983), 'Melodrama: Postmortem for a Phantom Genre', *Wide Angle*, 5 (3): 24–31.

Miller, Jade L. (2011), 'Producing Quality: A Social Network Analysis of Coproduction Relationships in High Grossing Versus Highly Lauded Films in the US Market', *International Journal of Communication*, 5: 1014–33.

Miller, Toby (2018), *El trabajo cultural*, Buenos Aires and Barcelona: Editorial Gedisa.

Miller, Toby, Nitin Govil, John McMurria, Richard Maxwell and Ting Wang (2005), *Global Hollywood 2*, London: British Film Institute.

Monsiváis, Carlos (1999), *Del rancho al Internet*, México: Instituto de Seguridad y Servicios Sociales de los Trabajadores del Estado.

Morawetz, Norbert, Jane Hardy, Colin Haslam and Keith Randle (2007), 'Finance, Policy and Industrial Dynamics – The Rise of Co-Productions in the Film Industry', *Industry and Innovation*, 14 (4): 421–43.

Obiaya, Ikechukwu (2012), 'Behind the Scenes: The Working Conditions of Technical Workers in the Nigerian Film Industry', in Andrew Dawson and Sean P. Homes (eds), *Working in the Global Film and Television Industries*, 109–20, London and New York: Bloomsbury.

Proimagenes (2019), 'Audiovisual Infrastructure', http://locationcolombia.com/guia-de-produccion/informacion-audiovisual/infraestructura-audiovisual/?lang=en.

Ricoeur, Paul (1970), *Freud and Philosophy: An Essay on Interpretation*, trans. Denis Savage, New Haven and London: Yale University Press.

Rivera, Jéronimo (2019), *El papel del cine colombiano en la escena latinoamericana*, Chía: Universidad de la Sabana.

Rocha, Carolina (2018), 'La productora colombiana Dynamo: Del cine nacional al transnacional?', *Studies in Spanish and Latin American Cinemas*, 15 (3): 349–67.

Salazkina, Masha and Enrique Fibla-Gutierrez (2018), 'Introduction: Toward a Global History of Amateur Film Practices and Institutions', *Film History: An International Journal*, 30 (1): v–xxiii.

Smets, Kevin and Ahmet Hamdi Akkaya (2016), 'Media and Violent Conflict: Halil Dağ, Kurdish Insurgency, and the Hybridity of Vernacular Cinema of Conflict', *Media, War & Conflict*, 9 (1): 76–92.

Solanas, Fernando and Octavio Getino (2000), 'Towards a Third Cinema', in Robert Stam and Toby Miller (eds), *Film and Theory: An Anthology*, 265–86, Malden and Oxford: Blackwell.

Stam, Robert (2003), 'Beyond Third Cinema: The Aesthetics of Hybridity', in Anthony Guneratne and Wimal Dissanayake (eds), *Rethinking Third Cinema*, 31–48, New York and London: Routledge.

UNESCO Institute for Statistics (2013), *Emerging Markets and the Digitalization of the Film Industry: An Analysis of the 2012 UIS International Survey of Feature Film Statistics*, Montreal: UNESCO-UIS.

Uribe-Jongbloed, Enrique (2016), 'El cambio mediático de la televisión: Netflix y la televisión en teléfonos inteligentes', *Palabra Clave*, 19 (2): 358–64.

Vanstone, Gail and Brian Winston (2019), '"This Would be Scary to Any Other Culture … But to Us It's so Cute!" The Radicalism of Fourth Cinema from *Tangata Whenua* to *Angry Inuk*', *Studies in Documentary Film*, 13 (3): 233–49.

Villegas, Andrés and Santiago Alarcón (2017), 'Historiografía del cine colombiano 1974-2015', *Historelo*, 9 (18): 346–81.

Wayne, Mike (2001), *Political Film: The Dialectics of Third Cinema*, London: Pluto Press.

Yúdice, George (2016), 'Músicas plebeyas', in Graciela Maglia and Leonor Hernández Fox (eds), *Memorias, saberes y redes de las culturas populares en América Latina*, Bogotá: Universidad Externado de Colombia, Facultad de Ciencias Sociales y Humanas.

Zuluaga, Pedro Adrián (2018), 'Contemporary Colombian Cinema: The Splintered Mirror of a Country', trans. Gabriella Muñoz, *Senses of Cinema*, 89 http://sensesofcinema.com/2018/latin-american-cinema-today/contemporary-colombian-cinema-the-splintered-mirror-of-a-country/.

# INDEX

*1717 Km of Summer* 218–19
*17th Parallel: Vietnam in War* (*Le 17e parallèle: La guerre du peuple*) 95
*4 Months, 3 Weeks and 2 Days* (*4 luni, 3 săptămâni și 2 zile*) 17, 164, 175–8, 180

Adorno, Theodor 15, 86, 96–7
*Adversary, The* (*Pratidwandi*) 15, 86–9, 92–6
Aguirre, Mirta 34
Alvarez, Santiago 30, 34, 171, 221, 224, 240
Antonioni, Michelangelo 15, 64, 70, 71, 74, 79, 263, 270
Aparicio, Yalitza 266
Autor, Nika 218–19, 223, 225, 227–8, 230

Bakhtin, Mikhail 66, 190, 210
*Bamako* 236, 237, 238–9, 241, 244–5, 247, 251
*Battle of Chile, The* (*La batalla de Chile*) 141–59
Bazin, André 268
Bethânia, Maria 75–7
Bhabha, Homi 15, 64–5, 204
Brenez, Nicole 214, 220

Cabrera, Sergio 281–2
*Calcutta '71* 87
Calzatti, Alexander 26–7, 31, 39
Castro Junior, Manoel 278
Castro, Fidel 26–30, 34, 39, 41–2, 47, 50, 55, 58
Castro, Raul 30–1

Cech, Vladimir 38, 41, 54
Césaire, Aimé 238–9, 246, 249–51
*Children of Men* 256
*Chircales* 281, 285
*Company Limited, The* (*Seemabaddha*) 87, 89
*Cronica Cubana* 41, 55–6
Cuarón, Alfonso 18, 255–72
*Cuba '58* 37

*Dare, The* (*O desafio*) 15, 64–81
De Havilland, Olivia 69
Debord, Guy 207–9
Deleuze, Gilles 152, 194, 225, 235, 242–3, 247, 248–9, 251
Diawara, Manthia 237–40, 242, 250

Eisenstein, Sergei 33–5, 237
Engels, Friedrich 7, 20, 136, 138, 199, 264
Eshun, Kodwo 216, 242
Espinosa, Julio García 3, 29, 31–2, 34–5, 37, 41–2, 57, 93, 105, 113, 229, 269
*Estrategia del Caracol, La* (*The Snail's Strategy*) 281–2
Evtushenko, Evgeny 25–6, 37, 42, 47, 54

Fanon, Frantz 4–5, 131–2, 198, 202–3
FARTAC (Tupac Amaru Revolutionary Agrarian Federation of Cusco) 105–8
Fellini, Federico 270
Fraga, Jorge 37

# INDEX

Gabriel, Teshome 8, 12, 173, 184, 240–1, 244–5
Gachev, Georgi 28–9, 38, 51, 57
*Game, The* (*Le jeu*) 236, 241, 250
Garcia Ascot, Jose Miguel 37
García Hurtado, Federico 15, 99–115
Gatti, Armand 30, 32, 41, 55–6
Getino, Octavio 1–3, 12, 16–17, 69, 87, 93, 105, 121–2, 128, 142, 157, 164, 170, 171, 175, 177, 179, 190, 194, 213, 220, 231, 240, 263, 270–1, 275, 277, 279
Godard, Jean-Luc 32, 201, 242, 263, 270
Goethe, Johann Wolfgang von 9
Gramsci, Antonio 42–3, 276, 279
*Gravity* 256–8, 268–9
Gray, Ros 216, 242
*Great Expectations* 256–7
*Guerrilla Fighter, The* (*Padatik*) 87
Guevara, Alfredo 31, 34, 37–9, 41
Guevara, Ernesto 'Che' 4–5, 121, 123, 134, 138
Gutierrez Alea, Tomas 30, 32, 34–7, 41–2, 51, 171
Guzmán, Patricio 16, 141–61

*Hablemos de Cine* 16, 105, 109, 112–14
*Harry Potter and the Prisoner of Azkaban* 256
Ho Chi Minh 4–5
*Hour of the Furnaces, The* (*La Hora de los hornos*) 2–4, 16, 95, 121, 171–2, 240, 241, 275
*Huayanay Case: Part Testimony, The* (*El caso Huayanay: testimonio de parte*) 16, 102, 111–14
Huillca, Saturnino 101–2, 106–7

ICAIC (Instituto Cubano del Arte e Industria Cinematográficos) 29–31, 37–9, 41, 50, 57, 101, 104, 108, 111
*India '67* 84
*Insurrection of the Bourgeoisie, The* (*La insurrección de la burguesía*) 16, 141–59
*Interview* 15, 86–8, 93–6

Iutkevich, Sergei 50
Ivens, Joris 47, 95, 240

Kaganof, Aryan 17, 202–3, 205, 207–9
Kalatozov, Mikhail 14, 25–7, 30–5, 37–8, 41, 43, 45, 48, 51, 53–6, 171
*Karl Marx Among Us* 217, 220–3
Keti, Zé 75, 77
Khouri, Walter Hugo 15, 63–5, 69–71, 74, 79
Kristeva, Julia 66
Kuroki, Kazuo 57

*Laulico* 16, 102, 108–11
Lenin, Vladimir 39, 43, 108
Levi, Pavle 230
Levinas, Emmanuel 245–6, 247, 251
*Life on Earth* (*La vie sur terre*) 236–44, 249–51
*Little Princess, A* 256
Loach, Ken 17, 195–6, 199, 201–2
*Lucia* 17, 164, 171–4
Lukinsky, Ivan 50

Maetzig, Kurt 41, 47, 54
Marti, Jose 43
Marx, Karl 2–4, 6, 9, 42, 87, 132–4, 136, 138, 152, 192, 194–5, 201, 264
Mbembe, Achille 202, 203, 208, 235, 246, 248, 249–50
Meden, Jurij 217–20, 222–3, 226
*Metalepsis in Black* 17, 189, 202–10
*Middleman, The* (*Jana Aranya*) 87, 89
Mulvey, Laura 169
Mungiu, Cristian 17, 164, 175–82

Nancy, Jean-Luc 235, 246–8
*Newsreel 55* 223–5
*Newsreel 57: We Should Ask Ourselves* 226
*Newsreel 62* 227–9
*Night Games* (*Noite vazia*) 15, 64–75, 77–9
Nolan, Christopher 258
Nollywood 276, 278, 283, 286

*October* (*Octobre*) 236–7, 244, 249
*Only with Your Partner* (*Sólo con tu pareja*) 256
*Other Christopher, The* (*El Otro Cristobal*) 30, 32, 55–6

*Paisan* 37
Perón, Juan Domingo 123–7, 130
Pineda Barnet, Enrique 25–6, 34, 37, 45, 47
*Preludio 11* 29, 47, 53–4
Pudovkin, Vsevolod 35

*Que viva Mexico* 33–4

*Rambo in the Amazon and the Professor's Rescue* (*Rambo da Amazônia o Resgate da Professora*) 278
Ray, Satyajit 15, 83–98
Reagan, Ronald 4
*Revolution and Land* (*La revolución y la tierra*) 99
Robbe-Grillet, Alain 69, 72
Roca, Pilar 15, 99–115
*Roma* 18, 255–72
Rossellini, Roberto 37
*Rostov-Luanda* 236, 238–9, 244, 249

*Sabriya* 236
*Salvador Allende* 16, 142–59
Sang-in, Cheon 50
Saraceni, Paulo César 15, 64–5, 70, 72, 74–5, 77–9
*Save the Children Fund Film* 17, 189, 195–202
Scorsese, Martin 27, 39, 48
Sen, Mrinal 15, 85–8, 93–6
SINAMOS (Peruvian National System for Social Mobilization) 101–3, 105
Sissako, Abderrahmane 18, 235–51
Solanas, Fernando 1–2, 11–12, 16–17, 69, 87, 93, 97, 105, 121–38, 142, 157, 164, 170, 171, 175, 177, 179, 190, 213, 231, 240, 242, 263, 270–1, 275, 277
Solas, Humberto 17, 58, 164, 171–5
*Song of the Little Road, The* (*Pather Panchali*) 91, 94–5
*Soy Cuba* 14–15, 19, 25–41, 43–9, 51–7
Spielberg, Steven 258

Thatcher, Margaret 4, 144
*Timbuktu* 18, 236–9, 241, 244, 249–51
*Tiya's Dream* 236
Trump, Donald 7, 255, 270

Ulive, Ugo 41, 55
Urusevsky, Sergei 26–7, 30–3, 35, 37, 48, 53

Valdes Rodriguez, Jose Manuel 34
*Vampires of Poverty, The* (*Agarrando Pueblo*) 281, 285
Velasco Alvarado, Juan 99, 100, 103–8
Veloso, Caetano 67, 75
Vertov, Dziga 50

wa Thiong'o, Ngũgĩ 196–8
*Waiting for Happiness* (*Heremakono*) 236–7, 239, 241, 244, 249, 251
Wang Bin 17, 166–8
Waugh, Thomas 222
Wayne, Mike 214–15, 276
*Where the Condors Are Born* (*Kuntur Wachana*) 16, 102–3, 105–8
*White Haired Girl, The* (*Bai mao nu*) 17, 163–4, 166–71, 174, 179
*For Whom Havana Dances* 29, 38, 54, 56

Yimou, Zhang 164–7, 169–70
*And Your Mother Too* (*Y tu mamá también*) 256–8

www.ingramcontent.com/pod-product-compliance
Lightning Source LLC
Chambersburg PA
CBHW052112010526
44111CB00036B/1781